A Guide's Guide to Philadelphia

Julie P. Curson

CURSON HOUSE, INC.
Philadelphia

ISBN 0–913694–06–1
Library of Congress Catalogue Card Number: 91–071426
Printed in the United States of America
First Edition, First Printing March 1973
First Edition, Second Printing July 1973
Second Edition — January 1975
Third Edition — February 1978
Fourth Edition — March 1982
Fifth Edition — September 1986
Sixth Edition — June 1991

Typography by Commcor Communications Corp.
Cover design by Elliott Curson.
Cover photograph: see page 228.
Illustrations by Wally Neibart.
Maps by SANCHEZ.
Research Assistant: Eden Pontz.

Contents

Maps

INTRODUCTION

Since I began writing the first edition of this book, Philadelphia has had many occasions to celebrate. The nation's bicentennial was celebrated here in 1976. The city's tricentennial was celebrated in 1982. The bicentennial of the Constitution of the United States was celebrated in 1987. And now we celebrate the same anniversary of the Bill of Rights.

But a special occasion is just one reason to write a guidebook. And, while Philadelphia has hardly escaped the problems common to big cities of the 1980s that saw a growing population of homeless people, an increase in crime and drugs, and finances being sapped by unanticipated needs brought on by these problems, there are still countless reasons to be proud and positive about the city. So here's my sixth edition.

Philadelphia is a city of history worth knowing and exploring. It's the city where the United States was born.

Philadelphia is a city with great culture. There are probably more major museums and cultural organizations here than anywhere in the country.

Philadelphia is a city of learning. There are more than 30 colleges and universities and six medical schools.

Philadelphia is a city with a major league team for every major sport, and Philadelphians are highly supportive and vocal fans. It's a city with ethnic diversity, a melting pot for a multitude of nationalities.

Philadelphia is a city with three flowing waterways and a major port. It's the city with the largest municipally maintained park in the world.

And it's a city that looks to the future.

Redevelopment of center city has moved at a rapid pace in the past decade. Towering new buildings have changed the city's skyline dramatically. Old neighborhoods are reborn. New world-class hotels have opened and a new Convention Center is underway.

Creative new restaurants continue to open along with the tried and true, and Philadelphia has justifiably gained a national reputation as a "restaurant city." Over 200 restaurants are described in Chapter 18.

This sixth edition of *A Guide's Guide to Philadelphia* brings you up-to-date on everything that's happening in Philadelphia. It tells you about attractions and events for everyone, the young and old, families and groups, tourists and natives. The comments are mine, and I tried to be objective.

If something is overlooked, or if you have any comments, please write to me. Address all correspondence to: Julie P. Curson, 250 South 18th Street, Philadelphia, Pennsylvania 19103.

Have fun!

Julie P. Curson

Capsule Summary Code

Every attraction in this book has a capsule summary of information that you need to know. This is what you should look for.

NAME OF ATTRACTION
Address with Philadelphia ZIP code
Telephone (area code 215, unless noted otherwise)

Hours: Opening and closing times for you to visit on your own and with no specially planned guided tour. The amount of time you should allow for a visit (not including time you might have to wait).

Tours: Regularly scheduled or specially arranged guided tours for individuals or groups; the group procedures, restrictions and method of reservations. How long will your tour be? In some cases, Philadelphia Public School teachers can make special arrangements, and this will be indicated here. In some instances, it's necessary to write or call in advance, even though you're not requesting or getting a specially planned guided tour.

Cost: How much is the admission? To get group rates, sometimes it's necessary to call ahead, and it's always better if one person pays for the entire group. Sometimes it's required. Information about membership plans.

Lunch: This information is provided when facilities are available.

SEPTA: These are the routes that go closest to the attraction. If you're not sure how to get there, call SEPTA at 580-7800.

Other: Gift shops, programs and special events are listed here. Also any unusual suggestions or requests.

E & D: This is information especially for the elderly or disabled. It includes wheelchair accessibility, indication of steps and excessive walking, or anything else that might hinder or help you to plan and take the tour. Special facilities for the blind and hearing disabled are included where available. More information is in Chapter 16.

Note

Things happen fast in Philadelphia, so there might be some changes since this book came out. Inflation is also a factor. Federal and municipal budget cuts have caused many temporary (and, unfortunately, some permanent) limits on staff and facilities, resulting in changed of hours an attraction is open. If you're going to a particular place, call ahead to be sure it will be open.

An **asterisk (*)** indicates that the same place or event appears elsewhere in the book with more details. You'll find that place in the **Index.**

Chapter 1.
Transportation and Tours.

Philadelphia

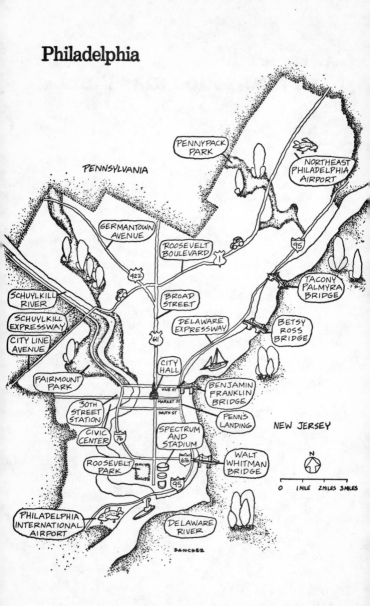

Philadelphia is on the move—and you can move with it, under it, around it and through it.

This chapter tells you how you can sit back, relax and enjoy the sights while someone else does the driving.

At the end of the chapter, you'll read about tour and guide companies that plan a tour for you, and perhaps even escort you with your transportation or theirs.

Tourist Information

PHILADELPHIA VISITORS CENTER
The Philadelphia Convention and Visitors Bureau
1525 John F. Kennedy Boulevard—19102
636–1666 or 800–321–9563

Hours: Daily except Christmas, 9 to 5; till 6 in summer.
SEPTA: Buses 2, 12, 17, 27, 32, 33, 38, 44, Ben Frank-Line route 76; Market–Frankford Subway–Elevated, Broad Street subway or subway–surface trolleys; SEPTA Regional Rail commuter trains to Suburban Station. Several Trolley–Bus tours also originate here.
Other: A gift shop sells postcards, books, T-shirts and all sorts of Philadelphia memorabilia.
E & D: There are 8 steps at the entrance, as well as a long ramp.

The Philadelphia Visitors Center is the place to go for information about what there is to see and do in Philadelphia.

You can go there for brochures about Philadelphia, listings of hotels, restaurants and current events, or to have questions answered. Aside from information, there's a possibility that you can get free tickets to some of the events that are being held.

If you can't get to the Visitors Center, call (from a touchtone phone) the Donnelley Directory **Philadelphia Events Hotline** at **337–7777 ext. 2540** for a recorded message on what's happening in Philadelphia today.

Local Transportation

SEPTA
580-7800

That's the Southeastern Pennsylvania Transportation Authority, Philadelphia's public transportation system, which operates some 140 bus, trolley and rail routes.

SEPTA routes going to points of interest are listed throughout this book. But you can also call SEPTA for specific directions. Be ready to tell them where you are and where you want to go.

The SEPTA system includes nearly 2,500 buses, articulated buses, trolleys, trackless trolleys, highspeed trains, subway trains and an elevated train that goes over and under the city. SEPTA also controls the extensive Regional Rail commuter system. You'll learn more about some of these vehicles later in this chapter.

A SEPTA **Customer Service Center** is at 841 Chestnut Street in center city. It's open on weekdays from 8:30 A.M. to 4:30 P.M. Schedules are available, and senior citizens and handicapped riders can get SEPTA identification cards which enable them to ride at special fares.

A SEPTA **Customer Service and Sales Office** is in the underground concourse at 15th and Market Streets in center city. Agents are on duty Monday to Friday from 7 A.M. to 6 P.M. They can answer your questions, provide schedules and brochures and sell you tokens, a TransPass or a SEPTA Visitor Key.

Most of the SEPTA fares in Philadelphia are $1.50, and exact change is required. A transfer is $.40 extra. Senior citizens can ride free of charge during the day except during peak hours (6 to 9 A.M. and 3:30 to 6:30 P.M.)when they pay the regular fare. Two children under 42 inches can ride free if they're with a fare-paying rider.

If you're planning to ride SEPTA often, their $16 weekly or $58 monthly Transpass is a good idea.

You can also use a token in place of exact fare. SEPTA tokens are $1.05 and they're available at several subway–elevated stations and at SEPTA depots. Call SEPTA for the exact locations, or stop at the SEPTA Sales Office at 15th and Market Streets or in the Market Street East station.

SEPTA information for the disabled is in Chapter 16.

All SEPTA bus and trolley stops are clearly marked along their routes. Look for the SEPTA transit stop signs attached to poles at mid-block or street corner locations.

An interesting and inexpensive way to see Philadelphia is to ride from one end of the city to the other. The Route 32 bus goes from Broad and Spruce Streets, around City Hall, up the Parkway, through Strawberry Mansion, East Falls and Roxborough to Andorra, at the city limits. You'll go from the center city business district to scenic residential sections in one hour. This 15-mile trip costs $1.50, and the buses run frequently.

We can boast that the nation's longest trolley route is right here in Philadelphia. You can ride the Route 23 trolley from 11th and Bigler Streets in South Philadelphia through center city, North Philadelphia, Germantown, Mt. Airy and on to Chestnut Hill via Germantown Avenue. The 25-mile round-trip takes over two hours and costs $1.50 each way. You'll see some of Philadelphia's richest, poorest, newest and oldest sections.

The downtown **Route 76 Ben FrankLine** bus (formerly called the MidCity Loop) is a unique way to get around center city between 3rd and Chestnut Streets and the Philadelphia Museum of Art. Buses run every day, every ten minutes from 9 A.M. to 9 P.M.

Philadelphia is really an easy city to find your way around in, and the Route 76 Ben Frankline bus makes it even easier. Route 76 travels between the Visitor Center at 3rd and Chestnut Streets, in both directions on the Chestnut Street Transitway to 16th Street, and in both directions on the Benjamin Franklin Parkway between the Philadelphia Visitors Center and the Art Museum.

The Route 76 Ben FrankLine is part of SEPTA's Visitor Route Network. A special brochure maps out the route and is available at stops along the way. Other tour brochures are also available on board the Route 76. Or for more information, you can call SEPTA's Visitor Route Network at 580–7676 or 580–7800.

Bus Route 38 is also part of SEPTA's Visitor Route Network. It operates daily between Independence Hall and Bala Cynwyd, making stops at 17 historic, cultural and visitor-related center city sites before heading to the western suburbs.

If you're spending a few days in Philadelphia, SEPTA's

Visitor Key is a great idea. For $7 you get 5 tokens, maps, tourist information and hundreds of dollars worth of discount coupons. Buy your Visitor Key at a SEPTA Sales Office, center city hotels, museums, or by mail. Call SEPTA for additional information.

SEPTA's **Airport High Speed Line** R1 provides nonstop train service between the four domestic air terminals and the international terminal at Philadelphia International Airport and all three center city rail stations: 30th Street Station, Suburban Station at 16th and John F. Kennedy Boulevard, and Market East—just north of Market between 10th and 12th. Trains run every half-hour, every day from 6 A.M. to midnight. The ride takes less than 30 minutes from Market East to Terminal E at the airport. Buy your ticket before boarding and the one-way fare is $4.75 for adults, half-fare for children under 12 and free for children under 5. It's $5.75 if you wait to pay on board.

Plane Rides and Airport Tours

Philadelphia International Airport is in the southwest section of the city, less than a half-hour drive from center city. Flight information is available by calling 492–3181. Airlines serve Philadelphia International Airport with flights to every major American city and several foreign capitals. Commuter flights connect Philadelphia with nearby cities.

All major airlines have ticket offices in center city, as well as at Philadelphia International Airport.

PHILADELPHIA INTERNATIONAL AIRPORT
Industrial Highway west of Island Road—19153

Tours: Call 937–1930 Ext. 1587 or 1588 at least 2 weeks in advance to schedule groups of 10 to 40, grade 3 and older, for Monday to Saturday at 10 A.M. Allow 90 minutes. One adult must accompany every 10 youngsters. Scouts and other groups can sometimes be scheduled at other times.
Cost: Free.
Lunch: Some 20 food and beverage concessions serve everything from haute cuisine to ice cream. Some have seating; others are stand-up.

SEPTA: Buses U, 37, 68; Airport High Speed Line R1.
E & D: Wheelchair access for entire tour. There's a lot of walking.

Your tour of the Philadelphia International Airport starts with a 12-minute slide show on the history of aviation and airport operations.

Then you'll take a walk through the terminal to see the ticketing and check-in procedures, a concourse and the baggage claim area. A stop at a security check-point emphasizes the importance of airport security.

And, finally, you'll take a mini-tour of the airfield and learn about landing and take-off procedures and what it takes to get a plane ready for departure.

HORTMAN AVIATION SERVICES
Northeast Philadelphia Airport
Red Lion and Norcom Roads—19114
969–0311

Hours: Daily, June through September, 7 A.M. to 9 P.M.; October through May, 8:30 A.M. to 6 P.M. Evening hours can sometimes be arranged.
Tours: Call 3 days ahead for a weekday flight; call a week ahead for a weekend flight. Planes accommodate a maximum of 3 adults.
Cost: Depending on the aircraft, $62 to $85 per hour with a minimum half-hour flight.

You have a choice of single engine planes when you fly with Hortman: a low-wing Piper Archer, a low-wing Piper Warrior, or a high-wing Cessna 150 that's great for taking aerial photographs but takes only one passenger.

If you have a special plan in mind, talk to your pilot before you take off. Otherwise, a popular flight plan takes you on an aerial "U" tour from the Northeast, across Roosevelt Boulevard and over to the Betsy Ross Bridge. You'll wave to William Penn in center city, swoop down over New Jersey and then head up the Delaware River back to the airport.

NORTHEAST AVIATION
Northeast Philadelphia Airport
Main Terminal Building
Grant Avenue and Academy Road—19114
677-5592

Hours: Daily, 9 A.M. till dusk, weather permitting.
Tours: Call at least 2 days in advance. Single engine planes take a maximum of 3 adults. Children 2 years and older must occupy their own seat.
Cost: $37 per half-hour.

Go sightseeing from the sky with Northeast Aviation and choose your own route. Head north over the Delaware River and get a bird's-eye view of Sesame Place or Bucks County. Head south and get an aerial look at the center city skyline, Fairmount Park, the zoo, Veterans Stadium, the Naval Base, Penn's Landing and more.

See Philadelphia from a whole new perspective. Be above it all, and don't forget your camera!

STERLING HELICOPTER
Penn's Landing Heliport, Pier 36 South
Delaware Avenue and Catherine Street—19147
271-2510

Hours: Saturday, 1 to 5.
Tours: No reservations necessary, but call ahead to be sure. Copters seat either 3 or 4 passengers and the pilot.
Cost: $20 per passenger. $40 minimum for larger copter (seats 4); $20 minimum for smaller (seats 3). Discounts available for children (they must be with an adult).

On weekdays, Sterling Helicopter provides flight training and aerial services for companies like KYW–TV, Sunoco Traffic Update–Shadow Traffic Network, the Associated Press, The Philadelphia Inquirer and the Daily News.

But on Saturdays, you can go in the same helicopters for an exciting aerial tour of center city Philadelphia.

From one-thousand feet at speeds of 100 miles per hour, the view is breathtaking and the picture-taking possibilities are endless. You'll lift off from the pier and swoop across the Delaware to Camden before crossing over the Ben Franklin Bridge. From there it's a bird's-eye view of Independence Mall, center city, the Art Museum, Boat House Row and Fairmount Park. Then you'll head south

over the University of Pennsylvania, across the Schuylkill, over Rittenhouse Square and eastward toward Washington Square and Penn's Landing.

The trip takes about eight minutes. The chances are
good you'll want to do it again.

Train Rides and Station Tours

Philadelphia has one of the most comprehensive railroad commuter networks in the country. And it's the most
important intermediate stop on AMTRAK's busy New
York–Washington corridor.

The Penn Central and Reading railroads were taken
over by ConRail back in 1976. ConRail currently runs
eight regional rail commuter trains under contract to the
Southeastern Pennsylvania Transportation Authority.
Most of the commuter lines run into attractive suburban
areas, as far north as Trenton, New Jersey and as far
south as Wilmington, Delaware, and they're all modern
air-conditioned electric trains. For train information, call
SEPTA at **580-7800.**

A handsome commuter tunnel, opened late in 1984,
connects the old Penn Central and Reading lines from
12th to 16th Streets. The new Market East Station, below ground (just north of Market Street between 10th and
12th) replaces the old Reading Terminal Station. Don't
miss the 880-foot-long ceramic mural expanding the
length of the Market East platform. Its 62 colors on
250,000 tiles suggest the great outdoors. See if it reminds
you of trees, grass, streams, shrubbery and a beautiful
blue sky.

AMTRAK runs the heavy inter-city traffic from
Washington through Philadelphia to New York, Boston,
Chicago and other points, as well as the Harrisburg commuter trains. More than half of the trains to Washington
and New York are the famous Metroliners, which run at
speeds up to 110 miles an hour. Other trains offer sleek
new Amfleet service. Board the **AMTRAK** trains at **30th
Street Station**. For information, call **824-1600.** For
Metroliner Service reservations and information, call the
Metrophone, 800-523-8720. Hearing disabled persons
with access to a teletypewriter should call 800-562-6960
in Pennsylvania or 800-523-6590 in the rest of the United States.

AMTRAK tickets can be purchased at Suburban Station, 16th and Kennedy Boulevard; at 30th Street Station; at the AMTRAK Rail Travel Center at 1708 Kennedy Boulevard (weekdays only); or from a travel agent.

Can you think of anything more exciting than taking youngsters on their first visit to a train station? And then a round-trip ride on a silverliner commuter train to one of Philadelphia's lush suburbs? You probably remember your first train ride.

Philadelphia's early railroad executives built their grand homes in the western suburbs along the tracks of their "main line" to Paoli. Today, the **Main Line** has some of America's most beautiful estates. They're in Overbrook, Merion, Narberth, Wynnewood, Ardmore, Haverford, Bryn Mawr and Paoli. Localites remember the names of these communities along the route of the Paoli Local with the help of this expression: "Old Maids Never Wed And Have Babies. Period."

In addition to taking train rides, you can go on a fascinating tour of 30th Street Station.

30TH STREET STATION
30th and Market Streets—19104
895-7122 (Passenger Service Office)

Hours: You could visit on your own anytime, day or night. Groups can be scheduled Monday to Saturday, except holidays, 10 to 3, and contingent on the station schedule.

Tours: For groups of 10 to 20, at least 1st grade. Allow 20 minutes to an hour. Call at least one week ahead.

Cost: Free.

SEPTA: Buses 9, 30, 31; subway–surface trolleys 10, 11, 13, 34, 36; Market–Frankford Subway–Elevated; or any of the regional rail commuter trains to or from Suburban Station.

E & D: People in wheelchairs are able to tour the station's main floor.

30th Street Station is the main railroad station in Philadelphia. It's a monumental structure that was built with opulence in the early 1930s and added to the National Register of Historic Places in 1979. A meticulous and resplendent $75 million renovation of the main station began early in 1989 and restores the building to its original grandeur.

Every day, hundreds of passenger and freight trains pass through Philadelphia to New York, Boston, Washington and points beyond. Each month, 300,000 intercity rail passengers go through 30th Street Station.

An equal number of regional rail commuter cars ride the rails to Philadelphia's scenic suburbs.

What else is there to see in the station besides trains? This tour is especially beneficial to youngsters who've never been "trained." They'll learn how to read the schedule board, buy a ticket, check a bag and go to the proper platform.

All aboard!

PATCO HIGH SPEED LINE
Port Authority Transit Corp.
922–4600

We recommend this computer-operated train ride, even though it takes you out of Philadelphia and into New Jersey. Or, you can take it for a quick ride from 8th and Market Streets to 16th and Locust Streets.

The man who controls the computer sits in the front car. Don't hesitate to ask him how the train works.

These air-conditioned high-speed trains travel at speeds up to 75 miles per hour. The 14½-mile route takes only 23 minutes.

Trains leave every 10 minutes or less from any of four underground stops in Philadelphia: Locust Street at 16th, 13th, or 10th, or 8th and Market Streets. You'll be underground until you get to the Benjamin Franklin Bridge. And wait till you see the view from there!

The view from the bridge alone is worth the fare ($1.60 one way for the entire trip, or $.75 from Philadelphia to Camden, $1.40 to Collingswood). Nine stops are made in New Jersey, as far as Lindenwold.

Special fares can be arranged for senior citizens and riders with disabilities during off-peak hours. Call PATCO for details.

ZOO MONORAIL*
34th Street and Girard Avenue
386–9088 or 243–1100 Ext. 297

Hours: Daily from March 15 to November 1, 9:30 to 4:30
  weekdays, till 5 weekends; weather-permitting.
Cost: Weekdays: adults, $3.50; children under 12, $3.
  Weekends and holidays: $.50 more. Group rates for 15
  or more: $.50 less.
E & D: People in wheelchairs should board at the south
  end near the Wolf Woods where there's a ramp entrance.
  You'll have to transfer to the monorail seat.

This is a one-of-a-kind transportation in Philadelphia.
The zoo monorail has canopied, open-air cars that circle
the 42-acre zoo. Live narration along the route makes you
familiar with the creatures and their habitats below.

The 15-minute ride is a nifty way to orient yourself to
everything that the Philadelphia Zoo has to offer. You can
read more about the zoo in Chapter 7.

Boat Rides

R & S HARBOR TOURS
Penn's Landing
Delaware and Lombard Street
928–0972

Tours: May to November, on the hour weekdays, 10 to 4;
  weekends, 12 to 6; also weekend and holiday 2-hour
  sunset cruise at 7:30. Reservations are necessary in advance for groups of 10 or more. Call ahead to be sure
  the boat is sailing. Write or call for information, charter
  parties or reservations. (Pier 9 North, Delaware and
  Race Streets, Phila., PA 19106)
Cost: 1-hour: adults, $5; children 12 and under, $3.
  2-hour: adults, $7; children, $4. Groups of 10 or more
  should call or write a month ahead for reservations and
  group rates.
Lunch: Sodas, hot dogs and light snacks are sold aboard,
  or you can brown bag it.
SEPTA: Bus 5 or 40 to 2nd and Lombard; bus 21 to Penn's
  Landing and Walnut St. Parking is available at dock.
E & D: There's wheelchair access to the top deck.

All aboard the 100-passenger "Rainbow" for a delightful, narrated sightseeing cruise of the Delaware River!

A 50-minute cruise heads south on the river as far as
the Walt Whitman Bridge before turning around and
heading back north to the Ben Franklin Bridge. The two-
hour trip goes all the way to the Philadelphia Naval Base.

You'll see scenic Penn's Landing and ships from around
the world. And you'll see why we boast that the Port of
Philadelphia is the world's largest freshwater port.

SPIRIT OF PHILADELPHIA
Penn's Landing
Delaware River at Market Street
923-1419; groups of 20 or more, 923-4993

Tours: For brunch, lunch, dinner and dancing in the
moonlight. Reservations required.
Cost: Varies with the cruise. Children's and group rates
available.
E & D: Wheelchair access on boarding deck only, and the
wheelchair cannot be used on the gangplank.

The 600-passenger "Spirit of Philadelphia" cruises the
Port of Philadelphia while providing live entertainment,
dancing, food and drinks. The captain points out famous
landmarks along the way. The ship has both open and
closed decks, and since it's really a restaurant, you can
read more about it in Chapter 18.

EMPRESS DINING CRUISES
Penn's Landing   **Note:**
Delaware River at Lombard Street   See page 437.
425-1400

Tours: May through October, weekdays for lunch, 11 to
1; weekends for brunch, 1 to 3; nightly dinner-dance 7
to 10; Wednesday to Sunday, moonlight cruise, 11:30
P.M. to 2 A.M. Reservations required. Call or write to
Empress Dining Cruises, 1080 N. Delaware Avenue,
Phila., PA 19125.
Cost: For sightseeing only, varies with the cruise. Special rates for children and groups of 20 or more. Full
service table dining with a la carte or fixed price menu
is additional.
E & D: Wheelchair access to main deck with assistance
necessary to upper decks.

Welcome aboard an elegant replica of what might have been a turn-of-the-century Hudson River steamboat.

The canopied top deck is ideal for sightseeing the Port of Philadelphia from Penn's Landing south to the Navy Base. Your captain points out the sights along the way.

The enclosed main and second decks are for dining, which you can read more about in Chapter 18.

Bus Tours and Terminals

The **Greyhound-Trailways** (931–4000) transportation center in center city Philadelphia is at 10th and Filbert Streets across from the Market East train station. **New Jersey Transit** (569–3752) buses that connect with nearby New Jersey communities and beach resorts also depart from here.

Every important city in the world offers sightseeing bus tours, and Philadelphia is no exception. So take a **Gray Line Tour** (569–3666) of Philadelphia and let your driver do the talking.

An assortment of tours with varying schedules and prices are offered. They're daily from April through October and highlight historic and cultural Philadelphia. If you have a group of 30 or more, call 568–6111 for charter information.

Trolley Rides

SEPTA's fleet of trolleys, which is the largest in the nation, covers a good portion of Philadelphia with 8 routes. You've already read earlier in this chapter about the Route 23. SEPTA also has three suburban trolley routes. All three are fun to ride, and they originate at 69th Street Terminal in Upper Darby, just west of the city. Just hop the Market–Frankford Subway–Elevated and ride to the end of the line at 69th and Market Streets.

The Norristown High-Speed Line Route 100, which runs frequent service on its 13.5 mile line through the picturesque Main Line suburbs, is America's original high speed line and the last interurban trolley line in the country.

The Media trolley line Route 101 is also interesting to see. It runs 8.5 miles west to Media, the county seat of Delaware County*. The line takes you through pretty suburban areas and winds up trundling down the middle of Media's main street.

The third line, Route 102, runs 5.3 miles to Sharon Hill.

Call 580–7800 or 574–7777 for fares, schedules and maps for each route.

You can take an old-fashioned trolley ride on the **PENN'S LANDING TROLLEY** and, at the same time, see Philadelphia's waterfront,  Queen Village, Society Hill and Old City from a beautifully restored, turn-of-the-century trolley car.

The round-trip excursion along Delaware Avenue between the Benjamin Franklin Bridge and Fitzwater Street takes 25 minutes. You can board at Dock Street or Spruce Street after you buy a ticket from the platform dispatcher, and your ticket is good for unlimited rides for the entire day.

The fare is $1.50 for adults and $.75 for children under 12. Call 627–0807 for group rates and charter information. Penn's Landing trolleys run from 11 A.M. to dusk, weekends from Easter Sunday to Thanksgiving, plus Thursdays and Fridays in July and August.

Trolley-Bus Rides

You've read about tours by trolley. You've read about tours by bus. Now you can go on a trolley-bus tour. What's a trolley-bus? I'll explain.

Between 1896 and 1946, Philadelphians were taken to Fairmount Park in open-air trolleys. Today's trolley-bus is a replica of these trolleys. The 31 seaters have open-air sections, leather strap-hangers, clanging bells and colorful red exteriors. They're modeled after their predecessors, except they don't need trolley tracks. The 39 seaters are all enclosed and air-conditioned.

American Trolley Tours (925–4567) take you through 20th century Philadelphia and back to the 18th and 19th centuries as well. Step aboard while your costumed guide explains the history and local lore and you see the Benjamin Franklin Parkway, center city, Independence

National Historical Park, Antique Row, Society Hill and more, making several stops along the way.

Four tours daily depart from the Visitors Center at 16th and Kennedy Boulevard at 9:40 and 10:10 A.M., 2:10 and 2:40 P.M. Or, you can arrange in advance to be picked up at the Visitor Center at 3rd and Chestnut Streets or your hotel along the route. The entire tour lasts two-and-a-half to three hours. The cost is $14 for adults, $12 for seniors and $6 for children under 12; $2 less for groups of 20 or more seniors or adults. Call for reservations, additional departure locations and times.

Another charming way to tour by trolley-bus is with a Park House guide from the Philadelphia Museum of Art. Take a **Park Houses Special Tour**.

Escape to sprawling Fairmount Park and three of its 18th century park houses (see Chapter 8) for two hours on a summer or fall afternoon. Tours depart at 1 P.M. from the Visitors Center at 16th and Kennedy Boulevard. They stop 10 minutes later at the Philadelphia Museum of Art and then head into Fairmount Park. Cost is $6. Call the Park House office at 787–5449 for reservations and additional details.

Clang, clang, clang goes the trolley.

Carriage Rides

Horse-drawn carriage rides were revived in Philadelphia for the Bicentennial back in 1976. Tourists and Philadelphians alike love the carriages. They love to clip-clop around the cobblestone streets of Old Philadelphia just as the colonists did more than 200 years ago.

You have a choice of companies and a variety of "vis a vis" (face to face) Victorian-style carriages to make your tour. All have driver-guides (sometimes in colonial garb; sometimes in formal Victorian attire) to narrate your trip. Don't worry about the horses; they only go out when the weather permits.

These companies are licensed by the Pennsylvania Public Utility Commission. Their rates are controlled and supposed to be equal. They offer a 15- to 20-minute ride ($15 for up to 4 people), a 30-minute ride ($25 for up to 4 people), or a 60-minute ride ($50 for up to 4 people). The rate for the 15- to 20-minute ride goes up to $20 after 6 P.M. An additional charge per person over 4 people is $3,

$6 or $10 for each of the 3 tours. Standard pick-up points are Independence Hall and Head House Square (2nd and Pine or Lombard Streets). Tours are given daily from 9:30 to 5:30; till 8 on weekends from Independence Hall and till midnight from Head House Square. Day or evening taxi service is provided by reservation, and a reserved carriage will pick you up anywhere in center city.

Five companies offer these tours: **Ben Franklin Carriages, Outback Carriages, Philadelphia Carriage Co.** (922–6840), and **Society Hill Carriages. '76 Carriage Company** (923–8516) also has larger carriages available that can seat up to 25. Special rates are quoted when making reservations.

Get a horse!

Ups and Downs

CITY HALL TOWER*
Broad and Market Streets (enter at northeast corner)
686–1776

Hours: Weekdays, 9 to 4:30. Closed some holidays.
Tours: No tours, and reservations are not necessary. It's first come, first served. Children under 12 must be with an adult.
Cost: Free
E & D: No wheelchair access.

You're used to traveling back and forth. Now travel up and down.

At City Hall, the glass-front elevator goes up the newly refurbished 548-foot William Penn Tower in one-and-a-half minutes. On the way up you'll see the various levels, the workings of the 23-foot wide clock, and the 604 steps that circle the elevator shaft. (No, you can't use the stairs. If you want to exercise, you could go for a run along Kelly Drive.)

You may have been on bigger elevators than this one. But have you seen any that are as exciting?

More Ins and Outs of Getting Around Philadelphia

Additional information can be obtained by consulting the Yellow Pages or your travel agent.

All major rent-a-car companies are located in center city, at suburban hotels and at Philadelphia International Airport. There are limousine services available from the airport to Philadelphia, Wilmington, Atlantic City and Fort Dix. You'll see drivers or "hot line" telephones at the airport terminal. Limousines also go from the airport to center city, City Line, Northeast Philadelphia and suburban hotels.

Limousines are also available for hire. (The companies are listed in the Yellow Pages.) If you're a movie star, or would like to pretend you're a movie star, rent a limo for a day and have the driver show you Philadelphia.

Radio taxicab service is available in all areas of Philadelphia. Yellow Cab, United, Crescent, Society Hill, Quaker City and Victory are the most common.

How Else Can You Tour?

Several small, private companies provide a variety of tours of Philadelphia and its suburbs. In most cases, you'll have to provide your own transportation.

They're listed here, objectively, in alphabetical order, with a brief description of their individual services. Call or write to them for more details.

ABC Bus & Walking Tours 2929 Gelena Road, Phila., PA 19152 (677–2495). Choose from six planned tours of Historic Philadelphia, the Italian Market or Valley Forge, or itineraries that are customized for your group. Multilingual. Reservations only.

Access Philadelphia 250 S. 18th Street, Phila., PA 19103 (732–7139). Business people and their families who are relocating to Philadelphia can benefit from the services provided by Access Philadelphia to corporations and non-profit organizations. All facets of living in Philadelphia are considered. It'll certainly make your move easier.

At Your Service 302 Old Lancaster Road, Devon, PA 19333 (296–2828). Half- or full-day custom tours of Old or Contemporary Philadelphia, or surroundings areas. For large or small groups. Multilingual. Reservations only.

AudioWalk & Tour Norman Rockwell Museum, 6th and Sansom Streets, Phila., PA 19106 (925–1234). You can tour eight blocks of historic Philadelphia at your own pace with your own rented cassette and player and accompanying map. The tour lasts 80 minutes. Start anytime after 10 A.M. Monday to Saturday or 11 A.M. Sunday, and return the equipment by 4 P.M. Cost is $8 for an individual and $16 for 2 or more.

Black History Strolls and Tours 339 S. 2nd Street, Phila., PA 19106 (923–4136). Walking tours of Old Philadelphia and bus tours with emphasis on black history, business, religion, education, the arts. Day or night life. Multilingual. Reservations only.

C & C Associates, Tours and Special Events 1919 Chestnut Street, Phila., PA 19103 (568–0676). Customized tours for large and small groups of Old Philadelphia and surrounding attractions. Multilingual. Reservations only.

Centipede Tours 1315 Walnut Street, Phila., PA 19107 (735–3123). Scheduled walking tours and warm-weather evening Candlelight Strolls* of Old Philadelphia, Society Hill and Franklin's Philadelphia with colonial-costumed guides. Call for schedule and reservations. Bus tours, group and convention planning by reservation. Multilingual.

Choo Choo Trolley Co. 456 Rhawn Street, Phila., PA 19111 (745–4014). Hire your own 39-seat red trolley-bus for a custom charter tour. 3-hour minimum.

Culture Tour 9733 Bustleton Avenue, Phila., PA 19115 (947-8991). Personalized half- or full-day tours for large or small groups to area museums and historic sites. Multilingual. Reservations only.

Discovery Tours Philadelphia Museum of Art, P.O. Box 7646, Phila., PA 19101 (787–5498). A 3½ hour Philadelphia Highlights Tour is one of 9 art-oriented group bus tours presented by the Art Museum. Price includes museum guide, an escort, reading materials, admissions and private tours. Their bus or yours. 20-person minimum. Reservations only.

Gilboy Tours 234 Pine Street, Phila., PA 19106 (925–7868). Half- or full-day custom bus or walking tours of Philadelphia, Valley Forge, Brandywine or Amish Countries with guides in 18th century dress. Multilingual. Reservations only.

Foundation for Architecture Tours One Penn Center at Suburban Station, Suite 1665, Phila., PA 19103 (569–3187 or 569–TOUR). Reservations are suggested for individuals who want to join any of the Foundation's scheduled architectural walks. 25 different tours are offered including Around City Hall, Old City, the University of Pennsylvania campus, Skyscrapers, Littlest Streets, or the neighborhoods of Chestnut Hill, Spruce Hill, Society Hill, Victorian Germantown, Rittenhouse Square and Washington Square. The organization is devoted to promoting Philadelphia to natives and visitors as a museum of architecture. Most tours cost $5 for adults and $4 for children. Members of the non-profit Foundation get a discount along with other benefits including events that are planned mornings, afternoons, evenings and weekends throughout the year. Take a walk!

Friends of Independence National Historical Park 313 Walnut Street, Phila., PA 19106 (597–7919). One-hour guided walking tours of the National Park depart daily at 7 P.M. from July 1 to Labor Day, except July 4th, from Independence Hall. Rain or shine; first come, first served. Free.

Hospitality PhiladelphiaStyle 1234 Market Street, Suite 2030, Phila., PA 19107 (568–3351). Personalized itineraries for out-of-town civic and cultural groups are the specialty of this non-profit corporation. They'll take you to the forefront and behind-the-scenes of your favorite interest.

I.V.C. 34th Street and Civic Center Boulevard, 3rd floor Civic Center Museum, Phila., PA 19104 (823–7261). Groups of foreign visitors can schedule custom tours of Philadelphia with an international flavor. Reservations only. Multilingual. Read more about this organization in Chapter 12.

Philadelphia Open House 313 Walnut Street, Phila., PA 19106 (928–1188). Turn to May in the Calendar of Annual Events and read about this unique opportunity to participate in unusual tours of Philadelphia.

Philadelphia Tours 719 Dickinson Street, Phila., PA 19147 (271–2999). Customized group tours with a Centipede guide aboard a 49-passenger coach, 21-passenger mini-bus or 14-passenger van. Also, an authentic English double-deck tour bus for summertime sightseeing above the rest. Reservations only.

Julie Curson (that's me!) I plan tours, and sometimes I take groups on tours of Philadelphia. Reservations only. Call me at 735–2775. Or write to me at 250 S. 18th Street, Phila., PA 19103.

Chapter 3.
Neighborhoods.

Philadelphia is a city of neighborhoods. There are at least a hundred of them.

In Philadelphia, people closely identify with their neighborhoods. You can tell that when you see celebrities on The Tonight Show with Johnny Carson: They always tell what section of Philadelphia they're from.

Many neighborhoods bear names that were derived from the earliest settlers in that area.

The Lenni Lenape Indians are responsible for names like **Passyunk**, meaning "in the valley"; **Wyalusing**, from "old man's place"; **Poquessing**, from "place of mice"; or **Manayunk**, meaning "place where we go to drink."

Other neighborhoods derive their names from an activity that was prominent at the site. **Fishtown** was a popular place for fishing along the Delaware River in the 18th and 19th centuries. **Roxborough** was referred to in the late 1600s as a place where foxes burrowed in the rocks. **Fox Chase** is what you guessed it is.

Many neighborhoods took their names from people's estates. **Holmesburg** was the section where William Penn's surveyor and friend, Thomas Holme, settled in 1682.

Logan was the estate of Penn's secretary, James Logan. **Wynnefield** is where Penn's physician, Dr. Thomas Wynne, decided to build his home. (If your ancestors were friendly with William Penn, there would be a neighborhood named after your family.)

Some neighborhoods are known for their ethnic character. (More about that in Chapter 12.) **South Philadelphia** is the southern section of the city between the Delaware and Schuylkill Rivers. This neighborhood has a large Italian population. In fact, it's Philadelphia's largest foreign-born population segment.

South Philadelphia is famous for its bakeries, bocce, the Italian Market* and many Italian restaurants. (See Chapter 18 for more on these restaurants.) In recent years, "Rocky" has made South Philadelphia even more famous.

Chinatown is a community within center city Philadelphia. It's in the area of 8th to 11th around Race Street. At least a quarter of the 4,000 or more Chinese who make their homes in Philadelphia live in this section. Their origins here date back to 1870 when Philadelphia's first Chinese laundry opened at 9th and Race Streets.

The greatest attraction in Chinatown is the dozens of fine restaurants and the numerous shops that carry food delicacies, gifts and imported goodies. A magnificent Chinese Gate spans 10th Street, just north of Arch. It was dedicated in 1985. Read more about Chinatown in Chapter 12.

Eastwick is one of Philadelphia's newer neighborhoods, brought about by 20th century planning.

Eastwick is approximately four square miles of southwest Philadelphia. It's bounded roughly by 58th Street south of Tinicum National Environmental Center* and Philadelphia International Airport west to Dicks Avenue and Cobbs Creek where it abuts Delaware County.

Eastwick was conceived in 1954 by the late, great Greek city planner Constantinos Doxiadis. It's supposed to be the largest urban renewal project in this country.

Work began in the early 1960s to build Eastwick. To date it is a neighborhood with thousands of new homes, schools, shopping centers and recreation facilities.

Franklin Town is a 50-acre, privately developed community within center city Philadelphia. It's bounded by Spring Garden, Race and Vine Streets between 16th and 21st Streets. Franklin Town began in the 1970s. So far there are highrise apartment buildings, Korman Suites*, the Wyndham Franklin Plaza Hotel*, Community College of Philadelphia*, lively restaurants, restored homes, new homes and plans for additional housing and office development.

And so it goes.

The original two-square mile City of Philadelphia that was founded by William Penn in 1682 was incorporated under Penn's Proprietary Charter of 1701. Then, for over a hundred years, dozens of little independent towns sprouted up in Philadelphia County.

In 1854, the City was consolidated with its surrounding towns and the City and the County became one and the same. The boundaries were the same 130 square miles of Philadelphia we know today.

This chapter is about a few of the neighborhoods that have played significant roles in the history of Philadelphia and the United States. Several other neighborhoods are mentioned throughout the book as the locations of various attractions.

Germantown

CHESTNUT HILL
2¼ MILES

SEPTA 23
ROUTE

CLIVEDEN
6401

UPSALA
6450

CONCORD
SCHOOL HOUSE
6313

JOHNSON
HOUSE
6306

MENNONITE
CHURCH
AND
GRAVEYARD
6121

EBENEZER
MAXWELL
MANSION

UPSAL
STATION

WYCK
6026

GERMANTOWN
STATION

GERMANTOWN
HISTORICAL SOCIETY
5503

TULPEHOCKEN
STATION

VERNON
MANSION
5708

DESHLER-MORRIS
HOUSE 5442

SEPTA
RAIL
LINE

CHELTEN AVE
STATION

CLARKSON-
WATSON
HOUSE
5275

GRUMBLETHORPE
5267

SEPTA
RAIL
LINE

FISHERS
STATION

LOUDOUN
4650

STENTON
MANSION

WAYNE JCT
STATION

ROOSEVELT EXPRESSWAY

SANCHEZ

0 1000 2000 3000 4000 5000'

Germantown

In 1683, William Penn deeded an area of land six miles northwest of Philadelphia to a group of German settlers. Francis Daniel Pastorius led the first group of 13 families to what we now call Germantown. They were anxious to pursue Penn's dream of a "Holy Experiment." To prove their spirit, they built one of the first industrial towns in America.

America's first paper mill opened here in 1690. Six of the old stone houses and a barn survive today at RittenhouseTown*, where three centuries ago the mill section of Germantown flourished. Read more about RittenhouseTown and its Homestead in Chapter 8. In 1691, Germantown was made a borough within the County of Philadelphia.

Germantown was on the main route from Philadelphia to Reading, Bethlehem and points west. The road was heavily traveled by traders, Indians and settlers. In the 1760s, the stagecoach started its route through Germantown to Wilkes-Barre, Buffalo and Niagara Falls.

By the mid-18th century, Germantown was an established community with many schools and churches. America's first paper mill was built in Germantown in 1690. A Market Square was built in 1703 for food merchants. A firehouse, a jail and stocks were also built. The Square is still a picturesque site at Germantown Avenue and School House Lane.

Various trades and professions of Germantown homeowners were represented along the Germantown road.

Weavers, carpenters, shopkeepers, tanners and doctors lived side-by-side. Long gardens occupied the lots behind their homes. Many of the homes were large and gracious, set back on considerable plots of land.

We're sure you've heard about the Battle of Germantown. During the Revolutionary War, most of Germantown was occupied by the British. Battle scars still remain in some of the homes that became troop headquarters and fighting grounds. The successful American advance was halted on October 4, 1777, by soldiers who occupied Cliveden*, a mansion that proudly stands at 6401 Germantown Avenue.

The yellow fever epidemic that struck Philadelphia in

1793 was a boon to Germantown. Many of the city's residents escaped to this suburban town where prosperous Philadelphians built their summer retreats.

In fact, Germantown was temporarily the nation's capital in 1793 while President George Washington stayed at the Deshler-Morris House*.

Many historic buildings still stand along the old Germantown Road—now called Germantown Avenue.

In 1969, the U.S. Department of the Interior designated Germantown Avenue a Registered Historic Road. The three mile stretch from Loudoun to Cliveden is particularly historic. You should try to spend at least one afternoon in Germantown to go on an unusual tour of its colonial homes and landmarks. You can visit Germantown on your own, or with a group.

Tours: You can experience three centuries of historic Germantown on a private bus tour arranged by calling two to three weeks ahead to Cliveden, Ebenezer Maxwell Mansion or Wyck. You'll be reading about those attractions in the next few pages. Lunch is included at a nearby restaurant, so plan to spend about six hours on this delightful combination tour.

Philadelphia Open House* sponsors two Germantown tours in May. There's a guided walking tour of Victorian homes and a bus tour of 18th century Germantown homes followed by a candlelight dinner. Call Philadelphia Open House (928–1188) for the exact dates and ticket information.

SEPTA: If you're going to Germantown on your own, Regional Rail trains run from center city to stations on or near Germantown Avenue. Trolley 23 goes up and down Germantown on the nation's longest trolley line. It originates at 10th and Bigler Streets in South Philadelphia, then heads north along 11th Street through center city making the 12.8-mile one-way trip to Germantown Avenue and Bethlehem Pike.

Note: Flat shoes are requested to prevent damage to the floors of the colonial homes.

E & D: The gardens and first floors of most homes are wheelchair accessible. Call ahead to be sure, though. At Stenton, for example, arrange to have a ramp placed at the step leading to the house. The barn entrance is at ground level.

The following sites are listed in order as if you were going north on Germantown Avenue.

STENTON MANSION
18th and Windrim Streets
329-7312

Hours: April to December, Tuesday to Saturday, 1 to 4. Closed January through March. Special arrangements can be made for group tours at other times. Allow at least one hour.

Tours: Groups of no more than 40 can be scheduled by calling a few weeks in advance.

Cost: Adults, $3; senior citizens and children 14 and older, $1.50; children under 14 and Philadelphia Public School classes accompanied by their teachers, free.

SEPTA: Trackless Trolley 75.

Other: A gift shop in the spinning room wing of the kitchen offers charming items (embroidery, needlepoint, note paper and the like) that reflect Stenton's lifestyle.

Stenton was designed and built from 1723 to 1730 by James Logan, a young chap who came to Pennsylvania as William Penn's secretary. At that time it was a 500-acre summer residence. Today there are only five acres.

The house complements the man who built it. Logan was a scholar, a statesman and a businessman. He served the Penn family for 50 years. He was an adviser to Benjamin Franklin, and he also served as Chief Justice of Pennsylvania.

Among Stenton's spacious rooms was the finest library in the Commonwealth. The children's room has pint-size furnishings, an original cradle and dolls. There's also a fully furnished three-story built-in doll house.

Stenton is still flanked by the original weaving shed and barn. The barn was recently restored and now houses colonial farm tools and charts explaining how Stenton's gardens and crops were planted.

LOUDOUN
4650 Germantown Avenue
685-2067

Hours: April through mid-December, Tuesday, Thursday, Saturday, 10 to 4. Closed mid-December through March. Special arrangements can be made for group tours at other times. Allow about one hour.
Tours: Call at least a week ahead for groups of no more than 40.
Cost: Adults, $1.50; senior citizens and children, $1.
Lunch: Groups of 12 or more can make special arrangements for a prepared salad luncheon to be served. Call a few weeks ahead to schedule in conjunction with group tour. If you bring your own lunch, you're welcome to use Loudoun's grounds, but please don't leave any trash.

The stately Loudoun mansion is high above Germantown Avenue. It was built in 1801 by Thomas Armat. The Greek portico was added in 1830. Loudoun was willed to the city in 1939 by Maria Dickinson Logan, Armat's direct descendant, after being owned and occupied by five generations of the same family. Some visitors say that her ghost is still in the house. Philadelphia Magazine calls Loudoun "one of only 33 houses in the entire United States with documented, historically certified hauntings."

Furnishings are exhibited on three floors, including the basement kitchen. Most of the items are from the 18th century and belonged to the Armat, Dickinson and Logan families. There's also a recently restored underground spring house that dates to the mid-1700s.

Continuing north on Germantown Avenue, at 4821 is the **MEHL HOUSE**, dating back to 1744. Generations of the Mehl family occupied the home until the early 1900s. It's privately owned now.

Several of Germantown's early settlers are buried in the **LOWER BURIAL GROUND** at 4900 Germantown Avenue (at Logan Street). Gravestones date back to 1708.

More buildings from the 1700s survive on the 5200 block of Germantown Avenue. A good example of the local style of Federal architecture from 1796 remains at 5214, while the house at 5275 was built around 1745 and restored to look as it did in 1793 during the time of the yellow fever epidemic when Thomas Jefferson lived here. 5208, 5218, 5222 and 5226 Germantown Avenue all date from the 18th century as well and have colorful histories.

GRUMBLETHORPE
5267 Germantown Avenue
843–4820

Hours: April through mid-December, Saturday, 1 to 4. Closed mid-December through March. Special arrangements can be made for group tours at other times. Allow 45 minutes.
Tours: Call 2 weeks in advance for groups of more than 20, at least 4th grade level.
Cost: Adults, $3; senior citizens and students, $2; children under 6, free.

John Wister, a wealthy merchant, was the first Philadelphian to build a summer home in Germantown: Grumblethorpe. (How did he ever come up with a name like that?) This home, which dates back to 1744, is a fine example of simple colonial architecture.

The building materials were completely local. The stone for the walls came from Wister's woodlands. Wister was a noted horticulturalist, and his garden is still maintained.

Grumblethorpe's furnishings are from the middle 1700s. The summer kitchen has barely changed since its original use. The cupboards are full of unusual old things. If you're interested in privies, Grumblethorpe's has been recently restored.

During the Revolution, Grumblethorpe was converted into soldier's quarters by the British. In fact, a bloodstain from British General Agnew's wound still shows up on the front parlor floor.

Note: If you're looking for ghosts, ask about Grumblethorpe's spooky Halloween tour.

DESHLER-MORRIS HOUSE
5442 Germantown Avenue
596–1748

Hours: April to mid-December, Tuesday to Sunday, 1 to 4. Closed mid-December through March and major holidays. Special arrangements can be made for group tours at other times. Allow 45 minutes.

Tours: Groups of up to 50 can be scheduled by calling at least 2 weeks in advance. Any group of 8 or more must call in advance for reservations, whether or not you want a guided tour.

Cost: Adults, $1; students, $.50.

We think of the White House in Washington, D.C. as our President's official residence. But did you know the "White House" was once in Germantown? Well, it was.

In 1793, when the yellow fever epidemic struck Philadelphia, President Washington and his wife moved to what is now the Deshler-Morris House. Cabinet meetings and official dinners took place that November in the Deshler-Morris front parlor.

The Washingtons enjoyed the house so much that they returned for six weeks the following summer along with Mrs. Washington's two grandchildren.

The other famous resident at Deshler-Morris was Sir William Howe. He made the home the headquarters for his British command after the Battle of Germantown in 1777. David Deshler, a shipping merchant, built the house in 1772. It was later owned by the Morris family between 1834 and 1948, when it was bequeathed to the Federal government. It now belongs to Independence National Historical Park*.

Eleven rooms of Deshler-Morris have been expertly restored and furnished. You'll see period and original pieces, beautiful woodwork, Pennsylvania marble and Delft fireplaces, Oriental rugs, a room filled with toys and an 18th century kitchen complete with a walk-in fireplace.

The garden is lush with flowers, shrubs and trees, some of which date back to Washington's time.

Imagine how royally the colonial notables were entertained in this White House. Yes, this is one place where Washington actually slept.

If you look across the street, you'll see the **GERMANTOWN MARKET SQUARE** and the former **FROMBERGER HOUSE** that dates from just before 1800. Now, it houses the Germantown Historical Society where you can go back in time to explore the neighborhood's colonial life.

GERMANTOWN HISTORICAL SOCIETY
5503–05 Germantown Avenue
844-0514

Hours: Tuesday, Thursday, 10 to 4; Sunday, 1 to 5. Closed
some holidays. Special arrangements can be made for
group tours at other times.
Tours: Call at least a week ahead.
Cost: Adults, $2; senior citizens and students, $1.50.
E & D: Call ahead for a ramp to be placed at the court-
yard entrance so the 1st floor is accessible.
Other: Stationery and books about Germantown are sold.

The Germantown Historical Society was founded in
1900 to preserve and display Germantown's colonial past.
Its vast collections include furnishings, costumes for
everyday and special occasions, quilts, china, silver, tools,
farm implements, fire-fighting equipment, and a wonderful assortment of dolls, toys and antique playthings.
Changing exhibitions give an overview of Germantown's colorful history while you get an idea of how folks
lived here in the 17th, 18th and 19th centuries.
A comprehensive Library and Archives of the Society
make for interesting research of Germantown and its residents. Read more about this opportunity in Chapter 11.

VERNON MANSION
5708 Germantown Avenue

Vernon Mansion's facade is in typical early 19th century Federal style with marble steps balanced by iron railings and large fluted Doric columns. The house dates
back to 1803.
In 1812, John Wister (the grandson of the Grumblethorpe John Wister) bought the mansion and named it
Vernon. Wister was a botanist, and some of the rare
shrubs and trees he planted still grow in the large public park that surrounds the house.
A statue of John Wister is out front. He's dressed in
plain Quaker clothes and the hat he always wore in
public.
There's also a monument bearing the statues of Francis Daniel Pastorius and the 13 families who were the
original settlers of Germantown.
Vernon Mansion is closed to the public.

WYCK

6026 Germantown Avenue
848–1690

Hours: April to mid-December, Tuesday, Thursday, Saturday, 1 to 4. Closed mid-December through March. Special arrangements can be made for group tours at other times. Allow one hour.

Tours: Groups of up to 40 can be scheduled by calling a few weeks ahead. Don't forget, you can plan a 3-centuries combination tour of Germantown described at the beginning of this section.

Cost: Adults, $2; senior citizens and children, $1.

One section of Wyck dates from around 1700, making it the oldest home in Germantown. In fact, the earliest section of Wyck was built seven decades before its neighbor Cliveden, and almost a century before George Washington became President.

Architect William Strickland designed alterations to Wyck in 1824 giving it the subtle touch of Greek Revival style that remains unchanged today.

For 283 years Wyck was owned and occupied by nine generations of one family. Many of their heirlooms and furnishings can be seen in six rooms on the first floor. Over 10,000 objects comprise the collection, so exhibitions are always changing.

In colonial times Wyck was surrounded by 20 acres of woods and farmland. Today it's on two-and-a-half acres along with an original smokehouse and ice and carriage houses. Wyck is most pleasant in warm weather when its magnificent formal rose garden is in bloom, the woods are green and the vegetable garden is sprouting.

If you'd like to visit what is one of the oldest homes in this country that has been occupied by the same family (and also where Revolutionary soldiers were hospitalized in 1777, and where the Marquis de Lafayette was formally honored at a reception in 1825), then you've come to the right place!

MENNONITE CHURCH AND GRAVEYARD
6121 Germantown Avenue
843-0943

Hours: Tuesday to Saturday, 10 to 4. Special arrangements can be made for group tours at other times. Allow at least 30 minutes.
Tours: Call or write at least a week in advance for groups of no more than 50. Arrangements can also be made for a slide show on Germantown's Mennonite history and to visit other Mennonite sites in the area.
Cost: Free, but donations are accepted.
Other: A book shop offers books about Amish, Mennonite and Germantown history, along with a selection of fraktur stationery.

The Germantown Mennonites, or German Quakers, were the first Mennonites to establish themselves in the colonies. In 1708 they built a log cabin to worship on this very site. The present stone meetinghouse replaced the log cabin in 1770. Its tiny chapel looks as it did in the 1800s. The basement with its drinking well has been restored to its 1770 appearance.

The church museum has memorabilia of Mennonite and Germantown history. A library* is available for reference on the same subjects.

A small graveyard fills the church's front yard. Its oldest stones date from the 1730s, and most of them belong to early settlers of Germantown.

EBENEZER MAXWELL MANSION
200 W. Tulpehocken Street (at Greene Street)
438-1861

Hours: April through December, Wednesday to Sunday, 1 to 4. Group tours of the mansion, its gardens and the neighborhood can be scheduled in advance at other times. Allow one hour.
Tours: Groups of up to 40 should call at least 2 weeks ahead. Don't forget about the combination tours with **Cliveden** and **Wyck** described at the beginning of this section.
Cost: Adults, $4; senior citizens, $3; students and children (including schools), $2. Groups of 10 or more, $3.
SEPTA: Bus H, XH, 53, 65; trolley 23; or Regional Rail train to Tulpehocken Station.

Go two blocks west of Germantown Avenue at Tulpehocken Street (6200 block) for a look at 19th century
Philadelphia. You've come to Philadelphia's only house-
museum of the Victorian period.

Ebenezer Maxwell had his Norman Gothic-style suburban villa built in 1859. Only one other family occupied
it since the Maxwells, and little has changed since the
original construction. Odd-
shaped high windows, a
gingerbread slate roof and
three-story tower
dominate the
exterior.

Large, sunlit and functional family rooms are gradually
being restored and furnished from the period. Chunky
Rococo Revival-style pieces dominate the library, parlor
and formal entertaining rooms downstairs, depicting life
in the 1860s. The functional kitchen is chock-full of
gadgets reflecting the Industrial Revolution. A separate
exhibit here explains the stages and processes of restoration used at the Mansion.

Magnificent examples of Victorian stenciling can be
seen along the stairway and on the upstairs walls and
ceilings. A children's room includes a magnificent three-
story dollhouse, also furnished to reflect the period. Here
on the second floor, restoration reflects life in the 1870s.
See if you can note the subtle differences.

When you visit the Ebenezer Maxwell Mansion, keep
in mind that this was a prestigious suburban section of
Philadelphia when the Maxwells lived here. The man of
the house was among the first center city merchants to
commute daily on the Reading Company's new line to
town.

The two gardens surrounding the house have proper
Victorian landscaping. Again, two distinct periods are
represented: the mid- and the later 19th century. A guide
to the plantings is available. A restoration resource
library is described in Chapter 11.

Does the Ebenezer Maxwell Mansion remind you of the
mansion in the Charles Addams cartoons? Well it should.
Because this is said to be what inspired him.

JOHNSON HOUSE
6306 Germantown Avenue
843–0943

Hours: By appointment only, Tuesday to Saturday, 10 to 4. Special arrangements can be made for group tours at other times. Allow at least one hour.
Tours: Call or write at least 2 weeks in advance for groups of no more than 50.
Cost: Adults, $2; children under 12, $1; special rates for school groups with advance reservations.

The Johnson House, owned by the Mennonite Church and Graveyard Corporation, is typical of the homes built for well-to-do Germantown families in the 1760s.

The Johnson House became the scene of major fights during the Battle of Germantown. If you want proof, look, or rather hunt, for the bullet holes and cannon ball scars.

The house had a unique function before the Civil War. It was the underground railroad station. Slaves were temporarily camped here when they were smuggled north from the Southern states.

Today, Johnson House is furnished and looks as it did in colonial days.

CONCORD SCHOOL HOUSE
6313 Germantown Avenue
843–0943

Hours: By appointment only, March through November, weekdays, 10 to 4.
Tours: Call ahead for groups of no more than 25.
Cost: Adults, $3; children, $2.

You know that schools weren't always the sleek and modern buildings that they are today. Now you can go back into history to see where children spent their school days at the time of our independence.

The Concord School House is a tiny one-room school built in 1775. The original school bell is housed in the belfry. The original books and desks are in the schoolroom.

A plot plan on the wall identifies the occupants of the **UPPER GERMANTOWN BURYING GROUND**. Peek out the window and see the graves of many early Germantown settlers and Revolutionary War victims.

CLIVEDEN
6401 Germantown Avenue
848–1777

Hours: April through December, Tuesday to Saturday, 10 to 4; Sunday, 1 to 4. Closed January through March, Easter, Thanksgiving, Christmas. Allow at least one hour.

Tours: Call a few weeks in advance to schedule for up to one busload, and no more than one school class at a time. Tours led according to youngsters' age levels. Special 2-hour programs can be scheduled for school groups. And don't forget the combination tours with **Ebenezer Maxwell Mansion** and **Wyck** described earlier.

Cost: Adults, $4; students, $3; National Trust members and children under 6, free.

Other: A gift shop features reproductions of 18th century decorative arts, items of the National Trust, games, and books on Philadelphia and colonial cooking.

E & D: Complete access, but call ahead for special assistance.

Note: Start your visit in the restored 18th century barn. It's now a reception center and small museum.

This historically important house was built in the 1760s by jurist Benjamin Chew. The Chew family owned and occupied the mansion until 1972. Now it's open to the public, and it's one of a select group of houses that is owned and maintained by the National Trust for Historic Preservation.

Before you go inside, walk around the six-acre block for an outside look at what was once Germantown's most elaborate 18th century home. Cliveden was built as a summer home. The stables, coach house, cook and wash houses are still in the yard. They're built with the same solid masonry as the Georgian style house. The British were so impressed with Cliveden's sturdy construction that they made it a fort during the Battle of Germantown. The home took quite a beating, but it managed to withstand the attacks led by George Washington himself. Musket fire and cannonball marks are still visible in walls and ceilings. Many of the marble statues in the garden are scarred by bullets.

Cliveden's elegant furnishings reflect the outstanding

taste of each generation that resided here. Many pieces are documented to important 18th century craftsmen.

UPSALA
6430 Germantown Avenue
842–1798

Hours: April through December, Tuesday and Thursday, 1 to 4. Closed January through March. Special arrangements can be made for group tours at other times. Allow at least 45 minutes.
Tours: Call one week ahead to schedule groups of no more than 25, at least elementary school age. Two adults must accompany youngsters.
Cost: Adults, $3; children under 12, $1.

Upsala was built in 1798 on the site the Continental troops camped on during the Battle of Germantown.

The Upsala facade is similar to the Vernon Mansion, in that it's the classic Federal style. You'll recognize the similarities of the stone front with Doric columns and marble steps.

The wood in Upsala is from the neighborhood. The mantlepieces, floors, stairs and doors are all original. And the structure hasn't been altered since it was built. Seven of Upsala's rooms are filled with period furnishings.

If you continue along Germantown Avenue, you'll pass more 18th century homes, churches and school buildings (including some that haven't been listed here).

The 6500 block has three more interesting homes. **BARDSLEY HOUSE,** at No. 6500, was originally one room deep. As you'll see, there have been many additions to the white stucco frame. The house was named for its owner, John Bardsley, who achieved a fair amount of fame in the 1870s importing English sparrows to eat the caterpillars that plagued neighborhood plants.

The **BILLMEYER HOUSE,** at No. 6504, and the double house across the street at No. 6505–07, also date back to the late 1700s.

On the next block, at No. 6613, is the original building of the **CHURCH OF THE BRETHREN**. It was built in 1770 by the first group of Dunkards that gathered in Pennsylvania. (Their name comes from the unusual way in which members are immersed at baptism.)

The **SCHOOL**, at No. 6609, was built in 1740 by **ST. MICHAEL'S LUTHERAN CHURCH**. Founded in 1717, the Church now occupies its third building on the site. Services are still held in German on Sunday mornings, followed by a version in English.

Continue north along Germantown Avenue and you'll come to another Philadelphia neighborhood, **CHESTNUT HILL**. This is the highest point in Philadelphia and was once abundant with chestnut trees.

Chestnut Hill is one of Philadelphia's finest residential sections. It's famous for its exclusive shops. The galleries, restaurants, farmers markets, boutiques and stores of Chestnut Hill are among the most charming in the country.

It's always fun to explore Chestnut Hill on your own. A unique way to visit the neighborhood is the day-long bus tour offered in May by Philadelphia Open House*. The Foundation for Architecture* also schedules guided walks of Chestnut Hill among its choice of neighborhood tours. Some of the **restaurants** convenient to Germantown and Chestnut Hill are described in Chapter 18.

Manayunk

Manayunk's roots go back to William Penn's time. About four miles west of his City of Brotherly Love, Penn owned land along the Schuylkill that was called Flat Rock by the English settlers who staked it off in 1683. (You'll probably get to Manayunk by following Kelly Drive parallel to the river, to Ridge Avenue West, to Main Street. Or go by bike on the path that goes adjacent to Kelly Drive.) The first stone house was built in 1736, and gradually a small community grew. George Washington's troops marched through towards Valley Forge in September, 1777, followed soon after by the British.

Manayunk's growth coincides with construction of the Schuylkill Canal begun in 1818 and the Manayunk Canal section that was completed in 1822. With the river navigable, it was natural that industrial development should follow. Manayunk sprouted as a mill town specializing in textile production.

In 1824, Flat Rock was renamed "Manayunk" from the

Indian expression meaning, "place where we go to drink." (Today, we still go to drink and dine at restaurants overlooking the Schuylkill and along Main Street in Manayunk.)

When a train linking Philadelphia with Pottstown began operation in 1842, a swath of rail lines cut through Manayunk and signaled the beginning of the end for canal travel. But, industry thrived, more mills were built, and more immigrants were lured here to work. They built their rowhouses on the hills above the Main Street and across the train tracks. The mill owners built their larger homes at the tops of the hills with sweeping views of the city and the river below. Churches were built by the English, Irish, German, Italian and Polish settlers. They all remain active today as new generations stayed on in the neighborhood.

Manayunk was consolidated into the City of Philadelphia in 1854. By the 1880s the Main Street was booming, lined not only with mills, but also hotels, stores, theaters and banks. By the turn of the century, a new trolley line linked Manayunk with the city. Keeping pace with advancing technology, it continued as an industrial center till the 1920s.

When you visit Manayunk today, you might think of San Francisco. At the base of the community, parallel to the river, Main Street is alive again with colorful shops, restaurants and galleries. Many of the original 19th century stone mill buildings along Main Street have been restored in the past few years as apartments and trendy commercial spaces. Remnants of the old mills survive, too, as wool spinners, felt and dye works, chemical and paper producers. Above Main Street, a 19th century rowhouse community climbs high towards the rocky cliffs. In some places, steep stairs cut into the rocks so you can navigate on foot to the top. The 19th century ambiance remains.

Rejuvenation of Manayunk was spurred by the rehabilitation in 1979 of its canal system and construction of the towpath and boardwalk. The Main Street area, the canal and adjacent Venice Island were designated a National Historic District in 1983. Manayunk became internationally known in 1985 with the advent of the CoreStates Championship*, described along with other Manayunk annual events, in Chapter 19. Manayunk **restaurants** are described in Chapter 18.

Don't miss the ups and downs of Manayunk. You can tour it with a Foundation for Architecture Tour* or spend time browsing on your own. Walk along the boardwalk and Main Street. Head for the hills and ask a localite for directions to Silver Street where there's a mid-19th century house just eight feet wide. Walk "the wall" on Levering Street and imagine what it must be like to pedal up it eight times in the CoreStates race. Climb some stairs in the cliffs. Talk to some "yunkers" and you'll get to feeling why they proudly call their neighborhood an "urban village."

Old City

Old City is in the shadow of the Ben Franklin Bridge, from Vine Street to Chestnut and from the Delaware River to 5th Street. This was the heart of William Penn's Philadelphia. Elfreth's Alley*, the nation's oldest continuously occupied residential street, is here. So are several of the 18th century churches (see Chapter 5). Here, too, are Fireman's Hall* and the Betsy Ross House*. An Old World charm remains.

In recent years, Old City was a commercial area for industry and wholesale distributors. Their structures are excellent examples of late 18th and early 19th century architecture. No fewer than 60 examples of cast iron building facades remain, mostly from the 1850s.

Since the late 1960s, many of these commercial loft buildings have been rehabilitated to provide expansive, well-lit living and working areas for artists and architects. They also have retail spaces on the street level.

Old City's resident population has quadrupled in the past decade.

Some examples of apartment and condominium conversions are Little Boys Way at 209 Cuthbert Street (once a sewing notions factory), St. Charles Court at 3rd and Arch Streets (formerly a hostelry for the Arch Street Friends), The Sugar Refinery at 225 Christ Church Walkway (built in 1782 and once the country's largest sugar refinery), The Wireworks at 301 Race Street (built at the turn-of-the-century for a factory that made insulated electric wire), The Chocolate Works at 231 N. 3rd Street (comprising five buildings from the early 20th century that

housed the Wilbur Chocolate Company), and the Hoop-
skirt Factory at 309 Arch Street (built in 1875, and you
can guess what they made there until 1894).

What Soho has been to New York City, Old City has become to Philadelphia.

Art galleries have discovered its lofty spaces and flocked
to the area. Design studios have proliferated, especially
along 3rd Street from Arch to Race. The Clay Studio* at
139 N. 2nd Street provides work and exhibition space for
craftspeople in the Second Street Art Building. Drama
groups and small theaters have assembled a la Greenwich
Village. The Painted Bride Art Center* moved to Old City
from South Street in 1981.

You'll want to stroll through Old City to see its historic
attractions and its recent changes and additions. Here,
too, you can take a guided tour with the Foundation for
Architecture Tours* or Philadelphia Open House*.

SEPTA routes to the area include any of the Market
Street bus or subway lines to 2nd Street, the Ben Frank-
Line route 76, bus 5 running north on 3rd Street or south
on 2nd Street, and bus 50 running north on 5th Street and
south on 4th Street.

As the population comes to a neighborhood, so do **restaurants**. Several of Old City's eating and drinking
places are described in Chapter 18.

Check out what's new in Old City.

Queen Village

This neighborhood is in the oldest part of Philadelphia.
It was settled by the Swedes prior to 1640. It was originally called Wiccaco. Then it was named Southwark, for
its English counterpart south of London. The newest
name, Queen Village, honors Swedish Queen Christina's
role in promoting the area's original settlement.

Queen Village is directly south of Head House Square
in Society Hill. Its borders are Front to 6th Street and
Lombard to Washington Avenue.

Queen Village was a separate neighborhood that became part of Philadelphia when the City and County
were consolidated in 1854.

Queen Village has many of Philadelphia's oldest
houses, and they, too, are being restored. The Shippen
family developed Kenilworth Street between Front and

2nd Streets in the 1740s. The neighboring homes belonged to sea captains, mariners, riggers and ropemakers who worked hard to make Philadelphia a major 18th century seaport.

New houses, as well, have sprouted in Queen Village. Striking individual townhomes and contemporary clusters are throughout the neighborhood.

If you want to see some interesting homes, look on Monroe, Pemberton, Fitzwater, Catharine and Queen Streets. Also look at the Court at Old Swedes development facing the Delaware River at Queen Street.

America's first naval yards were on the Delaware at the foot of Federal Street. They're long gone, but at one time frigates were outfitted and repaired in Southwark. The waterfront activity made this a bustling neighborhood.

The historic sites in Queen Village include Old Swedes' Church (Gloria Dei)*. This is the oldest church in Pennsylvania. The famous **SHOT TOWER** at Front and Carpenter Streets was built in 1808 to manufacture shotgun ammunition. It remained an arsenal for 100 years, and was the first arsenal in the country. By today's standards, the manufacturing process was relatively simple. Lead was dropped from the top of the 175-foot tower through screens with different size holes. The hot lead fell into cold water vats and then hardened into bullets. Some of the bullets are still on display at Old Swedes' Church. Shot Tower is now a recreation center.

A colorful part of the neighborhood is **SOUTH STREET** from 2nd to 7th, and extending a block north and south to Lombard and Bainbridge Streets.

Starting around 1970, old, dilapidated stores from another era were bought or leased by young people who converted them into craft houses, book stores, second-hand shops, leather shops, restaurants, cafe theaters, antique shops and coffee shops.

South Street was once one of Philadelphia's most popular shopping streets. Today, some 20 years after its renaissance began, it's similar to Greenwich Village in New York. Older Philadelphians are shocked to find that this longtime run-down area has become strong and viable again. As success came once again to South Street, many of the pioneers in its renaissance have been forced out by increased property values. In many locations, larger established retailers have taken over where individuals could no longer survive.

You can comfortably spend a few hours dining and browsing here. Most of the shops and restaurants are open daily from late morning till late in the evening. South Street is especially lively on weekends and for nightlife.

The South Street area is a mecca for good, imaginative restaurants. Read about several of them in Chapter 18.

Society Hill

Directly south of Independence National Historical Park lies a neighborhood known as Society Hill. It's loosely bounded by Walnut and Lombard Streets and Front and 7th Streets.

Society Hill got its name because it was land that William Penn granted to a stock company called the Society of Free Traders. Their goal was to promote trade in Pennsylvania. The Delaware waterfront at Front and Pine Streets was a hill. And that's why it's called Society Hill.

For many years, Society Hill was a meeting place and parade ground. The hill gradually disappeared over the years, but the name remained. (In the 1960s it became an "in" place for prominent Philadelphians to live.) Churches rose in the neighborhood, along with a market place and a community center.

Today a great deal of Society Hill looks as it did in colonial times. It's one of the nation's finest examples of urban renewal, and it's virtually impossible to buy a home here for less than $200,000.

The blight of the Industrial Revolution has rapidly disappeared. The major force for renewal came in June, 1959, when the antiquated Dock Street Markets were closed. (A modern Food Distribution Center* opened simultaneously at its sprawling new site in South Philadelphia.) The three Society Hill Towers luxury apartment buildings were completed in 1964.

Over 900 homes from the 18th and 19th centuries have been restored and rebuilt with loving care to resemble their original condition. Even the new homes in Society Hill have been designed to look colonial or to blend with their surroundings.

Many of the new homes are built in clusters around a common courtyard. Delancey Mews is at 2nd and Delancey Streets; Addison Court is at 6th and Pine Streets;

Bingham Court is at 4th Street and St. Joseph's Walk; Lawrence Court is tucked between 4th and 5th Streets and Spruce and Pine.

Colonial style brick walkways weave through Society Hill. You can stroll on the major streets or these walkways to see historic homes, recent courtyard developments, colonial churches and small parks. (My father built Delancey Park between 3rd and 4th Streets on Delancey.)

Some of the Society Hill homes are open to the public. You can visit Hill Physick Keith House*, Powel House* and "A Man Full of Trouble Tavern"*.

Stop at Head House Square* and NewMarket*. (You'll read about them in a minute.) See the 18th century-style street lights, cobblestone streets, narrow alleys and brick sidewalks. Have a frozen yogurt or some oven-fresh cookies.

Guided tours can be arranged with some of the guide services listed in Chapter 1.

SEPTA routes close to 2nd and Pine Streets are buses 5, 40, 42, 90 or the Ben FrankLine route 76. Route 50 buses go north on 5th Street and south on 4th.

The **HEAD HOUSE** stands proudly at 2nd and Pine Streets. This little red brick structure was built at the northern end of the colonial 2nd Street marketplace in 1804. Firefighting equipment was kept behind the large green double-doors that face Pine Street. An early 18th century man-drawn fire wagon is still here. The 2nd floor was used as a meeting place and community center.

The open-air market in the center of 2nd Street between Pine and Lombard was originally built in 1745 and known as "New Market." The stall dividers have been reconstructed at the **2ND STREET MARKET** so you can picture how Ben Franklin, George Washington, Thomas Jefferson and the rest of the fellows went to buy their provisions.

The market area of Head House, as it's called today, is the focal point of Society Hill.

Both sides of 2nd Street from Pine to Lombard are now lined with delightful shops, cafes, restaurants and intriguing sights. Some of the shops are restored, while others are recently built. The activity continues to bustle at Head House during the summer. Visitors come by car, carriage, bicycle, stroller and foot to dine, shop, browse and have fun.

Local artists, craftsmen and entertainers come to the marketplace for 10 weekends from late June till early September. The **Crafts Market** hours are noon to midnight on Saturdays and noon to 6 on Sundays. Workshops for children are on Sunday afternoons. Today's **NEW-MARKET** encompasses an entire block on the east side of Head House Square, from Pine to Lombard, Front to 2nd Streets. It's a multi-level commercial complex that combines the old and new with massive wood sculpture, stacked glass cubes and a see-through elevator. New-Market took 18th century homes on the 2nd Street side and combined them with an ultra-modern glass facade on the Front Street side.

A year was dedicated to archaeological exploration of the block before the restoration began. The thousands of items that were found indicate that a marketplace and homes were on the site in the 18th century. Period restorations show Georgian, Federal and Victorian architectural styles.

Unfortunately, much of NewMarket is currently vacant. We're waiting for NewMarket to renew. . .again. But what's there is worthy of your perusal. You can dine internationally at NewMarket and Head House Square. **Restaurants**, from informal to elegant, are described in Chapter 18.

University City

University City gets its name from the many educational facilities within its boundaries, from the Schuylkill River west to 44th Street and from the river north to Powelton Avenue. This neighborhood's history can be traced to five years before William Penn appeared on the scene. In 1677 William Warner, an Englishman who's said to have been Philadelphia's only Puritan, purchased from the Indians 1,500 acres in the area. Warner called his estate Blockley.

In 1734, Philadelphia lawyer and counsel to the Penn family, Andrew Hamilton, purchased a 250 acre tract that was among his land holdings later inherited in 1747 by his grandson William. The latter proceeded to build here between 1787 and 1790 a handsome Federal-style mansion surrounded by fabulous gardens. When William Hamilton died in 1813, his estate was considered one of the finest in America. Nearly 80 acres of its grounds were laid out in 1840 to become the rural garden **Woodlands** Cemetery. Today, the partially restored mansion is a National Historic Landmark, and the cemetery itself is designated as Woodlands Heritage National Recreation Trail. It's open weekdays from 8 A.M. to 4 P.M. The entrance gates are at 40th Street and Woodland Avenue. Stop by the office in the mansion and pick up a brochure with map of the grounds and a list of the distinguished persons who are buried here. Among them are several members of the Drexel family, architect Paul Cret (designer of the entrance gates), sculptor William Rush and artists Thomas Eakins and Rembrandt Peale. In many cases, the monuments are as noteworthy as the people they memorialize.

But, back to the neighborhood. Settlement grew in the area, especially after bridges were built to span the Schuylkill. Private estates covered entire blocks and summer villages sprang up in clusters. By the mid-19th century, Philadelphia's western suburbs prospered. University City was incorporated into the City in 1854.

Hundreds of homes and no less than 50 churches remain from that period and from subsequent decades. Over the years, however, much of University City's grand suburban residential atmosphere has been altered by the growth of great institutions including the Veterans Hospital and the Civic Center complex.

The University of Pennsylvania moved in 1872 from the center of Philadelphia to a campus that hasn't stopped growing in University City. A few blocks east, Drexel University (formerly known as Drexel Institute of Technology) was founded in 1890. The Philadelphia College of Pharmacy and Science moved in 1928 to its campus bordering the Woodlands Cemetery.

University City Science Center was founded in 1965 with the backing of 28 Philadelphia area colleges, universities and health centers. Its research and office buildings on 16 acres along nine blocks of Market Street make Philadelphia an internationally recognized "think tank" on just about any scientific subject.

When completed, the University City Conference Center will further expand the Science Center's capability and attract multilingual and international meetings. A huge auditorium, conference rooms, seminar halls, restaurants, retail shops, recreation facilities and a 300-room hotel will be the newest addition to the University City Science Center along the north side of Market Street from 36th to 38th Streets.

This combination of private and institutional wealth and resources has blessed University City with a variety of outstanding architecture. Many of the neighborhood's historic mansions have been adapted by the University of Pennsylvania for educational use. Blocks of unusual single homes, twins and rowhouses exist throughout the western section of University City on Locust, Spruce and Pine Streets, Larchwood and Osage Avenues, St. Mark's Square and Woodland Terrace. Powelton Village is seeing a rebirth northwest of the Drexel campus.

The Penn campus (I'm partial to my alma mater) has been a magnet for great architects. There is a unique blending of buildings designed by Frank Furness, Cope and Stewardson, Eero Saarinen, Louis Kahn and Mitchell and Giurgola, to name a few.

Drexel University's original and main building is the home of the Drexel Museum collection* at 32nd and Chestnut Streets. It was designed by the Wilson Brothers, finished in 1891, and is still spectacular. And it would be remiss not to mention the contemporary architecture of Children's Hospital on 34th Street and the International House*.

A good way to explore University City and West Philadelphia is a Foundation for Architecture Tour* of the University of Pennsylvania or nearby Spruce Hill Victoriana. You can call the West Philadelphia Partnership for information about the "University City Guide" they publish along with the West Philadelphia Chamber of Commerce. The University City Historical Society (387–3019) and the University City Arts League (382–7811) also sponsor ongoing programs in the community.

Several **SEPTA** routes traverse University City. They include the Market-Frankford Subway-Elevated; buses 21, 30, 31, 40, 42; trolleys 10, 11, 13, 34, 36; and the regional rail trains to 30th Street Station.

Some of the **restaurants** in University City are described in Chapter 18. There are also several campus-favorite sandwich shops, fast food establishments and cheerful cafeterias in the University Museum, hospitals and university facilities. Many of the people in University City are from the academic world and are very friendly, so feel free to ask them what's nearby.

You can see from this brief description and throughout this book that University City offers all kinds of cultural events, recreational facilities, hotels, office complexes, world-renowned medical centers, residential communities and campus environments. It's no wonder that the people of University City call their neighborhood Philadelphia's "Other City."

Chapter 4.
Museums and Historic Sites.

It's only natural that the city where the country was founded would be rich in historic attractions. You've read about the sites of Independence National Historical Park. Now examine the dozens of museums, 18th century homes, taverns, a colonial street and a Revolutionary fort. Some concentrate on a specific theme such as shoes, some dwell on a particular period in history, some are devoted to a prominent person and some are more general in their appeal. But you'll surely want to visit at least a few.

In some cases, art and artifacts overlap with objects and places of antiquity. So some of the attractions described in this chapter might be equally appropriate for the section on Art Museums in Chapter 9, and vice versa. Or the historic sites of Fairmount Park that appear in Chapter 8 might just as well be included here. You get the point. To know about all the terrific things in Philadelphia, you should read the whole book.

"A MAN FULL OF TROUBLE TAVERN"
127 Spruce Street—19106
922–1759

Hours: 2nd Sunday of every month, 1 to 4 P.M. Other times by appointment only. Candlelight tours can be scheduled from 7 to 9 P.M. Allow at least 45 minutes.
Tours: Call the tavern at least one week in advance.
Cost: Adults, $1.50; children under 16, $.50. Groups: $25 minimum charge for group of 15, and $1.50 for each additional visitor.
Lunch: No facilities. Special arrangements can be made for groups who want to bring their own.
SEPTA: Buses 5, 40, 42, 90, Ben FrankLine route 76.
E & D: No wheelchair access.

"A Man Full of Trouble" is the only remaining 18th century tavern in Philadelphia. It's a Society Hill landmark that dates back to 1759.

The Knauer Foundation restored the tavern with period furnishings that include Delftware, pewter and finds from nearby excavations.

As in most colonial dwellings, the kitchen is in the cellar. The first floor was formerly used by guests for food and drink. The bedrooms and a sitting room are on the second floor, and typical 18th century tavern bedrooms are on the third floor.

AFRO-AMERICAN HISTORICAL AND CULTURAL MUSEUM
7th and Arch Streets—19106
574-0380

Hours: Tuesday to Saturday, 10 to 5. Closed holidays. Allow at least one hour.

Tours: All exhibits are self-explanatory. Groups of 20 or more should call a week ahead to schedule visits and special rates. Philadelphia Public School teachers call 574-3127 for study programs and to arrange visits.

Cost: Adults, $3.50; senior citizens, handicapped and children under 12, $1.75. Groups rates for 20 or more when scheduling visit. Membership entitles you to free admission, shop discounts, a newsletter and invitations to special events.

SEPTA: Bus 48, Market Street routes or a short walk from Independence Hall.

Other: A gift shop sells African artifacts, jewelry, books and clothing. Cultural programs are scheduled throughout each month in the museum's auditorium. Call to find out what's planned.

E & D: Complete wheelchair access.

Philadelphia's Afro-American Historical and Cultural Museum was the first built by a major city in this country to house and interpret collections of Afro-American culture. It opened in 1976 during America's Bicentennial celebration.

The museum's galleries are used for changing exhibits to portray the Afro-American experience in Philadelphia, Pennsylvania and the United States.

"Let This Be Your Home" (through 1991) vividly portrays the migration experience of Afro-Americans from the South to Philadelphia in the years 1900 to 1940. What made them leave? What brought them here? What did they find here? What were the effects on South, North and West Philadelphia? What were the effects on Philadelphia's sports, culture and politics? You'll trace the personal experiences of individuals and families making the journey north to a new home.

Other galleries have exhibitions that change every few months. Stop by or call ahead to find out what's being shown now.

Don't leave the area without observing the museum's two outdoor sculptures. "Nesaika" is an African deity, and the 13 "Whispering Bells" honor a black patriot, Crispus Attucks, who was the first casualty of the Revolutionary War. (See the section of Chapter 9 on Street Art.)

AMERICAN-SWEDISH HISTORICAL MUSEUM
1900 Pattison Avenue—19145
389-1776

Hours: Tuesday to Friday, 10 to 4; weekends, 12 to 4. Closed holidays. Allow one hour.
Tours: Call 2 weeks in advance to schedule groups of 10 to 40, at least 4th grade level. A special 90-minute program can be arranged for school groups.
Cost: Adults, $2; senior citizens, students, $1; children under 12 with an adult, free; school groups with reservations for special program, $1.50. Memberships are available.
Lunch: No indoor facilities, but in nice weather you can picnic in the surrounding park.
SEPTA: Buses 17, C, G; Broad Street Subway to Pattison.
Other: Festivals are celebrated in April, June and December (see Chapter 19). A small gift shop sells Swedish crafts, knickknacks, stationery, jewelry and books.
E & D: No wheelchair access.

The American-Swedish Historical Museum resembles a 17th century Swedish manor house which is very much at home in Philadelphia's Franklin D. Roosevelt Park.

Its 14 rooms have artifacts from early Swedish settlements along the Delaware River. (The museum's site was part of New Sweden in the 1600s.) The displays honor Swedish and American-Swedish contributions to the cultural, economic, social and technological development of the United States.

"Before Penn: New Sweden Colony" portrays with paintings, maps, and colonial Swedish and Indian artifacts the history of the region prior to Penn's arrival.

The John Erikson Room contains its namesake's contributions to science. The Jenny Lind Music Room has memorabilia from her American concert tour that ran from 1848 to 1851.

The Pioneer and Arts and Crafts Rooms are enchanting for youngsters. One simulates an 18th century Dalarna farmhouse. The other contains jewelry, ceramics and a collection of 28 Swedish costumed dolls—all hand-made in Sweden and dressed in colorful authentic peasant costumes.

ATWATER KENT MUSEUM
15 South 7th Street—19106
922–3031 or 686–3630

Hours: Tuesday to Saturday, 9:30 to 4:45. Closed holidays. Allow 45 minutes.
Tours: You're on your own.
Cost: Free.
SEPTA: Buses 9, 21, 42, Ben FrankLine route 76, Market Street routes.
Other: A wide variety of unique tours, lectures, workshops and family activities are scheduled each season. Pick up the museum's "News and Notes" calendar of events.
E & D: There is a ramp at the rear entrance, off the Liberty Walkway. Once inside, all floors can be reached by elevator. All of the restrooms are accessible to wheelchairs; a parking lot is next door.

The Atwater Kent Museum is a wonderful place to learn about Philadelphia's early growth and progress.

The main gallery portrays Philadelphia from 1680 to 1880: from William Penn to the Centennial celebration. There are objects from every aspect of life in Philadelphia: weapons, model ships, model railroads, model houses, model streets, clothing, furniture, books, dolls, musical instruments, silverware, crafts and cockroach traps. (As I said, it has *every* aspect.)

"The City Beneath Us: A Gallery Devoted to the City Archaeological Collection" contains changing exhibits of archaeological finds that have been unearthed in Philadelphia.

Another gallery shows some aspect of "The City in Two Dimensions: Selections from the Print, Painting and Photograph Collection."

Two other small rooms trace the development of Philadelphia's municipal services. The water and gas utilities are in one exhibit and the police and fire departments are in another. Be sure to see the 1890 Rogues

Gallery with its old mug shots of local anarchists and horse thieves.

You won't want to miss a marvelous display on the second floor of antique toys and dolls native to this area.

BELLAIRE MANOR
20th Street and Pattison Avenue—19145
664-8456

Hours: By reservation only, daily, 10 to 4. Allow one hour.
Tours: Guides in colonial costume will escort you. Children must be with an adult. Call 2 weeks ahead.
Cost: Adults, $2; senior citizens and children under 12, $1.50. Group rates arranged in advance.
Lunch: No food is allowed in the house, but you can picnic in the park.
SEPTA: Bus 17, C, G.
E & D: There's one step at the entrance to each building. Arrangements can be made in advance for a ramp to be put down.

Built in 1714, Bellaire Manor is among the oldest of the Fairmount Park houses and one of the oldest houses in Philadelphia. It's tucked away in Franklin D. Roosevelt Park (near the American-Swedish Historical Museum), a section of Fairmount Park in the southern part of the city.

A visit to Bellaire takes in a description of its early Georgian architectural style, and the colonial lifestyle of the area's early Swedish settlers. You'll see five rooms that are furnished with period pieces and reproductions representing two centuries of occupants at the property.

The bake house is also restored, functionally furnished, in use and part of the tour. If something smells real good, it might be fresh bread in the kiln or hot soup in the cauldron.

The authentic colonial Rivinus herb garden is behind the bake house. I know you're familiar with parsley, sage, rosemary and thyme. But you might also recognize aloes, hyssop and lamb's leg. And, in warm weather, don't miss the colonial flower garden with its petunias and old-fashioned roses.

Remember: An **asterisk (*)** indicates that the same place or event appears elsewhere in the book with more details. Look in the Index for additional pages.

BENJAMIN FRANKLIN BUST
Arch Street east of 4th

Don't miss, or rather you can't miss, the bigger-than-life bust of Benjamin Franklin while you're walking through historic Philadelphia. Ben overlooks Arch Street and the Arch Street Friends' Meeting House*, only a block away from Franklin's grave in the Christ Church Burial Ground*.

Franklin came to Philadelphia in 1723 when he was 17. His contributions to Philadelphia, the colonies and later the United States and the world are renowned.

As a statesman, Franklin was United States emissary to France during the Revolution. He wrote the "Franklin Almanack" and published a daily newspaper, "The Pennsylvania Gazette."

As a civic leader, he started the colonies' first fire insurance company, the first circulating library and the first hospital. As an inventor, he experimented with electricity. (You remember the kite and key story.)

Franklin was an extraordinary man. When he decided he needed bifocals, he invented them.

You'll learn more about Franklin's wit and genius when you visit Franklin Court*, the Benjamin Franklin National Memorial at the Franklin Institute* and various of the institutions around town with which he was associated.

Back to the bust. This 16-foot-high statue was made out of 80,000 copper pennies. They symbolize one of Franklin's most famous sayings: "A Penny Saved is a Penny Earned." Most of the coins were donated by Philadelphia school children and youngsters of employees of the Philadelphia Fire Department.

BETSY ROSS HOUSE
239 Arch Street—19106
627–5343

Hours: Daily, except Monday, 10 to 5. Closed Thanksgiving, Christmas, New Year's. Allow 20 minutes.
Tours: You're on your own. No reservations taken.
Cost: Free.
SEPTA: Buses, 5, 48, Ben FrankLine route 76, or Market Street routes.
Other: There's a large souvenir shop. An annual celebration is held on **Flag Day, June 14.**
E & D: Wheelchair access to the adjacent park only. The house has 4 floors.

You'll know you're at the right house when you see a 13-star flag waving outside. The flag is a copy of the original "Old Glory" with 13 stars in a circle on a blue field. You'll enter through Atwater Kent Park, a neo-colonial retreat with brick and wrought iron, rhododendrons, azaleas, English ivy, magnolia and hawthorne trees.

The remains of Betsy Ross and her third husband, John Claypoole, were re-buried here in 1975.

This tiny two-and-a-half story red brick structure was built in the early 1700s as the Ross family's home. We think it's the place where upholsterer and flag-maker Betsy Ross, at George Washington's request, stitched together the first American flag.

Five rooms are handsomely decorated with period and original furnishings. Life-sized models depict Betsy Ross' busy life as a seamstress, musket ball maker for the Continental Army, home-maker, wife and mother of seven daughters.

Notice how small the house is.

It's a good thing we only had 13 states then, instead of 50. Betsy would have needed more space.

CIGNA CORPORATION MUSEUM
S.E. corner 17th and Arch Streets—19103
523-4894

Hours: Weekdays, 9 to 5. Closed some holidays. Allow one hour at the ground floor exhibits.

Tours: You're on your own with no reservations necessary to see ground floor exhibits. Inquire about guided group tours of the gallery collections at CIGNA's new Two Liberty Place offices (after September 1991).

Cost: Free.

SEPTA: Buses 2, 27, 32, Ben FrankLine route 76, Kennedy Boulevard or Market Street routes.

E & D: There's a ramp at the Arch Street entrance enabling complete wheelchair access.

America's first stock and marine insurance company was founded in 1792 at Independence Hall and was one of the first companies to underwrite fire insurance. You can see a fascinating collection of marine and fire artifacts that commemorate CIGNA's historic as well as innovative past.

The ground level public exhibits include fire fighting memorabilia ranging from hats, buckets and brigade equipment to antique fire apparatus stationed on a realistic brick and cobblestone street. The full-size pieces are visible at all hours through the glass walls of CIGNA's contemporary building at 17th and Arch Streets.

A wonderful collection of model ships, model fire engines, firemarks, old insurance documents, portraits, maritime art and lithographs, engravings and watercolors of 19th century Philadelphia are among the thousands of items in CIGNA's museum collection. These can be seen by appointment only, as noted above.

CIVIL WAR MUSEUM AND LIBRARY
1805 Pine Street—19103
735-8196

Hours: Daily, except Sunday, 10 to 4. Closed holidays. Allow 45 minutes or more.

Tours: Individuals and groups will be guided on arrival. Groups of no more than 25, at least 10 years old, can be scheduled. Children must be with an adult, and all groups are requested to call ahead.

Cost: $3. Organized groups, school classes, senior citizens and servicemen in uniform, $2; children under 12, free.
SEPTA: Buses 2, 17, 90.
E & D: No wheelchair access. There are 4 floors of exhibits reached by stairs.

Welcome to a showplace for Civil War mementos. The Military Order of the Loyal Legion was founded by three Philadelphia Union Army officers on April 15, 1865, the day President Abraham Lincoln died. Their intent was to perpetuate Lincoln's ideals. Hence, this magnificent collection. Hundreds of war items as well as an extensive library fill the four-story townhouse museum.

The only known collection of military escutcheons lines the entrance hallway. These hand-painted insignias were made popular by local artists after the Civil War. Each painting contains symbols and words detailing a soldier's entire military history.

One room is devoted to Ulysses S. Grant. His full dress uniform and personal items are encased. His portraits, photographs and correspondence cover the walls.

One section of the Lincoln Room recalls the President's assassination with newspaper front pages, mourning handkerchiefs, funeral badges and a walking stick retrieved from his box at Ford's Theater on April 14, 1865.

Other exhibits in the museum include soldiers' field gear, saddles, uniforms, flags, medals, Confederate money, artillery and Civil War weapons.

If you're a Lincoln buff, or a Civil War buff, you don't want to miss this museum.

ELFRETH'S ALLEY
Between Arch and Race, Front and 2nd Streets
574–0560 (Museum)

Hours: Elfreth's Alley is a public thoroughfare. The museum is open daily, 10 to 4. Call ahead to be sure, since it's manned by volunteers. Closed Thanksgiving and Christmas through New Year's. Special arrangements can be made in advance for groups to visit at other times.
Tours: You're on your own, except on **Elfreth's Alley Day** (see below).
Cost: Free.
SEPTA: Bus 5, 48, Ben FrankLine route 76, or a short walk from any Market Street route.

Other: Souvenir postcards, jewelry and mementos of the Alley are sold at the museum.

E & D: No wheelchair access to the museum, but the street itself is brick and cobblestone and wide enough for a car.

Elfreth's Alley is a charming little street hidden among modern-day warehouses and wholesale stores. It's lined with 33 houses that date back to the early 1700s. It's the oldest continuously occupied residential street in America. And it's a National Historic Landmark.

The people who lived along Elfreth's Alley were tradesmen. Jeremiah Elfreth, the street's namesake, was a blacksmith. See if you can tell the difference between these colonial homes in Old City* and the elegant residences of Society Hill.

No. 126, Mantua Makers House, is the **ELFRETH'S ALLEY MUSEUM**. The two downstairs rooms have period furnishings. At the second floor photo gallery you can view pictures of the interiors of some of the alley's preserved homes, as well as changes to the alley itself through the years. A third floor bedroom is also restored. A colonial garden is in the backyard.

Elfreth's Alley Day is celebrated the first weekend in June when residents of the street don colonial dress and hold open house for the public. There's music of the period, crafts demonstrations and other colonial activities. Hours are 12 to 5. There's an admission charge for adults; children 12 and under tour free but must be with an adult.

FIREMAN'S HALL
2nd and Quarry Streets (between Arch and Race)—19106
923–1438

Hours: Tuesday to Saturday, 9 to 5. Closed holidays. Allow 45 minutes.

Tours: You're on your own. Firemen are on duty to answer questions. Groups of 20 or more are requested to call a week ahead, and guided tours can usually be scheduled.

Cost: Free, but donations are accepted.

SEPTA: Bus 5, 48, Ben FrankLine route 76, or a short walk from any Market Street route.

Other: A gift shop sells memorabilia related to fire fighting and its history.

E & D: Complete wheelchair access.

In addition to all of his scientific and diplomatic achievements, Ben Franklin also organized the nation's first fire company: the Union Fire Company, founded in 1736.

Several rival volunteer groups followed until 1871, when all of the companies finally merged and became the professional Philadelphia Fire Department. This was another nation's first that happened in Philadelphia.

Fireman's Hall is a splendid restoration of an 1876 firehouse that belonged to Engine Company 8. A modern wing with multi-media exhibits was added in 1976. Together they provide a memorable tribute to the Philadelphia Fire Department and fire fighting history.

Engine Company 8 is the direct descendent of the Union Fire Company. The first exhibits you'll see here explain the early volunteer companies, the role played by insurance companies and the early methods of fire fighting. Two floors of exhibits include all kinds of apparatus from leather buckets to hand-drawn, horse-drawn and motor-driven vehicles, some of which you can climb on.

Clever historical displays feature firemarks, uniforms, helmet frontispieces, hand tools, hose sections, ladders, scale model fire engines and a "jump" net. A "dateline" of the development of fire fighting advancements winds through the museum.

Walk into the chief's office and firemen's quarters and see furnishings of the day, listen to typical firehouse banter and grasp the authentic brass pole that would whisk firemen to the floor below. Step up to the wheelhouse and direct a fireboat along the waterfront.

You'll want to observe the original "Joker System" as it receives and records fire alarms. At the same time, you'll hear any alarms that might be sounded in the city during your visit.

Four films are available that run up to 15 minutes each. You can request to watch about the importance of smoke detectors, fighting fires in Philadelphia or the city's emergency and rescue services.

This is an easy way to learn about the importance of home safety and fire prevention. Pay attention to these exhibits so the local firemen won't have to visit you!

FIRST TROOP,
PHILADELPHIA CITY CAVALRY
"First City Troop" Armory
23rd and Ranstead Streets—19103
564-1488

Hours: Weekdays, by appointment only. Allow 45 minutes.
Tours: Groups of no more than 15, at least 4th grade level, are scheduled by calling a few days in advance.
Cost: Free.
SEPTA: Buses 7, 12, Market or Chestnut Street routes.
E & D: There's one step at entrance. Call ahead for assistance and to use elevator to get to museum on 2nd floor.

You always thought the first 13-stripe flag was the American flag. Right? Here's the place where you'll be told you were wrong.

The "First City Troop" was founded on November 18, 1774. Their flag had 13 stars and stripes. The original "Old Glory" will be shown to you during your tour. Was Betsy Ross guilty of plagiarism? Or was it coincidence?

The "First City Troop" is the oldest continually active military company in the United States. The members parade through center city three times a year—on horseback—on their anniversary in November, the anniversary of George Washington's death in December and George Washington's birthday in February.

The armory's museum also includes a collection of militaria and important art by Eakins, Peale, Rembrandt and Pennington. The uniforms worn by members of the troop from the time of the Revolution through the Vietnam War are on exhibit. If you'd like to know more about the troop's history, call for a tour. If you want to see a parade, call for an exact schedule.

GLEN FOERD
On the Delaware
5001 Grant Avenue—19114
632-5330

Hours: Weekday tours, 10 A.M. and 2 P.M.; Sunday by reservation only, 10 A.M. and Noon. Closed holidays. Allow one hour for tour. Groups should call a few weeks in advance.

Cost: Adults, $4; senior citizens and students, $3. Group rates arranged when making reservations.

Lunch: Ask about catered luncheons available for groups.

SEPTA: Buses 19, 84; Regional Rail R7 to Torresdale stop and then a two block walk.

Other: A gift shop sells books, crafts, stationery and Philadelphia memorabilia. Ask about tour packages combining Glen Foerd with Andalusia* and Pennsbury Manor* and perhaps a Delaware River lunch or dinner cruise.

E & D: The side entrance has five steps. The tour is on two floors.

Welcome back to imagining life at the turn of the century on an 18-acre grand estate complete with 25-room mansion, formal rose garden, restored "gas house" that's now a cottage, carriage house, 1820s gate house, towering riverfront oak trees more than 300 years old and a weeping hemlock that's said to be the country's oldest and Pennsylvania's largest.

The original 3-story section of Glen Foerd was built in 1850 by Charles Macalester, founder of Torresdale, and financial adviser to several U.S. presidents. It reached its present size in 1902 when an art gallery was added by its then owner, Robert H. Foerderer, a member of Congress.

Your tour includes the gallery, a look at the huge pipe organ, original furnishings, rugs and art objects. You can't miss the Tiffany-style skylights, stately mahogany grand staircase and paneling throughout, ornamental ceilings and rich parquet floors. Picture how life must have been at Philadelphia's only surviving riverfront estate! (Relive it by renting Glen Foerd to have a party of your own.)

Glen Foerd was bequeathed to the Torresdale community in 1972 by the Foerderers' daughter and added to the National Register of Historic Places in 1979.

**GRAND ARMY of the REPUBLIC
CIVIL WAR MUSEUM**
4278 Griscom Street—19124
289-6484

Hours: First Sunday of each month, and every Sunday in January, 12 to 5 P.M. Special arrangements can be made in advance for groups to visit at other times. A Civil War "Round Table" is the 3rd Monday of each month, 8 to 9:30 P.M. Call ahead for the program.

Tours: Exhibits are self-explanatory and volunteers are available to answer questions. Call at least 2 weeks ahead to schedule groups of no more than 25.

Cost: Free, but donations gratefully accepted to maintain the museum.

SEPTA: A short walk from buses 3, 5 or Church Street stop of Market-Frankford elevated train. Free parking is available on private lot directly behind the museum.

Other: A Civil War Souvenir Shop sells books, flags, toy soldiers and swords, authentic Civil War 58 cal. bullets, and Union and Confederate caps.

E & D: There are 10 steps at the main entrance or 2 low steps at the rear from the parking lot. Exhibits are on 3 floors.

Here's another must-see for every Civil War buff.

The Grand Army of The Republic was founded after the Civil War as a social and political organization open to any soldier who fought in the years 1861 to 1865. Locally, they established a museum and library to collect and preserve artifacts and memorabilia from the war. Later, the membership and museum responsibility was opened to male descendants, then female descendants as well, and more recently to all interested persons.

Today, exuberant volunteers carry on the tradition. They're at the museum donned in exact replicas of Union and Confederate uniforms, waiting and eager to tell visitors about the era and the collections.

The G.A.R. Civil War Museum and Library is housed in the 1796 Georgian-style mansion built by Dr. John Ruan in what was then suburban Frankford. It's the last remaining example of a large house built in the neighborhood prior to 1800, thus ranking a place in the National Register of Historic Places. Three floors are packed with relics of the Civil War.

Among the objects to look for are cases full of ordnance, items retrieved from a Confederate prison camp, shoes and uniforms worn to battle, flags, photographs, medals, and handcuffs that belonged to John Wilkes Booth.

The G.A.R. also takes its show on the road (see "Tours to Go" in Chapter 13) and has a fascinating library (see Chapter 11).

HENRY GEORGE BIRTHPLACE
413 South 10th Street—19147
922–4278

Hours: Monday and Wednesday to Friday, 1 to 4. Closed holidays. Allow 20 minutes.
Tours: Visit on your own, or no more than 10 can be scheduled at once (larger groups will be divided). Groups should call or write at least a week in advance.
Cost: Free.
SEPTA: Buses 40, 47; trolley 23.
E & D: No wheelchair access.

This unpretentious two-and-a-half story, Federal-style townhouse is where Henry George was born in 1839 and lived his first ten years. George was a well-known 19th century American economist and social philosopher. The house is now a museum, a library and the Philadelphia branch of the Henry George School of Social Science. It was completely renovated to its original plan in 1989. Some of George's furnishings are exhibited.

Henry George spent his youth in Philadelphia, headed to California in search of gold, worked there as a journalist, and finally returned East and settled in New York City. It was while George lived in California that he developed his economic theories, culminating in 1879 with the publication of "Progress and Poverty." His writing is the text and basis for the Henry George School.

George advocated a single tax. He theorized that all men have an equal right to work, but the land on which they work can vary in value. Therefore, he said, it is the land that should be taxed, and not the men or the industry working on the land.

George spent his last 20 years as a lecturer on economics, returning several times to speak in Philadelphia. He was the mayoral candidate in New York City twice, losing the first time in 1886 and dying six weeks before the election in 1897.

Visit the Henry George Birthplace if you'd like to find out about his economic philosophy.

HILL PHYSICK KEITH HOUSE
321 South 4th Street—19106
925-7866

Hours: Tuesday to Saturday, 10 to 4; Sunday, 1 to 4. Closed holidays. Allow 30 minutes.

Tours: At 11 A.M., 1:30 and 3 P.M., or by appointment. Scheduled in advance for large groups that are divided into smaller groups of no more than 20. Children must be accompanied by an adult. Call at least a week in advance if you're coming with a group of 10 or more, to schedule group tours and to arrange group rates.

Cost: Adults, $3; senior citizens and students, $2; children under 6, free. Groups of 10 or more adults, $2.

SEPTA: Buses 50, 90, Chestnut or Walnut Street routes to 4th Street.

Other: An annual plant sale takes place one weekend in late April. If you have a green thumb, call for details.

E & D: No wheelchair access. There are 6 steps at the entrance and 2 floors to visit.

Dr. Philip Syng Physick owned this 22-room house from 1790 till his death in 1837. Dr. Physick was one of the first doctors to practice at Pennsylvania Hospital*. In fact, he's referred to as the father of American surgery. Among his famous patients was Chief Justice John Marshall.

This three-story single home with surrounding gardens was built in 1786. It's an outstanding example of architecture and furnishings of the Federal period.

You can visit the drawing room, study, dining room, bedroom and a small room that contains many of Dr. Physick's instruments. In addition to the elegant furnishings, there are artwork, china and silver collections.

THE HISTORICAL SOCIETY
OF PENNSYLVANIA*
1300 Locust Street—19107
732-6201

Hours: Tuesday to Saturday, 10 to 5. Closed holidays. Allow one hour. (See Chapter 11 for Library hours.)

Tours: Exhibit is self-explanatory. Group tours for no

more than 30, at least 6th grade, scheduled by calling in advance to the Education Department (Ext. 247).

Cost: Adults, $2.50; senior citizens and children 18 and under, $1.50. Special rates for groups scheduling tours in advance. (Membership enables free admission to exhibits and library, behind-the-scenes tours, subscriptions, special events and shop discount.)

SEPTA: Buses 9, 21, 42, 90 or Broad Street routes.

Other: A small Port Folio shop sells stationery, historical books, prints, jewelry, toys and novelty items.

E & D: There are 6 steps at the main entrance. Complete wheelchair access by calling ahead to use the 13th Street ramped entrance. Elevator to 2nd floor for library and research facilities.

The Historical Society of Pennsylvania was founded in 1824 for the purpose of "elucidating the history of the state." It still performs that function, as well as expanding its focus to include the 13 original colonies and their surrounding states. The research facilities, collections and exhibition here are unparalleled.

The Society's storehouse is divided among manuscripts, newspapers, art and artifacts. More than 6,000 objects and artworks are in the museum collection, including furnishings and personal possessions from the likes of our forefathers William Penn, Benjamin Franklin, George Washington and Thomas Jefferson, department store founder John Wanamaker, and 19th-century actor Edwin Forrest. At least 1,000 oil paintings from the 18th and 19th centuries include portraits and landscapes by the Peale family painters, Edward Savage, Benjamin West, Gilbert Stuart, Thomas Sully and Joseph Wright.

The manuscript collection, alone, is among the greatest depositories of its type in the world. It has over 14 million items. A few of the highlights are the Penn family archives, President Washington's and Buchanan's papers and a wealth of information on Pennsylvania's most important colonial families.

The Society's newspaper collection is equally impressive. Every era of printing technology that has been used in this country is represented. There are 8,000 bound volumes of newspapers along with hundreds of rolls of microfilm. Individuals using the Society's Reading Rooms (see Chapter 11) have access to many of these materials.

The Society is also the repository for the Genealogical

Society of Pennsylvania, but there's more about that, too, in Chapter 11.

Currently, **FINDING PHILADELPHIA'S PAST: Visions & Revisions** is the Society's remarkable exhibition that asks you to explore three centuries of Philadelphia's history from new perspectives. More than 500 artifacts along with multimedia displays tell you that, like wearing Ben Franklin's bifocals, there's more than one way to view the past. You're challenged to create your own point of view.

Travel through periods of Philadelphia's history from early Quaker visions to the 20th century, and experience life through the eyes of our nation's earliest leaders and its most ordinary people.

William Penn's wampum belt, the first draft of the U.S. Constitution, maps, photographs, oil paintings, weapons, furnishings, textiles, silver and china collections are some of the objects to see. Audio tapes enable listening to insights from the past. And board the recreated Market Street ferry to travel any of six video routes through Philadelphia and its suburbs at the beginning of this century.

This is one trip you don't want to miss!

**NEW YEAR'S SHOOTERS
AND MUMMERS MUSEUM**
Two Street and Washington Avenue—19147
336-3050

Hours: Tuesday to Saturday, 9:30 to 5; Sunday, 12 to 5. May through September, till 10:30 on Tuesday nights (concerts are at 8: see Chapter 10). Closed Thanksgiving, Christmas, New Year's. Allow at least one hour.

Tours: Groups of 20 or more should call at least 2 weeks ahead to arrange special rates and for a mummer or volunteer to guide you through.

Cost: Adults, $2; children under 12, students and senior citizens, $1. Group rates for 20 or more: adults, $1.25; senior citizens, $.75. Membership enables free admission, newsletters, shop discount and other privileges.

SEPTA: Buses 5, 50, 64.

Other: A gift shop sells Mummerabilia.

E & D: Complete wheelchair access.

Finally, the Mummers have been immortalized in their own museum.

Mummers, in case you didn't know, evolved from the pre-16th century word "mum" meaning to be silent. (Mum's the word.) In an old English custom, villagers in costume enacted pantomimes at Christmas like "Old Father Christmas" and "St. George and the Dragon." The early settlers brought these customs to the colonies.

Long before the Civil War, these settlers held open houses at New Year's. They called on friends and neighbors in costume. On January 1, 1876, individual groups paraded to Independence Hall and then to other parts of the city. The custom grew. In January, 1901, Philadelphia's City Council formally recognized 42 Mummers clubs and gave them permission to parade for cash prizes.

Nearly every child in Philadelphia looks forward to seeing the colorful Mummers "cake walk" up Broad Street on New Year's Day to the tune of "Oh, Dem Golden Slippers."

Now you can enjoy "Mummermania" all year long at the Mummers Museum.

You've probably wanted to know about Mummers, but didn't know who to ask. Now you can find out how many clubs there are, how many men participate in a club, how you can join, how themes are chosen, how costumes are made, what they weigh and what they cost.

You'll relive Mummers history, you'll take part in a parade and you'll learn how to strut and properly hold an umbrella. By pushing a few buttons, you can compose the string-band music of accordions, banjos, saxophones and bell lyres.

Nobody leaves without knowing "what's 2.55 miles long, 69 feet wide, 12 feet high and covered with feathers?" And nobody leaves without humming "Oh, Dem Golden Slippers."

OLD FORT MIFFLIN
Fort Mifflin Road near International Airport,
on the Delaware River—19153
492–3395 or 492–1881

Hours: April through November, Wednesday to Sunday, 10 to 4. Special arrangements can sometimes be made for tours at other times. Allow at least 30 minutes to tour inside the Fort, and 30 minutes to see the surrounding grounds.
Tours: Take a guided tour or watch a Uniform and

Weapons Demonstration, alternating on the hour. Also, a special event takes place one weekend each month. Call at least 2 weeks ahead to schedule group tours which can sometimes include cannon firing demonstrations and special programs on different war eras.

Cost: Adults, $2; children 6 to 12, $1. Group rates for 20 or more when making advance reservations.

Lunch: There are sodas for sale and picnic areas.

SEPTA: Bus 68 to Island and Enterprise Avenues, and then a half-mile walk. Go by car to the same intersection and follow brown and white signs to the Fort. There's plenty of free car and bus parking.

Other: A small gift shop sells flags, books and assorted mementos of colonial history.

E & D: The grounds are all wheelchair accessible, but it would be difficult to negotiate some of the old buildings. Photo albums are available to view sites that are inaccessible.

The British started to build Fort Mifflin in 1772. It was completed in 1776 by the Revolutionary forces under the direction of Benjamin Franklin.

The story goes that Fort Mifflin's 400 brave soldiers attacked the British ship "Augusta" and the gunboat "Merlin" in 1777. This small band boldly resisted over 2,000 British troops and 250 ships that sailed up the Delaware. The Fort was finally conquered after days of constant battering by British warships. About 250 Revolutionary soldiers died in the battle.

In 1797 the Fort was rebuilt. In the 1860s it was converted into a prison for Civil War military deserters, bounty jumpers and political prisoners. The 49-acre site was used to store ammunition as recently as the Korean War.

Today you can visit scenic Old Fort Mifflin and imagine life there as a soldier. You can picture the hardships and the eventual defeat of its fighting men. You can understand why it's been named a National Historic Landmark.

See the authentic and exact reproduction cannons and carriages of the war, the Arsenal, Officers' Quarters, hospital, mess hall, Soldiers' Barracks housing an exhibit "Defense of the Delaware," Blacksmith Shop and museum displaying artifacts and mementos of the Fort's two centuries.

Just outside the Fort sits what is thought to be Philadelphia's oldest house, built in the 1660s by a Swedish settler. It was hit by American cannon fire during the siege of Fort Mifflin and thus called Cannonball Farmhouse.

PENNSYLVANIA HOSPITAL
800 Spruce Street—19107
829–3971 (Marketing)

Hours: The Pine Building is open weekdays, 9 to 5, and you can browse on your own. Closed holidays. Allow at least one hour.

Tours: By reservation only, weekdays, 9 to 5. Call at least one week ahead to schedule groups of no more than 35, at least 12th grade level, and with 2 adults accompanying students.

Cost: Free.

SEPTA: Buses 47, 90.

E & D: There's wheelchair access to everything but the 3rd floor amphitheater. Call ahead to make arrangements. Some steps are involved.

Pennsylvania Hospital was founded by Benjamin Franklin and Dr. Thomas Bond in 1751. It's the oldest hospital in the country. Its original building, the Pine Building, is one of the finest remaining examples of colonial architecture. The interior recently underwent a major (and magnificent) restoration.

Visitors learn all about the hospital's history. You'll walk through the Great Court and see a 19th century portrait gallery of great men associated with Pennsylvania Hospital. You'll examine early American medical instruments, art objects and the rare book library.

You'll also see the country's first surgical amphitheater. (You've seen amphitheaters similar to this one in the movies.) The round amphitheater with its domed skylight was built in the hospital's Central Pavilion in 1804. It was last used in 1868, and it's the only amphitheater of its type left in the country. As many as 150 students bought tickets to sit on the edge of their seats in the three tiers of galleries and observe operations which could only be performed on bright sunny days.

Also, look in the Gallery Pavilion for Benjamin West's famous painting of "Christ Healing the Sick in the Temple."

The **HISTORY OF NURSING MUSEUM** is also in the Pennsylvania Hospital, and you'll see this as part of your visit.

Exhibits include class books, photographs, pins, uniforms, caps, correspondence and assorted memorabilia from the area's nursing schools. An early hospital wing has been reconstructed.

Note: The hospital's medical facilities are not included on this tour.

PHILADELPHIA CONTRIBUTIONSHIP FOR THE INSURANCE OF HOUSES FROM LOSS BY FIRE
212 South 4th Street—19106
627–1752

Hours: Weekdays, 9 to 4:30. Closed holidays. Allow 20 minutes.
Tours: You're on your own. Call ahead if you're planning to come with a large group or want to see the upstairs.
Cost: Free.
SEPTA: Buses 9, 21, 42, 50, 90.
E & D: There are 6 steps at the entrance, or arrange in advance to enter through the garden where there's one step.

You might have noticed the "Hand-in-Hand" firemarks nailed on the front of historic properties in Philadelphia. The clasp of four crossed hands symbolizes strength, and the firemark on the building indicates that property is insured by the oldest fire insurance company in America.

Ben Franklin helped found the Philadelphia Contributionship in 1752, and he signed the parchment scroll of policyholders that's carefully displayed under glass in the company's museum.

Philadelphia Contributionship's handsome Greek Revival-style headquarters were designed and built by Thomas U. Walter in 1836.

A small, charming museum includes fire fighting and insurance memorabilia, firemarks, speaking horns, the original company seal, beautiful old furnishings and "Franklinobilia." That's a word I invented to describe exhibits of all the things he thought of first.

If you arrange in advance for a guided tour, you'll also get to see the upstairs board rooms and dining room.

Point of interest: Another popular firemark in historic Philadelphia is the "green tree." It indicates a property insured by The Mutual Insurance Company (also known as The Green Tree), founded in 1784 to insure property owners who had trees in front of their buildings. If you don't know the significance of a firemark, you haven't been to Fireman's Hall*.

PHILADELPHIA MARITIME MUSEUM
321 Chestnut Street—19106
925-5439

Hours: Tuesday to Saturday, 10 to 5; Sunday, 1 to 5. Closed Easter, Thanksgiving, December 24, Christmas, December 31, New Year's. Allow one hour.

Tours: Groups of no more than 40 can be scheduled for guided tours by calling the Education Department at least a week in advance. A variety of 90-minute programs are available for all age levels, including tours for special education, gifted and handicapped groups.

Cost: Adults, $2.50; senior citizens and children, $1. (Admission fee includes entry to the Museum's Workshop on the Water described in Chapter 6.) Group rates available when scheduling tour. Membership entitles you to free admission, films, newsletters, monthly events, research assistance and more.

SEPTA: Buses 21, 42, 50, Ben FrankLine route 76, Market Street routes.

Other: A small gift shop features books, graphics, games and maritime objects that you're not likely to find elsewhere.

E & D: Complete wheelchair access. A variety of special programs available through Education Department.

Those of you who are curious about the sea, life at sea, or the Port of Philadelphia should head straight away to the Maritime Museum and see three floors of contemporary and well-designed exhibits.

In the first floor "Man and the Sea" gallery, one huge wall is devoted to a cut-a-way view of the "Philadelphia," a frigate that set to sea in 1800. Charming illustrations depict the activities on each deck. A fabulous collection of some 185 miniature silver ship models fill a showcase the length of the gallery. Other glimpses at the mariner's world include tools, instruments and assorted treasures.

"Dr. Franklin Sets Sail" occupies (through 1991) the

other first floor gallery. Join Ben Franklin on video as he arrives at the Market Street wharf in October 1723. Then, choose from eight topics and spend some time with Ben on his first day in Philadelphia. Did you know, among his many interests, Franklin also wrote about ships and the sea?

Displays upstairs from the museum's permanent collections include historical items such as charts, prints, paintings, scrimshaw, ship models, weapons, a wonderful shell mosaic sailor's valentine, and the painted wood statue of "Samuel Sailor" who advertised the nautical instruments shop at 310 Market Street for a century till the 1970s.

What you don't see on exhibit here can be seen in the Philadelphia Maritime Museum's "visible storage." It's a fascinating look through glass at what's behind the scenes in a museum, and clearly addresses major issues of conservation and preservation.

The Philadelphia Maritime Museum also maintains a library for serious researchers and a Workshop on the Water*, at Penn's Landing boat basin.

There isn't a better way to learn about ships, the seas, and the Port of Philadelphia.

Ship ahoy!

POWEL HOUSE
244 South 3rd Street—19106
627-0364

Hours: Tuesday to Saturday, 10 to 4; Sunday, 1 to 4. Closed Easter, July 4, Thanksgiving, Christmas, New Year's. Allow 45 minutes, and arrive at least 30 minutes before closing time.

Tours: All visitors are accompanied by a guide. Groups of 10 to 50, at least junior high school level, are scheduled by calling 2 weeks ahead.

Cost: Adults, $3; senior citizens and students, $2; children under 6, free. Groups of 10 or more adults, $2.

SEPTA: Buses 5, 90, Ben FrankLine route 76, or Walnut Street routes.

E & D: No wheelchair access. There are 5 steps at the entrance and 2 floors to visit.

Samuel Powel was the Mayor of Philadelphia before, during and after the Revolution. His Society Hill home, built in 1765, was certainly appropriate for a man of his position. The exterior facade is typical Georgian style. A formal colonial garden adjoins the house.

Pretend you're one of Mayor and Mrs. Powel's most honored guests as you visit the lavish dining room, the drawing room and the elegant ballroom with its magnificent crystal fixtures and damask fabrics. This is one place where George Washington actually danced.

Would you like to see what it's like to live in Society Hill splendor? Then rent the Powel House for an evening for a party or a catered dinner. Or combine your group tour with afternoon tea or an evening wine-tasting session.

RYERSS MUSEUM
Cottman and Central Avenues—19111
745-3061

Hours: Weekends, 1 to 4; other times by appointment only. Allow one hour.

Tours: Philadelphia Ranger Corps leads tours at 1:30 and 3 P.M. Call at least 2 weeks in advance to schedule a guided tour for groups of 5 or more.

Cost: Free

Lunch: There's a pavilion, tables and benches in Burholme Park if you want to picnic. Large groups need a permit: call 726-4377 (RANGERS).

SEPTA: Buses 16, 24. There's plenty of free parking.

E & D: There's a ramp at the entrance. Exhibits are on 2 floors, and there's an elevator.

The Ryerss' family mansion was built in 1859 to resemble an English country estate. A tower built in 1890 enabled its residents to see center city Philadelphia—a distance of 10 miles. The museum wing was added in 1920.

In 1976, the Ryerss Museum was placed in the National Register of Historic Places. It was completely restored in 1980.

This Victorian home has a number of fascinating collections. There are period clothing, Oriental arts including many ivory pieces, a case of footwear from around the world, old children's playthings and even suits of armor.

The dining room and parlor are restored and furnished with period pieces including an unusual "square" piano.

The Ryerss Museum and Library (see Chapter 11) is in the Burholme Park section of Fairmount Park in the Northeast. The building and grounds belong to the City of Philadelphia.

SHOE MUSEUM
Pennsylvania College of Podiatric Medicine*
8th and Race Streets (enter on 8th)—19107
6th floor
629-0300 Ext. 219 (Public Relations), Ext. 185 (Museum)

Hours: Weekdays, 9 to 4. Closed holidays. Allow 45 minutes.

Tours: Exhibits are self-explanatory, but arrangements must be made in advance to visit 6th floor, preferably Wednesday or Friday. Groups of no more than 25, at least 4th grade level, should call 2 weeks ahead. You can combine your visit with a scheduled tour of the College (see Chapter 13).

Cost: Free.

SEPTA: Buses 47, 61.

E & D: Wheelchair access.

Put your best foot forward and surround yourself with "Footwear Through the Ages."

Nearly 500 pairs of footwear are in the collection; some 200 items are on display.

There are burial sandals from Egypt, two-heeled shoes from Morocco and Japan, slippers from China, Eskimo snowshoes, Dutch wooden sabots (if you don't already know, ask where we got the word "sabotage"), Indian boots and more.

There are First Lady's shoes worn by Mamie Eisenhower, Ladybird Johnson, Betty Ford and Nancy Reagan. Sandy Duncan's "Peter Pan" boots are here, along with Lucille Ball's red brocade dancing shoes and another pair worn by a feline star in "Cats."

And speaking of celebrities, Joe Frazier's boxing shoes are here, Billie Jean King's tennis shoes are here, Bernie Parent's skates are here, and Dr. Baruch Blumberg and the late John B. Kelly, Jr.'s jogging shoes are here.

As Ed Sullivan used to say, "It's a really big shoe."

TUN TAVERN
2nd and Spruce Streets—19106

Ground was broken November 10, 1990 to rebuild Tun Tavern just a short distance from its original location.

The original Tun Tavern was built around 1700. It was one of Philadelphia's most popular inns until it was demolished by fire in 1781.

Tun Tavern was chosen as a recruiting station site soon after the Continental Congress decided there should be a force of "sea soldiers." Thus Tun Tavern is considered the birthplace of the Marine Corps. The date associated with the event is November 10, 1775.

The tavern's proprietor was appointed as a recruiting officer and given the rank of captain. He enlisted 300 men.

Tun Tavern will celebrate 216 years of the Marine Corps when it reopens late in 1991 as a living history museum.

VIETNAM VETERANS MEMORIAL
Spruce Street between
Front Street and Delaware Avenue

SEPTA: Buses 5, 42, Ben FrankLine route 76.

Some 20,000 Philadelphians served in Southeast Asia during the Vietnam era from August, 1964 to May, 1975. Hundreds of them never came home.

Philadelphia's Vietnam Veterans Memorial honors those who served in all branches of the U.S. armed forces during the Vietnam War. The 641 names of those killed or missing in action are inscribed on black stone here at the memorial's semi-circular south wall. The north facing wall across the outdoor amphitheater shows maps and battle scenes etched in granite.

Philadelphia's Vietnam Veterans Memorial was dedicated at this Society Hill site in 1987.

Chapter 5.
Churches and Religious Sites.

How many times have you heard people talk about the churches they went out of their way to see in Europe? Well, Philadelphia has many historic churches that should be visited. In fact, Philadelphia probably has more churches of historic significance than any other city in America.

Philadelphia's churches aren't as old as the European variety, but many of them are very old by American standards—founded by the first Philadelphians and worshipped in by the founders of our nation.

Philadelphia was the birthplace of religious freedom. It was here that William Penn brought to reality his dream of a "Holy Experiment," a place completely free from religious persecution. And so you can visit here the first Quaker meeting house in America, the first synagogue, the first Methodist church and many other firsts.

Religion was a very important part of life in Colonial Philadelphia. Most of the 18th century churches remain active and have their own congregations right up to the present day. Many of them are fascinating to visit. You can do this on your own, or you can join the Foundation for Architecture for one of its theme tours (described at the end of Chapter 1).

Old Philadelphia Churches

Thirteen churches of colonial origin have formed the Old Philadelphia Churches Historic Association. They include seven Protestant churches, four Roman Catholic churches, one Quaker meeting house and one synagogue. They're all interesting, and most are within walking distance of Independence Hall.

A descriptive sign on the sidewalk outside of each church gives more of its history and background.

ARCH STREET MEETING HOUSE
4th and Arch Streets—19106
627-2677 or 627-2631

Hours: Monday to Saturday, 10 to 4. Weekly Meetings are Sunday at 10:30 and Thursday at 10.
Tours: A guide is always on duty to answer questions and lead groups.

William Penn donated this plot to the Society of Friends in 1693. By 1804 there were enough members to require the construction of a meeting house as you see it today.

Many Quakers in England chose to go to prison rather than worship according to the dictates of the Church of England. William Penn, himself, was confined in England for insisting on the Quakers' rights to hold their own worship service.

You know the rest of the story. Pennsylvania was Penn's "Holy Experiment," where everybody could worship in freedom. If you want to brush up on the story, there's a 15-minute slide show here on "The Life of William Penn."

The Arch Street Meeting House is still used regularly by the Quakers. The Philadelphia Yearly Meeting is held here every spring.

Take a look at the original hand-hewn benches and see the simplicity of the interior. The Exhibit Room has clothing, Bibles and examples of Quaker life. Don't miss the gigantic "dollhouse" of a typical Quaker home during the Revolutionary period. Or the enormous Quaker quilt that dates from 1844 and has a fascinating story.

CHRIST CHURCH
2nd and Market Streets—19106
922–1695

Hours: Monday to Saturday, 9 to 5; Sunday, 12 to 4. Allow 15 minutes. Visitors are welcome at services daily at 9 and 11 and Wednesday at noon.

Christ Church, founded in 1659, is the birthplace of the Protestant Episcopal Church in the United States. A clause in Penn's Charter of 1681 from King Charles II provided that as soon as 20 residents of the Colony requested a minister, one would be sent by the Bishop of London.

The font in which William Penn was baptized in 1644 was sent to Philadelphia in 1697. It's the larger of Christ Church's two baptismal fonts.

Fifteen signers of the Declaration attended Christ Church. You can sit in George Washington's, Robert Morris', Benjamin Franklin's and Betsy Ross' pews.

The present Christ Church structure was built between 1724 and 1754.

Bishop William White was appointed rector of Christ

Church in 1779. He was consecrated Bishop in 1789. You can visit the Bishop White House* a few blocks away on Walnut Street.

CHRIST CHURCH BURIAL GROUND
5th and Arch Streets (enter on 5th Street)

Hours: April 1 to October 1, daily, 9 to 4:30. Closed the rest of the year except by appointment. Call Christ Church for special arrangements.

If you come here when the Burial Ground gates are closed, walk to the corner of 5th and Arch Streets so you can see four graves: Benjamin Franklin's, his wife Deborah's, and their children's. A bronze plaque outlines Franklin's illustrious life.

Local tradition says that fame and fortune will come to you if you toss a Franklin penny on Ben's grave. (We try it occasionally. If you buy another copy of this book for a friend, we'll know that the tradition works.)

Seven other signers of the Declaration are also buried in the churchyard or in the Christ Church graveyard. Christ Church and its Burial Ground are part of Independence National Historical Park*.

GLORIA DEI CHURCH (Old Swedes')
Swanson (below Front) and Christian Streets—19147
389–1513

Hours: Daily, 9 to 5.
Tours: You're on your own, but call ahead if you're bringing a group.
SEPTA: Bus 64.
Other: The Lucia Fest is at Old Swedes' in December. See Chapter 19 for details.

Organized in 1642, Gloria Dei is the oldest church in Pennsylvania. It's probably the oldest building in Philadelphia. Their congregation worshipped in a log cabin before the present building was completed in 1700.

Gloria Dei is also known as Old Swedes' Church. It was designated a National Historic Site in 1942. Old Swedes' was admitted to the Episcopal Diocese of Pennsylvania in 1845. It is also part of Independence National Historical Park*.

Gloria Dei has a Parish Hall, an old Caretaker's House,

a Rectory, an 18th century Guild House and a graveyard —all around a pleasant grassy courtyard.

The church has barely changed over the centuries.

It has to be the only church with model ships suspended from the ceiling. They're the "Key of Kalmar" and "Flying Griffin," the ships that brought the first Swedish settlers to America.

Old Swedes' is filled with relics and religious artifacts. The font and altar carvings date from 1642. Queen Christiana's 1608 Bible is in the sacristy, and there are mementos of Jenny Lind, who sang at Old Swedes' in 1851. Also, look at the samples from the nearby Shot Tower* which are exhibited in the vestry.

HISTORIC ST. GEORGE'S METHODIST CHURCH
235 North 4th Street—19106
925-7788

Hours: Daily, 10 to 4. Visitors are welcome at Sunday services at 11 A.M.

Tours: Volunteer guides are always on duty. Groups of 10 or more should call ahead. Allow up to an hour.

Other: A gift shop has items relating to St. George's and a selection of non-religious merchandise.

The original Philadelphia Methodists who organized here in 1767 bought this building from a German Reformed Congregation. Historic St. George's is the oldest continuously used Methodist Church in the world. The only break in its activities occurred during the British occupation of Philadelphia, when it was used as a riding school for cavalry.

Francis Asbury preached his first sermon at St. George's in October, 1771. He was sent to America by John Wesley, Methodism's English founder, to enlarge the church in the colonies. The church looks almost the same today as it did when Asbury preached there.

A **Methodist Historical Center** adjoins the church. Your guide will take you to the museum where exhibits relate the story of Methodism and the church. Historic St. George's is also part of Independence National Historical Park*.

As far as we know, this is the only church that ever influenced the location of a bridge. The plans for the construction of the Benjamin Franklin Bridge had to be altered to prevent the demolition of Historic St. George's.

HOLY TRINITY ROMAN CATHOLIC CHURCH
6th and Spruce Streets—19106
923–7930

Hours: For Mass only, Sunday at noon.

Holy Trinity was the first Catholic church in the United States founded especially for German- and French-speaking Catholics. Germans accounted for a large portion of the local 18th century Catholic population.

Holy Trinity's present building was constructed in 1788, the third Roman Catholic church in Philadelphia. Few alterations have been made to the original structure, so you'll see it almost exactly as did those who attended its first Mass in 1789.

The church's exterior is one of Philadelphia's best examples of Flemish bold, the alternating red and black brickwork style.

Holy Trinity is administered by Old St. Mary's Roman Catholic Church*.

MIKVEH ISRAEL SYNAGOGUE

44 North 4th Street—19106
Independence Mall East
922–5446

Hours: Visitors are welcome at services Saturday at 9 A.M., and in conjunction with tours of the National Museum of American Jewish History*.
Tours: Groups of 20 to 100 should call 10 days ahead to schedule. Allow 30 minutes.

Colonial merchant Nathan Levy brought the Jewish community of Philadelphia together in 1740 to found Mikveh Israel Synagogue. Today it's the oldest synagogue in Philadelphia and the second oldest in the U.S.

Mikveh Israel became a rallying point for all American Jews during the Revolution as they fled from British-occupied cities. Among its early congregants were Haym Salomon and the Gratz family.

Although most of the members today are of Ashkenazic (Middle and Eastern European) background, Mikveh Israel still maintains its Sephardic (Spanish and Portuguese) traditions. Men and women are seated in separate sections.

Mikveh Israel was originally at 3rd and Cherry Streets. It recently moved to its new home on 4th Street, sharing a modern brick structure with the National Museum of American Jewish History*. Tours of the museum also include a visit to the synagogue.

Don't leave before viewing exhibits in the lobby showcases that pertain to Mikveh Israel's history. And take a few minutes to admire the magnificent five- by ten-foot needlepoint tapestry, "Gateway to Heaven." Interior and exterior views of Mikveh Israel's three prior locations in 1825, 1860 and 1909 were meticulously created in 1.3 million stitches.

Two outdoor sculptures are noteworthy here, in addition to those mentioned under "Street Art" in Chapter 9. "Entebbe Jonathan Netanyahu" by Buky S. Schwartz pays tribute to the Israeli commander who lost his life leading an assault on July 4, 1976 to save 103 Jewish hostages. "Religious Liberty" by Sir Moses Ezekiel was carved from one enormous piece of marble to commemorate the centennial anniversary of American independence.

MOTHER BETHEL A.M.E. CHURCH
419 Richard Allen Avenue
(formerly South 6th Street)—19147
925-0616

Hours: By reservation only, Tuesday to Friday, 10 to 4. Visitors are welcome at 10:45 A.M. Sunday services which are followed by a tour at 1 P.M.
Tours: Call at least a week ahead to schedule groups of no more than 100. Allow 30 to 45 minutes.

In 1782, at the age of 22, Richard Allen bought his freedom from slavery to a Germantown family. Five years later he led 40 black worshippers from St. George's Methodist Church to become a "Free African Society." They founded a new church, Mother Bethel African Methodist Episcopal, which is today the "mother church" for an international denomination numbering five million. Allen bought the present church site in 1794.

Mother Bethel was one of the first institutions established by blacks in America. The church stands on the oldest property continuously owned by blacks in America. It's now a National Historic Landmark.

In 1816, Richard Allen was the nation's first Negro to be named a Bishop. He died in 1831, and you can see his tomb and his wife's in the church basement just outside the Richard Allen Museum where several church relics and religious documents are displayed. (The basement was a station on the underground railroad prior to the Civil War.)

A tour of Mother Bethel also includes a description of the magnificent stained glass windows.

OLD FIRST REFORMED CHURCH
4th and Race Streets—19106
922-4566

Hours: Weekdays, 9 to 3; Sunday, following worship at 11 to which visitors are welcome.
Other: The third Friday of each month, from 11 to 7, a Festival at Old First ties in with the season to present foods, crafts, festivities and perhaps an ethnic celebration closest to the date. The Church also provides accommodations for youth hostelers during July and August (see Chapter 20).

The First Reformed Church was organized in 1727 by German refugees seeking religious freedom in Philadelphia. Three different houses of worship have since been built at the present site.

The current church dates from 1837. It combines the designs and original materials from the two earlier churches. As the neighborhood became commercial, the location was abandoned in 1887, and the building became a paint warehouse. In 1967 the congregants returned to the original Old City* site.

The building has been beautifully restored, and the furnishings are either originals or exact duplications of the originals.

You have to see the churchyard the last two weeks of December. The nativity scene has props in a natural setting with live animals. It's a work of art. Old First Reformed deserves an award for its imagination and creativity. The least it warrants is 30 seconds on the evening news.

114

"OLD PINE" PRESBYTERIAN CHURCH
4th and Pine Streets—19106
925-8051

Hours: Weekdays, 9 to 5; call ahead to be sure. Visitors are welcome at Sunday services at 10:30. A coffee hour follows.

Built in the late 1760s, this is the only remaining colonial Presbyterian building in Philadelphia. The lot was donated to the First Presbyterian Church in 1764 by William Penn's sons, Thomas and Richard Penn.

John Adams attended church here while in the Continental Congress. Later, during the British occupation of Philadelphia, the church was used as a hospital and then as a cavalry stable. Many prominent colonists are buried in "Old Pine's" churchyard.

OLD ST. AUGUSTINE'S ROMAN CATHOLIC CHURCH
243 N. Lawrence Street—19106
(North 4th Street below Vine)
627-1838

Hours: The 15 minutes before each Mass. Daily Mass is weekdays at 7:30 and noon; Saturday at 5:15 and 11:30 P.M.; Sunday at 8 and 11 A.M. Call ahead for special arrangements to visit at other times.

Old St. Augustine's was founded in 1796 as a place of worship for the German and Irish Catholic residents of Philadelphia's northern section. Commodore John Barry, George Washington and Stephen Girard were among the contributors to its first building fund.

When it was completed in 1801, Old St. Augustine's was the largest church in Philadelphia, and the fourth Catholic church in Philadelphia.

The original structure was destroyed by fire in May, 1844, after three days of anti-Catholic street rioting.

The new building was designed by Napoleon LeBrun, who was also the architect for the Academy of Music* and the Cathedral Basilica of SS. Peter and Paul*. Old St. Augustine's was rebuilt on the original site in 1847.

This was the original "mother house" of the Augustinian Fathers in the United States. It was also the site in 1811 of what is now Villanova University, the oldest Catholic institution of higher learning in the country.

OLD ST. JOSEPH'S CHURCH
Willings Alley near 4th and Walnut Streets—19106
923-1733

Hours: Visitors are welcome daily, 10 to 4. Mass is daily
at 12:05; also at 5:30 on Saturday; and 7:30, 9:30 and
11:30 A.M. on Sunday.

This is the oldest Roman Catholic Church in Philadelphia, and Mass has been celebrated at Old St. Joseph's
for well over 200 years.

Religious freedom in America was born at Old St.
Joseph's. From 1733 to 1763, Old St. Joseph's was the only
Roman Catholic Church in the city. In fact, Catholic worship wasn't permitted in the colonies or in England except at Old St. Joseph's.

The present building is the third one for the church. It
dates back to 1838 and is part of Independence National
Historical Park*.

OLD ST. MARY'S CHURCH
252 South 4th Street—19106
923-7930

Hours: Daily, 9 to 5. Mass is Saturday at 5 P.M.; Sunday
at 9 and 10:30 A.M.

Old St. Mary's was established in 1763 as the Roman
Catholic Church expanded in Philadelphia. It's Philadel-
phia's second oldest Catholic church, and was the main
Catholic church during the Revolution.

Members of the Continental Congress attended Mass
here on July 4, 1779, to celebrate the third anniversary
of the Declaration.

John Barry, General Stephen Moylan and other noted
colonists are buried in the graveyard.

ST. PETER'S CHURCH
3rd and Pine Streets—19106
925-5968

Hours: Tuesday to Saturday, 9 to 4. Visitors are welcome
at Holy Communion on Sunday at 9 and 11 A.M., and
Holy Eucharist-Evensong on Wednesday at 5:30 P.M.

St. Peter's was established in 1753 as a new "South
end" chapel for Christ Church, the mother church at 2nd
and Market Streets.

St. Peter's looks the same today as it did when it was
built in 1760 on land that was given by Thomas and
Richard Penn. George and Martha Washington attended
St. Peter's during 1781 and 1782. So did Mayor Samuel
Powel and his family. They occupied Pew 41.

Some of the many patriots buried in the churchyard include naval hero Stephen Decatur, artist Charles Willson Peale and John Nixon, who first read the Declaration
of Independence to the people.

More Churches and Sites
of Religious Interest

Philadelphia's religious heritage of the 18th century
has been preserved and enriched in the 19th and 20th
centuries. There are additional churches of the 18th century and several of later origin that are also noteworthy
for their religious beliefs or their architecture.

Several historical societies and museums have taken
the historic documents from the religious edifices and
have made them available to the public through exhibitions and library collections.

Many of these collections could also be appropriately
included in Chapter 12 on International Philadelphia.
Their ethnic appeal is obvious.

William Penn would have liked that.

BETH SHALOM SYNAGOGUE
Old York and Foxcroft Roads
Elkins Park, PA 19117
887–1342

Tours: By appointment only, Monday to Wednesday, 11
to 3; Sunday, 9 to 1. Allow 45 minutes. Groups will be
scheduled by writing ahead to the chairman of tours.
Others must call ahead.
SEPTA: Bus 55.

Frank Lloyd Wright designed only one synagogue in his
lifetime, and this is it. Built in 1959, the unusual Beth
Shalom Synagogue was Wright's last major completed
work.

The structure rises from a hexagonal base. Its asym-
metrical dome juts 110 feet into the air, and from inside
the sanctuary you can look through the dome.

Your guide will explain the architect's symbolism of the
opaque dome, the steel beams and the fountain pool.

BRYN ATHYN CATHEDRAL
Route 232 (2nd Street Pike) and Papermill Road
Bryn Athyn, PA 19009
947–0266

Hours: Monday to Saturday, 11 to 5; Sunday, 1 to 5.
Visitors are welcome at services Sunday at 11 A.M. and
a Family Service at 9:30 A.M.
Tours: Groups can be scheduled for guided tours by call-
ing a few weeks ahead.
Cost: Free.
E & D: There's a level entrance and wheelchair access.

If you're interested in Gothic architecture, it's worth a
trip 15 miles north of center city Philadelphia to see one
of the area's architectural and scenic wonders.

Construction of Bryn Athyn Cathedral was begun in
1914, in the style of medieval craft guilds. You'll be given
an explanation of this, along with descriptions of the
stained glass windows and the overall design. The
Swedenborgian faith will be described for those who are
interested.

Just to give you an idea of the Cathedral's size, the entire population of Bryn Athyn can gather inside.

And while you're in the neighborhood, you really

should combine your visit to the Cathedral with a tour
of Glencairn (see Chapter 17).

CATHEDRAL OF IMMACULATE CONCEPTION
816 N. Franklin Street—19123
922–2222

Hours: Open for services only. Divine Liturgy is Sunday
at 8:30, 10 and noon; Saturday at 5:30 P.M.
Tours: Scheduled weekdays for groups of up to 100. Call
ahead and allow 30 minutes.
SEPTA: Bus 47.

If you've been to the William Penn Tower*, you may
have noticed a glowing golden dome as you looked to the
northeast. It belongs to the largest Ukrainian Catholic
cathedral in the world—the Cathedral of the Immaculate
Conception of the Blessed Virgin Mary.

This is also the "mother church" of all Ukrainian
churches in America. In Philadelphia alone there is a
closely-knit community of about 45,000 Ukrainians in
the northern part of the city. Pope John Paul II came here
to visit the church and its parishioners on October 4,
1979.

The tour here includes the church, the chancery office,
the school annex and a look at several other Ukrainian
establishments within the block. If you would like to see
and learn more about the Ukrainian culture and folk art,
visit the **UKRAINIAN HERITAGE STUDIES
CENTER**. It's located on the Manor Junior College campus at Fox Chase Road and Forrest Avenue in Jenkin-
town, Pa. Call 885–2360 for details. Their colorful Palm
Sunday and October festivals are described in Chapter
19. Nearby at 700 Cedar Road, the **UKRAINIAN EDU-
CATIONAL and CULTURAL CENTER** offers a complete schedule of cultural events, as well as a library
that's described in Chapter 11. If you'd like to know more,
call 663–1166.

Remember: An **asterisk (*)** indicates that the same
place or event appears elsewhere in the book with more
details. Look in the Index for additional pages.

CATHEDRAL BASILICA OF
SS. PETER AND PAUL
18th and Race Streets—19103
(enter through Chapel on north side)
561–1313

Hours: Daily, 9 to 3:30. Visitors welcome at daily Mass in Chapel at 7:15, 8 A.M., 12:05 and 12:35 P.M. Sunday Mass is at 8, 9:30, 11, 12:15 and 5. An Anticipated Mass is Saturday at 5:15.

The imposing Roman-style church facing Logan Circle on the Benjamin Franklin Parkway is the head church of the Philadelphia Archdiocese. Almost 2,000 worshippers can be seated here at once. There are over 300 Roman Catholic churches in Philadelphia.

Construction of SS. Peter and Paul was begun in 1846, and it was completed and dedicated in 1864.

The Cathedral of SS. Peter and Paul was designated a Basilica in 1976 following its major role in the 41st International Eucharistic Congress which brought over a million Catholics to Philadelphia in an eight-day period.

Six of Philadelphia's last nine bishops and archbishops are buried beneath the altar of SS. Peter and Paul.

CATHOLIC HISTORICAL SOCIETY
263 South 4th Street (headquarters)—19106
925–5752
667–2125 (Seminary library)

Hours: Weekdays, by appointment only.

Society Hill's Catholic Historical Society maintains one of the country's largest collections of books relating to Catholicism. The Society receives more than 5,000 newspapers and periodicals pertaining to their faith.

The collection is housed in the museum and library at the St. Charles Seminary, 1000 E. Wynnewood Road in Overbrook.

If you're involved in research into Catholic history, call the archivist in the library at the Seminary to find out if the information you want is available.

FREE QUAKER MEETING HOUSE
Independence Mall
5th and Arch Streets—19106
923-6777

Hours: Memorial Day to Labor Day, daily except Monday, 10 to 4; Sunday, 12 to 4. Allow 20 minutes.
Tours: You're on your own, but guides are present to answer questions.
E & D: There are 4 steps at the entrance limiting wheelchair access.

The Free Quaker sect was founded in 1781 by a group of 200 "Fighting Quakers." These Quakers were disowned by the peace-loving Society of Friends because they supported the Revolution. Thus they needed their own place of worship and built this brick meeting house in 1783.

The Free Quakers met here till 1834. By then the Revolution was long over, the Quakers were reunited and the Free Quaker members had dwindled to a handful.

In later years, a second floor was added to the interior and the building served as a library and a school and for commercial use. When Independence Mall was created in the early 1960s, the Free Quaker Meeting House was moved a short distance to its present site and completely restored. Almost two centuries of alterations were removed so the building now looks as it originally did in 1783. It's no longer used for worship but is a museum and part of Independence National Historical Park*. The simple wooden benches are back, as well as the three-sided balcony.

The Junior League of Philadelphia has its offices on the lower floor, and its members serve as guides. A continuous five-minute slide show provides historical background on William Penn, the Society of Friends and the dissenting Free Quakers.

HOLOCAUST AWARENESS MUSEUM
c/o Gratz College
Old York Road and Melrose Avenue—19126
635-6480

Hours: By appointment only, Monday to Thursday, 9 to 5; Sunday morning, 10 A.M. Allow 90 minutes.
Tours: Call at least 3 weeks ahead to schedule groups of 10 or more, at least 12 years old.

Cost: Free; donations accepted.
SEPTA: Bus 55.

Come to the Holocaust Awareness Museum to learn about a brutal period in world history when six million European Jews lost their lives at the hands of the Nazis. The aim of this teaching facility is to be sure future generations don't forget what happened in the concentration camps of World War II and the era from 1933 to 1945.

A wall of captioned photographs, documents, newspapers, personal possessions retrieved from survivors and deceased, items from Hitler's desk, a German gas mask and weapons are some of the grim reminders.

A visit to the museum includes three segments: a Holocaust survivor will address the group, a guided tour of the exhibits, and a talk from a concentration camp liberator. There's also an opportunity for questions and answers.

A reference library has materials for research on the Holocaust as well as films. Very large groups can arrange for a similar program from the museum at their auditorium (see "Tours to Go").

MIKVEH ISRAEL CEMETERY
Spruce Street between 8th and 9th
922-5446

Hours: You'll get a good view anytime by looking through the entrance gates.
Tours: Special arrangements can be made to open the gates by calling in advance.

The Mikveh Israel Cemetery was founded in 1738, two years before Mikveh Israel Synagogue*.

Nathan Levy originally acquired the ground from William Penn in 1738. He wanted it to be his family burial plot. The Levy family expanded the cemetery and donated it to the synagogue in 1766 so members of the Jewish community could be buried together.

Among the distinguished American Jews buried here are Nathan Levy (his ship "Myrtilla" carried the Liberty Bell to Philadelphia) and members of his family, Haym Salomon (patriot and financier of the Revolution) and Michael Gratz (who helped expand the U.S. into the West).

Rebecca Gratz's stone has an interesting story behind it. Sir Walter Scott is said to have modeled his Rebecca in the novel "Ivanhoe" after Rebecca Gratz.

Mikveh Israel Cemetery is maintained by Mikveh Israel Synagogue. It's part of Independence National Historical Park*.

NATIONAL MUSEUM
OF AMERICAN JEWISH HISTORY
Independence Mall East
55 North 5th Street—19106
923-3811

Hours: Monday to Thursday, 10 to 5; Friday, 10 to 3; Sunday, 12 to 5. Closed Thanksgiving, New Year's and Jewish holidays. Allow 30 minutes.

Tours: Docents are available to lead tours. Groups should call ahead to schedule tour of exhibits and adjoining Mikveh Israel Synagogue*.

Cost: Adults, $1.75; students and senior citizens, $1.50; children, $1.25; under 5, free. Discounts are available to groups planning a tour. Membership enables free admission, special programs and other privileges.

Other: A museum shop offers one-of-a-kind artwork, ceremonial objects, jewelry and unusual mementos. It's especially terrific for holiday shopping.

E & D: Complete wheelchair access.

The National Museum of American Jewish History, adjoining Mikveh Israel Synagogue*, opened in 1976. It's dedicated to telling the story of Jewish participation in the growth and development of America.

A permanent gallery, "The American Jewish Experience: From 1654 to the Present," is divided into periods showing how events affected the social, political, economic and cultural life of Jews in the nation. And vice versa. More than 300 items in the exhibit include ceremonial objects, religious artifacts, furnishings from the home of Rebecca Gratz, photographs, theater memorabilia, an eight-minute video and distinguished paintings.

Two smaller galleries have changing exhibits. A crafts show of "Contemporary Artifacts" by local and national artists is every fall.

Other programs available to groups include films shown at the museum followed by discussion and a tour, and "Walking Tours of Old Jewish Philadelphia." Call for details if you know a group that might enjoy any of these.

PHILADELPHIA JEWISH ARCHIVES CENTER
At Balch Institute
18 South 7th Street—19106
925–8090

Hours: Weekdays, 9 to 5. Closed Federal and Jewish holidays.

The Philadelphia Jewish Archives Center is an educational institute for the collection and preservation of the public and private records of the Philadelphia area Jewish community. Established in 1972, it is a service of the Jewish Federation of Greater Philadelphia.

Material is donated to the Center by Philadelphia area organizations, institutions and individuals. Among its records are those of the Jewish Publication Society, Association for Jewish Children, Hebrew Sunday School Society and Hebrew Immigrant Aid Society. A small non-circulating library and a photograph collection are also available to researchers.

Most of the archives here date from the mid-19th century, with a few items from earlier periods.

PHILADELPHIA MUSEUM OF JUDAICA
615 N. Broad Street at Mt. Vernon—19123
627–6747

Hours: Weekdays, 10 to 4; Sunday, 10 to 12. Closed Jewish holidays.
Tours: Exhibits are self-explanatory. Call in advance to arrange a guided tour.
SEPTA: Bus C; Broad Street Subway to Spring Garden Street and walk 2 blocks north.
E & D: There are 6 steps at the entrance.

Founded in 1795, Congregation **Rodeph Shalom** (Reform) is the oldest Ashkenazic synagogue in the Western hemisphere. It also houses and operates the Philadelphia Museum of Judaica.

The museum has a permanent collection of Jewish ceremonial art, artifacts and historical documents dating from 2000 B.C. to today. Three times a year there are major photography, sculpture, lithograph or painting exhibitions related to Judaism.

When you visit the museum, look at the synagogue's sanctuary and notice the architecture. This 1927 building is considered to be one of the country's outstanding examples of Byzantine design.

PRESBYTERIAN HISTORICAL SOCIETY
425 Lombard Street—19147
627–1852

Hours: Weekdays, 8:30 to 4:30. Closed holidays.
Tours: Call a few weeks ahead to schedule groups of up to 50, at least 7th grade level. Children must be accompanied by adults. Allow 30 minutes.

This is a non-circulating archives and research center in an impressive colonial structure. The resources on American and foreign Presbyterian and Reformed Church life are extensive. There's a permanent artifacts display and changing exhibitions. Many fine oil paintings and sculptures relating to the Presbyterian Church are shown.

Six larger-than-life statues dominate the exterior of the building; they're famous Presbyterians done by Alexander Stirling Calder.

ST. PETER'S ROMAN CATHOLIC CHURCH and ST. JOHN NEUMANN SHRINE
5th Street and Girard Avenue—19123
627–3080 or 627–2386

Hours: Daily, 7:30 to 6. Mass is Monday to Saturday at 7:30, 12:15 and 5:30; Sunday at 7:30, 9:30, 11 (in Spanish), 12:30 and 3 P.M. Novena Devotion in honor of St. John Neumann followed by 3:30 Mass. Hours at **St. John Neumann Shrine** are same as for Church.
Tours: Call in advance to schedule groups daily. Visit includes a tour of the Shrine, Mass (if requested), blessing with the relic and a talk on Saint John Neumann.
SEPTA: Bus 50; trolley 15.
Other: A gift shop is open daily, 9 to 4.

St. Peter's has gained international prominence for its **St. John Neumann Shrine** at 1019 North 5th Street. The Shrine was completely renovated in 1989.

St. John Neumann was the fourth Bishop of Philadelphia from 1852 till his death at age 49 in 1860. He was a founder of America's first parochial school system which was here in Philadelphia. He is the first American male to be canonized a saint (June 19, 1977) by the Roman Catholic Church.

St. John Neumann's remains are visible in a glass-sided crypt beneath the church's altar table. Artifacts of his life, including a rosary, chalice, copies of sermons and a will, are exhibited. Twenty-six stained glass windows tell the story of his life. Pope John Paul II visited the Shrine on October 4, 1979.

TEMPLE JUDEA MUSEUM
OF KENESETH ISRAEL
Old York and Township Line Roads
Elkins Park, PA 19117
887-8700

Hours: Monday to Wednesday, 1 to 4; before and after Friday services at 8:30 P.M. Group tours at other times by appointment. Closed Federal and Jewish holidays. Allow an hour or more.

Tours: Call at least one week ahead to schedule no more than 40 adults or school children.

SEPTA: Bus 55.

E & D: Complete wheelchair access.

When Temple Judea merged with Keneseth Israel in 1982 a museum was established to exhibit the Judaica collections of both synagogues. The ark of the former Temple Judea is a permanent feature of the displays, along with antique and contemporary ceremonial and art objects.

Exhibits, which change every few months, focus on religious holidays, festivals and life-cycle events.

A tour can also include a visit to the sanctuary with a detailed description of magnificent stained glass windows by Jacob Landau.

Center City Places of Worship

If you're visiting Philadelphia, or looking for a change of pace, the following places of worship are within walking distance of the various center city hotels. Call ahead to confirm their specific schedules of services.

Arch Street Presbyterian Church 1724 Arch Street, 563-3763. "The Church of Penn Center." Built in 1855, its grand interior is done in Greek Revival style. Services Sunday at 10:45 A.M.

Arch Street United Methodist Church Broad and Arch Streets, 568–6250. "The City's Central Church" has Sunday worship, Sunday organ recitals, occasional community dinners and other events. Tours follow Sunday morning service.

Central Philadelphia Monthly Meeting 15th and Cherry Streets, 241–7260. The 1856 Meeting House of classic architecture has been joined with a contemporary three-story brick and glass structure to form the Friends Center Complex. Included are the offices of several Quaker organizations, a library and a Quaker Information Center. Weekly Meeting is Sunday at 10:30 A.M.

Fifth Church of Christian Science 1915 Pine Street, 545–2899.

First Baptist Church 17th and Sansom Streets, 563–3853. Built in 1898 in Byzantine and Romanesque styles to resemble the Church of St. Sophia in Constantinople. A frequent site for concerts and community events. Open for "prayer and quietness," weekdays 11:30 to 1:30.

First Presbyterian Church 21st and Walnut Streets, 567–0532. The "Mother Church" of American Presbyterianism; established in 1698. Sunday services at 11 and occasional Thursday evenings and holidays.

First Unitarian Church 2125 Chestnut Street, 563–3980. Built in 1885 (their fourth home) after being established in 1796 as the first "Unitarian" American church.

Holy Communion Lutheran Church 2110 Chestnut Street, 567–3668.

Holy Trinity Episcopal Church 1904 Walnut Street, 567–1267. Sunday, Thursday and holiday services. Popular site for concerts and special events.

Philadelphia Ethical Society 1906 Rittenhouse Square, 735–3456. September to May, Sunday 11 A.M. meeting of Ethical Culture Movement stresses ethics and good living over theology.

St. Clement's Episcopal Church 2000 Cherry Street, 563-1876. Completed in 1859 with later additions of the present high altar, wrought iron gates and stained glass windows. Tours are available by appointment. Daily services.

St. George Greek Orthodox Cathedral 256 South 8th Street, 627-4389.

St. John's Catholic Church 21 South 13th Street, 563-5432. Several Masses daily.

St. Luke and the Epiphany Episcopal Church 330 South 13th Street, 732-1918. Built in 1840, and the site of a pre- and post-Civil War conference between Northern and Southern members of the Episcopal Church to preserve its unity. Services Sunday at 9 and 11 A.M.

St. Mark's Episcopal Church 1625 Locust Street, 735-1416. Built in the 1850s, and "The Church of the English Actors Union." Daily services.

St. Patrick's Roman Catholic Church 242 South 20th Street, 735-9900. Several Masses daily.

Society Hill Synagogue (Conservative-Reconstructionist) 418 Spruce Street, 922-6590. An early 19th century historical landmark designed by Thomas U. Walter as a Baptist Church. Bought by a Rumanian Jewish congregation at the turn of this century; its early 20th century qualities have been preserved. Services Friday evening and Saturday morning; frequent programs to which community is invited.

Temple Beth Zion-Beth Israel (Conservative) 18th and Spruce Streets, 735-5148. Formerly a 19th century, Gothic-style church, and transformed into a synagogue in 1954. Daily morning and evening services.

Tenth Presbyterian Church 1700 Spruce Street, 735-7688. Services Sunday at 9:15 and 11 A.M.; 7 P.M.

Vilna Congregation (Sons of Abraham Synagogue) 509 Pine Street, 592-9433. Daily and Saturday morning services.

YM-YWHA (Conservative) 401 S. Broad Street, 545-4400. Services Friday evening and Saturday morning, holidays and festivals from September to May.

Chapter 6.
The Waterfront.

The English explorer, Henry Hudson, discovered a river in 1609, and the next year it was named in honor of Virginia's first governor, Baron Thomas de la Waare. Today it's the Delaware River.

William Penn quickly saw the strategic importance that both the Delaware and Schuylkill Rivers could play in his dream of a "Holy Experiment," and when he laid out the plan for Philadelphia in 1682 the two rivers became the east and west boundaries of the city. The Schuylkill remained the western border until 1854, when the Borough of West Philadelphia was merged into the city.

Its situation on the Delaware River today enables Philadelphia to boast of the largest fresh water port in the world, and the second busiest port in the nation. It's the largest petroleum port on the East Coast, and a major center for grain, ore, iron ore and coal. Ships from all over the world can be seen on the Delaware, and it's a rare day when you don't spot a large freighter on the move. (You'll want to watch the ships from Penn's Landing.)

Four bridges span the Delaware River to connect Philadelphia with New Jersey.

The **Tacony-Palmyra Bridge** (opened in 1929) links Northeast Philadelphia with Burlington County, and it costs only 25 cents to drive across. It's a drawbridge, so be prepared to wait if there's a ship approaching.

The **Betsy Ross Bridge** (opened in 1976) connects the Bridesburg section of the city with Pennsauken, New Jersey. The **Walt Whitman Bridge** (opened in 1957) links South Philadelphia and Gloucester City.

The most interesting of the four spans is the **Benjamin Franklin Bridge**. It runs from center city Philadelphia to Camden. When it was built in 1926, it was the largest single-span structure in the world, boasting of 8,291 feet from portal to portal. More recently, in 1987, the Ben Franklin Bridge got "turned on." Some 592 lamps light its steel cables every night from dusk till midnight (and 2 A.M. on Saturday and Sunday). Every ten minutes, when a PATCO* train crosses over and triggers a computer, the lights appear to wiggle and dance. Don't miss a look at one of Philadelphia's newest nighttime landmarks.

You can drive across the Ben Franklin Bridge for 90 cents or you can ride a PATCO train for 75 cents. But the most energetic way to cross is on foot or by bicycle. There's a 10-foot wide walkway along the bridge's south side, which is open to hikers and cyclists from 7 A.M. until dusk. The view is fabulous, the picture-taking possibilities are excellent, and—best of all—it's free. Call the Delaware River Port Authority (925–8780) to make sure it's open on the day you want to cross.

Penn's Landing

Penn's Landing is one of Philadelphia's newer attractions. William Penn would certainly never recognize the sleek marina and riverside esplanades as the same place along the Delaware where he landed his small ship "Welcome" more than 300 years ago.

Dozens of ugly, run-down piers were demolished to make way for marinas, walkways, overlooks, a sculpture garden and parks. You can drive to Penn's Landing, arrive at the marina by boat, or you can handily walk from the adjacent Society Hill, Old City and Queen Village neighborhoods.

Penn's Landing currently extends from Market Street south to Lombard Street and covers 37 acres.

The construction of Penn's Landing began in 1967, and there's more work to be done. Additional recreation space, riverwalks, apartments, townhouses, restaurants, hotel and office buildings are underway or on the drawing board.

The Penn's Landing development has spurred growth beyond its boundaries. What were once commercial piers just north of the Penn's Landing site are now luxury residential properties. The Philadelphia Marine Center incorporates 15 acres of water and piers 12 to 19 north to include a 340-slip marina, boat show, sales and service centers. The Penn's Landing Marina at the Delaware and Spruce Street has 56 boat slips.

Penn's Landing itself has become an ideal site for special events and celebrations. Queen Elizabeth docked her royal yacht "Britannia" at Penn's Landing when she paid a visit to Philadelphia. Many of the world's "Tall Ships" paid a courtesy call when they participated in the Bicentennial's Operation Sail and to celebrate Philadelphia's 300th birthday in 1982. They returned again to commemorate "Freedom Sail International" in July of 1986. And we hope they'll return for more celebrations.

Displays along the Penn's Landing esplanade will familiarize you with the port's history and her traffic. Look for the enormous murals at the Market, Chestnut and Walnut "Malls" depicting the Philadelphia waterfront in 1702, 1753 and 1876.

The three-and-a-half acre Great Plaza at Chestnut Street provides a tiered, terraced amphitheater facing the river. You'll get to know the Great Plaza as the site of spectacular summertime festivals and concert programs.

Pavement designs at the site depict the Delaware and a compass pointing overseas to Philadelphia's sister cities*. Graphs, charts and drawings near the river's edge explain the city's topography and the river's channel and depths. Colorful panels point out the ships you might see along the Delaware, their flags and funnel insignias.

One adventuresome and nostalgic way to get an overview of Penn's Landing is from the Penn's Landing Trolley. In case you missed it, go back to Chapter 1. Plans also call for revival of the ferryboat service that once linked Penn's Landing with Camden, New Jersey across the river. Look for it sometime in 1992.

A highlight of your trip to Penn's Landing should be a visit to a few of the ships permanently moored there.

E & D: Gangplanks and stairs make wheelchair access to the ships impossible. It's best to view the ships and the river from the flat esplanades of Penn's Landing.

SEPTA buses to Penn's Landing include the 21 to the foot of Chestnut Street, 5 and 42 to Front and Walnut or Locust Streets, the 17, 33 or 48 to Front and Market Streets, or the Ben FrankLine route 76 to Front and Chestnut then south to 2nd and Lombard Streets.

GAZELA PHILADELPHIA
ex Gazela Primeiro
Penn's Landing at Market Street
(In winter, adjacent to Pier 3)
923–9030

Hours: Weekends, 10 to 5, weather permitting. Groups at other times by appointment.
Tours: Call at least 2 weeks ahead to schedule groups of up to 80. Adults must accompany children under 16.

Cost: Adults, $1; children under 12, free. Group rates available when scheduling tour.

The Gazela Philadelphia is a 177-foot square-rigged sailing ship built in 1883. She's the last of a Portuguese fleet that fished for cod off Newfoundland as recently as 1969. She's the oldest and largest wooden square-rigged ship that still sails.

The Gazela came to Philadelphia in 1971 under auspices of the Philadelphia Maritime Museum. Today, she's lovingly maintained and operated by the Philadelphia Ship Preservation Guild.

She was the oldest of the 18 "Tall Ships" from around the world to participate in OpSail on July 4, 1976 in New York City. In 1984, she participated in the "Return of the Tall Ships" in Quebec, Canada. She again returned to New York harbor to celebrate the Statue of Liberty Centennial on July 4, 1986, and immediately following that event, the Gazela Philadelphia led the flotilla of "Tall Ships" to Penn's Landing for "Freedom Sail International." Now, she's a permanent working exhibit and sail training vessel in Penn's Landing, and a maritime ambassador for Philadelphia. The Gazela can fly 13 sails from her three masts, with a mast height of 94 feet and a sail area of 11,000 square feet.

Come aboard and relive the bygone days at sea. Listen for the sound of the crew singing sea chanteys. Imagine the pounding of waves and the spray of the briny deep. Marvel at the spartan living accommodations where sailors longed for the comforts of home. And view the hold where freshly caught fish were kept.

Note: You can tell the Gazela has an ambitious sailing schedule. In fact, she's scheduled to go to Europe in 1992 to join the re-enactment of Columbus' voyage to America. You might want to call ahead to be sure she's in port.

TUGBOAT JUPITER is also maintained by the Philadelphia Ship Preservation Guild and sits in the shadow of the Ben Franklin Bridge just south of Pier 3. She was built in Philadelphia in 1904 and worked for the Independent Pier Company along the Delaware till her retirement in 1980. Today, she's under continual restoration by a dedicated cadre of retired tugboat workers, and she's available for hire for floating parties of up to 45 would-be sailors. (The barge adjacent to the Jupiter is actually a floating woodworking shop occupied almost every weekday by ships' restorers.)

133

LIGHTSHIP #79 - BARNEGAT rests nearby in this floating museum collection. "Old Barney" was built at the turn-of-the-century across the river in Camden at the N.Y. Shipbuilding & Dry Dock Co. Originally steam-powered, her present diesel engine was installed in 1931. For 63 years till 1967 she proudly marked the coastal shipping lanes to the Port of Philadelphia, the last lightship operated by the U.S. Coast Guard. Her 13,000 candlepower light could be visible for nearly 20 miles. For her devoted service, "Old Barney" now ranks a listing in the National Register of Historic Places. She's 131 feet long, 30 feet wide and rode a crew of 14 to 17 men.

U.S.S. OLYMPIA
Penn's Landing at Spruce Street
922–1898

Hours: Daily, 10 to 4:30 in winter; 10 to 6 from Memorial Day till late September. Closed Christmas, New Year's.

Tours: Call a week ahead if you're bringing a group of 25 or more.

Cost: A combined rate for the Olympia and the Becuna: adults, $3; senior citizens, $2; children under 12, $1.50. Special rates are arranged in advance for groups of 15 or more.

Other: Souvenirs and refreshments are sold on board at the Ship's Store. Flat shoes are best for touring the historic ships.

Admiral Dewey's famous flagship at the Battle of Manila Bay in 1898 has been restored as a floating museum. This is the ship where Dewey gave the famous order: "You may fire when you are ready, Gridley."

The Olympia is the last survivor of the Spanish-American War. She served in World War I and ceremoniously brought the Unknown Soldier back from France in 1921 to be buried in Arlington Cemetery. The Olympia took her final cruise in June, 1976, from Pier 11 North in Philadelphia to her present berth at Penn's Landing. She's a National Historic Landmark.

Most of the Olympia's 16 cabins have been restored, and you can tour the entire ship from topsides to berth deck. The ship's restoration includes many exhibits relating to the Spanish-American War, including old naval weapons, uniforms and assorted mementos from the ship's crew.

U.S.S. BECUNA
Penn's Landing at Spruce Street
922-1898

Hours and Tours: Same as Olympia.
Cost: A combined admission rate with the Olympia.

What's that big black thing next to the U.S.S. Olympia?
It's the World War II submarine, U.S.S. Becuna.

The Becuna was commissioned in 1944 and saw action
in the South Pacific. She was transferred to the Atlantic
fleet in 1949 and then to the Mediterranean. In 1951 she
was converted to a streamlined fast underwater submarine known as a guppy-class and updated with sophisticated radar and torpedo equipment. Then she served in
the Atlantic and Mediterranean during the Korean and
Vietnam wars.

The Becuna finished active service as a training vessel and conducted more than 10,000 dives before being
decommissioned in 1969.

WORKSHOP ON THE WATER
Penn's Landing at Dock Street
925-5439 or 925-7589

Hours: Wednesday to Sunday, 10 to 5.
Cost: Adults, $1; children, $.50; or free with admission
to Philadelphia Maritime Museum. Children under 12
must be with an adult. Groups of 10 or more get special rate if scheduled ahead.
Other: An annual regatta, on an early fall weekend, recreates boating of bygone eras along the Delaware. Call
for specifics.

Did you ever wonder what kind of boats our forefathers
were accustomed to seeing along the Delaware? Well,
here's your chance to find out.

The 110- by 30-foot covered lighter barge from 1939,
which is permanently moored in Penn's Landing, is the
Philadelphia Maritime Museum's* Workshop on the
Water.

It houses changing exhibits that focus on historic water-

135

craft of Pennsylvania, New Jersey and Delaware.

And this is most definitely an ongoing workshop. (In fact, some visitors have been so hooked, they've joined workshops and started boatbuilding themselves.) At any given time, you're likely to see in current construction an example of the traditional small craft once sailed along the Delaware. (Participants in workshop activities study sailmaking, toolmaking, painting and all of the skills of boat building. If you'd like to participate, call or stop by for a schedule and details.)

After you've toured the ships, come ashore. There's a lot more to see at Penn's Landing.

A two-acre **WORLD SCULPTURE GARDEN** surrounds a gigantic sundial that was installed to commemorate Penn's Landing in 1682. If you ever wanted to guess the time in this ancient way, this is your chance to try it, unless you come on a cloudy day.

William Penn returned again late in 1982, this time to stay. He's cast in bronze by sculptor Carl Lindborg and looks as he did at age 38 when he arrived in 1682.

The stone sculptures include a 16th century sacred bull from India, a pair of five-foot pre-Columbian spheres from Costa Rica, a pair of late 17th century Korean tombstones, an Etruscan sarcophagus from Italy and an "inukshuk" (or sign post) from Canada. The late 19th century 20-foot totem pole watching over the garden is also from Canada.

The **PORT OF HISTORY MUSEUM** at Walnut Street is a City of Philadelphia showplace for exhibits that change regularly. They're from the city's varied collections and borrowed shows. It's also a popular locale for celebrations and special events.

The museum's hours are Wednesday to Sunday, 10 A.M. to 4:30 P.M. It's closed holidays. Admission is $2 for adults, $1 for children 5 to 12, free for children under 5. Call 925–3802 for a preview of what's happening.

What else is there at Penn's Landing?

You already know about Delaware River cruises to see the Port of Philadelphia, and the Penn's Landing Trolley that travels Delaware Avenue (refer back to Chapter 1), but there are also festivities throughout the summer.

The Penn's Landing Corporation sponsors "Down by the Riverside," nearly a hundred concerts and special events taking place from May through September at the Great Plaza and outdoor pavilion. They include a Jazz Series, Nationality Festivals, Big Band Concerts and a Singer-Songwriter Series, just to name a few. See the local newspapers or call 923–4992 (and see Chapter 10) for their schedule.

Fireworks light up the sky at Penn's Landing around July 4th. Check the papers for the time and date. Foreign and U.S. Navy vessels frequently drop anchor at Penn's Landing and invite the public on board. Call 923–4992 to find out who's going to be here.

By now you've got the point. Penn's Landing is an exciting place to visit.

You can easily come to Penn's Landing by car or chartered bus because there's plenty of space for parking. It's $5 ($6 on weekends) to park a car for the day. You can come by bicycle because there are places to park and lock your bike. You can also come by SEPTA as described at the beginning of this chapter.

If you own a boat, come by boat. Call the Penn's Landing Corporation (923–8181) mid-May through October, or Philadelphia Marine Center (931–1000) just north of Penn's Landing, for information. The docks are available on a first come, first served basis and there's a daily fee.

Come to Penn's Landing and board a boat for a leisurely lunch or dinner cruise, or enjoy the sparkling Chart House on the waterfront at Lombard Street. Or watch the waterfront while dining at the Riverfront or its dinner theater, or a restaurant along Front Street or Delaware Avenue (see Chapter 18). Or have a picnic in the sculpture garden or any of the comfortable seating areas.

A reminder for the elderly and handicapped: All of the open, level stretches of Penn's Landing are easily accessible to wheelchairs. Unfortunately, it won't be possible to board the historic ships.

Philadelphia's Other Waterfronts

Philadelphia has two waterways in addition to the Delaware: the **Schuylkill** and the **Wissahickon**. (If you're not a native Philadelphian, don't try to pronounce them.) Both rivers flow through Fairmount Park. Both are described in more detail in Chapter 8.

Penn's Landing (on the Delaware) is Philadelphia's newest waterfront attraction, but the Schuylkill and the Wissahickon offer a variety of recreational activities. You'll be reading about these pastimes in Chapter 14.

Chapter 7.
Science and Nature.

ACADEMY OF NATURAL SCIENCES
19th Street and Benjamin Franklin Parkway—19103
299-1020 (recording) or 299-1000

Hours: Weekdays, 10 to 4:30; weekends and holidays, 10 to 5. Closed Thanksgiving, Christmas, New Year's. Allow at least 2 hours.

Tours: School classes can schedule any of the Academy's 25 natural history lessons (most of them including live animals) for a weekday; call 299-1060 for reservations. Other groups call 299- 1027 for reservations.

Cost: Adults, $5.50; senior citizens and military personnel, $5; children 3 to 12, $4.50; under 3, free. Group rates at door for 10 or more: adults, $5; children 3 to 12, $4. Group rates paid at least 10 days in advance by mail: adults, $4; children 3 to 12, $3. Membership provides free admission, newsletters, library privileges, a magazine subscription and discounts for classes, field trips and the Museum Shop.

Lunch: The Eatery has machines for beverages, sandwiches and desserts. Or you can brown bag it. Group reservations are necessary on weekdays: schools, call 299-1060; other groups, call 299-1027.

SEPTA: Buses 32, 33, 38, Ben FrankLine route 76, or Market Street routes to 19th Street.

Other: The Museum Shop is a fun gift place for children and adults seeking the unusual. It's filled with ecology kits, educational books, jewelry, T-shirts, mineral specimens, fossils and rare shells.

E & D: The Parkway entrance has 7 steps, but the 19th Street entrance enables complete wheelchair access.

When you visit the Academy, you'll get a feeling of what it's like to be in the animal worlds of Africa, Asia and North America, because you'll see animals that are native to those lands. And you'll see them in their natural settings. Thirty-five groupings of stuffed animals from around the world are on display.

There are wonderful exhibits of birds, fishes, decoys, Egyptian mummies, insects, gems and crystals, endangered species and species from the past. A distinguished show comes to the Hall of Changing Exhibits on the Academy's first floor every few months.

The Academy was founded in 1812, and it's the oldest natural history museum in America.

A total renovation of the Academy has recently taken place, and Dinosaur Hall was unveiled in 1986. You'll meet the likes of a 15-feet tall, 40-feet long tyrannosaurus rex and a dozen other awesome creatures that roamed the earth long before man appeared. When did dinosaurs live? How long did they last? How fast did they grow? What made them become extinct? These are just a few of the questions you'll answer on a computer for dinosaur data and other ingenious exhibits. You'll sit in a footprint, dig a fossil, stop in the dinosaur weigh station and see "Magnificent Monsters," shown every 20 minutes in an informal theater. **Discovering Dinosaurs** is a fabulous, world-class, one-of-a-kind exhibit. Don't miss it!

And, as if that's not enough, the Academy is undergoing a huge expansion. Look for its new addition with enlarged exhibition, classroom, lunchroom and library space to open late in 1991.

The Academy's animal room has 90 "critters" to choose from for the half-hour live animal and slides show. It's presented in the auditorium several times each weekend. Check the listing of the day's special programs on arrival at the Academy. If you can't get to the Academy to see a show, look into "Eco Show on the Road" (see Chapter 13 on "Tours to Go").

There's also a popular film presentation, "Dinosaurs," and several mini-shows each weekend on changing topics. Check the program schedule for these activities, too, when you get there.

Right within the Academy is a mini-museum for children called **OUTSIDE IN**. There's more about that in Chapter 15.

Saturday classes for children and weeknight classes for adults are presented during the school year, and classes for children are presented weekdays in the summer. Call 299-1060 for details. The Academy's library is described later in Chapter 11.

Bird-watchers will be especially interested in a hot-line provided by the Academy and the **Delaware Valley Ornithological Club**. Call **567-BIRD** to keep up with the latest in local, unusual sightings.

You shouldn't miss the Academy.

Naturally.

ANDORRA NATURAL AREA
Northwestern Avenue south of
Germantown Avenue—19118
685–9285

Hours: Trails and natural area are open all daylight
hours. Tree House Visitor Center is open most weekends. Call ahead to be sure. Maps and porch exhibits
are available if the center is closed.

Tours: You're on your own, or groups of up to 20 can make
reservations at least a month ahead for a scheduled
program.

Cost: Free, except a minimal charge for a few of the special events.

Lunch: Picnic tables are available for those who bring
their own. Groups must make reservations and everyone is responsible to remove their trash.

SEPTA: Bus L to Northwestern and walk south 2 long
blocks; bus 27 and walk north 2 long blocks.

Other: A Maple Sugar Fest is in February and a Harvest
Fest is in the fall. Call for dates and details.

E & D: Tree House Visitor Center is not accessible and
no special facilities, but special nature programs and
walks can be arranged for groups.

Five miles of lush nature trails weave through the city's
northwesternmost section of Fairmount Park* that borders the Wissahickon Creek.

A Tree House Visitor Center at the Andorra Natural
Area houses exhibits to view and touch, along with a
menagerie of live animals to meet and greet. Displays on
the porch change with the season. Maps and literature
are available to make your visit more interesting and informative.

The center's porch seating area overlooks a popular
bird-feeding locale, making it a comfortable place to relax and look for bluejays, cardinals, chickadees, snowbirds
or woodpeckers who might fly by for a snack. (A little
birdie told me this is a fun place to celebrate a youngster's
birthday.)

Nature programs are scheduled throughout the year appealing to children and adults. Nature lovers of all ages
enjoy wildflower walks, bird nest studies, story-telling,
hikes along the Wissahickon (it's about three miles to
Valley Green*) and family strolls. Binoculars are handy,

cameras are useful and comfortable shoes are necessary. If you'd like to participate, call ahead for a monthly calendar of activities.

BARTRAM'S HOUSE AND GARDEN
54th Street and Lindbergh Boulevard—19143
729-5281

Hours: The house is open May through October, Tuesday to Sunday, 10 to 4; November through April, Tuesday to Friday, 10 to 4. Allow 30 minutes. The garden is part of Fairmount Park and is open dawn to dusk.

Tours: A staff member is always available to answer questions. Guided tours of the house and garden can be arranged for groups of 10 or more by calling the John Bartram Association several weeks ahead. A self-guided tour of the grounds is available for $.75. Ask about adult tours that can include a slide show, the house, the garden, and tea and goodies in the 18th century kitchen. Children's tours can focus on botany or colonial life and crafts such as apple pressing, butter churning, candle making or maple sugaring.

Cost: Adults, $2; children 6 to 18, $1; under 6, free. Group tour rates available when scheduling in advance for 10 or more. The garden is free. Members receive free admission, a newsletter, shop discounts and invitations to special events.

Lunch: A picnic pavilion, ball field and a playground are on the surrounding grounds. Gourmet box lunches can be ordered in advance for groups of 10 or more.

SEPTA: Bus 52; trolley 36.

Other: A museum shop sells books, pottery and tinware reproductions, and items related to the 18th century lifestyle.

E & D: First floor of house and entire grounds are wheelchair accessible.

Visit America's oldest botanical garden.

Only 44 acres of John Bartram's original 102-acre farm remain, but what's left is a garden oasis along the Schuylkill River in the industrial areas of Southwest Philadelphia. It's the oldest surviving botanical garden in the country. This is a small but significant portion of the sprawling Fairmount Park* system.

Romp around the grounds and look at the collection of more than 100 trees and shrubs associated with the

Quaker farmer who became King George III's Royal Botanist. There's an ancient ginkgo, oaks, pawpaws, persimmons, magnolias, Franklinias, and a yellowwood tree. Many specimens are labeled.

Bartram built his house between 1728 and 1731, and an addition in 1770. The gardening tradition was continued by his son William who resided in the house, also, and other descendants of the family who lived here and maintained the nursery till 1850. The house, now a National Historical Landmark, has recently been restored and filled with lovely antiques and 18th century furnishings.

Look outside over the window of Bartram's study for an inscription carved by John Bartram, himself, in 1770. He made certain that his religious philosophy was inscribed in stone for longevity.

DAVID RITTENHOUSE
LABORATORY OBSERVATORY
University of Pennsylvania
209 South 33rd Street—19104
(enter from 33rd Street, south of Walnut Street)
898-8176 (weekdays, 9 to 5)

Hours: Monday and Thursday nights: Mid-September through March, 7:30 to 9 P.M.; April through mid-August, 9 to 10:30.

Tours: No more than 20 can visit at once. Groups of 10 or more must call at least a week ahead. Children must be with an adult.

Cost: Free.

SEPTA: Buses 21, 30, 42.

Other: Dress comfortably. You'll be standing during the entire visit.

E & D: No wheelchair access. After taking elevator to 4th floor, there are 2 flights of steps.

The Departments of Astronomy and Astrophysics at the University of Pennsylvania provide a close-up look at the heavens for serious star gazers. Be sure to come on a cloudless night.

Various phases of the moon, constellations, star clusters, nebulae and other planets are often visible, depending on the time of the year, through the enormous eight-inch refractor telescope.

A University faculty member or graduate student will be on hand to read heaven's timetable and answer your questions.

FRANKLIN INSTITUTE
SCIENCE MUSEUM
20th Street and Benjamin Franklin Parkway—19103
448-1200

Hours: Monday and Tuesday, 9:30 to 5; Wednesday to Sunday, 9:30 to 9 (except Science Center closes daily at 5). Futures Center also open Tuesday till 9 P.M. from mid-June to Labor Day. Closed July 4, Thanksgiving, December 24, Christmas and New Year's. Allow at least 2 hours in any section; better yet, a whole day. And plan to come again.

Tours: Everything in the museum is self-explanatory. The interactive computer network activated with your bar-code admission card enables visitors of any age or interest to plan a personalized tour. Groups of 15 or more must call (448-1201) 30 days ahead for special rates and reservations. Philadelphia Public School teachers should call Museum Education at Board of Education, 299-7778, for special arrangements.

Cost: Rates vary for day (9:30 to 5) and evening (5 to 9); for combination tickets to multiple attractions (Science Center, Futures Center, Omniverse Theater, Fels Planetarium) or single attraction tickets; for adults, seniors and children 4 to 11. Daytime packages start at $8.50 for adults; $7 for seniors and children 4 to 11; children under 4, free. Omniverse tickets available at Franklin Institute or call ahead to Ticketron 1-800-233-4050 (there's an added service charge). Group rates available in advance for school groups of 10 or more, non-school groups of 15 or more, call 448-1150. Student, Individual and Family Membership (call 448-1231) provides free admission to the Science Center, Futures Center and Planetarium, discount to Omniverse Theater and for guests, discount in Museum Stores and for workshops, publications, special travel ventures and family programs. Admission is free to the Futures Center Atrium where you can dine at the Omni Cafe, shop, watch science demonstrations and informal entertainment.

Restaurants: Ben's in the Science Center serves fast-food family-style breakfast and lunch. Omni Cafe in the Futures Center features ethnic foods and drink for lunch (daily) and dinner till 8 P.M. (except Monday and Tuesday when Futures Center is closed at night). Call 448–1190 for information and reservations. The emphasis is on good nutrition and moderate prices. A lunchroom can be reserved (448–1201) weekdays by school groups of 10 or more and other groups of 15 or more.

SEPTA: Buses 7, 32, 33, 38, 48, Ben FrankLine route 76. There's metered street parking and the museum's 350-car underground garage at 21st Street with direct access into the museum.

Other: The 3 Museum Stores are filled with scientific toys, games, books, kites, jewelry, T-shirts, star maps and various innovative wonders, from inexpensive novelty items to the latest in high-tech adult "toys."

E & D: Use the ramp at the Winter Street entrance. Elevators stop at all floors, but certain display areas are separated by steps. Rest rooms and the restaurants are wheelchair accessible.

The Franklin Institute **Science Center** is a "touch me" place, and its exhibits invite you to push buttons, pull levers, spin wires and slide weights.

It's a fabulous way to learn about hard-to-explain things like the principles of science, technology, time, perception, measurements, meteors, aviation, communications and atomic energy. Learning is fun when you walk through a giant heart, "engineer" a train for a 24-foot round-trip excursion, or climb into the cockpit and "fly" a plane.

Pick up your "Schedule of Events" and museum map when you get there. Then, set out on an adventure of scientific exploration.

You're certain to be captivated by the Institute's demonstrations of liquid air, computers, weather reporting, the forces of light, static electricity, ships and waves.

Shipbuilding on the Delaware is where you can design a duck or set sail on your own while you learn about local shipbuilding from William Penn's time to the mid-20th century.

Help build a mountain in The Changing Earth as you discover the forces that shape our planet. Do optics interest you? Then make hand shadows, freeze your shadow, learn to focus and refract. Electricity comes alive with Franklin's daily electrical experiments. The Hall of Aviation leads you through the history of flight from man's dreams of flying gods and magic carpets to the reality of jets and supersonic transport. Math problems become fun and easy when mastered on a giant abacus or a roulette wheel.

And that's just the Science Center.

Now journey into the 21st century at the Franklin Institute's dazzling new **Futures Center**. Eight state-of-the-art exhibits invite you to see, touch, explore and experiment with your options for the next century. Future-Visions, FutureComputers, FutureSpace, FutureEarth, FutureEnergy, FutureMaterials, FutureHealth and Future and You are the themes. You're lured into a life-size model of a space station with all kinds of activity stations, through a giant model of a human cell, and into a man-made tropical rain forest complete with waterfall, live fish and a solar-powered fountain. Try tic-tac-toe against a computer, "paint your face" to a different you, compose synthesized music, add 20 years to your face in a matter of minutes and experiment with the materials likely to be worn in our futures.

The Future Careers Center wants students to explore with computers their interests and skills and the job market of the 21st century. At the Cutting Edge Gallery, new products are demonstrated and tested before they reach the marketplace.

As we said, welcome to the 21st century, where you can start today making the choices that will affect your tomorrow.

The 350-seat **Omniverse Theater** in the Futures Center is unlike any other theater in the mid-Atlantic states. It's Omnivax, which means the 70mm film surrounds you on a domed, four-story high, 79-foot wide wraparound screen that's the largest of its kind in the country. Sit back, relax if you can, and imagine you're part of the picture!

The 40-minute film at the Omniverse Theater is shown almost hourly (call 448–1200 for the daily schedule) and individual tickets are required for each performance. The feature changes twice a year, and it's a good bet you'll want to catch them all. An eight-minute "Philadelphia Anthem" short film precedes each feature presentation.

The **Fels Planetarium** is the way you can travel into the Universe to learn about the sun, the stars, the heavens and the evening sky. With the Planetarium's new state-of-the-art DIGISTAR projector, everything is graphically simulated in three dimensions. 35- to 45-minute shows about the constellations and patterns in the sky change twice a year and are presented several times daily for individual visitors and for groups. (Reservations are necessary for groups of 10 or more: call 448–1201.)

A special show for young children is presented twice a day on weekends. In addition to the shows already

described, a Live Constellation Show is presented for backyard astronomers on weekends at 1:15 P.M. The live program changes as the sky changes, so you'll be able to look up and recognize the stars. Call 563–1363 for a Sky Report.

The **Benjamin Franklin National Memorial** is a tribute to this great man with an illustrious lifetime. An exhibit of personal possessions and science artifacts called "Ben Franklin: Ideas and Images" surrounds the enormous Franklin marble sculpture by James Earle Fraser. It's the largest collection of "Frankliniana" anywhere. This area is free to the public (if you enter from 20th Street), but children have to be with an adult.

Science and Computer Workshops, which are programmed for pre-schoolers through adults, meet weekdays and weekends throughout the year at the Franklin Institute. The groups are small and everyone has a chance to build or experiment with computers, rocks, minerals, model airplanes and amateur radio. . .just to name a few things. There's a fee for these workshops. For information, call 448–1260; for registration, call 448–1286. The Franklin Institute also schedules special evening programs throughout the year and camp-ins where students can bring a sleeping bag and spend the night learning science in the museum. Call for information about these and other special events.

We can't say enough about the Franklin Institute Science Museum!

MEDICAL SITES

If you need medical care, Philadelphia is a good place to be. We can qualify as the medical capital of the world.

You can tour Pennsylvania Hospital, the nation's oldest (see Chapter 4), and you can tour Pennsylvania College of Podiatric Medicine, one of the nation's five podiatry schools (see Chapter 13).

Philadelphia is a major medical research and dissemination center. Numerous journals and texts originate here from the world's largest medical publishing houses.

A great many of our country's physicians get their education at one of Philadelphia's six medical schools: Hahnemann University, Medical College of Pennsylvania, Philadelphia College of Osteopathy, Temple University, Thomas Jefferson University and the University of Pennsylvania (the nation's first medical school).

Attractions with medical significance are detailed in this chapter and elsewhere in this book. Several others welcome individuals or small groups who are interested in careers in medicine and allied professions.

These tours are designed for adults, but they might be of interest to youngsters. If you're visiting here for a short period of time, it's a good idea to write ahead and plan a special tour.

AMERICAN COLLEGE OF PHYSICIANS Independence Mall West, 6th and Race Streets, 19106 (351–2400). 70,000 physicians specializing in internal medicine belong to this national medical specialty society. The administrative headquarters, along with the editorial offices of "Annals of Internal Medicine," are housed here in a striking 9-story neo-classical style building completed in 1989. Tours for medical professionals must be scheduled in advance by contacting the Office of News and Information.

FRIENDS HOSPITAL Roosevelt Boulevard and Adams Avenue, 19124 (831–4772). The nation's oldest private psychiatric hospital was founded in 1813 and is in Northeast Philadelphia. Tours are for medical professional people only; write three to four weeks in advance. The magnificent 99-acre grounds are open to the public during the last weekend in April and the first two weekends in May (see Chapter 19) for the Friends Hospital Garden Days.

HAHNEMANN ARCHIVES AND HISTORY OF MEDICINE ROOM 245 N. 15th Street, 19102 (448–7811). This country's first homeopathic medical college was founded in 1848 by Samuel Hahnemann. It continued with homeopathic and related elective courses till 1959. Today, Hahnemann excels as a university and hospital pioneering in heart study and treatment, cancer research, renal care, hypertension and mental health. The Lucy F. Cooke Room exhibits memorabilia of world-renowned doctors affiliated with Hahnemann, hospital and school archives, and reference collections on homeopathy and the history of medicine. Hours are by appointment, weekdays, 9 to 5.

HISTORICAL DENTAL MUSEUM OF TEMPLE UNIVERSITY SCHOOL OF DENTISTRY 3223 N. Broad Street, 19140 (221–2816). Anyone is welcome to tour the museum weekdays from 8:30 to 4:30. Call ahead to be sure it's open and then stop by at Room 460. The museum currently shares several rooms with the art and photography departments, so it's an eclectic gathering of antique dental furnishings and equipment as old as the early 1700s, artwork, memorabilia and photographs. The museum moves late in 1992 to new exhibition space on the first floor.

PHILADELPHIA COLLEGE OF PHARMACY AND SCIENCE 43rd and Kingsessing Avenue, 19104 (596–8967). The Joseph W. England Library and the relics of an old apothecary shop may be visited (at new campus location in 1992) by appointment. If you'd like to see a wonderful collection of antique apothecary jars, they're always on display on the first floor of Griffith Hall and in the library.

PHILADELPHIA COUNTY MEDICAL SOCIETY 2100 Spring Garden Street, 19130 (563–5343). There are no tours here, but this is where you should call or write for a schedule of lectures, meetings or special medical events that take place in Philadelphia. The Philadelphia County Medical Society also publishes "Philadelphia Medicine" and provides physician referrals.

TEMPLE UNIVERSITY SCHOOL OF PHARMA-CY'S KENDIG MEMORIAL MUSEUM 3307 N. Broad Street, 19140 (221-4990). See all of the equipment a druggist needed to dispense medicine before pills were mass produced. Weekday tours for small groups by appointment.

UNIVERSITY OF PENNSYLVANIA SCHOOL OF MEDICINE, HISTORY OF MEDICINE EXHIBIT John Morgan Building, School of Medicine, 2nd floor, 37th and Hamilton Walk, 19104 (898-5181). This permanent exhibit of medical records, instruments and equipment offers highlights in the history of the oldest medical school in the country. (It was founded in 1765.) And, it's the place to see Thomas Eakins' famous painting of "The Agnew Clinic." There are also changing exhibits taken from the school's noteworthy collection of medical memorabilia. Hours are weekdays, 9 to 5. You're on your own, but call ahead if a group visit is planned.

MORRIS ARBORETUM
100 Northwestern Avenue
(between Germantown and Stenton)—19118
247-5777

Hours: April to October, daily, 10 to 5; November to March, 10 to 4. Closed December 24, Christmas, New Year's.

Tours: For the public on Saturday and Sunday at 2. Call at least 3 weeks in advance to schedule groups of 10 to 15 per guide, at least kindergarten age. If under 14 years old, one adult must accompany each group of 10.

Cost: Adults, $3; children 7 to 14 and senior citizens, $1.50. Group rates can be arranged when scheduling tour. Individual and family memberships entitle you to free admission, special events, advice for your plants and discount to classes.

Lunch: No food is allowed on the grounds. Ask for directions to picnic grounds at Harper's Meadow in Fairmount Park. It's a half-mile walk from the Arboretum.

SEPTA: Bus L to Germantown and Northwestern, and then a very long walk. There's plenty of free parking.

Other: A gift shop sells items appealing to horticulturalists like posters, prints, honey, and garden books including the "Garden Passport Book" that enables discount admission to 13 gardens in the Delaware Valley region.

E & D: The main roads are paved.

This 175-acre estate in Chestnut Hill is administered by the University of Pennsylvania, to whom it was bequeathed following the deaths of its original owners, John Morris and his sister Lydia. It's a veritable outdoor museum of trees, plants and wildlife as well as an entry in the National Register of Historic Places. It's the official arboretum of the Commonwealth of Pennsylvania.

There are 3,500 varieties of exotic shrubs, native shrubs and trees. There are conifers, hollies, azaleas, magnolias, dogwoods, witchhazels (that's right!), an oak row, weeping beeches, ivies and a medicinal garden. The scenic Wissahickon flows through the magnificent estate.

The spring and fall flowerings and the summer rose garden are all beautiful. The stately evergreens and tropical fern house can be seen in winter. A Victorian garden and an English park are picture perfect.

Small animals roam the grounds, but don't pet them.

Contemporary sculpture dots the landscape, and with the new Sculpture Garden, Morris Arboretum qualifies as an outdoor art museum as well.

There's an ongoing program of lectures and courses in gardening, botany and horticulture. Brochures on special programs are available on request.

Note: If you have a green thumb, try to be here for the Plant Festival Sale on Mother's Day weekend.

MUTTER MUSEUM
College of Physicians
19 South 22nd Street—19103
563-3737

Hours: Tuesday to Friday, 10 to 4. Closed some holidays. Allow 45 minutes. Children under 14 must be accompanied by an adult.

Tours: Scheduled for groups of 10 to 30. Allow 30 to 90 minutes. Call 3 weeks in advance for reservations.

Cost: Free. Donations are suggested to offset museum expenses.

SEPTA: Buses 7, 12, or any Market or Chestnut Street routes.

E & D: There are 8 steps at the building's main entrance.

Call ahead to arrange access to a street-level, rear entrance. Once inside, everything is wheelchair accessible.

The Mutter Museum, housed in a grand Greek Revival style 1909 building, would interest students who are intrigued with medicine and its related fields. The museum's specialties are pathology, anatomy and medical history exhibits, primarily from the 19th century. A 15-minute slide show presents an overview of the College of Physicians and its Museum collections.

Founded in 1787, the College of Physicians is the oldest independent and private medical society in the country. Its library is described in Chapter 11. This is its fourth home.

At the newly renovated, two-story museum, you'll be face-to-face with over 300 skulls and two dozen skeletons, including a 7'6" giant and a 3'6" dwarf. You'll examine medical kits, X-ray equipment, walking sticks, hearing aids, thermometers, spectacles and stethoscopes, the likes of which you've never seen.

Be sure to see Chevalier Jackson's collection of items he removed from his patients: pins and needles and buttons and lockets. The cancerous tumor that was removed from President Grover Cleveland's mouth in 1893 is on display. There's a plaster cast made from the bodies of Chang and Eng, the Chinese Siamese twins who lived in the 19th century, and the actual liver removed from their bodies at autopsy.

If you've ever wondered what an upstate Pennsylvania doctor's office might have looked like in the early 20th century, here's your chance to find out. A desk, examining-surgery chair, treatment facilities, telephone and office equipment are here, awaiting your visit.

If you've never seen a death mask, you can see them here, too.

There are many oil paintings, sculptures and art objects associated with the medical field, and there are interesting collections of memorabilia relating to Madame Curie, Louis Pasteur, Joseph Lister, Benjamin Rush and other noteworthy members of the profession.

A formal medicinal herb garden (open weekdays 9 to 5) is maintained in the yard. At least 60 varieties of plants are labeled with their common and botanical names and their uses for healing.

PENNSYLVANIA HORTICULTURAL SOCIETY
325 Walnut Street—19106   100 N. 20th
625-8250

Hours: Weekdays, 9 to 5. Closed holidays.
Tours: Call ahead if more than 30 are coming together to the Society or its gardens. A program on "Indoor Gardening in the Classroom" is available for Philadelphia Public School teachers. A large selection of horticultural films is available for classroom use on a rental basis.
Cost: Free. Inquire about membership in the Society.
SEPTA: Buses 5, 9, 21, 42, 50, Ben FrankLine route 76.
Other: A small shop sells some nifty planters, stationery, books and appropriate gift items.
E & D: There are 2 low steps at the entrance. An elevator can be taken to 2nd floor library.

You'll find an imaginative nature exhibit at the Horticultural Society at any given time. It might be unusual flowers, a bonsai exhibit or a maritime show with seascapes, herbarium specimens and seaweed designs. The show changes each month.

The Society also provides expert advice to people who want to plant their own vegetable or flower gardens. If you're lucky enough to have a city garden, ask about entering it in the Society's annual contest.

Almost a hundred activities including plant clinics, demonstrations and garden visits are planned for members. The most ambitious project is the famous Philadelphia Flower Show which is held each March at the Civic Center (see Chapter 19).

By all means, don't miss the typical 18th century garden that's adjacent to the Society's headquarters. Its unusual trees, shrubs and flowers are representative of those that grew in Philadelphia before the year 1800.

The Pennsylvania Horticultural Society plays a major role in the greening of Philadelphia with its "Philadelphia Green" project. Plants and gardening information are provided free of charge to organized urban residents so they can improve their environment.

Individuals can read up on gardening and receive plant care advice from the Society's 14,000-volume library*, or by calling the **Horticulture Hot Line** at 922-8043 on weekdays from 9 A.M. to noon.

PENNYPACK ENVIRONMENTAL CENTER
Verree Road south of Bloomfield Avenue—19115
671-0440

Hours: The park is open dawn to dusk. The Center is usually open daily, 9 to 5. Call ahead to be sure, or orient yourself with maps that are posted outdoors.

Tours: Groups of 10 to 50 can be scheduled for indoor or outdoor nature programs on weekday mornings or afternoons. Call at least a week in advance. Read below about other programs.

Cost: Free.

SEPTA: Buses 16, 67.

Other: 4 festivals are held annually at adjacent Fox Chase Farm. Read more about them below.

E & D: There are some paved bike paths in the park, but otherwise no special facilities.

The Environmental Center in the heart of Pennypack Park* features indoor nature exhibits that complement this natural setting. Explore the park on your own and feast your eyes on dozens of varieties of birds, waterlife, deer, small game, trees and exotic wildflowers.

Stop by the "bird blind," a protected area where any of 15 species might be sighted feeding themselves from fall to early spring. Or, join a nature program that might include the study of bugs, birds, insects, the creek, the stream, nests, plants, wildflowers, tracks and signs of wildlife along the trails. Peaceful activity is the theme among nature's inhabitants of Pennypack Park.

Two, three or four programs happen each month and you can get the schedule up to two months ahead. Also, special crafts, nature workshops and programs can be scheduled in advance for weekdays throughout the year for groups of 15 or more.

Fox Chase Farm, at Pine Road and Pennypack Creek near the Environmental Center, is a 113-acre working farm owned by the City of Philadelphia and managed by the School District of Philadelphia's W.B. Saul High School of Agricultural Sciences. (How many big cities do you know where students have an opportunity like this?)

Four Saturdays during the year they hold festivals at the farm from noon to 4 P.M., and the whole family is invited. Maple Sugaring is the first Saturday in March,

Sheep Sheering is the third Saturday in April, Family Farm Day is the third Saturday in August, and Apple Fest is the third Saturday in October.

Tours of the farm and hayrides are part of the adventure. A donation is requested. Call Pennypack Environmental Center to learn more about these fun festivals, parking arrangements and the trolley-bus shuttles.

PHILADELPHIA'S PARKS
(Just to name a few.)

The world's largest municipal park is right here in Philadelphia. We think **FAIRMOUNT PARK** is so important that the next chapter is devoted to it.

Park land exists in every section of Philadelphia. Some sections of Fairmount Park, however, stand on their own as significant, large green chunks of Philadelphia. Some of the attractions have already been described above. And there's more.

PENNYPACK PARK spreads out over 1,300 acres in Northeast Philadelphia from Tacony State Road north to Pine Road, and on both sides of Pennypack Creek. Pennypack, named by the Lenape Indians, means "without much current."

The creek's banks are surrounded by unusual trees and wild flowers. It's a haven for small animals and birds. It's a place to rest from the tension of day-to-day activities. There are picnic areas, recreational facilities, bridle paths, walking trails, a 150-acre bird sanctuary and the Pennypack Environmental Center*.

FRANKLIN D. ROOSEVELT PARK is 365 acres in South Philadelphia across from the sports complex at Pattison Avenue, from Broad to 24th Streets.

It's the site of the American-Swedish Historical Museum*, Bellaire Manor* and numerous recreation facilities. You can swim or play golf, bocce and tennis. Or you can participate in track and field events. You can also attend the cultural events which are scheduled during the summer.

COBBS CREEK PARK is the biggest green portion of West Philadelphia. It is almost 800 acres with a 150-acre creek flowing across the city limits into Delaware County. Pennsylvania's first grist mill was built along this creek in 1643.

Aside from its densely wooded areas, Cobbs Creek Park is well equipped with recreational facilities for all kinds of ball sports, summer camping, golf, ice skating, horseback riding and supervised playgrounds.

FRANKLIN, LOGAN, RITTENHOUSE and **WASHINGTON**, the four green squares of center city Philadelphia, are ideal play and picnic areas. They all have drinking fountains and seating areas. They're perfect settings for shows, having your picture taken, exhibits and special events that are scheduled throughout the year. All four of the squares were named in 1981 to the National Register of Historic Places*. Each of the squares has its own history and character.

Franklin Square* (Northeast) greets the visitor approaching Philadelphia from the Benjamin Franklin Bridge. Its early history includes service as a colonial burial ground, ammunition storage base during the Revolution and later as a cattle marketplace.

Today Franklin Square houses a permanent 14-foot high memorial to Philadelphia police and firefighters who lost their lives in service.

Logan Square* (Northwest) sits midway on the Benjamin Franklin Parkway surrounded by grand cultural, municipal, religious and hotel dwellings. When the Parkway was built in the 1920s, Logan Square became a circle to ease the traffic flow, but we still call it a "square." You'll notice the resemblance to the Champs Elysees and the Place de la Concorde. Philadelphia's versions were designed by a Frenchman, Jacques Greber.

Logan Square is distinguished by its Swann Fountain, designed by sculptor Alexander Stirling Calder to depict Philadelphia's three major waterways, and magnificently restored and turned on again in 1990. This is a perfect setting for picnics or splashing after a visit to the Parkway attractions.

Directly across from Logan Circle, and facing the Cathedral Basilica of SS. Peter and Paul*, is **Sister Cities Plaza**. Flags and concrete markers signify Philadelphia's Sister City relationships with Florence, Italy, and Tel Aviv, Israel. Philadelphia is also the Sister City of Tianjin, China; Inchon, South Korea; and Douala, Cameroon.

On the Cathedral's south side, between Race Street and the Benjamin Franklin Parkway, is another grassy plot called Torun Triangle. It commemorates Philadelphia's Sister City relationship with Torun, Poland, which was the birthplace of astronomer Nicolaus Copernicus. A sundial monument to Copernicus is on the Triangle.

Rittenhouse Square* (Southwest) is surrounded by fashionable brownstone houses, highrise apartment buildings, hotels and shops. It's the stage for an annual clothesline art exhibition and a flower show.

Washington Square* (Southeast) in the 18th century was known as Potter's Field, the first public burial ground for the poor. Hundreds of Continental soldiers and British prisoners of the Revolutionary War were also buried here.

Today Washington Square is distinguished as the site of the Tomb of the Unknown Soldier of the American Revolution. An eternal flame burns at the memorial, watched over by a statue of George Washington.

PENN TREATY PARK, East Columbia Avenue and Beach Street, is where William Penn is believed to have signed his treaty with the Indians beneath a great elm tree. An oasis of some six green acres, the park is in the shadow of I-95, on the banks of the Delaware River at the 1300 block north on Delaware Avenue. An obelisk marks the site of the old elm tree that blew down in 1810. A statue commemorates William Penn. And the entire scene is immortalized in Benjamin West's famous painting of "Penn's Treaty with the Indians" that you can see at The Pennsylvania Academy of the Fine Arts*.

AWBURY ARBORETUM is a 55-acre park in Germantown. But it's not a part of Fairmount Park. The arboretum's rolling lawns and beautiful vistas filled with trees, plants, shrubs and wildlife are always a nice oasis to enjoy nature. An observatory enables you to watch birds during their spring and fall migrations. Nature programs are available in the summer and environmental education programs are scheduled the rest of the year. Awbury's entrance is at Chew Avenue and High Street. Call 849-5561 for additional information.

By now you get the idea: Philadelphia is a city of parks. They're all over. Enjoy them.

SCHUYLKILL CENTER FOR ENVIRONMENTAL EDUCATION

8480 Hagy's Mill Road (Upper Roxborough)—19128
482-7300

Hours: Monday to Saturday, 8:30 to 5; Sunday, 1 to 5. Closed holidays, and Sundays in August.

Tours: Scheduled in advance for groups of 20 or more and led by a staff of teacher-naturalists. Cassette players are available for visitors going on their own along 2 of the trails. Reservations are necessary for groups. An outstanding study program is available for all grade levels which is coordinated with follow-up materials. Call for a schedule, and call to arrange a classroom theme.

Cost: Adults, $5; children under 12, $3. Special rates for school groups; ask when making reservations. Individual and family memberships enable unlimited free visits, special programs, gift shop discounts, newsletters, library borrowing and guest privileges.

Lunch: No food is sold, but picnicking is allowed for members only in specified areas.

SEPTA: It's a long walk from the bus 61 stop at Ridge and Port Royal Avenues. There's plenty of free parking.

Other: There's a shop selling natural history items, and it's a good idea to bring your camera and binoculars.

E & D: Widener Trail is paved perfectly smooth, making it accessible for anyone in a wheelchair or requiring a level path. It also has special high curbs to guide the blind. Complete wheelchair access in the Discovery Museum.

This magnificent sanctuary of near 500 acres is made up of woodlands, fields, thickets, ponds and six miles of trails. You'll see birds, wild animals, plants and trees in a natural setting—untouched by the city.

The hands-on nature, natural history and ecology exhibits in the Discovery Museum correspond to what you'll see on your own, if you go in a study group, or if you go on a self-guided tour with your family or friends.

Special walk and talk nature programs are presented on Saturdays and Sundays. They're usually at 2 P.M., but it's wise to check in advance and then plan your visit with this in mind.

Adult and children's workshops are offered each spring and fall on appropriate subjects like weather and nature photography. They're usually one day or one weekend. Call for specifics.

If you're an educator in the Philadelphia area, Schuylkill Center's Teaching Resource Center provides help and loans materials for developing your own teaching program. Some 400 volumes are available to choose from. Ten times as many volumes are in the Center's library. Read about it in Chapter 11.

TINICUM NATIONAL ENVIRONMENTAL CENTER
86th Street and Lindbergh Boulevard—19153
365–3118

Hours: Main entrance is open daily, 8 A.M. till sunset. Visitor Center: daily, 8:30 to 4.

Tours: Guided nature walks are weekend mornings at 9. Call ahead for the topic. Groups can schedule at other times by calling at least 2 weeks ahead. Children should be accompanied by adults. Go on your own with a copy of the self-guided nature walk "Boardwalk Loop" that covers 2/3 of a mile in 45 minutes.

Cost: Free.

Lunch: There are benches around, but no food is sold and no cookouts are allowed.

SEPTA: Buses U and 37 go to 84th and Lindbergh. When driving, call for directions before heading out to Tinicum.

Other: Wear comfortable shoes, and bring binoculars if you can.

E & D: About 2 miles of dike roads are well-graveled. Pick up a pass at the Visitor Center that allows a car to be driven along the roads from 8 to 4.

Tinicum is a 1,200-acre preserve situated along Darby Creek. It's just a few miles from City Hall and a stone's throw from the Philadelphia International Airport. Forget about concrete sidewalks and skyscrapers and jet airplanes for a few moments, because Tinicum shows you what Philadelphia was like before man's arrival. It's the largest remaining freshwater tidal marsh in Pennsylvania.

The name Tinicum comes from the Indian word meaning "islands of the marsh." It refers to the time when marshes extended to the islands in the Delaware River.

Tinicum is a native habitat for marsh plants and thousands of birds—especially water fowl. Depending upon the season, you might see ducks, geese, heron, egrets, gallinules, muskrats, weasels, rabbits, turtles and snakes.

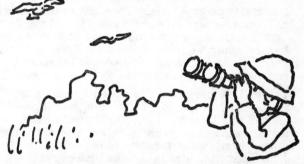

You can follow the lengthy nature trail on foot or by bike. You can launch a canoe, if you have one, into Darby Creek. And you can fish if you have a Pennsylvania Fishing License. (See Chapter 14.)

The best time for bird-watching is in the spring and fall when the birds are en route to or from the South. Call 567-BIRD for recent sightings. Since 1965, over 280 bird species have been sighted at Tinicum.

Nature charts and bird identification aids are available. There's an observation platform where your binoculars will come in handy, and there's a "photography blind" where up to 10 visitors can surreptitiously set up equipment or quietly view the flora and fauna.

Tinicum is administered by the U.S. Fish and Wildlife Service.

A note for Philadelphia and Delaware County educators: Ask about Tinicum's accredited 15-hour courses in environmental education.

161

WAGNER FREE INSTITUTE OF SCIENCE
17th Street and Montgomery Avenue—19121
763-6529

Hours: Tuesday to Friday, 9 to 4. Closed holidays. Allow 30 minutes. (Before going on a hot summer day, consider that there's no air-conditioning.)

Tours: Teachers of grades kindergarten to 7 can schedule in advance for a class lesson weekday mornings from September to June; 15 to 60 students. Otherwise reservations are not necessary.

Cost: Free.

SEPTA: Buses 2, 3.

Other: A series of evening lecture courses is offered to adults at Northeast Philadelphia and center city branches of the Free Library. Programs include ecology, geology, physical science, computers, diet and nutrition. Certificates are awarded upon completion. Call or write for a schedule.

E & D: No wheelchair access. There are 6 steps outside, exhibits are on 2nd floor and there is no elevator.

This will remind you of how museums used to be. It's one enormous exhibition hall, vintage 1865, neatly crammed with displays of over 21,000 specimens. In addition to the fabulous science collection, here's a museum of what Victorian era museums were like.

John McArthur, Jr. designed the Greek Revival-style building before he set his talents to City Hall (see Chapter 13). Everything inside remains in the original wood and glass display cases, and everything is labeled by hand. Virtually nothing on exhibit here has changed in more than a century.

The exhibits span the gamut of the animal kingdom from protozoa to man; from the tiniest bug to a dinosaur's hip. (Now, that's hip.) There are worms, insects, corals, fishes, birds, bones, minerals, crystals, mollusks, fossils, skulls, skeletons and you name it from every branch of natural science.

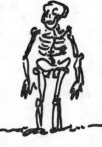

Wagner Free Institute's library is described later in Chapter 11.

WISTAR INSTITUTE MUSEUM
36th and Spruce Streets—19104
898-3708

Hours: Weekdays, 10 to 4. Closed holidays.
Tours: Groups of 12 or more should call for reservations a few days in advance. A 30-minute taped cassette tour can be requested on arrival. Children under 12 must be with an adult.
Cost: Free.
SEPTA: Bus 40; trolleys 11, 13, 34, 36.
E & D: There are 13 steps at the entrance on 36th Street. Arrangements can be made in advance to use a ground level entrance on Spruce Street.

This is another worthwhile museum for high school students who are interested in careers in medicine. It isn't a museum for the squeamish. There are exhibits on the human body, anatomy and biology. (The Wistar Institute is a world-renowned biomedical research facility.)

You'll see collections of skulls and skeletons. The first showcase explains the evolution of skulls from fish to man, a development that took 300 million years. Another exhibit shows the evolution of posture from a dog on all fours to a semi-erect monkey to man.

The museum's most historical displays are the "anatomical specimens of demonstration dissections" used by Doctors Casper Wistar and William Horner for studying and teaching in the 19th century. There's also a graphic explanation of the "Wistar strain" of rats.

Other exhibits and graphs compare the growth of boys and girls from birth to 20 years. Man's racial heredity and family-line inheritances are also charted. It shows why some of us are tall, why some of us are short, why some of us have brown, blonde or red hair.

ZOOLOGICAL GARDENS (Philadelphia Zoo)
34th Street and Girard Avenue—19104
(in Fairmount Park)
387-6400 (recording) or 243-1100

Hours: Weekdays, 9:30 to 5; weekends and holidays, 9:30 to 6. Closed Thanksgiving, December 24, Christmas, December 31, New Year's. Come for a whole day, any day, any weather!

Tours: Scheduled daily at 10 or 11 A.M., and additional times on weekends, for groups of 10 or more. Allow one hour. An adult must accompany each group of 10 children. To schedule a tour, call 243–1100 Ext. 317 at least 2 weeks in advance. Philadelphia Public School teachers can also call the Museum Education Department at the Board of Education, 299–7778, for special arrangements.

Cost: Adults, $5.75; senior citizens and children 2 to 11, $4.75; under 2, free. Groups of 15 or more: at entrance, $.50 less; prepaid 3 weeks ahead by mail or at least a day ahead at the zoo, adults, $4.50, senior citizens and children, $3.50. Admission to Treehouse is additional $1. All admission is free on Mondays (except holidays) December through February. Membership provides free admission, free parking, guest tickets, a magazine subscription, newsletter, shop discount, Members Day events and special events.

Lunch: There are picnic groves with tables, and many refreshment stands. The Impala Cafe seats nearly 200 indoors and outdoors by the impala fountain.

SEPTA: Bus 38; trolley 15. There's plenty of parking for $2.

Other: Strollers are for rent; film and souvenirs are sold. The ZooShop, near the 34th Street entrance, is a unique boutique for sophisticated animal-related items.

E & D: Wheelchairs are for rent. Everything at the zoo is accessible, including rest rooms. Printed descriptive material is available for the deaf; inquire at Education Department. Special tours are scheduled for groups of hearing impaired or physically disabled visitors. Van tours can be scheduled November to March for groups that arrive in their own vehicle. Call 243–1100 Ext. 224.

America's oldest zoo is a fun place to spend a day. Parents have been known to keep returning long after their children have grown.

The Philadelphia Zoo is an all-weather attraction with nine heated (and a few air-conditioned) buildings. The residents are particularly fond of winter visitors. In fact, they're known to make a bigger fuss when their audience is smaller!

The 42-acre zoo houses over 1,800 mammals, birds, reptiles and rare species from throughout the world. Every effort has been made to keep the animals in their natural settings.

The World of Primates puts visitors in the same natural one-acre landscape and jungle habitat as its permanent occupants—families of lemurs, gibbons, gorillas, monkeys and orangutans. A state-of-the-art Discovery House orientation center awaits you in the restored 1907 Kangaroo House.

Things really swing in the World of Primates—and in the Treehouse. But animals don't live in the Treehouse! It's the visitors who climb, crawl, crouch and swing to discover what it's like to see life as an animal. It's a wonderful rebirth for the 1874 Gothic-style Antelope House. Admission to the Treehouse is $1, and groups must make reservations in advance.

The five-acre African Plains exhibits let ostriches, cranes, geese, antelope, giraffes, zebras and their friends wander together as they would in the wilds of their homelands. The human eye will find it hard to detect that the massive rocks, caves and 40-foot baobab tree are synthetic.

Birds fly freely in the Birdhouse as they do in the tropics.

Bear Country always ranks among the zoo's most popular people lures. You'll be eye-to-eye with a polar bear if one should swim to you from their gigantic cliff-rimmed pool.

The Reptile House has an electronic rain forest thunder shower to make the snakes feel cozy. The rain storms are daily, on the hour, from 11 to 4 (and 5 in the summer). There's an exciting new fish exhibit here, too. Several aquariums have the varied species that are likely to be swimming in the nearby Schuylkill River.

Visit at meal time. Schedules are posted so you can watch when the lions and tigers, small cats, elephants, birds, penguins, reptiles and mammals are fed. But remember, please don't feed any of the animals yourself.

Look behind the glass walls of the zoo's nursery (near the apes' outdoor home) for babies receiving special care. Abandoned and rejected little animals in need of special care are hand-raised, weighed, doctored, fed baby food and treated as if they were human.

There's a zoo inside the zoo—a **CHILDREN'S ZOO***, where youngsters can get to know the little animals on a first-name basis. The animals can be touched, petted and fed. A zookeeper gives demonstrations every half-hour, from 11 to 4, from April through October. They might be sea lion performances, cow milking, sheep dog demonstrations or pony rides.

The **MONORAIL SAFARI*** is a 15-minute, mile-long aerial trip high above the tree tops. You'll hear descriptions about the buildings, the grounds and the animal collections. The monorail runs every day (weather permitting) from mid-March to November. The charge on weekdays is $3.50 for adults and $3 for children under 12. On weekends and holidays it's $.50 more. Groups of 15 or more pay $.50 less. Call 386–9098 or 243–1100 Ext. 297 for more information.

Chapter 8.
Fairmount Park.

Fairmount Park

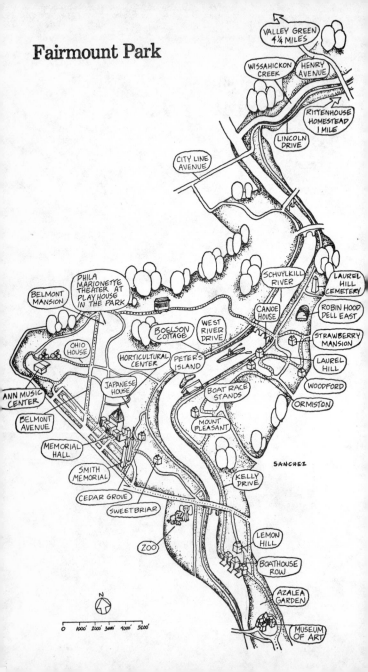

VALLEY GREEN 4¼ MILES

WISSAHICKON CREEK

HENRY AVENUE

RITTENHOUSE HOMESTEAD 1 MILE

LINCOLN DRIVE

CITY LINE AVENUE

SCHUYLKILL RIVER

LAUREL HILL CEMETERY

ROBIN HOOD DELL EAST

PHILA MARIONETTE THEATER AT PLAY HOUSE IN THE PARK

BELMONT MANSION

CANOE HOUSE

STRAWBERRY MANSION

BOELSON COTTAGE

WEST RIVER DRIVE

OHIO HOUSE

HORTICULTURAL CENTER

PETER'S ISLAND

LAUREL HILL

WOODFORD

ANN MUSIC CENTER

JAPANESE HOUSE

BOAT RACE STANDS

ORMISTON

BELMONT AVENUE

MEMORIAL HALL

MOUNT PLEASANT

SANCHEZ

SMITH MEMORIAL

KELLY DRIVE

CEDAR GROVE

SWEETBRIAR

ZOO

LEMON HILL

BOATHOUSE ROW

AZALEA GARDEN

N

0 1000' 2000' 3000' 4000' 5200'

MUSEUM OF ART

Fairmount Park is the largest and grandest landscaped park within a city anywhere in the world.

It owes its inspiration to William Penn.

Legend has it, that shortly after Penn arrived in Philadelphia, he went to the top of a hill overlooking the Schuylkill (a Dutch word meaning "hidden stream") to admire the view, and exclaimed, "What a beautiful faire mount this is." Penn's public relations consultant was with him at the time, and said, "Bill, that's a terrific name. We'll call this place Faire Mount. The people will love it." And thus it was known as Faire Mount on Thomas Holme's 1682 Plan for Philadelphia.

We already know that Penn envisioned a "greene countrie towne" with gardens, parks and open spaces.

But could Penn or his advisors possibly have imagined that by the 20th century Fairmount Park would grow to over 8,700 acres, with more than three million trees and stretching into every part of the city? Could Penn have envisioned that Fairmount Park would have 200 acres of waterways, with at least as many buildings? That it would be a "people's park," with 100 miles of nature trails, paved bikeways and bridle paths? And that it would be the site of hundreds of historic, cultural and recreational facilities?

The Fairmount area west of the city was a popular place for Philadelphia gentlemen to build their summer mansions. The first official City interest in the area happened in 1812 when the City of Philadelphia bought five acres near the hilly site where Penn had first surveyed the area. Construction began there immediately for what became the **FAIRMOUNT WATER WORKS** surrounded by landscaped gardens. This was the first steam-pumping station of its kind in America, and it provided Philadelphians with pure drinking water from the Schuylkill.

The pumping technique was gradually replaced by paddle wheels and water turbines, but the water works continued to function until 1911. The water itself was raised to an enormous reservoir on the "faire mount."

The original four water works buildings and pumping station still overlook the Schuylkill. They were designed by Frederick Graff in charming Greek Revival style, and were recently cited by the American Society of Civil Engineers as a national historic landmark in the development of American engineering.

From 1911 until 1962 the water works buildings housed

the Philadelphia Aquarium with its thousands of species of fish, reptiles and invertebrates. Today, the 19th century "faire mount" reservoir is the site of the Philadelphia Museum of Art*.

The water works buildings to the west of the Art Museum are undergoing major restoration, spearheaded by the Fairmount Park Commission, Philadelphia Water Department, the Junior League of Philadelphia and the Preservation Coalition of Greater Philadelphia.

Restoration began in the mid-1980s. The Watering Committee Building, once used by the Joint Committee on Supplying the City with Water, is completed and now a Visitors Center operated by the Philadelphia Ranger Corps. The Caretaker's House and the Old Mill House are also restored. Work is underway on the Engine House and should be finished by 1994 when a new interpretive museum will explain the original system and its effect on 19th century Philadelphia. Plans also call for an exciting new restaurant at the site overlooking the Schuylkill River.

Tours of the **Fairmount Water Works** are offered by the Philadelphia Ranger Corps and by the Philadelphia Water Department.

Members of the Philadelphia Rangers Corps conduct general tours of the old water works hourly on warm weather weekends starting at the **Water Works Visitors Center**. The Visitors Center is open weekends from 10 to 5 year-round, and daily from Memorial Day to Labor Day. An outstanding photographic exhibit and displays tell about the history and operation of the water works. A short slide show can be viewed at any time. A gift shop has books, educational games and appropriate novelty items. For information, call 581–5111 or 726–4377 (RANGERS).

Tours provided by the Water Department are more specialized and actually go underground into the construction site. (Dress accordingly.) The original Engine House pump has been entirely refurbished or replaced. A wet model shows how it worked at the turn of the century. To schedule this more technical tour, on a weekday from 10 to 4, call the Philadelphia Water Department at 592–6300.

(You'll read in Chapter 13 how you can tour Philadelphia's 20th century water treatment plants and pollution control facilities.)

The Fairmount Water Works can be reached by **SEPTA** bus 38 or the Ben FrankLine route 76 to the Philadelphia Museum of Art.

Be sure to take in the spectacular view of the Art Museum, Boat House Row outlined in lights, and the water works especially at night from across the river on the West River Drive or the Schuylkill Expressway.

The Schuylkill's scenic riversides lured early Philadelphians to build their country estates there. Several of these mansions survived the Revolution and others were built later.

By the mid-1850s civic and community leaders in Philadelphia were devoting a great deal of effort to acquiring those houses and park land to preserve it for the City. Their first purchase was Lemon Hill* in 1844, setting the course for Fairmount Park as we know it today.

More than 60 Fairmount Park buildings are historically certified and appear in the National Register of Historic Places. Several of the mansions stand majestically awaiting your visit.

Fairmount Park itself became a reality in 1855 when the Philadelphia City Council acted to make Lemon Hill part of a Fairmount Park for the use and enjoyment of the city's residents. The City formally received authority in 1867 from the General Assembly of Pennsylvania to buy more land for the park. Shortly thereafter a Fairmount Park Commission was established by the City to maintain and protect the park.

The park flourished and grew on both sides of the Schuylkill as more land was acquired by gift or purchase. From a five-acre tract in 1812, Fairmount Park has grown to more than 8,700 acres.

Sections of the park are scattered throughout the City, but the major tract of 4,000 acres stretches northwest along both sides of the Schuylkill from Penn's original "faire mount."

It was on 236 acres of this tract in West Philadelphia that the City hosted the huge international exposition to mark the country's Centennial* in 1876. Over 200 buildings went up on the fairgrounds. You can see a scale model exhibit in Memorial Hall*, the only major building that remains from the celebration. The Philadelphia Zoo* was also opened in time for the Centennial, and was the first zoo in America.

Peters Island, in the middle of the Schuylkill River, has been a wildlife preserve since 1969. Over a thousand geese, swans, ducks and red-crested poachers now make the island their home. The land is off limits to people, but the geese frequently swim across the river, and you can see them on the west bank near Montgomery Drive or on the east bank along Kelly Drive.

They say Fairmount Park's four-acre **Azalea Garden*** qualifies Philadelphia as the azalea capital of the world. Over 2,000 azalea bushes blossom each spring into summer along Kelly Drive behind the Art Museum. A full palette of pale to brilliant colors are found not only in azaleas, but also rhododendrons, hydrangeas, magnolias, red-berried hollies and franklinia orange blossoms, to name a few.

A short distance further along Kelly Drive, and just beyond the boat houses, look for the **Ellen Phillips Samuel Memorial Sculpture Garden*** and the **Glendinning Rock Garden**.

More than 200 statues are scattered throughout the park. If you have a group that's touring Philadelphia by bus, the Philadelphia Museum of Art will schedule a trained guide to escort you on a 90-minute **Sculpture Tour of Fairmount Park**. Arrangements must be made at least a month in advance by calling 787–5449. You'll pick up your guide at the Art Museum and then return her there after the tour.

More rustic sections of Fairmount Park are found along the **Wissahickon** and **Pennypack Creeks**. Wild flowers, trees and small animals are plentiful in these areas.

"Wissahickon" is the Indian word for "catfish creek." The creek stretches six-and-a-half miles from the Schuylkill to beyond the City's northwest boundary, and it's completely off limits to automobiles.

The **Valley Green** section of Fairmount Park is along the upper Wissahickon Creek. This is near the area that was settled by Francis Daniel Pastorius* and the German settlers. Valley Green is a miniature version of Colorado, with massive trees, rocky cliffs, boulders and steep paths.

Forbidden Drive is a popular five-and-a-half mile stretch along the Wissahickon. It has been designated by the U.S. Department of the Interior as a National Recreation Trail. It's great for hiking and horseback riding. There are marked paths for bikers, horsemen, joggers and nature walkers.

There's also a **Parcourse Fitness Circuit** along Forbidden Drive for people wanting to test their physical stamina and agility. It has 18 exercise stations along one-and-a-half miles. Another Parcourse is along the West River Drive near Montgomery Avenue. A half-mile exercise course is in Tacony Creek Park near Adams Avenue and Crescentville Road in the Far Northeast.

The Valley Green Inn is a quaint historic restaurant that has been open since 1850 (see Chapter 18). It sits beside the flowing creek that was once used by mills to make cornmeal, linseed oil, flour and paper. (William Rittenhouse's paper mill was the first of its kind in America, and its site is part of The RittenhouseTown* that has been restored nearby along the Wissahickon.)

Valley Green can be reached by winding dirt roads and bridle paths or by car. It's a pleasant gathering point to relax, hike, meditate and feed the ducks. You can fish for trout in the springtime, skate on the creek in winter and enjoy a pleasant meal in the old Valley Green Inn.

A rustic covered bridge spans the Wissahickon at Thomas Mill Road, north of Valley Green. The bridge is 97 feet long and 14 feet wide. It's the only covered bridge within a large American city. Bring your camera!

Did I make the point that Fairmount Park is brimming with history, art and horticulture? If I didn't, where have I gone wrong?

You can play baseball, football, cricket, tennis or golf. You can swim, hike, bike ride, ice skate, toboggan, go boating, attend concerts, watch shows and even go to a summer camp in Fairmount Park. You can dine at Valley Green Inn. All of these activities are described later in this book.

Other Fairmount Park attractions you should know about are the American-Swedish Historical Museum, Andorra Natural Area, John Bartram's House and Garden, Boat House Row, Bellaire, Chamounix, the Japanese Exhibition House, Mann Music Center, Pennypack Environmental Center, the police stables, Robin Hood Dell East, Ryerss Museum and Library and, of course, the spectacular Philadelphia Zoo. They're explained in other chapters; check the Index.

Remember: An **asterisk** (*) indicates that the same place or event appears elsewhere in the book with more details. Look in the Index for additional pages.

A new addition to Fairmount Park, already mentioned above, is the **PHILADELPHIA RANGER CORPS**. They're an elite group of recent Philadelphia high school graduates, now studying parks and recreation at Temple University (or graduates, and now career rangers), and dedicated to maintaining and promulgating Fairmount Park as the great resource it is.

You already know these handsomely uniformed and informed young men and women serve as guides at the Fairmount Water Works. They're also at Loudoun and Ryerrs Mansion (described in other chapters) and at Memorial Hall (described below). They lead warm-weather walking tours scheduled for the public, "Center City Connection," along the Benjamin Franklin Parkway, "Tales and Trails of the Wissahickon" along the Wissahickon Creek near Valley Green, and "Wetlands to Playlands" in Franklin D. Roosevelt Park*. You might spot them anywhere in the Fairmount Park system anxious to make your visit more educational and interesting.

Or, any Philadelphia group of no more than 40, preschoolers to adults, can plan an hour-long environmental education program, "Field, Forest and Stream," at a Fairmount Park locale. Bicycle tours of the Wissahickon or Pennypack sections of Fairmount Park can also be arranged for groups. And, for **E & D**, special tours are designed for the visually or hearing impaired or otherwise physically challenged small groups. If you still can't get to Fairmount Park for a tour with the Rangers, they'll try to accommodate and bring a program to you. See Chapter 13 on "Tours to Go."

All arrangements for specially planned tours must be made at least a month in advance with the Philadelphia Rangers Corps' Scheduling Officer.

For information about all of these and other free tours provided by the Philadelphia Ranger Corps, call 581–5111 or 726–4377 (RANGERS).

MEMORIAL HALL

N. Concourse Drive, near 42nd Street and
Parkside Avenue (West Fairmount Park)—19131
581–5111 or RANGERS

Hours: By reservation only to see Centennial exhibit,
daily, 9 to 4.
Tours: Call 2 weeks ahead to schedule group visit. Regularly scheduled tours during summer; call for times.
Cost: Free.
SEPTA: Buses 38, 40.
E & D: There are several steps at the entrance, or there
is a ramped entrance on the north side. The Centennial
exhibit is in the basement.

Memorial Hall was built in 1875 to serve as an international art gallery and to remain as a tribute to the
nation's 100th birthday celebration. President Ulysses S.
Grant officially opened the Centennial in its 150-foot high
"Great Hall" on May 10, 1876. It's the only major building that remains from the Centennial. You can hold your own celebration in Memorial
Hall's "Great Hall."
It's available to rent
for private
parties.

Memorial Hall has been designated a National Historic
Landmark. Its interior has been restored, and its Victorian ornamentation is carefully preserved. Today it houses
the Fairmount Park Commission's administrative offices,
police headquarters and recreation facilities. The Commission's office also serves as a **Fairmount Park Information Center**. You can stop by (enter at the building's
west side) for information and brochures on cultural
events and activities in Fairmount Park. And you can call
685–0000.

Memorial Hall's basement has an amazing exhibit. It's
an enormous 20- by 40-foot scale model of the Centennial
fairgrounds that shows all 249 buildings, roads and landscaping of the 1876 celebration site. On tour with a
Philadelphia Park Ranger, you'll see and hear a sound-and-light narrative about the events of the first world's
fair ever held in America.

A short walk down the road from Memorial Hall, at Lansdowne Drive, is the twin-towered **SMITH CIVIL WAR MEMORIAL ARCH**. It was built in 1896 with statuary honoring heroes of the Civil War.

Sit at one end of the curved stone bench and have a friend go 50 feet away to the bench's other end. Now whisper a message into the corner of the bench and your friend will hear you. That's why it's called the "whispering benches." How does it work? I would tell you, but I'm sworn to secrecy.

OHIO HOUSE is also nearby at Belmont Avenue and States Drive. The Ohio State Exhibition Building of the Centennial is the only other building, besides Memorial Hall, that still remains from the 1876 exposition. (The Philadelphia Ranger Corps is headquartered here.)

Ohio House was restored in the mid-1970s. The architectural style is Victorian Gothic. It's constructed with stones from dozens of Ohio quarries, each of which is engraved with the quarry's name.

BELMONT MANSION is among Fairmount Park's oldest surviving mansions. The earliest section of the now-Georgian style residence was a stone cottage dating to sometime in the early 1700s. Originally, a 400 acre site was granted by William Penn in 1684 to John Boelson and John Skutten. It passed through several owners till 1742 when Philadelphia lawyer William Peters became owner. His son, Richard, was born at Belmont in 1744 and resided there till his death in 1828. It was during this period that Belmont grew from a rustic cottage to the stately mansion you see today.

Two wings were added making Belmont a three-story residence worthy of entertaining the government, academic and religious leaders with whom both generations of Peters were associated. Richard Peters was also a lawyer, served several high government positions and for his last 37 years was a Judge for the U.S. Court for the district of Pennsylvania.

The entire Belmont estate was purchased by the City and incorporated into West Fairmount Park in 1867.

After years of use as a museum, various restaurants and abandonment, Belmont Mansion reopened to the public in 1986 under auspices of the American Women's Heritage Society. Their aim is to preserve and maintain it as a cultural, educational and social resource with special emphasis on women's contributions to these areas.

A tour of the house includes several formal entertaining rooms on the first floor including a tiny "sherbet room" where women would adjourn after dinner while men had their cigars. Elaborate plaster moldings and carved wood ornamentation have been preserved throughout.

Upstairs are several bedrooms, a charming little old-fashioned "kitchen" complete with a collection of antique utensils and pottery, and a gallery used for occasional exhibits highlighting local artists. A permanent collection of charcoal portraits by Samuel R. Byrd hangs, honoring prominent black women in Philadelphia history.

Belmont Mansion is open Tuesday to Friday, 10 to 5, and weekends by appointment. Call 878–8844. Groups of up to 40 are requested to call in advance to schedule a 45-minute tour. The suggested donation is adults, $3; children, $1. Group rates are set when scheduling tour.

Philadelphia's skyline about five miles away is a favorite picture-taking opportunity from Belmont Plateau. Don't miss the view. . .or rather, bring a camera, you can't miss the view!

BOELSON COTTAGE, built by a Dutchman sometime between 1678 and 1684, may be the oldest surviving house in Pennsylvania. It overlooks Peters Island and the Schuylkill from its perch along West River Drive just west of Montgomery Drive. What a lovely locale for its pioneer occupants! And what a charming headquarters for the Friends of Philadelphia Parks who completed its restoration in 1989 and share the little house with the Philadelphia Ranger Corps.

Built of field stone more than 300 years ago, Boelson Cottage blends Dutch and Swedish colonial architectural elements including a four-sided gambrel roof and some very small windows. The garden and pathways have been recreated to resemble what they might have been in the 17th century.

Call the Friends of Philadelphia Parks at 879–8159 for visitor information.

FAIRMOUNT PARK HOUSES
787–5449

The original estates of several prominent 18th century Philadelphians were completely restored in the mid-1970s and are beautifully furnished with authentic antiques. These seven are among the more than 20 historic homes that remain in Fairmount Park.

Each house reflects the personality and interests of its former owner. They range from simple brick row house style to elaborate mansions. All were summer homes for country living away from the hot city, and they take you back to a time when Philadelphia was the second largest city in the British Empire. Can you imagine that?

Hours: Wednesday to Sunday, 10 to 5.
Tours: There are 3 ways to visit the houses:
  1. You can visit individually with private transportation and a good map of Fairmount Park.
  2. You can arrange in advance to take a private tour (from one to 350 people) on the date of your choice with trained guides from the Art Museum. You'll visit one to seven houses taking up to a full day. Charges vary with the size and the type of group. Call for details. You provide the transportation.
  3. You can take a trolley-bus* tour with an Art Museum guide any Tuesday to Sunday at 1 P.M. They depart from the Art Museum, visit three of the houses, and cost $9.
Cost: To visit houses individually: adults, $1.50; children under 12, $1.
Lunch: Bring a picnic lunch and choose a nice quiet spot.
E & D: There are steps leading to most of the houses and a considerable number of stairs within all of them. The first floor of Cedar Grove and Strawberry Mansion are accessible.

CEDAR GROVE (787–5449), a Quaker farmhouse, was moved to West Fairmount Park in 1927 from its original 1748 construction site in Frankford.

You can see five generations of furnishings from an early Quaker family. William and Mary, Queen Anne, Chippendale, Hepplewhite and Sheraton styles are well represented.

There's an 18th century herb garden, and there are

rumors of a lady ghost living on the second floor. You can tell me if it's true.

LAUREL HILL (235-1776 or 627-1770), named for the clusters of laurel bushes on its surrounding East Fairmount Park hillside, has an original Georgian style center section dating back to 1760. An 1800 addition in the Federal style has an unusual octagonal room.

The mansion is often called Randolph after the family that occupied it from 1828 to 1869. Dr. Philip Syng Physick gave it to his daughter Sally when she married Dr. Jacob Randolph.

LEMON HILL (232-4337) was built in 1800 by Henry Pratt, who bought the 350-acre farm estate of Robert Morris. Pratt replaced Morris' 1770 farmhouse, "The Hills," with Lemon Hill as you see it today overlooking the Schuylkill. Pratt renamed his new home for the lemon trees that flourished in his gardens.

Lemon Hill has three floors, each with an oval salon. This architectural design exists in only three other buildings in the East; a clubhouse in Boston, the Thomas Jefferson Rotunda at the University of Virginia and the White House in Washington. (You're now one of the few people who know this.) Lemon Hill's furnishings are magnificent examples of the Federal style.

MOUNT PLEASANT (787-5449) was built by John MacPherson, a wealthy Scottish sea captain, in 1761. It's an important example of elegant, symmetrical Georgian architecture that was more common to buildings in Virginia than Pennsylvania. The front door and the back door are identical, so don't be confused.

The furnishings include the finest examples of Chippendale, along with antique pewter, china and porcelain.

An educational "touch-it" exhibit for children demonstrates colonial skills such as soap-making and weaving flax into fabric. You'll get a good idea of how 18th century life centered around the hearth.

Benedict Arnold purchased the house as a wedding present for his bride, Peggy Shippen, in 1779. But the following year, the Arnolds suddenly decided to take up residence in England.

STRAWBERRY MANSION (228–8364), the largest mansion in Fairmount Park, has a mixture of late 18th and 19th century furnishings that reflect its various owners' tastes. You'll see Federal, Regency and Empire styles.

Antique toys fill the attic. The Empire parlor has a fine collection of Tucker porcelain, the first true porcelain made in America. An elegant music room brings to mind beautiful colonial receptions.

SWEETBRIAR (222–1333) looks exactly as it did when it was built in 1797. This was one of the first riverside houses designed to be lived in all year.

Sweetbriar and its decor reflect the fine taste of the original owner, Samuel Breck, who came to Philadelphia from Boston after the Revolution to escape heavy taxes.

This is a classic example of Federal style architecture. Don't miss the floor-to-ceiling windows in the two gracious parlors overlooking the Schuylkill River. They'll give you an idea of the kind of windows Presidents look out of from the Oval Office.

WOODFORD (229–6115) was built as a one-story country residence in 1734 by Judge William Coleman, a patriot and friend of Benjamin Franklin.

The beautiful second floor Palladian windows were added two decades later by the new owners, a Loyalist family who frequently entertained the Tories here.

Again, there are outstanding examples of colonial furnishings. There's also an enormous Pennsylvania Dutch kitchen and delightful children's toys and games.

ORMISTON (763–2222) on Reservoir Drive in East Fairmount Park is undergoing restoration and maintenance thanks to the Royal Heritage Society of Delaware Valley, a non-profit organization founded in 1982 to preserve British heritage and memorabilia in Pennsylvania.

The Georgian-style brick house was built between Mount Pleasant and Laurel Hill in 1798 by Edward Burd, a lawyer who married the daughter of Chief Justice Edward Shippen. Burd named his country estate "after the name of his Grandfather's Seat near Edinburgh." Burd died in 1833, but the house was occupied by his family till 1869.

The furnishings are sparse in this spacious three-story mansion, but an exhibit each summer focuses on some aspect of Philadelphia's ties with England. The basement bake oven and open fireplace still work, and Ormiston is a popular site for private teas and receptions.

Ormiston is open June through August, Wednesday to Sunday, from 10 to 4. Admission is free. You can visit on your own or be an invited guest if you're lucky and have a friend who rents it for a private party. It's also open for the Park House Christmas Tours (see Chapter 19).

HORTICULTURAL CENTER
North Horticultural Drive, east of Belmont Avenue
(West Fairmount Park)
879–4062

Hours: Daily, 9 to 3. Closed holidays. Allow at least one
    hour to see the Center and the arboretum.
Tours: You're on your own.
Cost: $1 donation is requested.
E & D: Complete wheelchair access. Use any of the level
    entrances into the greenhouses.

Fairmount Park's Horticultural Center is on the grounds of the Centennial's Horticulture Hall, which stood until 1955. It's the showcase of a 22-acre arboretum that includes the Japanese Exhibition House* and magnificent Asian and North American trees that were planted during the Centennial in 1876.

If you love plants and flowers, you'll love the greenhouses here. Thousands of annuals and perennials are continually sprouting, waiting for transplanting to city parks, parkways, offices and museums.

One of the greenhouses is used for exhibition. Permanent planting beds and seasonal floral displays surround a lovely indoor fountain with sculpted cherubs dating back to 1876.

If you're looking for someplace to put your green thumb to good use, ask about volunteer programs at the Horticultural Center.

LAUREL HILL CEMETERY
3822 Ridge Avenue—19123
228–8200

Hours: Weekdays, 8:30 to 4:30; Saturday, 9 to 1. Cemetery office is open Monday, Wednesday and Friday mornings when you can purchase for $5 a self-guided tour book of Laurel Hill.

Tours: Stop by on your own during the day (park on Ridge Avenue) or join a tour sponsored occasionally by The Friends of Laurel Hill or as part of Fairmount Park happenings. 60- to 90-minute tours for up to 50 adults can be scheduled at least 3 weeks in advance by calling The Friends of Laurel Hill: 228–8817.

Cost: $5 per person (and minimum $50) for Friends guided tours.

Other: Be sure to wear flat, comfortable shoes.

Laurel Hill Cemetery adjoins East Fairmount Park and overlooks the Schuylkill River from above Kelly Drive. It spans 95 acres on both sides of Nicetown Lane. It was planned in 1835 by John Notman, making it the first architect-designed cemetery in America.

The park and garden landscaping were integral to the design. At least one specimen of every rare tree that could grow in the local climate was included. Many of them still remain.

Laurel Hill is noted for its magnificent mausoleums, monuments and sculpture. Works by Joseph A. Bailly, Alexander Milne Calder, Alexander Stirling Calder, John Notman, William Strickland and Thomas U. Walter, representing several architectural styles, are throughout the grounds.

Many prominent Philadelphians, including signers of the Declaration, authors, artists and merchants, are and continue to be buried here.

Guided tours can be scheduled with the Friends to focus on the architectural, literary or military aspects of Laurel Hill. The cemetery is listed in the National Register of Historic Places.

RITTENHOUSETOWN and the
RITTENHOUSE HOMESTEAD
207 Lincoln Drive—19144
(just south of Wissahickon Avenue)
843–0943

Hours: For house only: April through October: Saturday, 11 to 4. Other times by appointment.
Tours: A guide is available to answer questions and provide historic background. Groups are requested to call at least a week ahead.
Cost: Adults, $2; children under 12, $1.
Lunch: Picnic and play areas are directly across the road.

RittenhouseTown is a quaint part of historic Germantown nestled along the Wissahickon Creek, just a short distance from other historic homes along Germantown Avenue (see Chapter 3). This was the site of America's first paper mill, built in 1690.

William Rittenhouse, the first Mennonite minister in America, built his home here in 1707. Nicholas, the Minister's son, enlarged the house in 1713. Then, in 1732, it was the birthplace of David Rittenhouse.

David Rittenhouse grew up to be a patriot of the Revolution as well as a noted scientist and astronomer. Rittenhouse Square* and the Rittenhouse Observatory* were named for him.

A visit to RittenhouseTown and the house itself (the Homestead) offers a glimpse into the lifestyle of our colonial ancestors and the Mennonite life. View the downstairs of the little stone house with its period furnishings.

A smaller outbuilding is said to have the largest hearth in Pennsylvania.

It's fitting that the site of America's first paper mill is where you can see hand papermaking done before your eyes. Demonstrations are available for groups of up to 50 from late April to mid-September. Summer Papermaking Workshops are also available at all levels and in various aspects of the craft. For information about these unique opportunities, call the Friends of RittenhouseTown, 441-8789.

Chapter 9.
The Visual Arts.

If it's culture you want, you've come to the right city. Philadelphia's museums, galleries, film centers, dance troupes, theater companies, orchestras and musical groups have international reputations. So if you think the next two chapters on "The Visual Arts" and "The Performing Arts" are really big, it's only because Philadelphia has really big things to offer in the arts.

Additional programs for children are described later in Chapter 15.

This chapter deals with things you'll look at which, for the most part, are permanently in place. They include art, films, and sculpture that you'll come across as you wander around Philadelphia.

Art Museums and Galleries.
A Few Art Classes to Join.

ARTHUR ROSS GALLERY
University of Pennsylvania
220 South 34th Street—19104
898–4401

Hours: Tuesday to Friday, 10 to 5; weekends, 12 to 5. Closed Thanksgiving, Christmas, New Year's.
Tours: You're on your own. Groups of up to 25 can call a few weeks ahead to the gallery coordinator and arrange a tour.
Cost: Free.
SEPTA: Buses 21, 30, 42.
E & D: To avoid 10 steps at main entrance, call ahead to 898–4401 or 898–1479 and arrange to enter at ground level on building's south side and take elevator to gallery level.

It's worth a trip to the Penn campus just to see the magnificently restored 19th-century Furness Building that houses this gallery. In a former time (as recently as my days at Penn in the 1960s) the building housed the University's library. The gallery housed the Trustees' Board Room. This grand Victorian structure became a National Historic Landmark in 1985.

Over 4,000 works of art have been acquired by the University in its 250-year history. Four or five shows a year are drawn from Penn's eclectic collection, the Univer-

sity Museum's collections and major public and private
collections.

You could see anything from ancient arts to contemporary treasures. Call ahead if you'd like a preview. And
while you're on campus, take time to go to 36th and Sansom Streets to see the exciting Institute of Contemporary
Art* in its new home.

BARNES FOUNDATION
300 N. Latches Lane
Merion, PA 19066
667-0290

Hours: Friday and Saturday, 9:30 to 4:30; Sunday, 1 to
  4:30. Closed July, August and holidays.
Tours: You're on your own. Groups of 10 or more must
  have reservations. Call 664-1316 or write as far in advance as possible. Children under 12 not admitted.
  Young people 12 to 15 must be with an adult.
Cost: $1.
SEPTA: Bus 44 to Latches Lane and Old Lancaster Road
  and then a short walk. Barnes is 4 blocks west of City
  Line Avenue. Call for recorded driving directions.
Other: No cameras are allowed. You'll be asked to check
  your loose belongings. No spiked high-heel shoes permitted.
E & D: The first floor is wheelchair accessible if you can
  negotiate the 3 low steps at the entrance. There is no
  elevator to the 2nd floor.

In 1961 a court ruling forced the Barnes Foundation to
open to the public. Dr. Albert C. Barnes, an eccentric mil-
lionaire, died in 1951. But his temperament and influence
still prevail at his mansion gallery. His will prohibits the
reproduction or loan of any of the collection. And in accordance with Barnes' will, in 1988, the trustees of Lincoln University took control of the fabulous collection.

There are hundreds of paintings and sculptures in 23
rooms on two floors. Any one of these rooms would put an
art gallery on the map. Each room conveys the spirit of
France in the 1920s and 1930s because Parisian artists
were among Barnes' favorites.

You'll be startled by the enormity of the collection.
There are 180 Renoirs, 60 Matisses, 59 Cezannes, 19
Picassos and a good representation of works by van Gogh,

Seurat, Soutine, Modigliani, Rousseau, El Greco, Titian and Tintoretto. Matisse, himself, came to the mansion in 1932 to hang his 42- by 11-foot mural, "The Dancers."

One room is shared with the works of Horace Pippin, the one-armed black primitive artist from West Chester, PA, and William Glackens, Dr. Barnes' high school classmate. Elsewhere in the mansion is Pennsylvania Dutch bric-a-brac, Mayan Indian ornaments, pewter pieces and 16th century Chinese art.

Don't miss this opportunity to see one of the finest art collections in the world.

CAMPBELL MUSEUM
Campbell Place
Camden, New Jersey 08103
609–342-6440

Hours: Weekdays, 9 to 4:30. Closed some holidays. Allow one hour.

Tours: Gallery talks are scheduled for groups of up to 50. A 20-minute film, "Artistry in Tureens," can be included with your visit if requested in advance. Children must be supervised. All groups of 10 to 50 must call a few weeks ahead to schedule visit, a gallery talk or film. Light refreshments are served.

Cost: Free.

SEPTA: The museum is about one mile from the Camden City Hall stop of the PATCO High Speed Line which connects with many SEPTA bus and rail routes in Philadelphia. It is a 2-minute drive from the Ben Franklin Bridge and just off the Admiral Wilson Boulevard. It's a good idea to have directions before starting out.

E & D: The museum is all on one level, but there are several steps at the entrance.

"Soup's on!"

The Campbell Soup Company has a rare collection of 300 unusual tureens, bowls and ladles. When you come here, you'll get an idea of the many ways soup has been served over the past 2,500 years.

Anyone interested in food, the history of food service and the decorative arts will be fascinated by the assortment of porcelain, earthenware, gold, silver and pewter tureens. They're as innocent as a pair of porcelain rabbits, as opulent as a 100-pound ornamental bronze piece, as traditional as a lettuce topped with a playful toad and as bizarre as a life-size boar's head of 18th century porcelain.

The proof is all here that throughout the centuries the soup tureen has dominated the table as the biggest and most decorative service piece.

CITY OF PHILADELPHIA ART PROGRAMS
685–0152 (685–9740 in July and August)

No art-oriented youngster or adult should miss out on art lessons in Philadelphia. If you can't attend a class that's offered by a museum or art school, there are the Department of Recreation art classes.

A variety of arts and crafts programs are offered at recreation centers throughout the city. You can study painting, crafts, drawing, enameling or dabbling.

An annual Spring Arts Show presents the best of the year's creations by participants of all ages in programs representing everything from handicrafts to fine arts. Stop by the mall level of the Gallery at Market East, 9th and Market Streets, in late April or May to see some of the terrific work being done at city recreation centers.

Each summer the city sponsors an Arts Camp in Fairmount Park. Four two-week sessions are offered for boys and girls from the ages of nine to 17. A small fee covers costs for materials, lunch, field trips and bus transportation to and from camp. If you attend the city's Arts Camp, you'll get professional instruction in drawing, painting, graphics and sculpting. And, to stimulate your creativity, you'll visit area museums and exhibitions. The season ends with a show and celebration of the Summer Arts Camp that features the works of campers who attended any one of the encampments.

For additional information, call the Department of Recreation's Cultural and Special Events Section.

THE CLAY STUDIO
2nd Street Art Building
139 North 2nd Street—19106
925-3453

Hours: Gallery is open Tuesday to Friday, 12 to 6; weekends, 12 to 5. Closed Sundays in July and August.

Tours: Visit the gallery on your own. Tours of the studio and artists' floor can be scheduled during gallery hours or other times by appointment. Call at least 2 weeks ahead for groups of 7 to 20, 4th grade and above. Allow at least 30 minutes.

Cost: Free.

SEPTA: Bus 5, Ben FrankLine route 76 or any Market Street route.

E & D: Call ahead to use level entrance to gallery. A freight elevator enables access to studios and workshops.

Here's where you'll learn first-hand about the art of ceramics.

On the fourth floor, 12 competitively chosen resident artists work with clay in their own spaces. They use the various kilns in the studio, and also teach in the workshop program and exhibit in the gallery.

On the third floor, The Clay Studio School students work at basic pottery, sculpting, firing and glaze mixing. Classes, workshops and lectures are open to children and adults, both novice and advanced. Youngsters who tour the studio (with advance reservations for no more than 15 in a group) get a chance to play with clay and work a wheel. (Dress accordingly.)

On the street level, the gallery presents monthly shows; five by the resident artists, others are invitational and juried shows for potters from around the country, a student and a holiday exhibition.

DREXEL UNIVERSITY
DESIGN ARTS GALLERY
Nesbitt Hall
33rd and Market Streets—19104
895-2386

Hours: Weekdays, 12 to 5; weekends by appointment. Closed holidays, July and August.

Tours: You're on your own.

Cost: Free.
SEPTA: Buses 30, 31, 42; trolleys 10, 11, 13, 34, 36.
E & D: To avoid 6 steps at Market Street entrance, enter at north side on Lancaster Walk. Complete wheelchair access.

Eight shows are presented during the academic year at Drexel's Nesbitt College of Design Arts in their compact, neon-framed gallery that's neatly built into the school's ground floor lobby.

Four exhibitions present established artists of local or national acclaim; another is a faculty show; and three are works of students who aspire to the more professional categories.

An exhibit might comprise works of fine or applied arts. You could see sculpture, photography, costumes, graphics or paintings. A schedule for the year is available early in the fall. Plan ahead and attend a reception, dialogue or demonstration that usually goes with each show.

DREXEL UNIVERSITY, THE MUSEUM

Drexel University Main Building, Room 305
32nd and Chestnut Streets—19104
895-2424

Hours: Monday to Wednesday, 1 to 7; Thursday and Friday, 1 to 4. Closed academic and federal holidays.
Tours: Call at least 2 weeks ahead for groups of up to 25.
Cost: Free.
SEPTA: Buses 21, 30, 42, 125; or walking distance from 30th Street Station.
E & D: There are 13 steps at the Chestnut Street entrance, or call ahead to use street level entrance with easy elevator access on 32nd Street.

Drexel's Main Building, a National Historic Landmark which dates back to 1891, is a masterpiece in itself, but neatly tucked away on the third floor is an enormous sky-lit gallery where you'll discover many artistic masterpieces. The focus is on 19th century European academic paintings, sculpture and decorative arts.

Portraits of Drexel family members cover the walls. Many of them are by the 19th century family artist-turned-banker Francis Martin Drexel.

The floor is filled with fine furnishings of the period.

191

The showcases display ornamental silver, pewter, minia-
tures, antique toys, old wooden utensils, fine china collections and a service of Sevres china that was made for
Napoleon III.

The most historic clock in America is on display here.
It's the David Rittenhouse* clock, made in 1773. The
clock still ticks away the seconds, minutes and hours, as
well as the day and date of the month, the moon's phases,
the earth's and moon's orbits, zodiac signs and other technical data.

The Rincliffe Gallery, which adjoins the main gallery,
is devoted exclusively to what has to be Philadelphia's
largest collection of Edward Marshall Boehm porcelains.
These are the true-to-life sculptures of birds and animals
that are often chosen for gifts to royalty and heads of state.

A third facet of Drexel's Museum Collection is a changing exhibition gallery in Room 305. These displays are
related to the University through its alumni, faculty or
permanent treasures.

So don't miss these changing exhibits. And before you
leave, don't miss the bronze "Water Boy" by Auguste Bar-
tholdi, the French sculptor of the Statue of Liberty, or the
marble bust of Anthony Drexel by Moses Ezekial. They're
on the main floor of the Main Building.

ESTHER M. KLEIN ART GALLERY
University City Science Center
3600 Market Street—19104
387-2255

Hours: Weekdays, 9 to 5. Closed academic and federal
holidays.
Tours: Call a few weeks ahead to schedule groups of up
to 50.
Cost: Free.
SEPTA: Buses 30, 31, Market Street subway-elevated to
34th Street; trolley 10.
E & D: Complete wheelchair access.

Along with housing science research facilities and
offices, and in addition to the "Street Art" described later
in this chapter, there's a gallery for contemporary art in
the University City Science Center* complex. New and
emerging Philadelphia talent is displayed in the lobby
showplace of the science center's newest edifice.

Shows change every six weeks at the Esther M. Klein Art Gallery. You can call ahead to find out what's planned. Any medium might be represented, and opening receptions often combine with performance arts.

While you're in the neighborhood, walk next door to 3624 Market Street and view an exhibit from the science center's permanent collection of contemporary art.

FLEISHER ART MEMORIAL
709–721 Catharine Street—19147
922-3456

Hours: October to June: Monday to Thursday, 12 to 5 and 6:30 to 9:30 P.M.; Saturday, 1 to 3. Closed between exhibitions and July and August.

Tours: A gallery talk can sometimes be scheduled along with a brief description of the Sanctuary. Groups of 10 to 30 should call a few days ahead. And if you're coming for art classes, you'll have to sign up.

Cost: Free, excepted as noted below for some art classes.

SEPTA: Buses 47, 63.

E & D: Complete wheelchair access.

The Fleisher Art Memorial has three noteworthy divisions: the school, the galleries and the Sanctuary.

Art classes are free or nearly-free from October to July.

Adults can attend evening classes, and children from ages five to 17 can come any Saturday morning or afternoon. There's also an outdoor summer session (Saturdays in May and June) for landscape painting. This is a fabulous opportunity. You only pay for materials and you get first-rate instruction. (A $10 contribution is requested.)

The changing art exhibits are always open to the public. They may feature fine art, sculpture or graphics by a faculty member, alumni, a student or the "challenge" exhibitions presenting new local talent. Three artists are chosen by competition for each of these shows that are mounted five times a year. Call ahead if you want to know what will be exhibited on a certain date.

There's nothing in Philadelphia that's like Fleisher's Sanctuary. It's a late 19th century Romanesque Revival-style church building that houses a Russian icons collection, 14th to 16th century European paintings and sculpture, and a permanent exhibition of works by Nicola

D'Ascenzo, Robert Henri, John LaFarge, Violet Oakley and Samuel Yellin.

The striking Louis Kahn Lecture Hall designed by Siah Armajani is the site for lectures, critiques and community meetings. Fleisher is also "home" to the Philadelphia Folklore Project, a branch of Prints in Progress and the Hancock Chamber Players*. Ask for a schedule to see which of these might interest you.

GALLERY OF THE
ART INSTITUTE OF PHILADELPHIA
1622 Chestnut Street—19103
567-7080

Hours: Weekdays, 9 to 6; Saturday, 9 to 1. Closed some holidays. Allow 20 to 30 minutes.
Cost: Free.
SEPTA: Any route on Chestnut Street.
E & D: On street level with complete wheelchair access.

The Art Institute's home is a grand example of 1930s architecture. Much of its art deco splendor has been restored.

The school offers a continuous 24-month program to students aspiring to careers in commercial art, photography, interior design, fashion merchandising, and music and video production.

A contemporary storefront gallery features changing exhibits by students, faculty and leading designers and illustrators. Design professionals as well as the public will enjoy this opportunity to keep current with the state-of-the-visual arts.

GOLDIE PALEY DESIGN CENTER
Philadelphia College of Textiles and Science
4200 Henry Avenue—19144
951-2860

Hours: Tuesday to Saturday, 10 to 4. Closed major holidays and academic holidays.
Tours: Groups of no more than 40 should call 2 weeks ahead to schedule a one-hour tour. You'll be divided into smaller groups. You might want to combine this with a tour of the College (see Chapter 13).
Cost: Free admission; guided tour $2 per person.
SEPTA: Bus 32.

Other: A Gift Shop has books, stationery and posters, all related to textiles, as well as unusual scarves and handbags.

E & D: Complete wheelchair access.

The Goldie Paley Design Center is part of the Philadelphia College of Textiles and Science*, the oldest and largest college of its type in the country. Goldie Paley was an artist and she painted at her ranch-style home adjacent to the campus grounds. When she died in 1977, her family gave the house and grounds to the college as a living memorial.

The Design Center has four exhibition rooms, and the shows change every few months. The exhibits could be modern textiles, fabrics from various historic periods, textiles and traditional costumes from around the world, work by contemporary fiber artists or by the College's students and faculty.

This is a comprehensive textile museum and design resource center. More than a million fabric samples from American and foreign textile mills, from 1840 to the present, make up a study collection that serves as a fabric library and design resource. You'll get a glimpse at some of these stored materials, as well as Pre-Columbian and Coptic textiles, laces dating back to the 16th century, antique quilts, garments from the 19th century, 20th century designer clothing and a huge number of accessories including beaded handbags, gloves, shoes, hats, fans and parasols.

**GOLDIE PALEY GALLERY and
LEVY GALLERY FOR THE ARTS
IN PHILADELPHIA
Moore College of Art and Design**
20th Street and Benjamin Franklin Parkway—19103
568–4515 Ext. 1119

Hours: Tuesday to Friday, 10 to 5; weekends, 12 to 4. Closed academic and legal holidays.

Tours: You're on your own, but gallery talks and lectures are scheduled in conjunction with each exhibition.

Cost: Free. Friends of the Paley/Levy Galleries are invited to openings, gallery talks and special events, and receive an annual calendar and discounts on publications.

Lunch: The nearby student cafeteria is open to gallery visitors between 11:30 A.M. and 1:30 P.M.
SEPTA: Buses 32, 33, 38, Ben FrankLine route 76.
E & D: Complete wheelchair access.

Two outstanding galleries at Moore present provocative exhibitions of mostly 20th century art, crafts, sculpture, design, architecture and photography.

American and foreign artists not frequently shown elsewhere are showcased at the Goldie Paley Gallery. Here, traditional art is examined in a contemporary way, and contemporary work is reviewed in an historical context. Recent shows by the likes of Hanne Darboven, Josef Hoffman, Arnulf Rainer and Bill Traylor have drawn national acclaim to the gallery. Many of these shows have traveled to other cities.

Since opening in 1987, the Levy Gallery provides a showplace for Philadelphia area artists. Some are established; others are lesser-known. Some are traditional; others are avant-garde. All are imaginative. "Found Ground" presented works by several local artists who work on a variety of readymade surfaces. "Fieldworks: Collecting as Folklore" established dozens of unique private collections as artwork worth exploring. Levy Gallery is where Moore's students have their annual spring show and you get to see the textile designs, graphics, sculpture, painting and photography of future talents. A faculty show is held every few years.

Gallery talks, slide lectures, symposiums, family workshops and film programs are planned in conjunction with shows. Exhibitions generally run for five weeks. A yearly schedule is available in the fall.

Luckily for Moore students and for the public, the campus and galleries are directly across from the southwest corner of Logan Square. . .within a flower's scent of the Benjamin Franklin Parkway and its many attractions. Don't pass up a chance to see some of the gutsiest art shows in town.

INSTITUTE OF CONTEMPORARY ART
University of Pennsylvania
36th and Sansom Streets—19104
898–7108

Hours: Tuesday to Sunday, 10 to 5; Wednesday till 7.
Closed July 4, Christmas, New Year's.

Tours: Thursday and Sunday at 1 P.M. for an hour.
Groups of no more than 30 can be scheduled at other
times by calling the Education Coordinator at least 2
weeks ahead. Informal gallery talks are also scheduled
in conjunction with each exhibition.

Cost: Adults, $2; senior citizens, students and artists, $1;
University of Pennsylvania students, faculty and staff
and children under 12, free. Free for everyone on Wednesday. Group rates set when scheduling tour in advance. Members enjoy free admission, discount on I.C.A.
catalogues, and invitations to a variety of receptions
and special events.

SEPTA: Bus 21; trolleys 11, 13, 34, 36.

Other: Show catalogues and posters are for sale.

E & D: Complete wheelchair access.

The ICA, founded in 1963 and relocated to its exciting
new home in January, 1991, is Philadelphia's newest
showplace for contemporary art. And this is where tomorrow's art is exhibited today. The building itself is a work
of angular, contemporary, industrial-style design, by
Philadelphia architect Adele Naude Santos, planned to
minimize its own impact while accentuating the art work
inside in a two-level interconnected flexible gallery.

Four exhibits of American or internationally-known artists are presented at ICA during the course of the academic year. (ICA is an independent gallery affiliated with
the University of Pennsylvania.) You might see photography, video, performance, installation or visual art. Recent exhibitions have featured Laurie Anderson, David
Hammons, Robert Mapplethorpe, Cindy Sherman, The
East Village Scene, Siah Armajani, and Arquitectonica.

During each exhibit, one hour of a Saturday and Sunday morning on two weekends is devoted to young people five to 11. These Family Art Workshops include
geared-to-the-young gallery talks (which fascinate parents) and a supervised informal art happening where children have an opportunity to display their own creative
talents. Call the ICA in the fall for details.

LA SALLE UNIVERSITY MUSEUM
Olney Hall, 20th Street and Olney Avenue—19141
951-1221

Hours: Late September through April: Tuesday to Friday, 11 to 4; Sunday, 2 to 4. May through July: Monday to Thursday, 11 to 3. Closed August, holidays and academic holidays. Allow one hour.
Tours: Large groups are requested to call in advance. A printed, self-guided tour is available in each room.
Cost: Free. Donations accepted.
SEPTA: Buses 18, 26. There's parking on campus; inquire at the guard house where you enter.
E & D: You can avoid steps by entering at the street level and taking a self-service elevator to the gallery floor.

Each of the five period rooms at LaSalle's gallery exhibits works from a different century. The 16th to 20th centuries in Western art are represented with a collection of more than 200 paintings and over 2,000 prints and drawings. These exhibits are supplemented with special shows that change every few months.

The artists include Boudin, Bourdon, Corot, Degas, Eakins, Pissaro, Prevost, Raeburn, Rouault, West, Tanner and Tintoretto. Almost every style and subject matter is shown.

One of the gallery highlights is the Susan Dunleavy Collection of some 200 finely illustrated and printed Bibles from the 15th century to today. Catholic, Jewish and Protestant versions have the common quality of artistic beauty.

LLOYD P. JONES GALLERY
HARRY FIELDS GALLERY
University of Pennsylvania
Gimbel Gymnasium, 3701 Walnut Street—19104
898-6101

Hours: Weekdays, 12 to 3; Saturday, 2 to 5. Closed some holidays.
Tours: You're on your own, but call ahead if you're coming with a group of more than 10.
Cost: Free.

SEPTA: Bus 21.

E & D: There are 4 low steps if you approach from the adjacent parking lot. Gallery is on entrance level. Marked entrance on Sansom Street enables complete wheelchair access; ring the bell.

Each of the four people associated with this permanent exhibition shared a love of sports. Likewise, the gallery is bound to interest anyone interested in sports.

Lloyd Jones, a member of the University of Pennsylvania's class of 1907, was also a member of the 1908 U.S. Olympic Track Team. R. Tait McKenzie was a surgeon, Professor of Medicine and Director of Physical Education at the University from 1904 till his death in 1938. He also achieved world fame as a sculptor.

The Lloyd P. Jones Gallery displays 68 of Dr. McKenzie's sculptures. Most of them are bronzes, and almost all of them capture the stance, the equipment or the expression of an athlete or an athletic event. When you're at the Benjamin Franklin Parkway, also look at McKenzie's lifelike sculpture of "The Scout" standing proudly on the front lawn at the Boy Scouts of America Building*, 22nd and Winter Streets near the Parkway.

Harry Fields was also a noted doctor and surgeon, as well as a championship wrestler. He advocated good physical fitness as an antidote for good health. The Harry Fields Gallery of the Sculpture of Joe Brown was established in his memory after his death in 1987.

Joe Brown started his career as a professional boxer. He turned to sculpting as a means to create lasting tributes to athletes and apprenticed with R. Tait McKenzie. Among his realistic figures represented in bronze are a punter, soccer goalie, hockey player, discus thrower, hurdler, baseball, basketball and tennis players. You're sure to recognize many of the famous subjects. Over a hundred works are displayed. (Several of Joe Brown's sculptures are also listed later in this chapter under "Street Art.")

MORANI ART GALLERY of the
MEDICAL COLLEGE OF PENNSYLVANIA
Conference Center at EPPI—Room 305
3200 Henry Avenue—19129
842-4090 or 842-4116

Hours: Tuesday and Thursday, 2 to 4; 1st Sunday of each month, 2 to 4; other hours by appointment.

Tours: You're on your own, or call the curator at 843–8404 to schedule a guided tour.
Cost: Free.
SEPTA: Buses 32, R.
E & D: Complete wheelchair access. Gallery is on ground level.

Dr. Alma Dea Morani graduated in 1931 from what was then called Women's Medical College. She was one of the country's first female surgeons and in 1947 became the first woman member of the American Society of Plastic and Reconstructive Surgery. Dr. Morani is also a world traveler, an art collector and sculptor. She recently gave much of her collection to her alma mater, which, in turn, opened a gallery in her honor.

Among the items on exhibit are bas reliefs, sculptures, antique statuary, paintings, woodcarvings and artifacts from other times from throughout the world.

Some of the sculptures and bas reliefs are by Dr. Morani, some of the artwork is by members of her family, and some are by local artists whose work she collected. There are also sculptures from the Philippines, a Shiva from India, jade from China and Macau and landscapes from Japan, just to name a few.

Three or four special exhibits during the year feature area artists in some connection with the medical profession.

Note: The Morani Art Gallery will relocate early in 1992 to Ann Preston Hall on the MCP campus.

NORMAN ROCKWELL MUSEUM
Curtis Building, 6th and Sansom Streets—19106
922–4345

Hours: Monday to Saturday, 10 to 4; Sunday, 11 to 4. Closed Thanksgiving, Christmas, New Year's. Allow 30 to 45 minutes.
Tours: Scheduled for groups of 10 or more by calling in advance.
Cost: Adults, $2; senior citizens, $1.50; children under 12, free. Group rates for 10 or more, $1. A fee for class tours is set when reservations are made.
SEPTA: Any route to Independence Hall.
Other: The gift shop has the country's largest selection of Norman Rockwell prints, figurines, plates and limited editions ranging from $.50 to $350.

E & D: There are 14 steps at the entrance and then exhibits are on one lower level. Or use ramp at 6th and Walnut Streets to enter lobby and take elevator down.

What's as American as apple pie?
A Norman Rockwell illustration.
Where can you see a complete set of his 324 covers for *The Saturday Evening Post*?
In the Norman Rockwell Museum. And that happens to be in the very same building where *The Saturday Evening Post* was published. What else will you see here?
Reproductions of Rockwell's "The American Family" series, which was done for the Massachusetts Mutual Insurance Company, his Boy Scout drawings, the "Four Freedoms" posters and at least 50 more canvas reproductions of his work. The exhibit spans 60 years of Norman Rockwell's prolific career. The museum's only original is an unfinished drawing that sits on the easel in a simulation of Rockwell's studio in Stockbridge, Massachusetts.
An eight-minute video on Norman Rockwell's life plays continuously on a TV screen.

PENNSYLVANIA ACADEMY
OF THE FINE ARTS
Broad and Cherry Streets—19102
972–7600 or 972–7633 (recorded information)

Hours: Tuesday to Saturday, 10 to 5; Sunday, 11 to 5. Closed Thanksgiving, Christmas, New Year's. Allow one hour or more.
Tours: Regularly scheduled tours are Tuesday to Friday at 11 and 2, and weekends at 2. Groups of 10 to 60 must call at least 3 weeks ahead to schedule tours at other times. Museum lessons for school-age groups from kindergarten through high school must also be scheduled 3 weeks in advance. Choose from a variety of study topics and receive pre-tour classroom material and follow-up suggestions. Call 972–7608 for all group and bilingual tour arrangements.
Cost: Adults, $5; senior citizens, $3; students, $2; children under 5, free. Free on Saturday from 10 to 1. Group rates for 10 or more: adults, $4; senior citizens, $2.50; students, $1.50; Philadelphia school groups, free. Membership enables free admission and a wide range of special programs and events.

SEPTA: Any route to City Hall and walk 2 short blocks north on Broad Street to Cherry.

Other: The contemporary, bi-level triangular gift shop features art books, posters, stationery, slides, T-shirts, totes, ties and some nifty gift items.

E & D: Complete wheelchair access. There are 7 steps at the main Broad Street entrance, or ring bell at rear Burns Street entrance for level access. Wheelchairs are available. Special tours can be arranged in advance for the visually and hearing impaired; call 972-7608.

If architect Frank Furness were around today to see his creation, he would beam with delight.

This National Historic Landmark built in the Victorian Gothic style was completely restored for the Bicentennial in 1976. Every part of the building is as much a work of art as the masterpieces it displays. You have to see it to believe it.

The Pennsylvania Academy of the Fine Arts houses one of the world's finest collections of American paintings and sculpture. The Academy, founded in 1805, is the nation's oldest art museum and school. Its art ranges from the 1700s to today. It's known for its art by local painters like Charles Willson Peale (founder of the Academy) and his sons, Thomas Eakins (who taught at the Academy), Winslow Homer, Horace Pippin, William Rush, Andrew Wyeth and Gilbert Stuart.

The galleries on the second floor are reached by the great stairhall or by elevator. They have natural lighting and individual decors which are appropriate to their exhibits. The major shows change five or six times a year, and they range from historical to contemporary art. Among the hundreds of paintings on permanent display is Benjamin West's "Penn's Treaty with the Indians."

The special exhibitions in the first floor Morris Gallery feature one-person shows by contemporary artists with a connection to Philadelphia. The shows here change every eight weeks.

Other popular facets of the Academy are the concerts, lectures, film series, Saturdays for Children and Families, and special events which are throughout the year. Call the Academy to find out what's coming up next, and refer to the Index for other mentions in this book.

PHILADELPHIA ART ALLIANCE
251 South 18th Street—19103
545-4302

Hours: Weekdays, 11:30 A.M. to 9 P.M.; Saturday, 10:30 to 5. Closed holidays, between shows, and August through Labor Day. Allow 30 minutes.

Cost: Free for members. Suggested donations for non-members, $2. Ask about membership and all of its benefits.

Lunch: There's a lovely dining room for members.

SEPTA: Buses 2, 9, 17, 21, 42, 90.

E & D: There are 8 low steps at the entrance and exhibits are on 3 floors connected by stairs or elevator. Call ahead for ramp to be placed at entrance.

Note: As this edition goes to press, the Philadelphia Art Alliance is in a state of transition. Be sure to call ahead and confirm hours before making a visit.

This stately former center city dwelling overlooking scenic Rittenhouse Square is filled with seven galleries of exhibitions that change every six weeks. Even the hall cases and beautiful wooden stairway are utilized for displaying works of contemporary art.

Shows focus on three goals: to present new or established Philadelphia artists; show work of nationally renown artists who might not otherwise be seen in Philadelphia; and exhibit innovative work relating to contemporary issues.

At any given time you might be delighted to see sculpture, paintings, prints, photography, weavings, architectural design, jewelry, glass, metal or wood crafts. Several now-famous artists have been introduced to the public with shows at the Philadelphia Art Alliance. Andrew Wyeth was one.

Lectures, music and dance programs, poetry and play readings, and children's workshops are also on the agenda. Call the Art Alliance for details.

PHILADELPHIA MUSEUM OF ART
26th Street and Benjamin Franklin
Parkway—19101–7646
763–8100 or 787–5488 (recording of daily schedule)

Hours: Tuesday to Sunday, 10 to 5. Closed holidays. Allow as much time as you can, and then plan to return.
Tours: You have a choice of ways to visit the museum.
1) Visit on your own and get to know the museum.
2) Any individual can join the daily one-hour Museum Treasure Tours, Tuesday to Sunday at 10:15, 11, 12, 1, 2 and 3.
3) Family Programs are Sunday 11:30 A.M. to 2 P.M. (arrive when admission is free) for children of all ages. See Chapter 15.
4) Museum Treasure Tours or Family Tours, for groups of 10 or more, on a special subject or in a foreign language must be scheduled a week in advance. Call the Group Sales Office, 787–5498.
5) Members of the museum's professional staff present one-hour gallery lecture/spotlight talks from October to June, Tuesday to Saturday at 11, and Sunday at 12:30. The gallery and topic changes each week. Folding stools are provided. Reservations are not necessary. Call the Education Department (787–5455) for the current topics.
6) Philadelphia Public Schools: One-hour tours are scheduled for a class 2 weeks in advance on weekdays from 9 to 3. Call the Museum Education Department at the Board of Education, 299–7778, to arrange.
7) Parochial, private and suburban schools: similar tours are arranged by calling Museum Division of Education, 787–5455.
8) Scouts, church, neighborhood and other groups: 45-to 60-minute tours are scheduled 2 weeks in advance for groups of 5 to 100, at least 2nd grade level. Tuesday to Sunday from 10 to 3. Call the Group Sales Office, 787–5498.

Cost: Adults, $5; senior citizens, students with I.D. and children under 18, $2.50. $1 more for special shows. Free for everyone on Sunday till 1. Group rates are arranged when scheduling tour. Membership entitles you to free admission, special programs and events, the art rental gallery service, newsletters and shop discounts.

Lunch: The cafeteria is open Tuesday to Friday, 10 to 3:30, and weekends from 11 to 3:45. The restaurant is open Tuesday to Sunday, 11:45 to 2:15. A Student Center Cafeteria is available weekdays by reservation to school groups with a scheduled tour and bringing their lunch. Beverage machines are available.

SEPTA: Buses 7, 32, 38, 43, 48, Ben FrankLine route 76.

Other: There's an expansive Museum Shop. Inquire at the east or west information desks (or call the Education Department, 787-5455) about film and concert programs, family events, and an extensive gallery talk schedule. No flash, strobe or tripod photography is allowed. No pens are allowed to sketch or take notes. No smoking is allowed. Children under 12 must be with an adult. Wheelchairs and strollers are available.

E & D: There are 7 low steps at the west entrance. There is complete wheelchair access to the museum. A ramp entrance is on the museum's south side. Special parking spaces for the handicapped are marked off nearby. Group tours for senior citizens are scheduled through the Group Sales Office (787-5498). Tours for visually impaired are scheduled through the Education Department (787-5455). Tours for hearing impaired are scheduled through the Education Department (787-5455) or by calling on TTY phone 787-5458. The Education Department also offers a full schedule of Programs for Older Adults and Audiences with Special Needs.

It doesn't matter how old you are, or what you like in art, because there are things for everyone to marvel at in the Philadelphia Museum of Art.

When the nation celebrated its Bicentennial, the museum celebrated its Centennial with a major renovation of its classical Greco-Roman home that was built between 1919 and 1928. Over 300,000 art objects are displayed in 200 galleries covering 10 acres. The museum's map will be a big help if you're visiting on your own. Stop first at the museum's west lobby for information: the kiosk itself is a work of art, and scheduled guided tours depart from here.

Among the museum's most prized possessions are Van Gogh's "Sunflowers," Picasso's "Three Musicians," Rubens' "Prometheus Bound," DuChamp's "Nude Descending a Staircase," Renoir's "The Bathers," Cezanne's "The Large Bathers," Charles Willson Peale's sons in the artist's "Staircase Group," Benjamin West's "Benjamin Franklin Drawing Electricity from the Sky" and Brancusi's limestone sculpture "The Kiss."

The museum's 20th century wing and the Arensberg Collection make New Yorkers realize they don't have a monopoly at their Museum of Modern Art. Cy Twombly's "Fifty Days at Iliam" fills a gallery of its own.

If Renaissance art is more to your liking, don't miss the Johnson Collection represented by most of the great Italian and French masters.

The Philadelphia Museum of Art is more than paintings and sculpture. It's the home of the Kienbusch Armor Collection of weaponry and entire suits of metal, and a tapestry collection big enough to floor anyone.

The museum is also the "new home" of entire buildings, fountains and interiors that have been reconstructed as they were in their own time and place. Where else could you stay under one roof and walk through a 17th century Chinese Palace Hall, a 12th century French Cloister, a 16th century Indian Temple Hall, a Japanese Buddhist Temple and an authentic Tea House?

You can also visit Period Rooms from England, France and America or stand face to face with the 7th century statue of a Buddhist Lord of Mercy. Then visit Rural and Shaker Pennsylvania, see three centuries of magnificent handmade furnishings, glass and silver collections and the works of Thomas Eakins, Winslow Homer, Thomas Sully and Andrew Wyeth, to name a few.

Three pages here hardly does justice to the museum. You'll have to see it for yourself.

THE PRINT CLUB
1614 Latimer Street—19103
735-6090

Hours: Tuesday to Saturday, 11 to 5:30. Call for summer hours. Closed some holidays.

Tours: No tours, but groups of 10 or more should call in advance for reservations.

Cost: Free. Ask about General Membership that enables participation in lectures, special events, educational programs and discount purchases. If you're an artist, ask about the additional benefits of an Artist Membership.

SEPTA: Buses 2, 9, 21, 42, 90.

Other: The Gallery Store offers a wonderful selection of contemporary prints, photographs, hand-made books, unique fabric items, crafts and art objects. Several local art organizations are represented along with local, national and international artists.

E & D: There's one step at the entrance, and only the first floor is accessible to wheelchairs.

The Print Club is a non-profit educational and cultural organization that has been operating since 1915. It's a short block south of Locust Street in a charming, converted center city townhouse. The gallery features exhibitions that change frequently and present new and established artists from the Philadelphia area and around the country.

Members are also invited to partake in The Print Club's program of lectures, demonstrations and talks by exhibiting artists and visiting professionals. Schedules are available in the late summer, newsletters are sent to members, and you can check the newspapers for announcements.

RODIN MUSEUM
22nd Street and Benjamin Franklin
Parkway—19101-7646
763-8100

Hours: Tuesday to Sunday, 10 to 5. Closed holidays. Allow 30 minutes.

Tours: A public tour is the 1st and 3rd Saturday and 2nd and 4th Sunday of each month at 1 P.M. Adult groups of 10 to 50 can be scheduled any day from 10 to 3. Reservations must be made at least 2 weeks in advance through the Group Sales Office at the Philadelphia Museum of Art (787-5498).

Cost: A donation is requested.

SEPTA: Same as for the Philadelphia Museum of Art.

Other: A small Museum Shop sells slides, T-shirts, postcards and books, including a guidebook to the museum and all of its works.

E & D: A combination of 33 low steps and landings lead through the gardens and to the main entrance. Galleries are on one level. A level entrance is reached from the rear driveway at 22nd and Hamilton Streets. Buzz for guard to open the door.

The City of Philadelphia just saved you a trip to Paris to see the work of French sculptor Auguste Rodin (1840–1917). Philadelphia's Rodin Museum houses the largest single collection of Rodin's work outside of France. All aspects of his career are represented in every media.

You'll know you're there when you come upon "The Thinker" on the Parkway. Continue through the peaceful gardens to a chateau-inspired building, and revel first at "The Gates of Hell" dominating the museum's entrance.

The building itself was designed by architects Paul Cret and Jacques Greber and opened in 1929. It's a reproduction of the old Chateau D'Issy that Rodin himself had copied for his home at Meudon near his studio in France.

Inside are nearly 200 magnificent bronze, plaster and marble sculptures so lifelike they seem to breathe. Rodin's favorite themes were interpretations of various strong emotions and the hands and busts of his many famous friends. Several are of the French poet Balzac. The six bigger-than-life figures of "The Burghers of Calais" dominate the main gallery.

ROSENBACH MUSEUM AND LIBRARY
2010 Delancey Place—19103
732–1600

Hours: Tuesday to Sunday, 11 to 4, with last tour at 2:45 P.M. Closed August and federal holidays.

Tours: Everyone gets a tour at Rosenbach. Groups of 8 to 30, at least junior high school level, must be scheduled in advance.

Cost: Adults, $2.50 for a tour of the house and exhibits, or $1.50 to see only the exhibits; senior citizens, students and children under 12, $1.50. Group rates for 8 or more scheduled in advance. Memberships are available.

SEPTA: Buses 7, 12, 17, 40, 90 or Walnut Street routes.

E & D: There are 4 steps at the entrance and 3 floors of exhibits. No wheelchair access.

It's almost inconceivable that two bachelor brothers could have amassed such an outstanding collection of treasures. Abe Rosenbach collected fine literature and books. Philip concentrated on antiques and the decorative arts.

A foundation was established to maintain the Rosenbach treasures since the brothers' deaths in the 1950s, and the museum and library continue to acquire.

Their stately 1863 townhouse has valuable furniture, silver, antiques, porcelain, paintings, rare books and manuscripts. More about the library in Chapter 11.

One room reproduces the living room of poet Marianne Moore. Her furniture, books, bric-a-brac, souvenirs and baseball mementos are just as they were when she died.

Another room features the original drawings of Maurice Sendak, well-known author and illustrator of children's books. Trace the complete production of a Sendak favorite by viewing the artist's preliminary sketches, finished artwork, color separations and finished composition.

The museum is well known for its "Bay Psalm Book" (the first Bible printed in the Western hemisphere), the original manuscripts of Chaucer's "Canterbury Tales" and James Joyce's 877-page handwritten copy of "Ulysses." The works of art include Matisse bronzes, Daumier drawings and William Blake watercolors. And since you're interested in Philadelphia, don't miss seeing the first issue of Benjamin Franklin's "Poor Richard's Almanack."

ROTUNDA GALLERY at
COMMUNITY COLLEGE OF PHILADELPHIA
1700 Spring Garden Street—19103
751-8040

Hours: September to May, weekdays, 10 to 8; weekends, 10 to 5. Closed school holidays and between shows.
Tours: You're on your own.
Cost: Free.
SEPTA: Buses 2, 43.
E & D: Complete wheelchair access. Enter at ramp on 17th Street side of old U.S. Mint building and take elevator to gallery level.

Of the six shows presented here during the school year, one features work by the College's art faculty; another, by its students.

Other shows are brought to the gallery from the outside, but they're always tied in with some aspect of the curriculum at Community College.

The gallery is named because of its unique architecture. The glass-domed show area is at the core of the grand old United States Mint building.

Call ahead to ask what's being shown now. You might want to combine your visit to the gallery with a tour of the campus (see Chapter 13) or a concert or dramatic presentation (call the Student Activities Office, 751–8210).

STEPHEN GIRARD COLLECTION
Founder's Hall at Girard College
Girard and Corinthian Avenues—19130
787–2600

Hours: Every Thursday from 2 to 4; other times by special arrangement.
Tours: Groups of 10 or more must call ahead; groups of 10 to 50 can be scheduled for guided tours. Allow one hour.
Cost: Free.
SEPTA: Trolley 15 to the College entrance. There's plenty of free parking on the campus.
E & D: There are 11 marble steps to the porticoed entrance. Exhibits are on 2nd floor and reached by stairs.

Stephen Girard's name is almost as familiar to Philadelphians as Benjamin Franklin's. A bank used to be named after him, dozens of businesses and a street were named after him, and, of course, Girard College where his collection is housed.

Girard came from France to Philadelphia in 1776 and rapidly became one of the wealthiest men in America. As a result, he was able to hire the finest craftsmen and buy the best of everything. His furnishings attest to that.

Antique lovers shouldn't miss this display.

The collection includes 500 pieces of furniture, china, silver, crystal and personal items dating from 1780 to 1830. Everything is carefully documented and preserved by the excellent records that Girard kept.

The furnishings are displayed in six exhibit areas, simulating the rooms at Girard's Water Street home in Philadelphia at the time of his death in 1831.

Founder's Hall, designed by Thomas U. Walter and completed in 1847, is considered to be one of the world's finest examples of Greek Revival architecture. Among Walter's other designs were the four cantilevered stairwells in the

corners of City Hall*, the Society Hill Synagogue* at 418
Spruce Street, Andalusia* in Bucks County and the dome
of the Capitol building in Washington, D.C.

TEMPLE GALLERY
Temple University Center City
1619 Walnut Street—19103
787–5041

Hours: Tuesday to Saturday, 10 to 5; June through
    August, Tuesday to Friday, 10 to 5. Other times by ap-
    pointment. Closed holidays.
Tours: You're on your own.
Cost: Free.
SEPTA: Buses 2, 9, 21, 42 or any Chestnut Street route.
E & D: Complete wheelchair access.

The Temple Gallery of Temple's Tyler School of Art
came to Walnut Street's upbeat retailing district in 1985.
The gallery was designed by Robert Venturi, a leader in
today's post-modern architecture movement and a partner in Philadelphia's world-renowned architectural firm
Venturi, Rauch & Scott-Brown. The gallery is a welcome
respite from the hectic center city pace.

An expansive glass street-front facade invites you inside to view contemporary works by artists, sculptors and
craftspeople. They might be of regional, national or international repute, or they might be student or faculty
shows of Tyler's finest.

Shows change every month and have proven that art
can be fun, educational and a rewarding interlude.

UNIVERSITY OF THE ARTS
HAVILAND HALL GALLERIES
Broad and Pine Streets—19102
875-1116
MEDNICK GALLERY
333 S. Broad Street—19102
875-1020
ROSENWALD-WOLF GALLERY
333 S. Broad Street—19102
875-1116

Hours: Rosenwald-Wolf: weekdays, 10 to 5; Wednesday till 9; Saturday, 12 to 5; mid-May through August, weekdays only. Haviland Hall: weekdays, 9 to 6; Saturday, 12 to 5; mid-May through August, weekdays only. Mednick: weekdays, 10 to 5. All galleries closed academic and federal holidays.

Tours: Groups of up to 30 can be scheduled for any or all of the galleries by calling at least a week in advance.

Cost: Free.

Lunch: Cafe PCA in the Haviland-Strickland Building (Broad and Pine Streets) is open to gallery visitors.

SEPTA: Buses C, 27, 32, 40, 90; Broad Street Subway.

E & D: Complete wheelchair access. Call ahead for assistance at Haviland and Mednick Galleries.

A variety of galleries at the University of the Arts offer several fine opportunities to see what's new in contemporary art. Exhibitions exemplify the diversity of teaching and talent at the school in students, faculty and alumni, as well as from nationally and internationally recognized artists.

Rosenwald-Wolf Gallery occupies a glass-front street level space in a building that was stunningly restored by the University in 1985. Its opening was celebrated with the East Coast's first major show of "Memphis/Milano: Furniture, Furnishings, Experiments and Ideas in the New Design," just to give an idea of what you might see here. Art and design aficionados will appreciate the type of work exhibited.

Mednick Gallery, on the second floor, is a compact, one-room showcase for photography and film exhibits. It's certainly worth a visit while you're here.

You can't miss the Haviland-Strickland Building with its Doric-style portico across the way on Broad Street. Shows in the Haviland Hall Galleries are in conjunction with Rosenwald-Wolf or focus on student work. Additional exhibits line the ground-floor walkways on either side of Haviland's "Great Hall." It's well worth a look to see not only the art, but also the magnificent restoration in this historic building that was the school's home since the 1890s.

Shows usually run a month. The galleries close for a week between each show, but since the schedules overlap, you can always see at least two. And you can always see the "Window on Broad" at 333 S. Broad Street. It's where each month a local artist, student or faculty member is chosen to install a work designed specifically for the site. And you'll be amazed, amused, baffled or enchanted by what might fill the space that's some 12-feet high by 10-feet long and three-and-a-half-feet deep.

UNIVERSITY MUSEUM
University of Pennsylvania
33rd and Spruce Streets—19104
898–4000 or 222–7777 (recording of current programs)

Hours: Tuesday to Saturday, 10 to 4:30; Sunday, 1 to 5. Closed Sundays from late June till early September, July 4, Christmas. Allow one hour, at the very least.

Tours: You can visit on your own at any time. 45-minute gallery tours are September through May, Saturday and Sunday at 1:15 P.M. Groups of 10 to 30, at least 3rd grade, can be scheduled for a one-hour tour with a museum teacher by calling the Education Section (898–4015) at least 4 weeks in advance. These tours can be Tuesday to Friday at 10, 10:30, 11, 1, 1:30 or occasionally at other times by special arrangement. One gallery must be chosen from those described below, and preparation is suggested. Teachers conducting their own tours must reserve the desired gallery for after noon from Tuesday to Friday. Appointments for class reservations are made by phone in mid-September for the fall, and in mid-December for January through the end of the school year. Call Tuesday to Friday between 9 and 4.

Cost: Adults, $3; senior citizens and students, $1.50; children 6 and under, free. Membership offers free admission, lectures, newsletters, a magazine, gallery talks, special events and shop discounts. There's a charge for all tours led by museum teachers: $35 for groups from Philadelphia and within Pennsylvania; $45 for groups from out-of-state.

Lunch: The Museum Cafe offers a wide variety of international hot and cold foods at reasonable prices.

SEPTA: Buses 21, 30, 40, 42, 90.

Other: The Pyramid Shop is especially for children and school groups. The Museum Shop carries distinctive museum replicas, jewelry, crafts, books and unusual gift items.

E & D: You can avoid steps by entering from a driveway on the east side of the museum's new wing. Elevators connect all floors, and there is complete wheelchair access. Group tours for senior citizens and the handicapped are free and scheduled as noted above. The 33rd Street driveway entrance permits direct access to the museum's auditorium for special programs. Call ahead to make sure it will be open.

You can wander through thousands of years of history simply by exploring the primitive art and artifacts at the University Museum of the University of Pennsylvania. Many of the museum's relics have come from the almost 300 archaeological expeditions the museum has participated in since 1889. Among its most recent acquisitions is Jordan's Bicentennial gift, an ancient Roman column excavated from the ruins of the Jordanian city of Jerash. Annual special exhibitions bring treasures from around the world.

Choose your scheduled group gallery tour from any of the following areas: the ancient civilizations of Egypt, Mesopotamia, Greece, Rome, a combination of Greece and Rome, Palestine or General Archaeology; Africa, Oceania, Plains Indians or Woodland Indians; Buddhism, Diversity of a Great Tradition; or the culture of the Aztec, Maya, and Inca tribes.

Whether you're with a group tour or on your own, these exhibits give you a fairly good idea about man's daily existence in civilizations that go back thousands of years. Tools and weapons used by North American Indians as long as 3,000 years ago are on display, as well as African fetishes, masks and ceremonial objects.

There's a sphinx and Egyptian mummies from 2490 B.C., give or take a few years. You can "dig" through nine layers of Biblical civilizations from a "tell" that has been excavated at Gibeon near Jerusalem. And don't miss seeing the 2,000 objects (give or take a few) in the museum's Polynesia exhibition.

The museum's film programs are described later in this chapter, and its concerts are described in Chapter 10. Read about the museum's tours "to go" in Chapter 13, and its special programs for children in Chapter 15. And ask at the Information Desk when you enter for a museum floor plan and a schedule of the day's events at the University Museum. It's nice to combine a special program with your visit to the museum.

WOODMERE ART MUSEUM
9201 Germantown Avenue—19118
247–0476

Hours: Tuesday to Saturday, 10 to 5; Sunday, 2 to 5. Closed holidays. Allow 45 minutes for group tours.
Tours: Call at least 2 weeks in advance to schedule groups of up to 45. At least 2 adults must accompany children's groups. All groups should call ahead, and children under 14 must be with an adult.
Cost: Free.
SEPTA: Bus L. There's plenty of parking within the grounds.
Other: A gift shop (closed August through Labor Day) offers unique art objects, books, jewelry and novelty items.
E & D: Visitors in wheelchairs should call ahead. There's access to the main gallery and the upper level exhibits. Depending on the exhibit, gallery talks and tours can sometimes be planned especially for small groups of blind visitors allowing them to handle the works of art.

For 50 years, Woodmere has been showing fine 19th century paintings, sculpture, tapestries, Oriental rugs, Japanese ivories, vases, Meissen, porcelain and other objects of art from the valuable collections of the late Charles Knox Smith.

The original house was Smith's grand residence. You'll be a guest in the magnificent salon and dining room, with their priceless furnishings. Smith's collection was so large that selections are changed frequently.

With its spacious "new" wing, Woodmere is truly a

full-scale museum.

Special exhibitions every eight weeks feature artists from the Delaware Valley region. Plan your visit when you can see a special exhibit as well as the permanent collections. Call for a schedule.

Art classes are offered for children and adults in the spring and fall, and there are summer classes for children.

Woodmere also presents an annual concert series: Music at an Exhibition. A series of four performances take place weekend evenings in Woodmere's Kuch Gallery, followed by a reception with the musicians. Call for details on these unique opportunities.

Movie Theaters

Movie Theaters—Center City, Society Hill and University City—for first-run feature presentations, foreign films and occasional early afternoon specials.

AMC Midtown 2 1412 Chestnut Street, 567-7021.

AMC Olde City 2 Sansom Street Walkway between Front and 2nd Streets, 627-5966.

AMC Palace 1812 Chestnut Street, 496-0222.

AMC Walnut Mall 3 3925 Walnut Street, 222-2344.

Eric Rittenhouse 3 1907–1911 Walnut Street, 567-0320.

Eric 3 on Campus 40th and Walnut Streets, 382-0296.

Eric's Place 1519 Chestnut Street, 563-3086.

Ritz Five 214 Walnut Street, 925-7900. Frequent foreign films and "Movies to Talk About." Call 440-1183, noon to 10 P.M., to order tickets in advance with Visa or Mastercard for both Ritz theaters. Call at least 3 hours before showtime and up to 2 weeks ahead.

Ritz at the Bourse 4th Street north of Chestnut Street, 925-7900. More foreign films and "Movies to Talk About" on 5 screens.

Sameric 4 1908 Chestnut Street, 567-0604.

Sam's Place I and II 19th and Chestnut Streets, 972-0538.

United Artists Delaware Avenue and Dickinson Street at Riverview Plaza. 9 screens wth 2,500 seats, opening fall 1991.

Alternative Movie Theaters

Commercial movie theaters aren't the only places to go to see films in Philadelphia. Many of Philadelphia's cultural and civic centers show full-length feature films and shorts on a variety of subjects throughout the year.

In many instances, they're free. And you'll be able to see excellent films that the regular movie houses don't show.

So forget about the popcorn (or bring your own if you can't see a film without it) and take advantage of a continuous festival of fine films.

If you're a film buff, keep an eye out for announcements from area colleges, community centers, churches, synagogues, shopping centers and local gathering places that present occasional programs for young people and adults.

FILM FORUM/Philadelphia
509 S. Broad Street at Lombard—19147
732-7704 or (609) 854-3221

E & D: Complete wheelchair access.

FILM FORUM/Philadelphia is a club dedicated to the preservation and screening of classic foreign and American films. Their theater is the comfortable 125-seat auditorium of the contemporary Philadelphia Senior Center. Showtimes are Thursdays at 7:30 P.M. and Saturdays at 7 and 9:15 P.M.

Membership in FILM FORUM/Philadelphia is $10 annually and provides two free admissions, discounts to additional screenings and workshops and to most features at the Ritz Theaters, special events, and programs mailed to your home. Otherwise, general admission is $3.50; students and members pay $2.50.

Call for a preview of what's coming up and don't miss an opportunity to catch some of the great vintage films.

FREE LIBRARY OF PHILADELPHIA*
Central Library on Logan Square, and at Branches
686-5322 for general information

The Free Library has free films. Seating is on a first come, first served basis. The programs and times vary with the branches. A schedule with all of the library's programs is available monthly.

Pictures for a Sunday Afternoon (check the dates) are at 2 in Montgomery Auditorium at the Central Library. There are also occasional matinee and evening programs with a theme at the Central Library as well as many of the branch libraries. These might include a series of musicals, films by women, black filmmakers, foreign flicks or travel adventures.

The Free Libraries' films for children are described in Chapter 15. The Free Library also offers films "to go." See Chapter 13.

GEOGRAPHICAL SOCIETY OF PHILADELPHIA
563-0127

You probably yearn to see some far-off and exotic places, but you won't be able to swing it this year. So go by way of some beautiful and exciting travel films with live narration by professional film producers. Where would you like to go? London? Paris? The Orient? Australia? Or Africa?

The Geographical Society of Philadelphia conducts a series of travel lecture films at the Academy of Music*, 10 Wednesday evenings at 7:45 from October to April. Sometimes tickets are available for solo adventures at $7.

These armchair excursions are otherwise open to members only, who pay $50 dues annually. Membership entitles you to purchase additional tickets for guests, use the Society's extensive travel library, and take advantage of trips planned by the Society to places of historic, geographic and scenic interest around the world.

For information, call or write the Geographical Society of Philadelphia, Suite 909, 21 S. 12th Street, Phila., PA 19107.

NEIGHBORHOOD FILM/VIDEO PROJECT OF INTERNATIONAL HOUSE*
Hopkinson Hall
3701 Chestnut Street—19104
895-6542

An annual series brings American and foreign films, along with visiting filmmakers, to the International House. They could be premieres, classics, documentaries or experimental. The season is from September to April.

The program breaks when the semester breaks at the nearby University of Pennsylvania. It resumes again in June and July.

Showtimes are evenings at 7:30 and occasional weekend matinees. Tickets are $5 for adults, $4 for senior citizens and students, $2 for children under 12. A series pass is available for five films. There are group rates for 10 or more who call a few days ahead for reservations.

Programs for these outstanding Neighborhood Film/ Video Project series are available in advance. Or watch for listings in the neighborhood movie directory of the daily newspaper.

PENNSYLVANIA ACADEMY OF THE FINE ARTS*
Broad and Cherry Streets
972–7608 (Education Department)

Films at the Pennsylvania Academy of the Fine Arts are selected for screening because of their relationship with the current exhibition. That connection, however, is sometimes remote.

It's a nice chance to see a classic American or foreign film and a good art show in one afternoon for the price of admission to the museum. Showtime is an occasional Sunday afternoon at 3 P.M. in the museum's Hamilton Auditorium. Call ahead for a schedule.

PHILADELPHIA MUSEUM OF ART*
Van Pelt Auditorium
26th and Benjamin Franklin Parkway
763–8100 Ext. 281 or 787–5455

The museum's Division of Education features an occasional film series or films in conjunction with current art exhibitions. They're on Friday, Saturday or Sunday afternoons. Call or write (P.O. Box 7646, Phila., PA 19101) for information about upcoming events.

ROXY SCREENING ROOMS 1 & 2
2021 Sansom Street—19103
561–0115 or 561–0114 (recorded schedule)

E & D: Complete wheelchair access. Call ahead for assistance from theater staff.

Philadelphia's smallest commercial movie houses both have 137 comfortable seats. They screen foreign and

American repertory films and first-run films that generally don't reach Philadelphia audiences. There are occasional retrospectives and film festivals as well as revivals.

Admission to either Roxy is $5.50, or $3.50 for senior citizens or for the very first matinee performance daily. Programs are available each season, or consult the daily newspaper's movie directory.

TEMPLE CINEMATHEQUE
1619 Walnut Street—19103
787–1529 (recording of schedule)
787–4372 (to receive calendar)

E & D: Complete wheelchair access.

The Temple Cinematheque provides film buffs with a rare opportunity to view formerly lost, sometimes forgotten and rarely seen movies. It's located at the center city campus of Temple University, otherwise known as TUCC.

During the school year, showtime is 7:30 P.M. on Monday to Thursday; 7 and 9:15 P.M. on Friday and Saturday, but never on Sunday. The screening rooms are 501 and 505 on the fifth floor. Be there in plenty of time to get a seat for a film you might otherwise never get to see. During June, July and August there are performances every night at 7 and 9:15. The box office opens a half-hour before each performance.

The Temple University Film Society is a club whose members perpetuate the preservation of one-of-a-kind remaining and hard-to-find films. The Society meets on Tuesdays at 7:30 to view and discuss film classics. Join the club ($25 annually) and you'll contribute to that worthwhile cause. You'll also get four free admissions to the Cinematheque, reduced prices for all other admissions, discounts to workshops and film lectures, Cinematheque calendars and program notes.

Tickets to the Cinematheque are $4. Film society members, senior citizens and students with ID pay $3.

Pick up a film schedule at TUCC's Information Desk, or call to find out what's "in the can."

UNIVERSITY MUSEUM*
33rd and Spruce Streets—19104
898–4015 or 222–7777 (recorded schedule)

The film programs at the University Museum are free with museum admission and they're fun. An annual program is available in September by sending a long, self-addressed stamped envelope to the Museum's Education Section. Specify whether it's for children or adults. (The museum's film programs for children are described in Chapter 15.)

An Adult Entertainment Program features full-length motion pictures on Sunday afternoons from October through March at 2 P.M. These films are about anthropology, archaeology and classic dramas. Children attending these shows must be with an adult.

What other opportunities are there for viewing films of special interest? Several.

EXPLORATORY CINEMA AT ANNENBERG*, 3680 Walnut Street at the University of Pennsylvania, offers a rare chance to see classic and contemporary documentaries, features and short subjects from around the world. Most of the films that are shown are produced independently. They're shown weekday evenings during the academic year. Call 898–7041 for a schedule that's available in the fall.

The Gershman YM & YWHA Arts Council, 401 S. Broad Street at Pine, has presented since 1980 a popular annual **JEWISH FILM FESTIVAL**. The films are from around the world but all relate to Jewish experience in culture, history or heritage. Most are premieres for the Philadelphia area. Six films are presented from November to April each year and you can subscribe to the series or attend single screenings. The 8 P.M. Saturday presentation includes a noted actor or actress, film critic or educator to discuss the movie. The same film is shown again the following Sunday at 3 P.M. Call 545–4400 Ext. 241 for ticket and schedule information.

The **NATIONAL MUSEUM OF AMERICAN JEWISH HISTORY*** houses the Ralph Lopatin Film Library. Films are chosen from its vast and noteworthy collection on Jewish tradition and history for a January film festival and other screenings throughout the year. Private group screenings and discussion programs can also be arranged. Call 923–3811 to get their schedule or to make your own schedule.

The **PHILADELPHIA INTERNATIONAL FILM FESTIVAL**, founded in 1978, takes place during the last week of July. PhilaFilm screenings, for four consecutive days from noon through evening, are at the 180-seat theater of the Federal Reserve Bank of Philadelphia at 100 N. 6th Street and other theaters in the center city area. Here, too, is a chance to see independently produced full-length and short films and videos that you won't often get to see elsewhere.

The festival focuses on a new theme each year related to a timely social or human issue or an aspect of the film industry. Admission to programs at the Federal Reserve Bank is free. Call 977–2831 for details or look for newspaper announcements of the PhilaFilm schedule.

Street Art

There's so much sculpture outdoors in Philadelphia that the city's Fairmount Park Art Association has published a thick photo book entitled "Sculpture of a City," as well as an abbreviated paperbound edition called "Philadelphia's Treasures in Bronze and Stone."

The proliferation is partly due to a trend in major cities towards placing monumental contemporary works in public, outdoor places.

In Philadelphia, it's also due to an ordinance that requires one percent of costs for any municipal construction project be spent on artistic embellishment. These works must be approved by the Philadelphia Art Commission prior to purchase and installation.

The city's Redevelopment Authority has a similar requirement. The Authority has the right of eminent domain to acquire blighted land, then clear, package and sell it for public or private redevelopment. The purchasers of this land must agree to spend no less than one percent of their total construction cost for fine arts. In this case, the artwork must be approved by the Redevelopment Authority's Fine Arts Committee.

We're also lucky in Philadelphia because we're a regional district headquarters for the Federal government, and the General Services Administration has a policy requiring that three-eighths of one percent of total construction costs must be devoted to fine arts on new Federal buildings. That gives us even more street art.

These art requirements can be met with murals, mosaics, frescoes, stained glass, bas reliefs, tapestries or ornamental fountains. In the past few years, the definition of public art has expanded to include works involving the whole environment, such as landscape design, historic preservation and architectural restoration. The most popular and traditional, though, is statuary. I call it "Street Art" because most of it is outdoors.

The following list is restricted to works created since 1950. (A few exceptions are noted.) It's about sculpture and some works in other mediums that you'll come upon while walking in center city Philadelphia or visiting attractions that are described in this book. It also includes a few major pieces that are inside public buildings, but at least partially visible from the street.

The works are listed by their locations—from Old City to Society Hill and heading west to the Independence Mall area, Washington Square, around City Hall and Penn Center, the Benjamin Franklin Parkway, Franklin Town and University City. Sports fans will want to see the bigger-than-life sculptures outside Veterans Stadium* and the Spectrum*.

The site is followed by the artist's name, the year of installation (often a year or two after its completion) and the title of the work.

Delaware Avenue Piers 3 and 5
Residences at Pier Five
Andrew Leicester, 1990
"Riverwalk at
  Piers 3 and 5"

444 N. 3rd Street
Fred Fisher, 1980
Abstract metal sculpture

2nd and Locust Streets
Society Hill Towers Plaza
Leonard Baskin, 1965
"Young Man, Old Man, and
  the Future"

3rd and Locust Streets
Society Hill Townhouses
  Courtyard
Gaston Lachaise, 1963
  (sculpted 1927)
"Floating Figure"

210–212 Delancey Street
Harold Kimmelman, 1970
"Butterfly"

2nd and Pine Streets
Stamper-Blackwell Court
Margaret Wasserman Levy,
  1969
"Mustang at Play"

**Delancey Street
  between 3rd and 4th**
Delancey Park*
Sherl Joseph Winter, 1966
"Three Bears"

**North of Pine Street
  between 4th and 5th**
Lawrence Court
Harold Kimmelman, 1970
"Kangaroos"

4th and Willings Alley
Bingham Court
Richard Lieberman, 1970
"Unity"

330 Market Street
Royal Insurance Building
  (lobby)
George Persak, 1974
"Symbol of '76"

5th and Chestnut Streets
Independence National
  Historical Park
EvAngelos Frudakis, 1982
"The Signer"

**5th and Christ Church
  Walkway**
National Museum of
  American Jewish History*
Christopher Ray, 1976
"The Seed" (iron relief
  panel)

5th and Market Streets
CoreStates Plaza Building
Robinson Fredenthal, 1977
"White Water"
Joseph Bailey, 1977
"Gift of the Winds"

6th and Market Streets
Rohm and Haas Building
Clark Fitzgerald, 1965
"Milkweed Pod"

**Monument Plaza, 6th
  Street at Benjamin
  Franklin Bridge**
Isamu Noguchi, 1984
"Bolt of Lightning...A
  Memorial to Benjamin
  Franklin"

5th and Race Streets
Barbara Hepworth, 1980
"Rock Form"

6th and Race Streets
WHYY
Harold Lehr, 1976
"Clouds"
Eric Parks, 1976
"American Song"

6th and Arch Streets
Beverly Pepper, 1977
"Phaedrus"
Federal Reserve Bank*
East Courtyard
Alexander Calder, 1976
"White Cascade" (mobile)

6th and Market Streets
U.S. Courthouse*
David von Schlegell, 1977
"Voyage of Ulysses"
fountain
Louise Nevelson, 1976
"Bicentennial Dawn" (lobby)

7th and Race Streets
Police Administration Bldg.
Charles Parks, 1977
"Policeman Holding Small
Child"

7th and Arch Streets
Afro-American Historical
and Cultural Museum*
John Rhoden, 1976
"Nesaika"

615 Chestnut Street
One Independence Mall
George Segal, 1981
"Woman Looking Through
A Window"

6th and Walnut Streets
The Curtis Center
Tiffany Studios, directed by
Louis Comfort Tiffany,
1914–1916
"The Dream Garden" (glass
mosaic)

**7th and Washington
Square**
Hopkinson House
Oskar Stonorov and Jorio
Vivarelli, 1963
"Adam and Eve"

7th and Delancey Streets
McCall School Playground
Joseph J. Greenberg, Jr.,
1966
"The Bear"

9th and Market Streets
Market East—The Gallery
Harold Kimmelman, 1977
"Burst of Joy" (interior and
exterior)

900 block Locust Street
9th and Walnut Streets
Wills Eye Hospital
(entrance)
George Sugarman, 1981
90-foot grouping of free-
standing wall sculptures

9th and Walnut Streets
Brower Hatcher, 1990
"Starman in an Ancient
Garden"

10th and Walnut Streets
Thomas Jefferson University
Henry Mitchell, 1975
"The Ox"

10th and Market Streets
Market East—Stern's
David Lee Brown, 1977
"Amity"
Charles Madden, 1977
200-color abstract tapestry
(between 3rd and 4th floors)

11th and Market Streets
Market East—Gallery II
J.C. Penney's concourse level
Larry Rivers, 1983
"Philadelphia Then and
Now"
Market East Commuter
Tunnel
David Beck, 1984
880-foot-long ceramic mural

11th and Market Streets
ARA Tower (lobby)
Ronald Bateman, 1985
Three murals
Walter Erlebacher, 1985
Two bronze odalesques
"The Dream Garden"

1234 Market Street
Robinson Fredenthal, 1973
Three metal sculptures
"Falling Water" (two
interior, one exterior)

**Broad and Delancey
Streets**
Herbert Bayer, 1977
"Horizons"

**Broad Street and
Kennedy Boulevard**
Joe Brown, 1981
"Benjamin Franklin,
Craftsman"

**15th and Kennedy
Boulevard**
Municipal Services Building
Plaza
Jacques Lipchitz, 1976
"Government of the People"

**15th and Kennedy
Boulevard**
John F. Kennedy Plaza
Robert Indiana, 1976
"LOVE"

Henry Moore, 1964
"Three-Way Piece,
Number 1: Points"

15th and Cherry Streets
Friends Center*
Sylvia Shaw Judson, 1975
"Mary Dyer" (Quaker
martyr)

**City Hall West/Dilworth
Plaza**
Emlen Etting, 1982
"Phoenix Rising"

1500 Market Street
Centre Square*
Claes Oldenburg, 1976
"Clothespin"
Jean DuBuffet, 1976
"Milord La Chamarre"
("Man With a Fancy
Vest")

**15th and South Penn
Square**
One Meridian Plaza
Robert M. Engman, 1974
"Triune"

**17th and Kennedy
Boulevard**
Penn Center Plaza
Concourse
Alexander Calder, 1964
"Three Disks: One Lacking"
Seymour Lipton, 1963
"Leviathan"

17th and Chestnut Streets
Chestnut Street Park
Christopher Ray, 1980
"Wissahickon Valley Gates"

226

17th and Locust Streets
J. Seward Johnson, Jr., 1985
"Allow Me" ("Man with an
  Umbrella")

**210 W. Rittenhouse
  Square**
The Rittenhouse
EvAngelos Frudakis, 1989
"Welcome" (Lady with a
  Rose)
Michael Webb, 1989
"Fairmount Park"
mural (lobby Tea Garden)

**226 W. Rittenhouse
  Square**
The Dorchester
Arlene Love, 1988
"Winged Woman"

2300 Chestnut Street
Richard Haas, 1984
Trompe l'oeil wall painting
"William Penn, Ben
  Franklin, the B & O
  Railroad..."

**16th and Benjamin
  Franklin Parkway**
Jacob Lipkin, 1966
"The Prophet"

**16th and Benjamin
  Franklin Parkway**
Isaac D. Levy Memorial
  Park
Nathan Rapoport, 1964
"Monument to the Six
  Million Jewish Martyrs"

**17th and Benjamin
  Franklin Parkway**
Oskar Stonorov and Jorio
  Vivarelli, 1963
"The Tuscan Girl" fountain

**18th and Benjamin
  Franklin Parkway**
Cathedral of SS. Peter and
  Paul*
Walter Erlebacher, 1977
"Jesus Breaking Bread"

**19th and Benjamin
  Franklin Parkway**
Academy of Natural
  Sciences
Kent Ullberg, 1987
"Deinonychus"

**20th and Benjamin
  Franklin Parkway**
Youth Study Center Lawn
Walter Raemisch, 1955
"The Great Mother"
"The Great Doctor"

**17th and Callowhill
  Streets**
One Franklin Town
  Apartments
Nam June Paik, 1990
"Video Arbor"

**18th and Spring Garden
  Streets**
Museum Towers
Albert Paley, 1987
"Synergy"

20th and Hamilton Streets
Korman Suites at
Buttonwood Square (rooftop)
Stephen Antonakos, 1990
"Neons for Buttonwood"

**25th Street, foot of North
  Drive to Art Museum**
Khoren Der Harootian, 1976
"Meher"

The contemporary sculptors, representing a sampling of works outdoors around the Philadelphia Museum of Art*, include Jacob Epstein, Jacques Lipchitz and Louise Nevelson.

Continuing along Kelly Drive, you'll find dozens of statues. William Zorach's "Puma" reposes in the Azalea Garden*. The Ellen Phillips Samuel Memorial Sculpture Garden*, with works by 16 artists, is just a short distance west of Boat House Row and before you get to the Girard Avenue Bridge.

If you get to University City, look for the following:

34th and Civic Center Blvd.
Civic Center Plaza
Harry Bertoia, 1967
"Fountain Sculpture"

3500 Market Street
Monell Chemical Senses
Center
Arlene Love, 1975
"Face Fragment"

35th and Market Streets
University City Science
Center
(lobby mural)
Jennifer Bartlett, 1981
"In the Garden"

3600 Market Street
University City Science
Center
James Carpenter, 1989
"Refractive Light Spine"

3624 Market Street
University City Science
Center
James Lloyd, 1974
Untitled 14-foot fiberglas work
on granite base that
rotates periodically to
show revolution and change
Edith Neff, 1976
Untitled mural depicting life
in West Philadelphia (lobby)

34th and Walnut Streets
University of Pennsylvania
Claes Oldenburg, 1981
"Split Button"

34th and Spruce Streets
University of Pennsylvania
Chemistry Building (lobby)
Robert M. Engman, 1977
"After Invengar"

34th Street and Locust Walk
University of Pennsylvania
Alexander Calder, 1979
"Jerusalem Stabile"

36th Street and Locust Walk
University of Pennsylvania
Tony Smith, 1975
"We Lost"

**37th Street between Spruce
and Locust Walk**
University of Pennsylvania
George Lundeen, 1987
"Benjamin Franklin"
(see front cover)

33rd and Market Streets
Drexel University
Henry Mitchell, 1975
"Running Free"
George Rickey, 1985
"Two Open Triangles
    Leaning Gyratory"
(3rd floor parapet of library)

3700 Market Street
Founders Plaza
Timothy Duffield, 1976
"Dream of Sky"

3680 Walnut Street
Annenberg Center (lobbies)
Contemporary works by
    Harry Bertoia,
    Jose de Rivera,
    Michael Langenstein,
    Seymour Lipton,
    Sam Maitin

**39th Street and Locust
    Walk**
University of Pennsylvania
Alexander Liberman, 1975
"Covenant"

51 North 39th Street
Scheie Eye Institute
Christopher Ray, 1975
"Phoenix Tree"

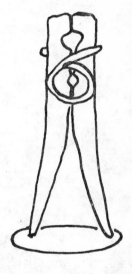

At the **Sports Complex** in South Philadelphia, look for
sculptor Joe Brown's two "Football Players" and two "Baseball Players" outside gates B, C, E and H of **Veterans Stadium**. On the south side of the **Spectrum** is Gilman B.
Whitman's hockey player in "Goal," portraying Gary Dorn-
hoefer's overtime score against Minnesota in 1973. "Kate
Smith" is by Marc Mellon and installed in 1987.

On the Spectrum's north side, movie boxing hero "Rocky
Balboa" was cast in bronze by A. Thomas Schomberg and installed late in 1982. "Julius 'Dr.J.' Irving—Athlete, Sports-
man, Gentleman" is by sculptor Barney Bright.

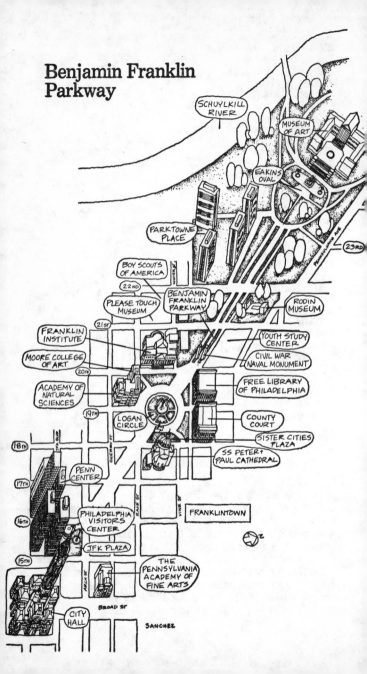

Chapter 10
The Performing Arts.

As we continue in the arts, this chapter tells you about arts where there's action. It's about performances alive with sound and movement in dance, music and theater. Additional programs for children are described in Chapter 15.

Setting the Stage

Some of the names and facilities have already appeared in the preceding chapter, and you'll come across them repeatedly in this chapter. That's because many galleries and theaters cater to more than one of the arts. And many of the performing arts companies can be enjoyed at a variety of locations. The following are some of the most popular. Spend some time in Philadelphia and you'll be familiar with them.

E & D: See Chapter 16 for additional information.

The **ACADEMY OF MUSIC** at Broad and Locust Streets (893–1930), home of the Philadelphia Orchestra*, is also a stage for other musical programs, opera, dance and film events. You can also tour the Academy (see Chapter 13). The Academy seats almost 3,000 in the orchestra pit, parquet, parquet circle, balcony, family circle and amphitheater.

The **ALL STAR-FORUM**, under the direction of Philadelphia impresario Moe Septee, brings concerts, dance and theater in individual performances and series to the Academy of Music. The Forum's offices are at 1521 Locust Street, Phila., PA 19102 (735-7506).

Every summer, the **CITY OF PHILADELPHIA Department of Recreation** sponsors cultural events that are scheduled during the day and evenings at several locations throughout the city.

Among the hundreds of happenings are the Mummers String Band concerts at the Mummers Museum on Tuesday evenings, and programs Wednesday evenings at Rittenhouse Square, Pastorius Park and Pennypack Park. The schedules include opera, Gospelrama, barbershop singers, dixieland bands, folk and rock concerts, theater and dance. There are series at parks and recreation centers throughout Philadelphia.

There isn't any charge to attend these performances, and one of the series will be convenient for you.

Most events with a constant schedule are included in Chapters 9 and 10. They're also announced in the Philadelphia newspapers. You can get additional information by calling the Mayor's Office for Information (686–2250) or the Department of Recreation (685–0151).

The CITY OF PHILADELPHIA Department of Recreation also has programs where young people and adults can join in workshops, classes and performances of their own. The activities during the fall and winter include ballet, ceramics, dramatics, folk dancing, music, painting, paper-mache and sketching.

Many of these programs continue during the spring and summer along with arts and crafts, bands, contemporary music, dramatics, harmonica and guitar lessons. The city also has outstanding cultural summer camps*.

For more information about these programs, call the Philadelphia Department of Recreation, 685–0151. And don't forget about all the special events that happen annually in Philadelphia. They're included in Chapter 19.

The **FREE LIBRARY OF PHILADELPHIA** at Logan Square is more than a place for books (see Chapter 11). It's a showplace for literary exhibits, films, the performing arts, story hours and whatever else those clever people can schedule for their auditorium. Several of these events are described elsewhere in this book. Refer to the Index.

You've already read in the previous chapter about the Neighborhood Film/Video Project at **INTERNATIONAL HOUSE**, 3701 Chestnut Street. Performing arts events here at the 500-seat Hopkinson Hall are brought to you year-round by the **Folklife Center**. Music and dance programs feature traditional ethnic talents from the Delaware Valley and around the world. Concerts are usually in the evenings with occasional weekend matinee workshops. For times and more information, call 387–5125.

MOVEMENT THEATRE INTERNATIONAL moved into Philadelphia in 1987. Their stage is as creative and clever as their performances. The venerable

Tabernacle Church edifice, across from International House at 3700 Chestnut Street, was built in 1884. More than a century later, MTI converted the building to use as a 300-seat center for performing arts. It's called **MTI Tabernacle Theater.**

What is movement theater? Anything that depends on motion: cabaret, clowning, dance, mime, puppetry, vaudeville, or any combinations thereof that might also include music, film, video and other surprises.

MTI imports artists from around the world, as well as staging local talent. Their shows are fun, inventive and exploding with rhythm and movement. Each month from September through April brings a five day, Wednesday to Sunday run. A biennial week-long Spring Festival accompanied by a month of master classes happens in June of "odd" years. This is a terrific opportunity to learn first-hand from international performers making a local visit.

Tickets for MTI shows start at $10.50 for members and $15 for non-members. Group rates are available in advance for 10 or more. Subscribe to three or more shows and you automatically become an MTI member with discount benefits, special invitations to meet the artists and other privileges.

Make your move now and call 382–0606 for a schedule.

SEPTA: Buses 21, 40; trolleys 11, 13, 34, 36 to 36th and Sansom Streets.

The **PAINTED BRIDE ART CENTER**, founded on a shoestring in 1969, has come of age and prospers at 230 Vine Street in Old City*. By day, the Painted Bride is an art gallery for month-long shows by area painters and sculptors. Gallery hours are Tuesday to Friday, 12 to 6, and Saturday, 2 to 6. At night it transforms into a 200-seat theater for seasoned and budding talent from the Philadelphia area or around the world to recite poetry, dance, sing, act, mime, do puppetry or give unique musical performances. More than 175 events and exhibits, sometimes off-beat and always fun, are presented each year. You'll want to bring the whole family to at least a few. The theater is casual and comfortable.

Most performances at the Painted Bride are Friday, Saturday and Sunday evenings at 8. Admission is usually $10 or $12. Members receive a discount on all tickets, invitations to special events and a newsletter with full calendar of activities. Subscriptions are available for a five-event series in theater/performance arts, dance or music. Or, you can subscribe to a combination series, mini-series of three Saturday night programs, or a super subscription of all 15 series events (at considerable savings). With a subscription, tickets for any show cost less than $10. Discounts are available to groups making reservations at least a week in advance. Tickets are also available from UPSTAGES, described in the next part of this chapter, "Getting Tickets." Watch the local newspapers, or call 925–9914 for a schedule.

SEPTA: Buses 5, 17, 33, 48, Ben FrankLine route 76; mid-way between the 2nd and Market Streets and Spring Garden Street stations of Market-Frankford Subway-Elevated train.

The **SHUBERT THEATER** at 250 S. Broad Street belongs to the University of the Arts*. It accommodates an audience of almost 2,000 in the orchestra, balcony and family circle. To find out what's appearing, watch the theater announcements in the local newspapers, or call the box office at 732–5446.

THEATRE OF THE LIVING ARTS at 334 South Street is an unusual, intimate 400-seat theater environment for musical acts of national acclaim. One or two-night stands bring jazz, folk and alternative musicians to Philadelphia's liveliest nightlife locale. This is where you might hear the likes of the Eric Burdon Band, the Mighty Lemon Drops or jazz performer Pat Metheney. What else would you expect from a theater that's in the heart of South Street? Tickets are from $15.50 to $22.50. Watch for newspaper announcements or call 922–1011 to find out who's booked.

You can count on the **Y ARTS COUNCIL** to bring to Philadelphians whatever is new and outstanding in films, chamber music, poetry readings and literature programs. Their stage for the performing arts is primarily the auditorium of the Gershman YM & YWHA at 401 S. Broad Street, Phila., PA 19147. The Borowsky Gallery for innovative artwork occupies a part of the first floor here. Arts Council events are usually scheduled from October to May. (The Jewish Film Festival is described in Chapter 9.) You can subscribe for the year, or purchase tickets for individual programs. Call 545–4400 for details.

ANNENBERG CENTER, the **FORREST THEATER** and the **WALNUT STREET THEATER** are described later in this chapter.

Getting Tickets

You can get tickets for the performing arts by subscription or for individual shows, directly from each company or its box office.

An alliance of three arts groups invites you to purchase tickets in advance from one location for any of their performances. **INNOVATION ARTS** includes **Relache, Wilma Theater** and **Zero Moving Dance Company**. All are described later in this chapter. Their combined box office is at 2040 Sansom Street (the Wilma Theater), 963–0345. If you subscribe to any one of the companies, you're entitled to discounts at the others.

Another alliance of performing arts companies has a box office at the Philadelphia Visitors Center* at 1525 John F. Kennedy Boulevard. **UPSTAGES** provides ticket service and information for performances by **American Music Theater Festival, Arden Theatre Company**, the **Painted Bride Art Center** and the **Philadelphia Singers**. Here, too, if you subscribe to one of the companies, discounts are offered to performances by the others. UpStages is open Tuesday to Saturday, 10 A.M. to 5 P.M. Call 567–0670 for 24-hour information.

Ticketmaster offers charge-by-phone for tickets to major concerts and family and sports events at the Civic Center and the Spectrum. Call the Talking Yellow Pages (on a touchtone phone) at 337–7777 Ext. 9258 to hear what's coming up. Call 336–2000 to order your tickets.

Ticketron is a computerized telephone ticket service that sells seats for sports events (Eagles, Phillies and 76ers games) as well as concerts and shows at most area theaters. Their information hotline number is 885–2515. To order tickets, call 800–233–4050.

Dance

Philadelphians are rising to their feet.

The local dance world is no longer dominated by a single ballet company. Several dance troupes have arisen in recent years and are being welcomed by growing audiences. The troupes represent diverse styles and goals, and they provide an opportunity for Philadelphians to attend traditional ballet, modern, improvisational, ethnic and young people's performances. Many of them will bring their performances directly to you (see Chapter 13).

In 1971 the **PHILADELPHIA DANCE ALLIANCE** formed an association of "smaller" companies dedicated to promoting dance in the Philadelphia area. Today its ranks have grown to more than 170 professional dance troupes and schools, from the most prominent to the small and up-and-coming. Dance students and devotees of dance are welcome to join.

Members of the Dance Alliance receive a monthly newsletter announcing public workshops, ticket specials, a professional "dance calendar" and general information.

National Dance Week is celebrated locally at the end of April. Watch for announcements of the special events. The Alliance also schedules occasional dance festivals at popular and convenient Philadelphia stage locales.

If you would like to know more about the Philadelphia Dance Alliance, contact them at 1315 Walnut Street, Suite 1500, Phila., PA 19107 (545–6344).

Several opportunities also exist for you to participate in the dance. So don't be a wallflower. And don't say no one ever asked you to dance.

CITY OF PHILADELPHIA DANCE PROGRAMS

The Philadelphia Department of Recreation has fall and winter classes in acrobatics, aerobics, ballet, jazz, modern and tap dancing for young people and adults. The best dancers are chosen to perform in a Spring Recital at a major performing arts center. A year-round children's program in conjunction with the Philadelphia Dance Alliance also takes place at sites throughout the city. Call 685-0151 to find out which dance classes would be the most convenient for you.

For those who would rather watch, semi-professional and professional dance companies perform in city-sponsored programs throughout the summer. Many of them are described elsewhere in this chapter.

DANCE CELEBRATION
898-6791 (Annenberg box office)
898-6683 (group sales)

Dance Celebration has been bringing Philadelphians the tops in contemporary dance since 1984. Performances are at Zellerbach Theater in the Annenberg Center*.

When we say tops, we mean the likes of Alvin Ailey, ISO & The Bobs, Merce Cunningham, Feld Ballet, Martha Graham, Bella Lewitsky, Jose Limon, Lar Lubovitch, Pilobolus and Twyla Tharp. Five companies visit for each year's Celebration, usually with a 7:30 P.M. Wednesday performance, 8 P.M. Thursday, Friday and Saturday, and a 2 P.M. Saturday matinee.

Tickets can be purchased for the series or, if you're lucky, for individual performances.

A New Dance Series of Dance Celebration introduces three new troupes to Philadelphians each year in one-night performances on Mondays.

FOLK DANCING

This is where the star dancing attraction is YOU. There are several places to go when you get the urge to dance. Try one of the following, or consult the dance listing of the weekend newspapers.

The **Folk Dancers at the Art Museum** do everything from the Virginia Reel to polkas, American ragtime and international tunes.

Would-be and seasoned dancers meet on Tuesdays at 8 P.M. from June through mid-October on the Art Museum Terrace at 26th and Benjamin Franklin Parkway. The action moves indoors to No. 1 Boat House Row (Plaisted Hall) on Kelly Drive on rainy summer nights. On Monday evenings from late October through April, they also meet at 8:15 P.M. at No. 1 Boat House Row. All of these dance sessions are sponsored by the city's Fairmount Park Commission.

The same group meets under auspices of the city's Department of Recreation on Thursdays at 8:15 P.M. from mid-October through April at the Water Tower Recreation Center, Hartwell Lane off of Germantown Avenue. (When the city celebrates a holiday, the dancers take the night off.)

No one judges your ability, but everyone is enthusiastic and has a good time. Some folks attend just to have an excuse to jump up and down. Bring a partner or come alone.

The word on these Folk Dancers is out, and people from all over the country mosey over to dosey-do when they're in this-here parts. There's circle dancing, line dancing, partner dances, no-partner dances and traditional square dances. Donations of $2 are requested to help defray the cost of records and sound equipment. Call 635–4295 if you have any questions.

The **Folk Dance Center of Philadelphia** meets for international folk dancing from September to June on Friday nights at the St. Michael's Lutheran Church, 6671 Germantown Avenue. Be there at 8 P.M. Admission is $1.50 for members and $2.50 for non-members.

Traditional dances are called, along with native folk dances of foreign countries. There's something for everyone, so stop by any evening. No partners are needed; it's mostly line and circle dancing. If you want to know more, call 624–4242 and ask for folk dance information.

The **Germantown Country Dancers** have been gathering since 1972. They dance at Calvary Episcopal Church, Pulaski and Manheim Streets, on the second and fourth Wednesday evening of every month, except August, from 8 to 10:30 P.M. You're welcome to join them on your own or with a partner, no matter what your skill is.

The Germantown Country Dancers are always learning new figures to English and American country dances done to live music. The fee is $3.50 per session, or you might decide to become a member.

Workshops, with guest callers, or country dance parties are held the first Saturday of each month. These are always fun, too. You can learn more about the Germantown Country Dancers by calling 247–5993, 283–0787 or 609–858-3385, or you can be one of the 25 to 50 enthusiasts who stop by at any of their gatherings.

If you would like to schedule a fully-costumed demonstration by the Germantown Country Dancers at your occasion, see Chapter 13.

For additional schedule information and notice of special events, and to learn about other opportunities for folk dancing in the area, contact the Folk Dance Council of the Delaware Valley, 7011 Sprague Street, Phila., PA 19119, or call them at 248-3521.

GROUP MOTION DANCE THEATER
928-1495

Group Motion is a modern, multi-media dance company that was founded in 1968. Their dance is highly improvisational, using innovative lighting and electronic music and requiring boundless energy. They present workshops, hold classes and perform at their studio (624 S. 4th Street) and at several other locations throughout the year.

Two series of programs are presented annually. The Visiting Artists Festival headlines out-of-town dancers and performers working in new techniques who come to Philadelphia for a week in the spring.

The Spiel Uhr Series presents emerging artists from the Philadelphia area one weekend a month from September through June.

All performances are at 8 P.M. and tickets are usually $8, or $6 for senior citizens and students. Call for a schedule or watch the newspaper for announcements.

PENNSYLVANIA BALLET COMPANY
551-7014

Philadelphia's resident ballet company since 1964 presents a season of new ballets, repertoire favorites and modern dance at the Academy of Music and the Shubert Theater from September to June. Christopher d'Amboise is artistic director.

You can attend single performances, or you can subscribe at discount rates (551-7000 Ext. 3035) to one of their varied series plans. Tickets for a single performance range from $10 in the amphitheater to $60 for a box seat. There are evening shows from Wednesday through Sunday and weekend matinees.

A once-a-year favorite for thousands of Philadelphians

is the Christmas performance of the "The Nutcracker" at the Academy of Music. Nearly 30 matinee and evening performances are given in the last two weeks of December. Children (and their parents) are known to return year after year.

Don't miss a chance to see a ballet company that is a major force in the local and national dance world.

PHILADELPHIA CIVIC BALLET COMPANY
564-1505

The Philadelphia Civic Ballet Company appears on prominent center city stages as well as going out to the community to entertain and introduce Philadelphians of all ages and all neighborhoods to the world of dance. Many of their performances are at area schools (see Chapter 13), and several throughout the year are available to the general public.

A dozen adults make up the P.C.B.C. Founded in 1955, this is a "veteran" among the local companies. They've appeared on television, in major theaters, at the Academy of Music, historic sites, playgrounds, parks and even in the streets. The Philadelphia Civic Ballet Company performs annually at the Free Library and at special events throughout the city and Delaware Valley.

PHILADELPHIA DANCE COMPANY
387-8200

The Philadelphia Dance Company, founded in 1970 by Joan Myers Brown, has a well-established reputation for exhilarating contemporary and modern dance.

Philadanco made a Lincoln Center debut in 1979, and has gone on to perform nationally at the Joyce Theater in New York, the 1986 Bermuda Arts Festival, the 1990 National Black Arts Festival in Atlanta, the 1990 and 1991 Houston International Festivals, Jacobs Pillow in Massachusetts, and the 1989 and 1990 Martin Luther King Celebrations in Atlanta.

Locally, Philadanco presents a May series of six concerts at Annenberg Theater, a December series of three concerts at Mandell Theater and an annual performance at Robin Hood Dell East*. Members of the company have appeared with the Philadelphia Orchestra, Young Audiences and a variety of programs hosted by the city. This is another dance company that goes into the neighborhoods for a full schedule of lectures and demonstrations at schools and recreation centers (see Chapter 13).

Call or check the newspapers for the Philadelphia Dance Company's next performance.

ZERO MOVING DANCE COMPANY
243-0260

ZeroMoving Dance Company was founded in 1972 by Hellmut Gottschild. Karen Bamonte is currently artistic director of the ten-member dance ensemble. Together, and independently, they both choreograph and dance in ZeroMoving performances. The quality and ingenuity of ZeroMoving's work has taken them on tour in recent years to Berlin, New York, San Francisco and as far as Eastern Europe.

Two major productions are done each year, the first week of December and a week in mid-April, each of five 8 P.M. shows from Wednesday to Sunday. Their stage is the MTI Tabernacle Theater*, 3700 Chestnut Street. The music is always live, and equally interesting. Single tickets are available for ZeroMoving, or you can subscribe to the series at a discount. And, you can get tickets to ZeroMoving from Innovation Arts described earlier in this chapter. Call for details.

Reminder: Other internationally-known dance companies appear in Philadelphia each year thanks to the ALL STAR-FORUM*. Call them (735-7506) to find out who will be here soon. These performances are usually at the Academy of Music.

Music

ALL STAR-FORUM
1521 Locust Street (office)—19102
735-7506

Every year between October and May, the All Star-Forum brings nine exciting concerts to the Academy of Music*, along with other special events. Most are at 8 P.M.; a few are Sunday matinees at 3 P.M.

Orchestras from Atlanta to Moscow have appeared. And stars like Isaac Stern, Itzhak Perlman, Christopher Parkening, Marcel Marceau, Robert Merrill, Roberta Peters, and Leontyne Price have also appeared.

The Great Performers Series enables you to choose six concerts in advance for preferred seats and savings. Subscriptions should be ordered by mail, or they can be charged by telephone. There may be tickets at the Academy of Music box office prior to a performance.

Special events are also scheduled by the All Star-Forum at the Academy. They might include such greats as James Galway, P.D.Q. Bach, Alvin Ailey American Dance Theatre or Judith Jamison.

CHORAL GROUPS

If you like vocal music, we've got it. You can either listen to it or participate in it.

The **CHORAL ARTS SOCIETY** was founded in 1982 under the direction of Sean Deibler. Members are carefully selected from the tri-state area; a third are professional musicians. They've grown to a 150-voice symphonic chorus that is recognized around the world. The Society's 1986 two-week European tour marked the first time a group of this kind performed in Warsaw, behind the Iron Curtain.

Back home, the Choral Arts Society performs at the Academy of Music and in its own subscription concert series at center city church locales. You can purchase tickets as a series or for individual concerts. Call 545–8634 for a schedule of performances and additional information.

The city's oldest mixed choral group, the **MENDELSSOHN CLUB OF PHILADELPHIA**, was founded in 1874. Alan Harler is their music director and conductor. Among the Club's 150 semi-professional singers are doctors, lawyers, teachers and housewives. They range in age from 17 to 75.

The Mendelssohn Club performs on various occasions throughout the year at the Academy of Music, churches and concert halls. Most of their selections are classical, many are major choral works that aren't often heard and some have been commissioned especially for them. The 35-voice **MENDELSSOHN SINGERS** are chosen from the Club to perform in chamber concerts. Call 735–9922 for audition or performance information.

PENNSYLVANIA PRO MUSICA, directed by Dr. Franklin Zimmerman, presents rarely heard music, especially from the Medieval, Renaissance and Baroque Periods, along with classics from the likes of Bartok, Beethoven and Mozart. Their repertoire comes into the 18th, 19th and 20th centuries as well.

The company varies with the programs. The concerts usually feature a chorale or solo singers, and they are often accompanied by a chamber orchestra. Occasionally, they're purely orchestral.

You can enjoy Pennsylvania Pro Musica at concerts in a fall or spring series or on special occasions throughout the year at the Church of the Holy Trinity on Rittenhouse Square or historic churches in Old Philadelphia. Tickets start at $10, with discounts for groups, students and senior citizens. For ticket and schedule information, call 222-4517.

The **PHILADELPHIA BOYS CHOIR AND CHORALE** sing at concerts and special events both in Philadelphia and around the world. Since their founding in 1968, they've travelled over a million miles and performed in 14 different languages on every major continent. Recently they've served as goodwill ambassadors in Israel and the Soviet Union. An annual Christmas and spring concert are on their busy schedule of some 40 concerts each year.

Dr. Robert G. Hamilton directs this highly acclaimed choir of 75 schoolboys from the ages of eight to 13. They're complemented with a young men's chorale of 25 voices.

Auditions are held throughout the year. If you know someone who would like to try out for this great opportunity, call 222-3500. If you'd like to see a choir that has performed for presidents and heads-of-state, call or watch the newspapers for concert announcements.

PHILADELPHIA SINGERS is a 30-voice all-professional chorus directed by Michael Korn. They perform from a repertoire of classical choral literature in a series from October to May at the Academy of Music or the Church of the Holy Trinity on Rittenhouse Square.

You can listen to them at home, too, since they've recently made a world premiere recording of Handel's "Roman Vespers" as well as "Christmas with the Philadelphia Singers and Benita Valente" and "Ceremonies of Carols with Benita Valente and Maureen Forrester," all on the RCA Red Seal label.

Tickets for the Philadelphia Singers can be ordered by phone, mail or picked up prior to each concert. (They're also available at UPSTAGES, the ticket service described at the beginning of this chapter.) Group, student and senior citizen discounts are available. Call 732-3370 for auditions, schedule and ticket details.

SINGING CITY, founded in 1948 by Dr. Elaine Brown who conducted them for 40 years, is a 100-voice group of talented amateurs now under direction of Graeme Cowen. They sing at community centers throughout the city and with the Philadelphia Orchestra at the Academy of Music. They've traveled as far as the Soviet Union to perform with the Leningrad Philharmonic and twice been to the Middle East to perform in Israel and Egypt. They'll capture your ear with a wide range of music from Hindu chants to Handel's "Messiah." Their music is as diverse as their membership. Call 561-3930 for schedule and ticket information.

CITY OF PHILADELPHIA
SUMMER MUSICAL PROGRAMS
685-0151

Thanks to the city's Department of Recreation, you have a choice of free musical events to attend almost every night of the summer. A few of the series are described later in this chapter. Here are some more.

They're all announced in the daily newspapers. If you prefer to plan ahead, the Department of Recreation can tell you the schedule for citywide locations so you can choose the programs according to your interest and the location.

Music comes to the Pennypack Park Festival, at Rhawn Street near Winchester Avenue, on 10 consecutive Thursdays at 8 P.M. from the last week in June. You'll enjoy symphony concerts, opera, a touch of dixieland, the big band sound, jazz or vocalists on any given warm summer night. Many of the same jazz and classical groups also appear at the eight Summer Evenings at Rittenhouse Square, 18th and Walnut Streets, Wednesdays at 8 P.M.

There's lots of music filling the air of lazy, hazy nights of summer. Call the Department of Recreation for other sites and schedules.

CONCERTO SOLOISTS
CHAMBER ORCHESTRA OF PHILADELPHIA
574-3550 (Walnut Street Theater)

Founded in 1964 under the direction of Marc Mostovoy, the Concerto Soloists offers an unusual opportunity to listen to distinguished chamber music. It's comprised of 15 strings and a harpsichord. Woodwinds, brass and percussion are added when necessary. Their name comes from the unusual practice of giving the performers a chance to play both solo and supporting roles.

Baroque and classical music are the Concerto Soloists' specialty, but it isn't the limit of their repertoire. They also play rarely heard music of the 19th and 20th centuries, and each year they premiere the work of a contemporary American composer.

Concerto Soloists presents two concert series. The Masterworks of Music Series is five concerts at the Walnut Street Theater on Mondays at 8 P.M. Marc Mostovoy or Max Rudolph conduct. The other is the Resident Artists' on the Square Series on five Sundays at 2:30 P.M. at the Church of the Holy Trinity on Rittenhouse Square. At these concerts the ensemble performs without a conductor and members are featured as soloists.

Tickets can be purchased in a choice of series plans (or individually before a concert when available) with reduced rates for students and senior citizens. Call for a schedule and the programs.

THE CURTIS INSTITUTE OF MUSIC*
1726 Locust Street—19103
893-7902
893-5261 (recording of program for upcoming concerts)

SEPTA: Buses 2, 9, 17, 21, 42, 90.
E & D: There are 8 steps at the 1726 entrance and then several more steps into Curtis Hall. If you enter directly into Curtis Hall at 1724 Locust Street, there are 2 low steps at the door and 3 steps into the auditorium. Call ahead and alert the security guard to assist and open the door at 1724.

This is a wonderful opportunity to hear the future great musical artists of the world because students from throughout the world come to Curtis to study virtually every musical instrument. Since its founding in 1924, the Curtis Institute of Music has trained nearly 3,000 musicians for concert performance. Students are given a strenuous audition and, once they're accepted, they receive the Institute's coveted free education.

Recitals in Curtis Hall include opera, chamber concerts, wind, percussion, piano and harp performances. They're at 8 P.M. on most Monday, Wednesday and Friday evenings from October to the first week of May, and there's no admission charge.

The Curtis Symphony Orchestra performs under the baton of world-famous conductors several times each year at the Academy of Music. Performances of the Opera Department are also popular productions among music lovers. There's a small charge, and tickets are required.

The Curtis schedule is available a month in advance. Call or stop in for information. Call 893-5261 to hear the program for the next scheduled concerts.

You're probably wondering who Curtis' famous graduates are. Well, among others they include Leonard Bernstein, Judith Blegen, Jorge Bolet, Gary Graffman, Eugene Istomin, Jaime Laredo, Gian Carlo Menotti, Anna Moffo, Peter Serkin and dozens of current members of the Philadelphia Orchestra.

MANN MUSIC CENTER
West Fairmount Park
George's Hill near 52nd Street and Parkside Avenue
567-0707

SEPTA: Buses 38, 40, 43, 85 and special Mann Music Center buses that go round-trip from center city. Call for schedule and route. There's plenty of free parking and special parking for Friends of the Mann Music Center.

Dinner: Bring a picnic and dine al fresco on the lawn before the concert. Refreshments are available at 2 food stands before each concert and during intermission.

E & D: Complete wheelchair access with rest rooms at ground level. An 8- by 130-foot ramp eliminates steep walking and steps. It goes from the top of the theater shell and parking areas directly into the balcony.

The **Philadelphia Orchestra** moves outdoors in summer. They've been making a joyful sound in Fairmount

Park since 1929. In 1976 they moved to the dramatic new Mann Music Center. Charles Dutoit was named Artistic Director and Principal Conductor in 1990.

The world's most popular guest conductors and soloists visit with the orchestra each season for 18 concerts in seven weeks. They begin the third week in June and continue on Monday, Wednesday and Thursday evenings at 8 P.M., except the week of July 4th.

Aficionados can take their choice between the "Starlight Terrace" of 4,599 free seats, or grassy slopes (bring a blanket and a picnic supper for before the concert). There's free seating for up to 10,000, but tickets are necessary. Coupons appear in The Inquirer three weeks prior to each concert. Mail the coupon with a stamped, self-addressed envelope and your tickets will be sent on a first come, first served basis. If you don't have a coupon which indicates a concert, give your concert preference. The address is Mann Music Center Concerts, Department of Recreation, P.O. Box 1000, Phila., PA 19105. There's a two-ticket limit for each concert requested.

You can have a reserved seat, under cover, by becoming a Friend of the Mann Music Center. An annual contribution entitles you to a seat at each concert.

For concert programs and additional information, call or write to Mann Music Center, 1617 John F. Kennedy Blvd., Phila., PA 19103.

Note: The entertainment continues at the Mann Music Center in August and in the absence of the Philadelphia Orchestra. There's ballet, opera, theater, pop and rock concerts. Watch for newspaper announcements, or call to find out who will be there.

OPERA

The history of opera in Philadelphia is as old as the Academy of Music. Its opening performance in February, 1857, was Verdi's "Trovatore" and for more than a century opera has flourished here.

Today you have a choice of opera companies. The grand scale, popular productions are presented by the **OPERA COMPANY OF PHILADELPHIA**, formed in 1975 when the local Grand and Lyric companies merged. This is where Luciano Pavarotti makes frequent guest appearances and judges an international voice competition. It's where English subtitles are projected over the stage.

The Opera Company of Philadelphia stages four operas a year at the Academy of Music from November to April. Each opera is performed on two evenings and a Sunday matinee in one week. Subscriptions go on sale the preceding spring from the company's office at 1500 Market Street, East Tower 26th floor, Phila., PA 19102. Individual tickets go on sale in September from O.C.P., and three weeks prior to each performance at the Academy box office. They range from $16 to $110 for individual performances. Call 732–5814 for details.

A new concept in opera was introduced to Philadelphia in 1975 by the **PENNSYLVANIA OPERA THEATER** and its artistic director, Barbara Silverstein. Their operas are in English and they stress drama as well as music. Their productions appeal to contemporary audiences of all ages. Recent choices have been Mozart's "Idomemeo," Strauss' "Die Fledermaus," and a world premiere of Greg Pliska's "The Secret Garden," specially commissioned by the Opera Theater.

The Pennsylvania Opera Theater stages three operas each year at the Shubert Theater, in fall, winter and spring, with three performances of each. The curtain goes up at 7:30 P.M. on Wednesday and 8 P.M. for Friday and Saturday performances.

You can subscribe to a series of two or three operas, or try and get tickets for a single performance. Individual tickets are $20 to $45. For schedule and ticket information, call 440–9797 or write the Pennsylvania Opera Theater, 1217 Sansom Street, 6th floor, Phila., PA 19107.

The nation's oldest amateur Gilbert & Sullivan troupe, **THE SAVOY COMPANY** was founded in Philadelphia in 1901. They, too, perform at the Academy of Music. Their performances are one Friday and Saturday each year late in May. It's a rare treat to see a fully-staged and authentic production of Gilbert & Sullivan. You'll see why Gilbert & Sullivan are two of America's favorite playwrights. Call the Academy or The Savoy Company (735–7161) for the schedule and ticket information. (All ticket proceeds benefit a different local charity each year.) If you miss them at the Academy in May, there's a repeat performance the following weekend in June at Longwood Gardens* in Kennett Square, PA.

Another opera series is presented each year by the **ACADEMY OF VOCAL ARTS**. They present in the native language three or four operas a year from November to May at their charming 150-seat Helen Corning Warden Theater at 1920 Spruce Street (four nights for each performance).

Tickets are $17, or $15 for senior citizens and students. Call 735–1685 for tickets and schedule information. (A note for **E & D:** Call ahead to use the ramped entrance on Delancey Street.)

We've already mentioned earlier in this chapter about opera productions by **CURTIS INSTITUTE OF MUSIC**. Don't say you don't have a choice of wonderful ways to enjoy opera in Philadelphia!

ORGAN CONCERTS

If you like organ music, and if you've never seen a pipe organ, the **JOHN WANAMAKER DEPARTMENT STORE** at 13th and Market Streets in center city is where you have a chance to see one. The Wanamaker pipe organ is the largest in the world and one of the finest ever built.

This huge instrument has 451 stops and 964 controls, all within the organist's reach. They're tied in with 30,000 pipes. The 100 gold pipes you see in the loft area overlooking Wanamaker's Grand Court are purely decorative. The real ones stretch out for seven floors behind them!

The Wanamaker organist gives 45-minute concerts every shopping day at 11:15 A.M. and 5:15 P.M. (The organ has been played at John Wanamaker every business day since its installation in 1911.)

You can be at any point in the Grand Court on the store's main floor to enjoy the music or on any of the upper floors where they overlook the Grand Court. Or you can be one of the lucky few to sit at the great console while the organist performs. A dozen guests, at the most, can be accommodated at one time. Go directly to the second floor on the 13th Street side of the Grand Court and ask a salesperson to direct you. For additional information, call 422–2450.

Another unusual opportunity to enjoy organ recitals is

at **IRVINE AUDITORIUM** at the University of Pennsylvania, 34th and Spruce Streets. Here, you'll hear the Curtis Organ, built in 1926 for Philadelphia's Exposition to celebrate America's sesqui-centennial, and then named for publishing giant Cyrus Curtis who bought the organ and gave it to the University.

The Curtis Organ ranks as the world's 13th largest with 10,731 pipes. It can produce every tonal quality of a full symphony orchestra. Recitals are during the fall and spring semesters on 10 Wednesdays at noon. They're free, and you're invited to bring lunch and brown-bag-it during the concert. And, if you've never been to Irvine Auditorium, it, too, is a work of art worth visiting. A once-a-year concert is in October (see Chapter 19).

For an exact schedule of these noontime recitals, call the Curtis Organ Restoration Society at the University of Pennsylvania, 898–2848.

PHILADELPHIA CHAMBER MUSIC SOCIETY
569–8587

Philadelphia's Music from Marlboro series was founded in 1965. It proved so popular that in 1986 it blossomed into the Philadelphia Chamber Music Society whose mission is to bring major international ensembles and soloists to Philadelphia.

The repertoire is mostly 18th and 19th century, but there are world premieres each year and works by Philadelphia composers specifically commissioned by the Society.

Musicians from Marlboro continue to be on the schedule as part of two International Chamber Music Series, as well as a Master Piano, Master String and Master Vocal Artist Recital Series.

All five series are held at the Port of History Museum* at Delaware and Walnut Street, from November through mid-May, and most concerts are at 8 P.M. (Four from the International Chamber Music Series are Sundays at 3 P.M.) There are several combinations of subscriptions from as few as three concerts to as many as 23. If you're lucky, single performance tickets may be available for $15.

For additional information, call or write the Philadelphia Chamber Music Society at 135 S. 18th Street, Box 101, Phila., PA 19103.

PHILADELPHIA CLASSICAL GUITAR SOCIETY
259-3767

Classical guitar music is unusual for many of us, so it's an interesting interlude. The Philadelphia Classical Guitar Society presents recitals at 7:30 P.M., usually on the fourth Sunday of each month from September to June (unless it's a holiday). They're often held at Jefferson Alumni Hall, 11th and Locust Streets, and other convenient center city locations, so plan to attend something unusual and interesting.

Selections for these recitals include a wide variety of classical music. Sometimes there's a lecture and discussion in conjunction with the concert. If classical guitar music is new to you, this will be a good learning experience.

Tickets are available in advance or at the door for $5 to $15. Members of the Society get ticket discounts and the opportunity to attend social and educational events as well. A schedule is available from the Society at the end of the summer.

PHILADELPHIA FOLKSONG SOCIETY
247-1300

Come and sing along when the spirit moves you!

Whether you sing along or just enjoy listening, this is another unique musical experience in Philadelphia. The music ranges from blue grass to a good sampling of international favorites. You'll probably find yourself humming a few tunes.

The concerts are held in Hopkinson Hall at the International House*, 3701 Chestnut Street, the second Sunday of each month from October to June at 8 P.M. You can call ahead to find out who's appearing. Concerts are followed by refreshments and an open sing-along. You should be able to make new friends, too.

Admission is $4, or free if you're a member of the Society or under 12 years of age.

The Folksong Society also sponsors the annual Philadelphia Folk Festival the last weekend before Labor Day. This is a three-day, rain or shine event with afternoon workshops, evening concerts and overnight camping at the Old Poole Farm campgrounds near Schwenksville, PA. Tickets are available from Ticketron or the Folk Society for the entire weekend or individual afternoon or evening events. Thousands of folk-lovers participate, so if you're interested be sure to get the details early so you won't be left out.

Just in case you can't make it in August, inquire about the Folk Society's annual Spring Thing that takes place during a weekend in May or the Fall Folk Festival that happens on a September weekend.

PHILADELPHIA ORCHESTRA

Academy of Music* (performances)
1420 Locust Street—19102 (offices)
893–1900 or 893–1930 (box office)

Hours: About a dozen series of subscription concerts are at 8 P.M. on Monday, Tuesday, Thursday, Friday and Saturday evenings. Matinees are Fridays at 2. The season is September to May. For summer schedule, read about the Mann Music Center.

Cost: Individual concert ticket prices are $9 to $39 (plus a $1 per ticket Building Renovation and Expansion Fee). They're available at the box office 8 weeks prior to a performance. Mail orders are also accepted 8 weeks ahead (include a stamped, self-addressed envelope with your request and check or money order). $2.50 General Admission tickets for the Amphitheater go on sale one hour prior to Friday matinees, Friday and Saturday evening concerts.

Box Office Hours: Weekdays, 10 to 9, or till 5:30 if there is no evening performance. Open Sunday only if a performance is scheduled.

E & D: See Chapter 16.

The Philadelphia Orchestra is said to be one of the finest orchestras in the world. (In Philadelphia, we say it's the finest.) When the first cultural exchange in decades between the United States and the People's Republic of China was planned, our orchestra was chosen to make the historic tour in September, 1973.

The Philadelphia Orchestra is as old as this century. Following the Leopold Stokowski era from 1912 to 1935, Eugene Ormandy took over direction of the orchestra in 1936. Riccardo Muti assumed the role of Music Director and Conductor of the Philadelphia Orchestra in 1980. Wolfgang Sawallisch takes over in the 1993–1994 season.

A distinguished list of additional guest conductors, instrumentalists and vocal soloists appear.

If you want to learn more about the Philadelphia Orchestra you can tour the Academy of Music (see Chapter 13). The orchestra's **Concerts for Children** and **Come and Meet the Music** are described in Chapter 15.

The Philadelphia Orchestra presents a series of pre-concert lectures that are open to the public free of charge. These **Orchestra Insights** take place in the Academy of Music Ballroom preceding several of the evening concerts. Another series called **Composer Encounters** enables you to chat with today's top composers in conjunction with concerts that include their works. This program also takes place in the Academy Ballroom following the concert and there's no charge. Call for details on both of these exciting opportunities to get really close to the music.

The Philadelphia Orchestra also presents a series of six **Chamber Music Concerts** from October through April. They're on Sunday afternoons at 3 in the elegant Academy of Music Ballroom. Take this opportunity to hear members of the orchestra in different ensembles and as solo performers in a more intimate setting. For ticket and schedule information, call 893–1926.

Note: Don't miss a look in the Academy's lobby at the magnificent model of the Orchestra's planned new home. The Philadelphia Orchestra Hall will be just a block south of the Academy of Music at Broad and Spruce Streets.

PHILADELPHIA YOUTH ORCHESTRA
765–8485

Talented young people between the ages of 14 and 21 can audition in May or September for this 100-piece orchestra which is conducted by former Philadelphia Orchestra member Joseph Primavera.

Since 1940, this talented orchestra has had a 35-week annual season of Saturday morning rehearsals at a center city location, community concerts, and an annual closing concert in late April or May at the Academy of Music.

The orchestra made its first major tour in 1981 when they travelled to Australia to perform in the Australia Youth Music Festival. They've since played at the Edinboro Festival in England, for over 50,000 people in China and Hong Kong, in South America, in East and West

Berlin, and at the 1991 International Youth Orchestra Festival commemorating the 700th anniversary of the founding of Switzerland.

The Youth Orchestra is the only full-sized symphony of its kind in the area. It's a treat to attend their concerts. It's a bigger treat to be a member. Call or write (P.O. Box 41810, Phila., PA 19101–1810) for information.

PHILLY POPS
735-7506

The Philly Pops was founded in 1980. Under the baton of Peter Nero, and with guest performers like Robert Merrill, Mel Torme, Tommy Tune and Tug McGraw (reciting "Casey at the Bat"), they were an overnight sensation.

The Philly Pops performs at the Academy of Music from October to May in a choice of four series of four concerts each. Two series are Sunday afternoons at 3 P.M.; one is Mondays at 8 P.M.; the other is a combination of Tuesday and Wednesday evenings at 8.

Tickets can be purchased individually from the Academy box office prior to each concert, if you're lucky, or in a series from the All Star-Forum, 1521 Locust Street, Phila., PA 19102. Call for programs and dates and try to see this fun-filled musical entertainment.

ROBIN HOOD DELL EAST
East Fairmount Park
Near Kelly and Strawberry Mansion Drives
477-8810 (summer months only)

SEPTA: Buses 7, 39, 54, 61, 85. There's plenty of free parking.
E & D: Anyone in a wheelchair can be seated comfortably at the Dell. Try to arrange in advance to park at the lot that's adjacent to the main entrance. Refreshments and rest rooms are accessible. A special section can be reserved for groups in wheelchairs. Call 685-0152 to arrange.

For spectacular outdoor musical events, come to "Essence of Entertainment" at Robin Hood Dell East, compliments of the city's Department of Recreation.

Any Monday, Wednesday or Friday at 8 P.M. in July or August might feature singers, dancers or musicians from Philadelphia or around the world. (Rain dates are on the following evenings.) Recent audiences were treated to jazz, folk and pop music programs with The Isley Brothers, Billy Eckstein, Lou Rawls, The Spinners and The Four Tops. Gospelrama, ethnic festivals with international flavor, ballet and opera are also on the schedule.

General Admission is $5; reserved seats are $8, $12 and $14. Watch for June and July newspaper announcements with the summer's schedule. Call for ticket information, or write to the city's Cultural and Special Events Office, Belmont and Parkside Avenues, Phila., PA 19131.

ROCK AND POP CONCERTS
Electric Factory Concerts
569-9400

The latest rock, pop, jazz and folk shows head straight to Philadelphia—all compliments of Electric Factory Concerts.

For the latest on who's appearing, when and where, you can call the **WMMR Concert Line** at **561-4080**.

Electric Factory Concerts stages many of its concerts at the Spectrum, and lines have been known to form for blocks around the building as fans anticipate the crush for tickets. You can call the **Spectrum** at **389-5000** for a recording of what's coming up there. Programs are also at the **Tower Theater (352-0313)** with approximately 3,000 seats at 69th and Ludlow Streets in Upper Darby, Academy of Music, Civic Center, Mann Music Center, Shubert Theater and Theater of the Living Arts. Refer to the Index for more information about these locales.

For more night club entertainment, see Chapter 18.

UNIVERSITY MUSEUM* CONCERTS
33rd and Spruce Streets—19104
898-4015

The **Museum String Orchestra**, under the direction of Philadelphia Orchestra member Donald Montanaro and other great artists, performs at this concert series that's usually held in winter and spring on occasional Sunday afternoons at 2:30.

The programs generally include music that is rarely heard in this area. There's also an annual tribute to Johann Sebastian Bach.

Admission is free and no tickets are necessary. Children who attend must be accompanied by an adult; these concerts are billed as "Adult Music Programs."

Call the museum for information, or send a long, self-addressed stamped envelope with your request for a "Music at the Museum" schedule. They're available in September.

Concerts & Croissants is a series of three Sunday morning at 11:30 concerts presented with a tasty breakfast in the museum's glass-walled cafe. The music is international and the menu is continental. Tickets can be bought as a series or for individual performances.

A festival of **Summer Music** from around the world is six consecutive Wednesday evenings in July and August. Folk artists and jazz musicians perform in a charming outdoor courtyard starting at 5:30 P.M. (Everyone moves indoors if it rains.) A light supper is available during intermission. These concerts, too, can be attended as a series or individually. Tickets for single concerts are $3.50 for adults, $2.50 for museum members, and $1.50 for children under 12.

The Summer Music Series and Concerts & Croissants are both very popular. Call the museum's special events office at 898–4890 for a schedule and plan to attend some of these delightful programs.

VALLEY FORGE MUSIC FAIR
Route 202 at Devon Exit
Devon, PA 19333
644–5000

The Valley Forge Music Fair is a 45-minute drive from center city Philadelphia (west on the Schuylkill Expressway Route 76 and south on Route 202 at King of Prussia). It's theater-in-the-round—open year-round.

There are one-night stands, weekend attractions and week-long runs of concerts and shows. The Music Fair bills only the best entertainment for its audience of 2,900. Tickets are sold for each show and they can be ordered by mail or phone with Visa or Master Charge once you know the date and ticket price of your choice. There's plenty of free parking for everyone and special group rates are available in advance. Call 647–2307 for group reservations.

To find out what's coming up, either call or look in the daily papers. **Children's Musical Theater** at Valley Forge Music Fair is described in Chapter 15.

MORE CONCERTS?
ENCORE. ENCORE.

There are a number of other orchestras and musical groups that periodically perform throughout Philadelphia. Here are some of them.

The **AMERICAN SOCIETY OF ANCIENT INSTRUMENTS**, the first of its kind in the United States, was founded in Philadelphia in 1929. This chamber orchestra is devoted to playing baroque and Renaissance music on authentic 18th century instruments. Performances take place at museums, cultural centers, college campuses and an Annual Festival held three Sunday afternoons in May at Old First Reformed Church* at 4th and Race Streets.

After each concert you have a chance to talk with the musicians and see their antique instruments. This is a rare opportunity to touch a pardessus de viole, viola da amour or viola da gamba and see if you can tell the difference from their contemporary counterparts. If you can't get to a concert and would like to see an exhibit of the instruments, they're on permanent display at the Fleisher Collection of the Free Library of Philadelphia*.

Tickets for the Annual Festival concerts are sold individually or for the series, with discounts for senior citizens and students. For additional information, call 635-3434.

The **CHESTNUT BRASS COMPANY** presents a series annually at First Presbyterian Church, 21st and Walnut Streets. Five players perform on two trumpets, French horn, trombone and tuba. They also use original antique instruments and program a variety of guest artists to appear with them. Four concerts are usually Mondays at 8 P.M. Admission is free. Call 787-6792 for the schedule, or, for additional information call the Temple University Esther Boyer College of Music at 787-8306 where Chestnut Brass Company is ensemble-in-residence.

CONCERTS BY CANDLELIGHT are five summer Sunday evenings at 7:30 at Laurel Hill* in East Fairmount Park. They usually feature soloists or chamber groups. A reception follows each concert. Tickets are $10.

For tickets and schedule information, call Laurel Hill at 235–1776 or Women for Greater Philadelphia at 627–1770.

1807 & FRIENDS, in conjunction with the Y Arts Council*, presents five chamber concerts each season from October to May at the YM & YWHA, Broad and Pine Streets. The setting is intimate for these Monday at 8 P.M. programs of music that might be old or new, but always adventurous and intriguing. Tickets are $10, or $8 for senior citizens, and $3 for students. The series of five concerts is $40. Call 473–4012 or 545–4400 for additional information.

Another variety of chamber concerts are performed each season by **HANCOCK CHAMBER PLAYERS** at Fleisher Art Memorial*, 719 Catherine Street. Not only is the sanctuary setting unique, but also this is America's only chamber trio of oboe, horn and piano. Formed in 1982 to showcase woodwind chamber music, Hancock Chamber Players draw from a repertoire of music covering the last three centuries. And they frequently perform with guest artists. For a schedule and additional information, call 688–1053.

The Folklife Center of International House*, 3701 Chestnut Street, presents an **INTERNATIONAL MUSIC SERIES**. Ten concerts, Thursday to Sunday nights at 8, offer a combination of innovative performances from around the world. This is a special opportunity to see and hear musicians and dancers (see the preceding chapter) making rare visits to Philadelphia. Tickets can be purchased in a series of five, or for individual concerts. Call 895–6537 for specifics.

Since 1952, the Philadelphia **MUMMERS STRING BANDS** have been "showing their stuff" each summer in a free weekly concert series. Top bands perform their well-known music along with instrumental solos and duets, vocalists, community singing and impromptu strutting.

Be at the Mummers Museum*, Two Street and Washington Avenue (336–3050) on Tuesdays at 8 P.M. from

May through September. But don't come if it rains. (The concerts are held outdoors.) Call the museum at 6 P.M., or listen to KYW–1060 Newsradio, for last minute announcements.

And be prepared to go away singing "I'm Looking Over a Four Leaf Clover."

NEW MUSIC AT ANNENBERG is a series of three mixed-media concerts co-presented each year by Annenberg Center at 3680 Walnut Street and Relache (you'll read about them in a minute). A recent season included a unique musical-theater work, a saxophone opera, and a film joined in concert with music by Philip Glass. Tickets are available by series or for individual concerts. If you'd like to hear some of the most imaginative music in Philadelphia, call the Annenberg box office at 898–6791 for additional information.

A group of professional and semi-professional musicians who wanted to practice and perform regularly, but didn't want a strenuous concert schedule, founded the **ORCHESTRA SOCIETY OF PHILADELPHIA** in 1964. Today they're highly respected innovators in the local musical arena, and they're the resident orchestra of Drexel University. Luis O. Biava, principal second violinist with the Philadelphia Orchestra, is music director and conductor.

The Orchestra Society encourages new compositions and performances by young soloists. They present unusual concerts like Mahler's Symphony 8 (the Symphony of One Thousand), rarely performed in Philadelphia.

You can see the Orchestra Society of Philadelphia at Drexel University, 32nd and Chestnut Streets, when they perform in the Main Hall Auditorium. Admission is free. Call 924–2196 or watch for newspaper announcements of the exact dates and programs. Auditions are also held regularly for talented musicians interested in joining the orchestra.

ORCHESTRA 2001 was founded in 1988 to focus on 20th century music. Their six concerts from September to May are at Mandell Theater at Drexel University and the Philadelphia Ethical Society at 1906 Rittenhouse Square. Programs often feature local composers and works specifically commissioned for Orchestra 2001.

Hence, you could be among the first to hear Philadelphia premieres and first performances of new music.

Professional musicians who belong to other local orchestras moonlight to compose Orchestra 2001. Each concert could have anywhere from six to 20 players, and you'll have a chance to talk to them about the music.

Tickets are $10, or half-price for senior citizens and students. You can buy them individually, or by subscription at a discount. Call 358–9556, or write to 1433 Gradyville Road, Glen Mills, PA 19342 for additional information.

If the sound of 17th and 18th century music played on period instruments is to your liking, then thrill to the sound of **PHILOMEL**. Their name is derived from a poetic word for the nightingale, whose male is known for his melodious song. Philomel has performed since 1976 in small ensemble with guest artists as well as a baroque chamber orchestra with chorus and vocal soloists.

Ten concerts are presented annually from October to May. Five are on Saturday evenings at 8; followed the next day at 3 with the same program at a different locale. Tickets are available for individual concerts or in series of three, four or five. There are discounts for senior citizens, students and groups. Call Philomel at 889–1692 for additional information.

The **RELACHE** Ensemble was formed in 1977 to present contemporary and experimental music from around the world. A core of 15 inspired musicians and vocalists develop and present programs that you might not otherwise have an opportunity to hear. Much of what they perform is experimental music. They call it "Music Without Boundaries."

Relache is "in residence" at Mandell Theater of Drexel University where they present a "Guest Performer/Composer Series" of three concerts annually on Saturday evenings at 8 P.M. They also present three concerts of "New Music from the Old World" each year at the Philadelphia Ethical Society, 1906 Rittenhouse Square. These programs are Fridays at 8 P.M.

Tickets for Relache concerts are $12, or $8 for students and senior citizens. You can buy them in advance or just prior to a concert. Call the Innovation Arts box office at 963–0345 for a schedule and to order tickets.

One more unique series of intimate concerts is performed each year at Woodmere Art Museum*, 9201 Germantown Avenue. **MUSIC AT AN EXHIBITION** invites an audience limited to 200 to hear guest ensembles and soloists on four weekend evenings at 8 P.M. A gallery reception for subscribers and performers follows each concert. For information, call 247-0476.

MORE MUSICAL EVENTS?
OF COURSE!

There are also musical celebrations that take place annually.

The **BACH FESTIVAL OF PHILADELPHIA**, under direction of Janice Fiore, is from October through early December at churches in Chestnut Hill*. World-famous vocalists and instrumentalists perform, many on authentic period instruments as they would have for Bach's 18th century audience. There are six major concerts, supplemented by lectures and recitals. Don't miss this rare opportunity. Tickets range from $11 to $30 per concert, with discounts for senior citizens, students and groups. Subscription information is available early in June. Call 247-BACH, or write to 8419 Germantown Avenue, Phila., PA 19118, in late spring for a schedule and ticket information.

There's an annual **MELLON JAZZ FESTIVAL** in Philadelphia that's held in mid-June. Some of the country's great jazz legends appear at the Academy of Music. Concerts are also at smaller theaters and clubs around the city. Some 40 events are included; many are free. Watch for newspaper announcements starting in late April. For ticket information, call the Academy of Music at 893-1930, or during the Festival, call the Mellon Jazz Festival Hotline at 561-5060. We don't miss a beat in Philadelphia!

MOZART ON THE SQUARE takes place for two weeks in May on and around Rittenhouse Square*. It's been an annual musical celebration since 1980 with chamber music, orchestral concerts and recitals. All of the noon events are free. Tickets for evening chamber and orchestral concerts are $10 and $15. There are senior citizen and student discounts. Call 988–9830 for festival information. Mozart would have loved this series.

A few final notes: If you're a fan of the late Mario Lanza, you'll want to stop by the **MARIO LANZA MUSEUM** housed in the Settlement Music School at 416 Queen Street in Queen Village* (468–3623). Hours are Monday to Saturday, 10 to 3:30. Admission is free.

Hundreds of photographs, personal effects and memorabilia of the operatic tenor and film star from South Philadelphia are exhibited. Mario Lanza was born just a few blocks from here in 1921. He died at age 38 in 1959.

The Mario Lanza Institute was organized to pay tribute to the singer and to provide inspiration and scholarship awards to aspiring young vocalists. The Institute also established this mini-museum in one big room on the third floor of the school where young Mario got his first musical training.

Dozens of celebrities have been honored for their contributions to Philadelphia's musical heritage since the **WALK OF FAME** was established in 1987 by the Philadelphia Music Foundation. Look for bronze plaques in the sidewalk on the west side Broad Street between Walnut and Spruce Streets, honoring the likes of Marian Anderson, The Four Aces, Samuel Barber, Anna Moffo, Ed McMahon and Leopold Stokowski. A title plaque is at Broad Street and Bach Place at the corner of the Shubert Theater. Please, watch your step, or you'll be walking on stars.

Theater

Where are the major shows and Broadway productions in Philadelphia? Many of Philadelphia's stages for the performing arts are described at the very beginning of this chapter. You've read about the **SHUBERT** and the **PAINTED BRIDE**.

The **FORREST***, 1114 Walnut Street (923–1515), was completely refurbished in 1989. It has 1,800 balcony, mezzanine, box and staggered orchestra seats.

Several theater companies present live theater for children. These are described in Chapter 15.

Where else can you see provocative and entertaining drama in Philadelphia? Read on.

AMERICAN MUSIC THEATER FESTIVAL
1400 South Penn Square, Suite 1302—19102 (office)
988–9050

Look for world premieres during this festival, and don't be surprised to learn that many of the shows go on to be hits in other cities as well. Since it was founded in 1984, 22 of A.M.T.F.'s first 28 productions were Philadelphia or world premieres and 17 went on to be staged elsewhere. Several have been recorded. Some of the big hits include Duke Ellington's "Queenie Pie," Philip Glass' "1000 Airplanes on the Roof," and "X" on the life and times of Malcolm X.

There are four productions from March through June and each runs for about three weeks of evening and matinee performances. Their mainstage is **Plays and Players Theater** at 1714 Delancey Street and occasionally another popular locale in town.

Special events are also planned, and a some performances include an opportunity to meet the artists after the show. Tickets range from $18 to $24, with discounts for senior citizens, students, members and groups. Watch for newspaper announcements, or call for festival information. Tickets are also available through UPSTAGES*.

ANNENBERG CENTER*

3680 Walnut Street—19104
898-6791 (ticket information and phone reservations)
898-6683 (school and group sales, study guides and post-
performance discussion arrangements)

SEPTA: Buses 21, 40; subway-surface trolleys 11, 13, 34,
36 to 36th and Sansom Streets.
E & D: See Chapter 16.

You can indulge yourself in a showcase of innovation
and classic drama at any of the Annenberg Theaters:
Studio (smallest, with 120 seats), **Harold Prince** (225
seats), **Annenberg School Theater** (382 seats) or **Zellerbach** (most frequently used, with 970 seats).

Six or seven plays are presented as part of Annenberg's
annual subscription series. Some are co-produced with
other Philadelphia area theaters and festivals. Some of
the stars who appeared here in recent seasons are Zoe
Caldwell, Jose Ferrer, Laurence Luckinbill, Estelle Par-
sons, Liv Ullman and Mary Ure. Occasionally, special
events are also scheduled.

The admission prices vary. Tickets are available individually or on a discount subscription plan. Group,
senior citizen and student discounts are available.

Annenberg Center Theater for Children and the
**Philadelphia International Theater Festival for Chil-
dren** are described in Chapter 15.

Zellerbach is also home for the Philadelphia Drama
Guild. Harold Prince is home for the Philadelphia Festival Theater for New Plays. You'll be reading about these
later in the chapter.

Be sure to get your seasonal program.

And don't say that Philadelphia doesn't provide unusual and exciting theatrical experiences.

ARDEN THEATRE COMPANY
St. Stephen's Alley
923 Ludlow Street—19107
829–8900

SEPTA: Any Market or Chestnut Street route to 10th Street.
E & D: There are 6 steps at the entrance. The main theater is on the 2nd floor and reached by stairs.

Two young men appeared on the Philadelphia theater scene in 1988 and made big things happen in a short time. In a joint development with historic St. Stephen's Episcopal Church, and already having produced several successful shows on other local stages, they opened a new performing arts center late in 1990. The main stage theater on the second floor at St. Stephen's Alley seats 150; a smaller studio stage seats 80 on the ground level. Ben Franklin is said to have done his kite experiment and discovered electricity near what is now 10th and Ludlow Streets. Arden Theatre Company likes to say lightning has struck the same site again.

Arden's mission is to "tell the greatest stories by the greatest storytellers of all time." Five shows are produced each season with a five week run for each. Seven performances are Tuesday to Sunday, including a Wednesday and Sunday matinee. Tickets are $15 and $17, with discounts for senior citizens, students, groups and subscribers. Call to find out more about these electrifying performances, or call UPSTAGES at 567–0670 for tickets.

CITY OF PHILADELPHIA'S
DRAMA GROUPS TO JOIN

The Department of Recreation conducts an extensive four-part drama program each fall and winter at its indoor facilities throughout the city.

Creative dramatics involves pre-schoolers to 12-year-olds in spontaneous acting out of stories, poetry and their daily lives.

Formal dramatics offers basic training in acting, movement, dialogue and stage craft. Skits and plays are the end result of practical exercises and classes in theory.

Environmental theater offers workshops in scenery, lighting, music, costumes, make-up and the like—all with the goal of being able to create a complete production.

Talent shows are conducted at local recreation centers, followed by district shows and a one-act play festival showcasing the city's top amateur talents. Who knows where the stars will go from here? After all, Philadelphia is a City of Stars. Just ask Bill Cosby, Joey Bishop, David Brenner, Fabian, Eddie Fisher, Jack Klugman, Lola Falana, Andrea McArdle, Wilt Chamberlain or Bobby Rydell.

The talent shows and dramatics workshops continue in summer months at local recreation centers on an individual basis. Call your neighborhood recreation center for their schedule, or the Department of Recreation's Cultural and Special Events Division (685-0151) to see if there's a program beginning soon near you.

Youngsters from ages six to 16 get together at neighborhood recreation centers each summer to write and produce original **Fire Prevention Plays**. They're based on an annual theme which is chosen by the Philadelphia Fire Department. Local fire battalions give helping hands.

Competitions are held in the districts and the winners compete at a citywide finals production. The top finalist groups present their plays on stage at the Free Library. You'll be surprised how amateur talents can dream up and act out imaginative stories about hazards like faulty heaters, oily rags and open flames.

Don't forget about the other **summer camp*** opportunities provided by the city. Of course, there are those that focus on sports and recreation. There's also Summer Visual Arts and Performing Arts Camps and a Carousel House Camp that combines a variety of recreational and cultural activities for handicapped youngsters.

DINNER THEATER
(See Chapter 18.)

FORREST THEATER*
1114 Walnut Street—19107
923-1515

SEPTA: Buses 9, 21, 42; trolley 23.
E & D: Theater entrance and orchestra seating are street level. There are 4 orchestra locations for people in wheelchairs. You must notify the theater in advance. Rest rooms are either up or down a long flight of stairs.

Four or five Broadway productions make up the Forrest Theater Subscription Series each year. Subscribers are guaranteed seats to see top stars in smash hits. Recent shows have been "Cats," "Cat on a Hot Tin Roof," "Les Miserables," "Other People's Money" and "Sarafina!"

Subscriptions to the Forrest Series are ordered c/o The Shubert Organization, P.O. Box 1006, Times Square Station, New York, NY 10108. For details, call 1–800–432–7780.

Showtimes are Monday to Saturday evenings, a weekday and Saturday matinees. Tickets are also available at the Forrest box office prior to and during each show's run.

The Forrest remains lit most of the year, even when it isn't alive with the Broadway series. Musical and dramatic hits are booked for short stays. Watch the newspapers for announcements, or call for a schedule.

FREEDOM THEATER
1346 N. Broad Street—19121
765–2793 or 800–836–0814

SEPTA: Buses C, 57; Broad Street subway to Girard Avenue.
E & D: No wheelchair access. The theaters are on the lower level and reached by stairs.

Freedom Theater is a unique showplace in the Heritage House, where the great American actor Edwin Forrest once lived. Forrest was born in Philadelphia in 1806 and we have a theater named in his memory. Freedom Theater, founded in 1966, is Philadelphia's oldest and most active black theater. There are actually two theaters: one seats 120, the other, 130.

A dozen or so talented actors and actresses stage six productions a year in addition to a special summer youth presentation, "Under Pressure," that deals with the realities of growing up to adulthood. There could be musicals, dance, drama, poetry, or who knows what.

Recent productions have been "The Colored Museum" and "Simply Heavenly." Many of Freedom Theater's performers have gone on to successful careers in television and theater. (You've probably seen Erica Alexander who stars as Pam on "The Cosby Show." She got her start here at Freedom Theater.)

Shows are usually Thursday to Sunday with a minimum four-week run for each. Tickets are $12.50 to $20, with discounts for students, senior citizens and groups.

Freedom Theater also brings its dramatic talents to schools and centers in the community (see Chapter 13). A school for performing arts is conducted at Heritage House for adults and young people. Auditions are held for all study programs, and there's an open casting for all of Freedom Theater's productions. If you're interested, call for specifics.

PHILADELPHIA DRAMA GUILD
563-7530 or 898-6791 (Annenberg box office)

The Philadelphia Drama Guild began in 1971 as the city's only professional production company. Five well-known plays and frequent premieres starring well-known talents are brought to **Zellerbach Theater** at Annenberg every year from October to May. Each show has a three-week run. There are evening curtains Tuesday to Sunday, and Saturday and Sunday matinees.

Tickets can be purchased prior to each show (if you're lucky) or by a season subscription that offers two shows free. The subscription hot-line is 563-PLAY. Discounts for students, senior citizens and groups are available in advance.

Call the Drama Guild for their schedule and brochure, or write to them at the Robert Morris Building, 100 N. 17th Street, Philadelphia, PA 19103, and watch for announcements in the local newspapers.

PHILADELPHIA FESTIVAL THEATER
FOR NEW PLAYS
3900 Chestnut Street—19104 (office)
222-5000

The Philadelphia Festival Theater for New Plays is professional, non-profit theater devoted to the production of new plays by American playwrights. Thousands are submitted from around the country, and four or five are selected each year. Almost seventy-five percent of the plays presented since the festival began in 1981 have since been published or presented elsewhere. They've included works by Jules Feiffer, Bruce Graham, David Mamet and Chaim Potok, to name a few.

Harold Prince Theater at Annenberg is the festival's stage. Each play has a three-week run with a choice of 21 performances. Subscriptions and group, student and senior citizen discounts are available, and series holders also can plan to attend performances followed by curtain call discussions with the playwright or cast members. For single ticket information, call 898-6791. For subscriptions and additional information, call the Festival Theater office.

THE PHILADELPHIA THEATER COMPANY
592-8333

The Philadelphia Theater Company was founded in 1974 to present Philadelphians with new plays by American writers. Their stage is the **Plays and Players Theater*** at 1714 Delancey Street.

Four shows are presented each year. Each has a three-week run. Tickets are $20 to $28, but if you subscribe to the series, you get a discount. There are also student and senior citizen discounts.

Among the company's recent Philadelphia premieres are David Mamet's "Speed-the-Plow," A.R. Gurney's "The Cocktail Hour" starring Celeste Holm, and "Pill Hill" by Sam Kelley.

If provocative, innovative drama appeals to you, call for a schedule, or write to The Philadelphia Theater Company, The Bourse, Suite 550, 21 S. 5th Street, Philadelphia, PA 19106.

PLAYS AND PLAYERS
1714 Delancey Street—19103
735-0630

SEPTA: Buses 2, 90, or a short walk south from Chestnut or Walnut Streets.
E & D: The entrance and lobby are level and a ramp leads to the theater. Wheelchair access.

This is the oldest continuing community theater in the country, and it certainly enjoys a fine reputation. The charming 324-seat structure on quaint Delancey Street is historically certified. (You should know by now that it's also home for The Philadelphia Theater Company and the American Music Theater Festival.)

Four shows are presented from September to June. They

run three weeks each with Thursday to Saturday evening performances at 8 and one Saturday and Sunday matinee at 2 for each show. The fare is comedy, light drama and suspense. Tickets are $11 for general admission, $10 for students and senior citizens. Inquire in advance about subscriptions and group rates.

Memberships to the Plays and Players Club are available at various levels: single, couple, student, out-of-towners and so forth. This is a great opportunity if you're interested in theater. The club has a cocktail hour on Friday evenings; the atmosphere is social and the talk is stimulating.

The **Children's Theater of Plays and Players** is described in Chapter 15.

SOCIETY HILL PLAYHOUSE
507 South 8th Street—19147
923-0210

SEPTA: Buses 47, 90.
E & D: The Main Stage Theater is on 2nd floor and there's no elevator. The Second Space is on the ground level. There are 2 low steps at the entrance.

An open acting company has been providing the drama at Society Hill Playhouse since 1960. It's thought of as Philadelphia's oldest professional off-Broadway theater. The building itself is almost as old as the century and the Main Stage Theater was completely renovated in 1985 to seat 223.

Shows are presented each year from October to mid-June. Tickets are $12 to $24.50, with discounts for groups. Recent productions have been "Pump Boys and Dinettes" and a very long and successful run of "Nunsense."

More intimate productions are staged in the cabaret-style Second Space that seats 60. Recent audiences saw "Noel Coward at the Cafe de Paris" by Will Stutts.

There are acting classes for adults and an opportunity to audition for the Playhouse's productions.

Call or watch for newspaper announcements to find out which shows might interest you.

PHILADELPHIA YOUTH THEATER performs at Society Hill Playhouse as well. This is an Alternative Program for students between the ages of 15 and 18 who live in Philadelphia or surrounding communities. Philadelphia high school students also make up the audiences. The productions are a group effort. It's a training ground in real theater for budding actors, actresses and technicians. In addition to acting, students get to work on sets, props and costumes.

Their approach to drama is young and fresh. A contemporary version of "Phantom of the Opera" was recently adapted by youth and for youth in this "almost adult" theater.

One play is produced early in December, Shakespeare is in February and another show is in the last two weeks of May. There isn't any charge to see these performances. And who knows what future stars you might get to see?

TEMPLE UNIVERSITY
Tomlinson Theater
13th and Norris Streets—19122
787-1122

SEPTA: Bus C on Broad Street; trolley 23 on 11th or 12th Streets. There's free attended parking in Lot #6 adjacent to the theater (enter on Diamond Street).

E & D: Special arrangements must be made in advance for people in wheelchairs to enter by side door. Otherwise, there are steps.

The productions at Temple theaters are under the auspices of Temple's Department of Theater. This is where you might see tomorrow's stars today.

Main Stage productions take place on Temple's main campus at the 480-seat Tomlinson Theater. Each show usually has a two-week run during the college year with evening curtain times and Sunday matinees. Musicals, comedies, classics and contemporary drama make up the season. Smaller productions take place at the more intimate Randall Theater or at Stage III (see below). Inquire about these, too.

Tickets can be purchased for Tomlinson and Stage III productions individually or in a series. Naturally, student discounts are available as well as special rates for senior citizens and groups.

Schedules for Tomlinson Theater and Stage III are available in the late summer. They can be mailed, or you can call or stop by the information desk at Temple University Center City, 1619 Walnut Street, to get yours.

Stage III
1619 Walnut Street—19103
787-1122 or 787-1619

SEPTA: Buses 2, 9, 21, 42; Market or Chestnut Street routes.
E & D: Entrance is level with street and there's an elevator to basement theater.

Temple University's Center City campus opened in 1973 and the 180-seat Stage III was inaugurated in the spring of 1974. For you Philadelphia trivia buffs, the theater was once the home of the Mike Douglas Television Show.

Many of Stage III's productions are Philadelphia premieres. They're presented two weeks at a time, and they have evening and Sunday matinee performances.

Stage III is also the locale for Novel Stages (you'll read about them soon) and other visiting and local acting companies, so call for a schedule of what you might see here.

WALNUT STREET THEATER
9th and Walnut Streets—19107
574-3550 or WALNUT-5

SEPTA: Buses 9, 21, 38, 42, 47, 61 or Ben FrankLine route 76.
E & D: See Chapter 16.

The Walnut Street Theater is the oldest continuously operating theater in the English-speaking world. It opened in 1808 with a gala circus performance and has a colorful history. It was designated a National Historic Landmark in 1964, and a two-year total renovation of the Walnut was completed early in the 1970s. It was the site of the historic first debate between then-President Gerald R. Ford and Jimmy Carter back in September, 1976.

The Walnut Street Theater Company produces five mainstage plays a year from October to May, including musicals and Shakespeare. Subscriptions are available (call 925-6885), and there are discounts for early purchases, students, groups and senior citizens. Tickets for individual performances are also available at the box office.

There are evening performances during the week and

Saturdays, as well as a weekday and weekend matinees. This is a popular series, so call in advance to find out what's scheduled.

In addition to its two-level, 1,052 seat theater, the Walnut has two more intimate theaters in its adjoining building at 825 Walnut Street where you can enjoy four plays a year. Most of the plays are new, as part of the Studio Theater series.

When the Walnut Street Theater Company isn't presenting plays, its stages are home to theatrical road shows, dance, opera and musical programs. The Walnut is a center for all of the arts.

THE WILMA THEATER
2030 Sansom Street—19103
963–0249

SEPTA: Buses 9, 17, 21, 42 or a short walk from Market Street routes.

E & D: There's one step outside. Call ahead for ramp to be placed. Complete wheelchair access in the theater.

The Wilma Theater also gives Philadelphians a potpourri of innovative drama in a cozy 100-seat theater. There are original works, multi-media presentations and staging that provokes the imagination. Four shows are presented each year from late September to June. Each runs for seven weeks.

Curtain is Tuesday to Saturday at 8 P.M. (except Opening Night Tuesday at 7); Saturday and Sunday at 2. Tickets are $19 and $24, and there are discounts for subscribers, students, senior citizens and groups. Call the Innovation Arts Box Office at 963–0345 for reservations.

Note: The Wilma plans to build Philadelphia's first new theater in six decades. Look for an addition to the Hilton Hotel at Broad and Locust Streets to include a 300-seat Wilma Theater at the northeast corner of Broad and Spruce Streets.

MORE THEATERS?
THE SHOW MUST GO ON.

There's something for everyone on stage in Philadelphia.

Many theaters and little groups in and around Philadelphia offer a variety of outstanding and unusual productions. They often look for localites to participate, as well as for audiences to enjoy their shows. Here's a few.

BRISTOL RIVERSIDE THEATRE opened its first season in 1988 at a sparkling contemporary 300-seat showplace situated on the Delaware River about 45 minutes north of center city. The address is 120 Radcliffe Street in Bristol, PA. Five plays make up the subscription series from September to May. They could be comedy, drama or fully-orchestrated musical theater. Performances are Wednesday to Saturday evenings, plus Wednesday and Saturday matinees. Individual tickets are $14 to $22.

When the curtain comes down in May, Bristol serves up special events, concerts and lighter dramatic fare during the summer. Children's Theater is two or three Saturday mornings each month during the season. Call 788–7827 for information and reservations, or write to P.O. Box 1250, Bristol, PA 19007 for subscription details.

BUSHFIRE THEATER at 52nd and Locust Streets in West Philadelphia was founded in 1976 as a writers and actors workshop and a forum for African-American playwrights. They're a professional equity theater who use mostly local talent to present five plays each year that are usually local premieres. Their stage is a 400-seat converted movie theater. Comedy, musicals and drama enjoy runs of two to four weeks from September to May. Each spring, over school vacation weeks, there's a special production for children and family entertainment. Tickets are $10 to $17.50, with discounts for senior citizens, students, groups and subscribers. If you'd like to submit a play or attend a play, call 747–9230 for details.

Four plays and popular children's theater are presented from October to July at the 140-seat **CHELTENHAM PLAYHOUSE** at 439 Ashbourne Road in Cheltenham, PA (379–4027). The schedule is available in late June. Tickets are available individually or by subscription. There are special rates for groups and parties. This is part of an extensive cultural program from the Cheltenham Arts Center (379–4660).

A charming old stone grist mill was converted in 1923 into the **HEDGEROW THEATER** at 64 Rose Valley Road in Moylan, Pa. It was completely restored again, to accommodate audiences of 135 to 150, after fire gutted the old Hedgerow in 1985. A dedicated resident company of nine is once again presenting their dramas, mystery and comedy at the airy "new" theater behind the historic facade.

Performances are every Thursday, Friday and Saturday at 8 P.M. Tickets are $10 and $12. Call 565–4211 for details. They also go on tour with mainstage productions and to area schools with delightful children's productions. The Hedgerow Playhouse also enjoys an outstanding reputation for their acting classes. They're really quite famous in Philadelphia.

NOVEL STAGES was founded in New York City in 1986 but, luckily for us, chose to move to Philadelphia in 1988. The stage for their novel performances is Stage III at Temple University Center City, 1619 Walnut Street.

Four world premieres are presented each season for runs of three weeks each. The titles might be familiar, but the interpretation is always new. Each play shares a unique collaboration with music or special stage effects. Showtime is 7 P.M. for Monday openings, 8 P.M. Wednesday to Saturday, and 3 P.M. on Sunday. Tickets for individual shows are available from the Novel Stages box office at 963–9775, or call 843–6152 for subscription information.

OLD ACADEMY PLAYERS presents six popular shows from September to June at their theater (which used to be a church) at 3544 Indian Queen Lane. Cake and coffee are served to 130 theater-goers at intermission.

Curtain for each show is at 8:30 P.M. on Friday and Saturday and 2 P.M. on Sunday for three consecutive weekends. Tickets are $7, with discounts available for groups.

This is a delightful way to see a favorite comedy, mystery or drama. For a schedule and reservations, call 487–0572.

Contemporary and classic drama is electrifying when it's performed by the **PEOPLE'S LIGHT AND THEATER COMPANY** located at 39 Conestoga Road in

Malvern, Pa. 19355 (644–3500). It's worth the 40-minute drive from center city Philadelphia to see this dynamic troupe in their dramatic country home: a magnificently converted 200-year-old stone barn that's now a top caliber 400-seat theater and a 200-seat Steinbright Stage Cabaret.

Four mainstage productions are presented annually, each with a six week run. Performances are nightly except Monday, with a matinee on Sunday (a nice time to picnic before the show). When the curtain is down on the mainstage, chances are good there will be a lively production in the cabaret.

Tickets for People's Light productions are $10.50 to $24, with discounts for senior citizens, students, children under 18 and groups. Call for additional information.

Four shows are presented annually by **PHILADEL-PHIA AREA REPERTORY THEATRE** at the charming Mask & Wig Theatre, 310 S. Quince Street in center city between Spruce and Pine, 11th and 12th Streets. The plays are paired to alternate performances in the spring and fall seasons on Wednesdays to Sundays. Tickets are $17.50, and discounts are available for senior citizens, students, groups and subscribers. Call 922–1038 or write to P.O. Box 54319, Phila., PA 19105 for ticket and schedule information so you can take PART in this masterful theatrical experience.

If you've never experienced mime, make it a point to see **THE QUIET RIOT COMEDY THEATER**. Their show includes verbal story-telling, mime and comedy. It incorporates clever costumes, dance, gymnastics, creative lighting and sound backdrops to tell the tale.

The Quiet Riot Comedy Theater has appeared at the Walnut Street Theater, the Philadelphia Museum of Art, the Philadelphia Folk Festival and almost every area college theater. They often appear on stage at the Free Library of Philadelphia . . . a logical place for a quiet performance. Shh!

The Quiet Riot Comedy Theater also brings its show to you (see Chapter 13). For information, call 885–8825.

The concept of **THEATER CENTER PHILADEL-PHIA** is unique in Philadelphia. Its current stage is the Shubin Theater at 407 Bainbridge Street, just one block south of the South Street district. Local playwrights arrange in advance to have script-in-hand readings of their new works at the weekly **Playwright's Workshop**. The public is invited to listen to and critique them on Tuesdays at 8 P.M. Admission is $3. Many of the pieces read in these open forums go on to become T.C.P. productions.

T.C.P. also stages modern and experimental plays that are rarely or never seen in Philadelphia. The works of Brecht, Pirandello, Sternheim and Wedekind are among those that have been "reinterpreted" at this informal theater where seating is arranged for each production to accommodate an audience of about 70. Tickets are $8 to $12, with discounts for students, senior citizens, groups and series subscribers.

Another facet of T.C.P. is its annual summer **Black Theater Festival**. Philadelphia or world premieres of works by African-Americans are staged from late June to September. The plays might be contemporary or revivals of classics. Showtime is Wednesday to Saturday nights at 8 and Sundays at 7, and ticket prices are the same as above.

If you've considered yourself a would-be actor or playwright, Theater Center Philadelphia is an ideal place to try out your talent. Call 336–3869 for additional information.

Seasoned performers, faculty and graduate students in Villanova University's Masters in Theater program are cast in five productions from October through April at the **VILLANOVA THEATRE** series. Situated on Philadelphia's Main Line* about 40 minutes from center city, Villanova Theatre is 235 seats in-the-round in the campus' Vasey Hall. Since the rows are only four deep, every seat is a good one. A unique new set is built for every show.

There are 10 performances of each play from Wednesday to Sunday in two consecutive weeks. Single tickets are $10 to $12; $6 for students; and there's a 20% discount for senior citizens, groups and subscribers. Call 645–7474 for a schedule and to order tickets for this popular series that recently celebrated its thirtieth anniversary.

Chapter 11.
Libraries.

A library is more than a place to do research and homework assignments. A library can be a source of fun. A place for enjoyment and self-improvement.

In Philadelphia, we're fortunate in having libraries of all types and sizes. Many are part of museums, cultural and historical attractions. Those listed in this chapter with an asterisk (*) appear elsewhere in this book with more details. Refer to the Index.

Some libraries require you do your reading there, while others allow you to borrow their books. In some cases you have to be a member to use the facilities. Some libraries even offer tours.

If you have questions on a particular subject, it's wise to call the library in advance to see if they can help you.

"The Fabulous Freebie"

FREE LIBRARY OF PHILADELPHIA
Central Library—Logan Square
19th and Vine Streets—19103
686-5322, for instant information

Hours: Monday to Wednesday, 9 to 9; Thursday and Friday, 9 to 6; Saturday, 9 to 5; Sunday, 1 to 5. Closed Sundays in summer and 15 holidays during the year. Hours vary with the branches and the season, so call ahead to be sure. All branch libraries are listed under "Free Library" in the White Pages of the Philadelphia Telephone Directory.

Tours: Scheduled a month in advance for groups of no more than 15 (larger groups will be divided) for weekdays from 9 to 4. Allow one hour. An adult must accompany students. For children through 8th grade, call the Office for Work with Children, 686–5372; for 9th graders through adults, call the Office for Work with Adults-Young Adults, 686–5345. Tours of the Rare Book Department are weekdays at 11; groups are scheduled at other times by appointment. Call 686–5416.

Cost: There is no charge for tours or any of the special events at the Free Library. Membership is available, free, to any resident of or student in Philadelphia, to workers who pay the City wage tax and non-residents over 65 years old. For anyone else, the annual cost is $15.

Lunch: The Skyline Cafeteria (with a terrific view) on the Central Library's 4th floor is open to the public weekdays, 9 to 4, and Saturdays, except in summer, 10 to 2. Brown-bagging is allowed. Groups are not permitted between 11 and 1:30.

SEPTA: Buses 32, 33, 38, Ben FrankLine route 76.

Other: The Library Store offers unusual stationery, jewelry, posters, books and items you'd like for your personal library.

E & D: See Chapter 16.

The Free Library of Philadelphia houses over four million bound volumes in the Central Library and 49 neighborhood branches. About one-third of those books are in the Central Library. The three regional branches are Northeast at Cottman Avenue and Oakland Street (685–0500), Northwest at Chelten Avenue and Green Street (685–2150) and West Philadelphia at 52nd and Sansom Streets (823–7424).

The Free Library has grown from its original three-room home in 1894 in City Hall to one of the country's largest library systems with a main building that's among the biggest of its kind in the country.

The Free Library is for you. Members of the Free Library may borrow as many as 12 books at one time for as long as 21 days, and sometimes for the entire summer. Besides having books, the Free Library has changing exhibits, displays and special programs.

A good place to start your visit to the Free Library is the General Information Department on the second floor. The knowledgeable staff answers thousands of questions each month by phone and to visitors. These people can make your research easier. General Information also houses all telephone directories for Pennsylvania, Delaware and New Jersey as well as for all U.S. cities with populations over 100,000.

The Data Base and Newspaper Center (686–2860) is also housed on the second floor. You have five minutes to search at no charge for news items from The Inquirer or Daily News on one of the Center's five different information systems. Over a million abstracts are stored in over a thousand data bases. The "V.I.C.S." system here and in the three regional branch libraries provides career information for high school students, people making career changes and those re-entering the job market. There's no charge for use of the V.I.C.S.

Are you looking for a particular newspaper? The Free Library subscribes to over 130 newspapers, including several foreign ones. This is a great way to practice a foreign language, to find out what's going on back home or to look up the news from an important day in your past. The Data Base and Newspaper Center is open weekdays from 9 to 5.

The Social Science and History Department's collection includes guidebooks to most major cities as well as a Map Collection of almost 100,000 maps and charts. It's also where you'll find the Regional Foundation Center to research fund-raising and proposal writing. An appointment is necessary (686–5423) if you're a first-time user of these resources.

There are more than 12,000 completely scored musical compositions in the Fleisher Collection of Orchestral Music, making this the largest collection of its kind in the world. Most of the classical, jazz or show music can be listened to on earphones.

The Free Library has one of the world's finest collections of literature on cars, motorcycles, bicycles and carriages in the Automobile Reference Collection. You'll be interested to know that almost all of the 10,000 or so annual U.S. government's publications are in the Government Publications Department.

We think every conceivable hobby and profession is covered in the Business, Science and Industry Department which shelves business books, financial books, magazines and popular literature.

The Rare Book Department is like a rich Uncle Henry's private paneled library. It's lavishly furnished to display hundreds of old manuscripts like Edgar Allan Poe's "Murders in the Rue Morgue" and "The Raven." And for those who have grown up to love her tales, Beatrix Potter's first editions and many of her original drawings are here. Special tours of the Rare Book Department are available as described above.

The Video and Film Center at the Central Library (and for videos at all branches) allows borrowers to take home 16mm films and video cassettes. And there are 2,000 films and over 3,000 videos from which to choose. There's more about this service in the section of Chapter 13 on "tours to go."

Most branches feature a Children's Department which you'll be reading about in 30 seconds.

Of course, the Free Library has fiction. With over 40,000 volumes, it's the largest collection in Pennsylvania. Over 125,000 books on all subjects are available for borrowing from the Central Lending Department. We could obviously fill a book on all of the departments, books, events and services at the Free Library. Is it any wonder it's called "The Fabulous Freebie?"

The Children's Department
Central Library
686–5369

Hours: Weekdays, 9 to 6; Saturday, 9 to 5; Sunday, 1 to 5, except when the Central Library is closed.

Tours: Call at least a month in advance to schedule groups of no more than 15 and up to 8th grade level. Allow one hour for story time, a short film and discussion of the library. Groups can visit the Rare Book Department and outside the Children's Department by special request.

Cost: There's no charge for tours. Membership is open, free, to any Philadelphia youngster who is able to write his or her full name. Up to 5 books may be borrowed at a time for a 3-week period.

E & D: See Chapter 16.

The shelves of the Children's Room are crammed with fairy tales, magazines, fiction, picture stories and other informative books for youngsters from pre-school to eighth grade. (There's a Parents Room and there are special collections for adults to use with children.)

This is the largest collection of books for children and for those studying children's literature in Philadelphia.

In Philadelphia, children are encouraged to become acquainted with books at an early age. The library holds Story Hours* for pre-schoolers, Picture Book Story Hours for kindergarten to second graders and Story Hours for school age children. An Annual Spring Book Review with displays, reviews and reading lists of the year's outstanding children's books is given to parents, teachers and librarians. A "Welcome Gifts" book list is available in mid-November for suggested holiday giving.

Every summer the library encourages youngsters from fourth through eighth grades to join the eight-week

Vacation Reading Club. The club has a meeting each week (at the Central Library and every branch library) where its members discuss books they've read from among specified categories of fiction and non-fiction. The members must read at least eight books to finish the program and receive a certificate.

At the same time, pre-school through third grade children are encouraged to join READ Time. Any parent, older sibling or care-giver can bring their youngster to the library, get them their own library card and help them choose any book to read during the summer. Every child who completes the program gets his or her own Really Exciting And Different Time certificate.

Book Concerts*, Story Hours*, Film Festivals* and an occasional Lecture Series are regularly scheduled at the Free Library. They're usually on Sunday afternoons at 2 at the Central Library. You can stop by any branch library to pick up a monthly calendar of events that includes activities at all of the libraries.

Or for more information about special events, the Vacation Reading Club and READ Time for youngsters, or other programs sponsored by the Free Library, call the Office for Work with Children (686–5369) or the Office for Work with Adults-Young Adults (686–5345).

General Interest

RYERSS MUSEUM-LIBRARY*
Cottman and Central Avenues—19111
745–3061

Hours: Friday to Sunday, 10 to 5.
Note: This library is not part of the ACCESS PENNSYLVANIA system.

In 1895, Robert W. Ryerss willed that his stately mansion's library be open free to the public. His trust gives area residents an opportunity to use its resources.

Membership at Ryerss is open to residents of the Burholme Park neighborhood and surrounding communities.

Ryerss is divided into departments for adults and children. Over 15,000 volumes of fiction, non-fiction and reference works make up the circulating collection.

There's also a very special collection of Victoriana and books about that era, as well as historic maps of the Burholme Park and Fox Chase areas, which are available for use at the library.

In case you didn't know, Philadelphia is a college town. It's the home of more than 30 colleges and universities. Among them are the University of Pennsylvania, Temple University, Drexel University, LaSalle University, St. Joseph's University, Thomas Jefferson University, University of the Arts, Bryn Mawr College, Haverford College and the Philadelphia Community College. All of these schools have outstanding libraries.

While you can't borrow their books if you aren't enrolled there, you're welcome to browse and do research.

Incidentally, many of these libraries are worth visiting just to see.

Searching for Your Roots

AMERICAN-SWEDISH HISTORICAL MUSEUM* (389–1776) has catalogued more than 20,00 volumes, manuscripts, rare books and genealogy charts to research American and Swedish history and immigration to the middle-Atlantic colonies. An appointment is necessary at the Nord Library (during museum hours) and it's helpful if you can read Swedish since a majority of the collection is in that language.

BALCH INSTITUTE* (925–8090) has a research library of more than 60,000 books, and most of them that were printed after 1900 are available through inter-library loan. Balch also has a vast collection of manuscripts, microfilms and newspapers representing ethnic and minority groups who have immigrated to North America. These resources are available to the public and there is no charge. The hours are 9 to 5, Monday to Saturday.

CATHOLIC HISTORICAL SOCIETY* (667–2125) is bound to have information for your research on Catholicism. See Chapter 5 for details.

The library of **GERMANTOWN HISTORICAL SOCIETY*** at 5503 Germantown Avenue (844–8428) goes into the past of Germantown and its residents. If you're tracing local history or genealogy, this is a good place to start. The collection also includes over 12,000 photographs. Hours are Tuesday and Thursday, 10 to 4; Sunday, 1 to 5. The user's fee for non-members is $2; senior citizens and students, $1.50.

JOSEPH HORNER MEMORIAL LIBRARY of the German Society of Pennsylvania* (627–4365) has more than 100,000 volumes, 85 percent in the German language. Annual membership entitles you to library privileges and regularly scheduled activities of the German Society. Library hours are Tuesday, Wednesday and Thursday, 10 to 4.

The **MENNONITE CHURCH LIBRARY*** (843–0943) will be of interest to researchers of Mennonite and Germantown history. Call for an appointment.

PHILADELPHIA JEWISH ARCHIVES CENTER* (925–8090) is what the name implies. See Chapter 5 for details.

PRESBYTERIAN HISTORICAL SOCIETY* (627–1852) is another religious archives center, specializing in Presbyterianism in the U.S. and abroad. Call ahead to see if they have the material you need, and make an appointment to do your research.

YEARLY MEETING LIBRARY at the Friends Center Complex, 1515 Cherry Street (241–7220), is of general interest to Quakers. Books can be borrowed by Friends School teachers, members and attenders of the Yearly Meeting and other Quaker affiliates. The public is welcome to use the books at the library. Ask about a library subscription if you'd like borrowing privileges. Hours are weekdays, 9 to 5, except a few weeks in August and holidays when the library is closed.

ATHENAEUM OF PHILADELPHIA
219 South 6th Street—19106
925–2688

Hours: Weekdays, 9 to 5. Closed holidays.
Tours: Groups of 10 to 30, 4th grade and above, are scheduled by calling at least a week ahead. Allow about one hour and specify if you want a general tour or emphasis on architecture or literature.
Cost: Free.
SEPTA: Bus 90 or Walnut Street routes.
E & D: There are 6 steps at the entrance. An elevator connects the 3 floors.

The Athenaeum welcomes you back to Victorian Philadelphia. This private library, named for the Greek goddess of wisdom, was founded in 1814. Charles Dickens and Edgar Allan Poe were among the famous writers who used its facilities.

Today the Athenaeum is one of the country's most complete 19th century libraries. Its strong points cover Victorian architecture, interior design, periodicals, literature, the French in America, travel, exploration and transportation. A new exhibition gallery will open in 1992.

Borrowing privileges are limited to members only, but students, writers and researchers are welcome to use the Athenaeum's books and reference works. Call ahead to see if the material you need is available, and to make an appointment.

Tours of the Athenaeum go beyond the literary collections. They focus on the distinctive period furnishings, artwork and architecture. The building was completed in 1847 and was one of Philadelphia's first "brownstones." It was also America's first major building in the Italian Renaissance Revival style. Now it's a National Historic Landmark and completely restored.

CIVIL WAR LIBRARY AND MUSEUM* (735–8196) specializes in books about Abraham Lincoln and the Civil War period. Many of the 12,000 volumes are old and one-of-a-kind so you won't be able to borrow them. The reading rooms are comfortable, though, and the surrounding exhibits get you into the appropriate mood. The hours are the same as for the museum. Call ahead if you want to use the library.

G.A.R. CIVIL WAR MUSEUM AND LIBRARY* (673–1688) is another outstanding source for information relating to the Civil War period. Its 2,500 volumes are non-circulating and available for research by appointment only (but NOT on the first Sunday of each month during the Museum Open House).

HISTORICAL SOCIETY OF PENNSYLVANIA* (732–6201) was the first of its kind in the state. It serves as a user-friendly center for research on Pennsylvania and American history. The Society has been gathering and preserving old documents since it was founded in 1824. Its staff is eager to help you with your research, whether it's academic or simply to discover facts of personal ancestry or neighborhood interest.

Scholars and book lovers from around the world come to see the treasures that start with the archives of the Penn family and continue through three centuries. Over 15 million pieces are included in the manuscripts collection. Another 8,000 bound volumes of newspapers relate to Pennsylvania history. There is also a superb collection of Pennsylvania maps.

If your ancestors were Pennsylvanians, you might be able to use the material here to trace your family tree. The collections include over 10,000 printed family ancestries, manuscripts, family, church and civil records.

The Society requires that reference work be done on the premises. This is a non-circulating library. The hours are Tuesday to Saturday, 10 to 5, and Wednesday till 9. It's closed on holidays.

There's a $5 daily fee for use of the reading rooms. Annual memberships starting at $30 allow limited free use of the reading rooms and also get you subscriptions to "The Pennsylvania Magazine of History and Biography" and "The Pennsylvania Correspondent."

LIBRARY COMPANY OF PHILADELPHIA
1314 Locust Street—19107
546-3181

Hours: Weekdays, 9 to 4:45. Closed holidays.
Tours: Groups of no more than 25 high school students or adults can be scheduled for hour-long tour that includes the current exhibit. Call at least a month ahead.
Cost: Free. Or you might consider purchasing a share in the library for a nominal amount. That is an old and honorable tradition shared by signers of the Declaration and distinguished citizens through the centuries.
SEPTA: Buses 21, 42, 90 or Broad Street routes.
E & D: The entrance is at ground level so there's wheelchair access.

In addition to everything else Benjamin Franklin founded, he also founded this library in 1731. It was the first of a long list of Franklin's "finds" to follow.

This is the oldest cultural institution in America. It was the country's first subscription library. The first books were brought here from England in 1732. The library currently houses over 500,000 books that tell you about America from Colonial times to the Civil War era.

Among the Library Company's treasures are Lewis and Clark's guidebook to their 1804 expedition, Thomas Jefferson's personal copy of his first published book and the James Logan collection, which was the most important library in the colonies.

The Library Company's building is an award-winning design of contemporary architecture. It's next door and connected to the Historical Society of Pennsylvania.

Note: This library is open to students, scholars and the curious for research purposes only, and their work must be done here.

LIBRARY HALL* (440-3400) is the venerable library of the American Philosophical Society. It's also part of Independence National Historical Park and described previously in Chapter 2.

NATIONAL ARCHIVES
Mid-Atlantic Region
9th and Market Streets—19107
597-3000

Hours: Weekdays, 8 to 5; 1st and 3rd Saturdays of each
month, 8 to 12. Closed holidays.
Tours: You're on your own to view exhibits and use
resources. Groups must call at least 2 weeks ahead to
schedule a 1- to 2-hour tour. See below for topics. Workshops on genealogy are offered in the spring and fall.
Call for dates, details and reservations.
Cost: Free.
SEPTA: Any Market or Chestnut Street route.
Other: Items for sale include books, postcards, posters
and games related to U.S. history as well as family-tree
charts and books related to family history.
E & D: Wheelchair entrance from Market Street side.

The National Archives of the United States in Washington, D.C. houses the records that document our nation's
history from 1775 to today.

All of the documents that are considered to be of permanent value from all three branches of the Federal
government are stored here. Among the millions of documents at the main branch of the National Archives are
the Declaration of Independence, the Constitution of the
United States and the Bill of Rights.

Several Federal depositories are located around the
United States, and Philadelphia is one of 11 field archives. The local holdings include federal records from
agencies in Pennsylvania, Delaware, Maryland, Virginia
and West Virginia; the U.S. District Courts; the U.S.
Court of Appeals for the Third and Fourth Circuits; the
U.S. Army Corps of Engineers and the U.S. Navy.

Microfilm holdings include census records from 1790 to
1910, Civil War records, Revolutionary War records, passenger list indexes from ships that arrived in Philadelphia from 1800 to 1948 and Baltimore from 1820 to 1952,
and indexes for Naturalization Petitions in the Federal
Courts of Baltimore, Pittsburgh, Philadelphia and Wilmington from 1795 to 1968.

These resources are all available for your use.

The museum exhibits are drawn from the Archives'
vast resources. The exhibits change twice a year.

Groups can schedule visits and choose from one of four topics. They'll learn what an archives is and how to use it. Original documents, microfilm, a slide show, tour and demonstration are part of the program.

You can focus on "Searching for Your Roots," "Introduction to Historical Documents," "Archives and the Three Federal Branches of Government" or a special program based on the current museum exhibit.

It's practically impossible to visualize the scope of the National Archives. A visit to the Philadelphia branch for the Mid-Atlantic Region will heighten your understanding and certainly aid any research in these areas.

Researching a Special Interest

Of course, all of the libraries described above are also likely sources for researching a special interest.

Many of the following libraries are also available in museums. Most of the museums have an admission charge, but the fee is often waived if you are visiting specifically to use the library.

ACADEMY OF NATURAL SCIENCES* (299–1040) has a research library specializing in biology, geology and the natural sciences. The public may use the reading room but books are loaned only to members. The hours are weekdays, 9 to 5.

The **COLLEGE OF PHYSICIANS OF PHILADEL-PHIA LIBRARY**, 19 South 22nd Street (561–6050), ranks among the top 10 collections of its kind in the United States. Dr. John Morgan, who formed the library in 1789, was a founder of the College of Physicians and the nation's first medical school at the University of Pennsylvania. Dr. Morgan donated 25 volumes to the library. Today there are almost 600,000 volumes, and almost 800 medical journals arrive here each year. You're welcome to use the library's reference materials in the library. There's a $2 per day user's fee for the reading rooms. Hours are weekdays, 9 to 5, except holidays when the College is closed. The **Mutter Museum*** is also here at the College of Physicians and worthy of your visit.

A small non-circulating library at the **EBENEZER MAXWELL MANSION*** (438–1861) enables study of Victorian architecture and landscape design and research on property restoration. There are photographs, journals and books. Hours are the same as for the mansion. Call ahead to check if the resources here could be helpful.

The **FEDERAL RESERVE BANK*** has a research library (574–6543) for people interested in banking, finance and the economy. There are current books and periodicals, as well as periodicals dating back to the early 1800s and all Federal Reserve publications. All research must be done at the library. Hours are weekdays, 9 to 4. A guard will direct you when you enter the building and sign in.

HENRY GEORGE BIRTHPLACE* (922–4278) contains a library devoted to economics and the particular economic philosophy of its namesake. There's also a small collection on Chinese language and philosophy. You're welcome to visit the house and browse through its books, but only students of the Henry George School of Social Science are permitted to borrow them.

An archival library at the **INSTITUTE OF CONTEMPORARY ART*** (898–7108) houses literature, publications, art and items relating to shows presented at the museum since its founding in 1963. It's a unique resource for in-house study on some of the most avant-garde work to be done in recent decades. Call ahead to determine if the collections can be of help in your research.

JENKINS MEMORIAL LAW LIBRARY (592–5690) is the place to go if you're interested in law. It's at 841 Chestnut Street and open Monday to Saturday, except holidays. Call ahead for specific hours. The stacks and comfortable reading areas are available to the public, and books may be borrowed by members of the library and the Philadelphia Bar Association.

The library at the **NEW YEAR'S SHOOTERS & MUMMERS MUSEUM*** (336–3050) contains historic Mummerabilia, a collection of English Mummers' plays and the latest in video-tape and copying equipment to aid in your research since you won't be able to borrow any of the materials. It's open by appointment only.

PENNSYLVANIA HORTICULTURAL SOCIETY*
(625–8261) maintains a growing library of books and periodicals about horticulture, plants and gardens. Members of the Society are welcome to borrow from its bulging shelves; others can dig into the books while there. If you thought about starting a garden, it is a good place to find out how to do it.

At the **PENNSYLVANIA HOSPITAL*** (829–3971) in the Old Pine Building, you'll find the country's most complete collection of medical books from 1750 to 1850, and some that go back as early as the 16th century. This was the first and finest medical library in the colonies, located here in 1847 and elegantly restored in 1977. There are over 13,000 volumes. Obviously, these books aren't available for loan. A compact new medical library is upstairs.

PHILADELPHIA MARITIME MUSEUM* (925–5439) has a non-circulating library for those of you doing research on maritime life. If you're a museum member or serious researcher, call ahead for an appointment, weekdays 9 to 5. There's a $4 charge for non-members.

The **PHILADELPHIA MUSEUM OF ART*** (763–8100 Ext. 259) has an extensive library of books on art, art history, decorative arts and art sales that museum members are welcome to use at the museum on Wednesdays, Thursdays and Fridays from 10 to 4. Members are admitted free. There's a $5 annual fee for teachers and graduate students, and it's $10 a year for anyone else having reciprocal arrangements to use the resources.

ROSENBACH MUSEUM* (732–1600) is a veritable gold mine of rare books, priceless manuscripts and the thousands of books collected by A.S.W. Rosenbach during his lifetime and by the museum and library established after his death. Read about some of them in Chapter 9, or, better yet, go there. You have to see it to believe it. Rosenbach's library is open by appointment, weekdays 9 to 5, for serious research only.

The library at **SCHUYLKILL CENTER FOR ENVIRONMENTAL EDUCATION*** (482–7300) is restricted to borrowing by members only, but anyone is welcome to use the resources here. The 4,000 books are all about nature, ecology and the environment. If you're interested in borrowing privileges and activities at the Schuylkill Center, inquire about membership.

The **UKRAINIAN LIBRARY** (663–8572) at the Ukrainian Educational and Cultural Center (see Chapter 5) has the only collection of Ukrainian and bilingual books in the tri-state area available for circulation. Some 11,000 volumes and 25 periodic titles are available representing general literature and specific areas for research. Hours are Tuesday to Saturday, 10 to 3, except Friday, 1 to 8 P.M. If this resource stirs your interest, call for membership information.

The reference library at the **WAGNER FREE INSTITUTE*** (763–6529) is valuable if you're doing research on natural history or scientific subjects. There are more than 25,000 bound volumes and 150,000 pamphlets, magazines and periodicals, including many foreign titles. The materials are available to scholars only, by reservation, during museum hours.

Chapter 12.
International Philadelphia.

Foreign Aid

This chapter is for visiting foreigners or anyone who seeks a taste of foreign lands.

If you're a visiting foreigner or have an interest in foreign lands and peoples, you have several sources of special assistance with tours and interesting programs. The most obvious source, of course, is the city's official VISITORS CENTER* on John F. Kennedy Boulevard at 16th Street (636–1666). Here are some others.

INTERNATIONAL HOUSE OF PHILADELPHIA
3701 Chestnut Street—19104
387–5125

This well-designed, modern high-rise is a home-away-from-home for 450 foreign and American residents and graduate students. A small number of short-term accommodations are also available for visitors interested in unique housing (see Chapter 20).

International House provides social and service programs for its residents, including at-home hospitality extended by Philadelphia hosts. In return, International House invites you to its outstanding facilities with a smorgasbord of happenings.

There's the Neighborhood Film/Video Project* and frequently scheduled cultural events with guest musicians, ethnic performers and speakers on international issues. Many of these events are described in Chapters 9 and 10 of this book.

There's a gourmet cafeteria restaurant, Eden, at International House. The International Bazaar sells jewelry and crafts from around the world.

All of this proves that you don't have to go far in Philadelphia to get a foreign taste. Most of the activity at International House is scheduled year-round. If you're interested, call for details.

Remember: An **asterisk (*)** indicates that the same place or event appears elsewhere in the book with more details. Look in the Index for additional pages.

INTERNATIONAL VISITORS CENTER
OF PHILADELPHIA
3rd floor, Civic Center Museum
34th Street and Civic Center Boulevard—19104
823-7261

The International Visitors Center of Philadelphia ar-ranges professional appointments, home hospitality, and tours led by multi-lingual Philadelphians for over 3,000 sponsored foreign visitors each year. IVC also refers for-eign visitors to service committees and organizations that could be of interest.

The International Visitor Program sponsored by the U.S. Information Agency is also administered locally by IVC. Some 125 former and current foreign leaders have visited America under the auspices of this program.

If you're a Philadelphian who would like to have the op-portunity to meet and help welcome foreign guests to your city, then call IVC and ask about being a member. This is truly a unique chance to offer social and professional hospitality to future world leaders.

NATIONALITIES SERVICE CENTER
1300 Spruce Street—19107
893-8400

If you're coming to live in Philadelphia from another country, you'll find that this agency can be very helpful.

The Nationalities Service Center is a United Way agen-cy that serves the social, educational and personal needs of immigrants and their descendants. It helps refugees and non-English-speaking people with problems result-ing from language or cultural differences.

The NSC teaches English as a second language to new-comers, provides social activities and prepares immi-grants and refugees for the naturalization process. They also have changing exhibits of foreign arts and crafts.

Foreign visitors and Philadelphians who need transla-tion or interpreter service can benefit from this agency. The NSC Translation Service operates weekdays from 9 to 5 for anyone needing translation of an official docu-ment. Call 893-8418 Ext. 116. The NSC Interpreter Serv-ice is a 24-hour hotline for anyone needing emergency translation or oral interpretations of refugee languages. Call 893-8418 Ext. 115 from 9 to 5, or 735-7022 at any other time. There is a fee for this service.

The NSC also founded the popular Philadelphia Folk Fair that's at the Civic Center on "even" years in April (see Chapter 19).

WORLD AFFAIRS COUNCIL
922–2900

Another opportunity for Philadelphians to get involved in foreign affairs is the World Affairs Council. It invites you to participate in its program of luncheons, dinners, special events, discussions, seminars, trips and tours. There's at least one event each week from which to choose.

World leaders, ambassadors, journalists, international business executives and notables in the arts and industry come to Philadelphia as guests of the World Affairs Council to address its members.

The World Affairs Council guarantees to stimulate your interest in international subjects. They keep you informed of what's going on in the world today. Call if you'd like to find out more about joining this dynamic organization.

Foreign Intrigue

Philadelphians and foreign visitors alike will be interested in touring "foreign" Philadelphia.

Architecture of the British colonial period dominates the historic area. The Benjamin Franklin Parkway, Logan Circle and City Hall have obvious French influences. There are also many classic examples of Greek Revival and Italian Renaissance styles, and they're mentioned throughout this book. Germantown* was predominately settled by Germans. The Swedes founded Old Swedes' Church, and they're highlighted in the American-Swedish Historical Museum*. Mikveh Israel* was the first synagogue in the colonies. The prominence of Ukrainians in Philadelphia is explored when touring the Cathedral of the Immaculate Conception (see Chapter 5). African-Americans can trace their roots at the Afro-American Historical and Cultural Museum*.

The tastiest way to pay a local visit to faraway lands is to sample their foods. And in Philadelphia you can almost dine your way around the world. You can have Chinese food (with chopsticks, of course), nouvelle cuisine from

France, German schnitzel, moussaka from Greece, Italian pasta, Vietnamese chicken sautéed with lemon grass, Japanese food with a tea ceremony, shish kebab from the Middle East or tacos and beans from Mexico.

Restaurants representing many different countries are plentiful in Philadelphia. You'll find them listed by nationality in the Yellow Pages, and you'll also find many of them in Chapter 18. You'll find many of them casual-style under one roof at the Reading Terminal Market*.

And now, more about International Philadelphia.

BALCH INSTITUTE
18 South 7th Street—19106
925-8090

Hours: Monday to Saturday, 10 to 4. Closed holidays. Allow one hour.

Tours: If you're on your own, everything is self-explanatory. Groups of 10 or more should be scheduled at least 2 weeks in advance. Programs are geared to any school level or to adults and can include a choice of films.

Cost: Adults and students, $1; children under 12, free. Groups of 10 or more students, $.50.

SEPTA: Any Market Street route to 7th Street, or a 2-block walk from Independence Hall.

E & D: Complete wheelchair access.

This is where you'll relive the experience of your parents, grandparents or great-grandparents when they immigrated to America. You'll sit on a bench immigrants once sat on when they came to Ellis Island. You'll see exhibits on new immigrants telling what it's like to be in America.

Since one-third of the 50 million immigrants to the United States between 1820 and 1980 entered through ports other than New York, you'll be interested in a major exhibition, "Freedom's Doors: The Other Ports of Entry to the United States." Important documents, clothing, household objects and cherished personal belongings brought by foreigners to America help tell the story.

This is where you can learn about your ethnic heritage. An hour here gives you the total immigration experience.

You can dig further for your roots at the Balch Library described in the previous chapter. Reference is available on more than 80 different cultural groups.

CHINATOWN

There are no regularly scheduled tours of Chinatown in Philadelphia, but you can explore this pocket of center city on your own and discover a wealth of Oriental lore and excitement. The neighborhood is centered around Race Street from 8th to 11th, and from Vine to Market Street.

The **Chinese Cultural and Community Center** at 125 N. 10th Street is worthy of your inspection. Its original structure dates back to the 1830s. It's designed after a Peking Mandarin Palace. The colorful tilework that decorates its facade is actually from China. Authentic New Year's Banquets are held here every winter in conjunction with the Chinese New Year. Every year, chefs are invited from different regions of China to present Philadelphians with a traditional 10-course dinner. Call 923–6767 for the schedule, price information and reservations.

South of the Community Center, spanning 10th Street north of Arch, is the spectacular 40-foot-high **Chinese Friendship Gate**. In 1983, a team of artisans from Philadelphia's sister city Tianjin, China, came here with 142 cases of colorful tiles to build and paint the gate in dazzling colors and symbols. It's a magnificent tribute to the friendship between two distant cities.

Chinatown is famous for its outstanding restaurants. The first restaurant opened in Chinatown in 1880. Today, there must be at least 40 restaurants serving Canton, Szechuan and Hunan cuisines as well as Japanese and Vietnamese fare.

You can shop for Oriental groceries and household items at a number of markets and gift shops on 9th, 10th, 11th and Race Streets. Be sure to stop for fortune cookies at Yep's Bakery at 127 N. 11th Street. Pick up chow mein or lo mein noodles from Ding Ho at 933 Cuthbert Street or New Tung Hop at 133 N. 11th Street. If your timing is right, you might see fortune cookies or noodles being made.

All of the streets of Chinatown are identified with signs in both English and Chinese. The phone company has thoughtfully placed pagoda-style booths on the sidewalks. The sidewalks themselves have a stylized Chinese symbol for long life called a "shou."

You'll get the flavor of the Orient just by strolling through Chinatown.

Good appetite!

GERMAN SOCIETY OF PENNSYLVANIA
611 Spring Garden Street—19123
627-4365

Hours: Weekdays, 10 to 4; Saturday, by appointment. Closed Saturdays in July; closed all of August.
Cost: Free.
SEPTA: Buses 43, 47.
E & D: No wheelchair access.

In Chapter 3 you read about Germantown and the early German settlement in Philadelphia. You might recall that Holy Trinity Roman Catholic Church* was founded for German-speaking Philadelphians in the late 18th century.

The German Society of Pennsylvania, founded in 1764, is the oldest of its kind in America. The Society provides its members with a cultural program of language classes, concerts, exhibits, films and lectures.

The German Society's Joseph Horner Memorial Library was founded in 1817. Call for additional information and see Chapter 11.

ITALIAN MARKET
9th Street, from Wharton to Christian Streets

Hours: Tuesday to Saturday, early mornings till about 6 at night. Some activity on Sunday mornings.
Lunch: There are several restaurants along 9th Street, or munch on fresh fruit, Italian bread and cheese.
SEPTA: Buses 47, 63, 64.
E & D: No stairs to climb, but the walking can be treacherous.

The Italian Market in the heart of South Philadelphia* is different from any market you've ever seen. The neighborhood merchants jam-pack their stores and display their overflowing merchandise on sidewalk tables and pushcarts.

The market is stretched along five city blocks with the hub at 9th Street and Washington Avenue.

You'll find anything that's in season. The stalls are decked with fresh fruits, vegetables, poultry, baked delicacies, pasta and cheeses. An assortment of skinned animals adorns butcher shop windows while chickens and rabbits wait in coops to be selected for someone's dinner.

Hucksters call out the merits of their cod, mackerel, octopus and crabs that are ready to be scooped up from barrels. Even clothing hanging from canopies is for sale.

The prices are reasonable, and the markets are a beehive of activity, especially towards the end of the week when the shoppers stock up. Most of the shops are closed on Sunday and Monday.

As a note of interest, every candidate for office campaigning in Philadelphia, from the President of United States on down, makes it a point to visit the Italian Market. You've also seen 9th Street in a number of movies. . . like "Rocky," "Rocky II," "Rocky III," "Rocky IV" and "Rocky V."

JAPANESE HOUSE and GARDEN
Fairmount Park Horticultural Center*
Lansdowne Drive east of Belmont Avenue
West Fairmount Park
685–0184

Hours: May to October, Wednesday to Sunday, 10 to 4. Call ahead to be sure. Allow 30 minutes or more.
Tours: Japanese guides in kimonos will greet you and explain the function and reason for each of the home's features. Call ahead if you're bringing a group.
Cost: Adults, $1.50; children under 12, $1.
Lunch: No food permitted within the house gates, but you can picnic nearby in Fairmount Park.
SEPTA: Walk from Bus 38 stop on Belmont Avenue. There's plenty of free parking.
E & D: Wheelchair access difficult within the gates; the walkway is narrow and there are a few steps.

Nestled among the trees in scenic Fairmount Park is an authentic replica of a 16th century Japanese home. It's known as a "shoin" and represents the typical living quarters of a scholar, priest or government official of the time.

It's surrounded by Japanese gardens, walkways, waterways and a pond. By today's standards, the house is modern and spacious. And the furnishings are authentic.

Sliding and removable screens separate the rooms to give an open, airy feeling. The "fusama" (sliding screen doors) and "shoji" (sliding paper doors) were restored and painted by Japanese artisans. Tables, chests and bedding are stored away when not in use. Floor cushions provide the seating, and they're covered with "tatami" (rice-straw mats).

The Japanese always remove their shoes before entering the house. It's considered unsanitary to wear shoes indoors, and it also prevents damage to the "tatami."

You might be lucky enough to see "Ikebana," the Japanese art of flower arranging; "Origami," the Japanese art of paper folding; or "Cha-No-Yu," the ancient tradition of the symbolic tea ceremony. If you're especially interested in one of these arts, call ahead for a schedule.

While you're at the Japanese House, don't miss the Horticultural Center that's just a stone's throw away.

POLISH AMERICAN CULTURAL CENTER
308 Walnut Street—19106
922–1700

Hours: January through April, weekdays, 10 to 4; May through December, Monday to Saturday, 10 to 4. Closed holidays.
Tours: Call a few days ahead for school groups and adults. Large groups will be divided. Allow 20 to 45 minutes.
Cost: Free.
Lunch: Arrangements can be made for groups of up to 50 to have a catered lunch with a Polish flavor. Call several weeks ahead.
SEPTA: Buses 9, 21, 42, 50 or a block walk from any route to Independence Hall.
Other: A gift shop sells dolls, books and Polish crafts.
E & D: There's one step at the entrance. Exhibits are in one large room on the ground level.

The Museum Exhibition Hall at the Polish American Cultural Center provides programs and displays that highlight contributions of Poles and Polish Americans to U.S. and world history and culture.

Portraits depict Polish musicians (Chopin, Paderewski), scientists (Madame Curie), writers (Mickiewicz, Sienkiewicz), religious leaders (Pope John Paul II), military leaders (Pulaski, Kosciuszko) and contemporary heros

(Walesa) while accompanying displays tell their stories. Historic photographs put in perspective noteworthy events of Polish life in the 20th century. One exhibit commemorates the 50th anniversary of World War II and the invasion of Poland by the Soviets and Nazis. Art objects, Polish crystal and crafts fill several display cases.

It's fitting that the Polish heritage is being kept alive here, just a few blocks from the Liberty Bell.

TALLER PUERTORRIQUENO
THE PUERTO RICAN WORKSHOP
2721 N. 5th Street—19133
426–3311

Hours: Tuesday to Saturday, 10 to 6. Closed holidays.
Tours: Call at least 2 weeks ahead for groups of up to 40. Ask about combining tour with a film, lecture on Puerto Rican history or an art workshop.
Cost: Free. Donations accepted.
SEPTA: Buses 50, 54.
Lunch: Ask about arrangements to bring in meals from a nearby Spanish eatery.
E & D: There are 2 steps outside and 5 more inside at the front door. Call ahead for people in wheelchairs to enter at rear where an elevator enables access to the 1st floor.

Taller Puertorriqueno was founded in 1974 to promote the arts and culture of Philadelphia's Hispanic population. Appropriately, it's located on the "golden block" of 5th Street, just north of Lehigh Avenue in the heart of the North Philadelphia Hispanic neighborhood. You can't miss the colorful "Three Vejigantes" festival characters who cover an entire facade to welcome you. You'll be captivated by the pulse of the community and the resources provided by the three-story center.

A spacious gallery is the setting for changing art exhibitions of works by professional, student and emerging artists. Lectures, receptions and workshops correspond to each show. A variety of art classes are held regularly for neighborhood youngsters. The bookstore is the largest in the region, featuring reading materials, records, and tapes in Spanish as well as English.

Special programs are also frequently scheduled to involve the community in cultural, historic and current events.

Vengan a visitarnos!

Chapter 13.
Philadelphia at Work.

This chapter takes you into the workings of Philadelphia's government, businesses and industries. It tells how you can tour various city and federal offices, private companies, public utilities and institutions.

Philadelphia is one of the country's leading cities in business and industry, and it's a regional headquarters for several agencies of the federal government. If your group is interested in a particular field that's not shown here, don't hesitate to call a company, institution or department in that area. Many of Philadelphia's prominent banks, brokerage houses, manufacturers, medical facilities and public agencies might accommodate you with special tours.

The last section of this chapter features people who will bring programs to your location.

It's called "Tours to Go."

Tours of City Installations

CITY HALL
Broad and Market Streets—19107
686–1776 (general information)

Hours: Weekdays, 9 to 5. The City Hall Tower* closes a half-hour earlier. Closed holidays. See below for specific activities.
Tours: Call 568–3351 for tour information, in addition to what's noted below, or stop by Room 143 for a "Do-It-Yourself Tour." One-hour guided tours are weekdays at 12:30, departing from Conversation Hall, Room 201, along the north corridor of the 2nd floor (enter through North Broad Street portal). Group tours are by appointment only. Philadelphia Public School classes grades 3 to 12 can be scheduled in advance by calling 686–2840.
Cost: Free.
SEPTA: Buses 12, 17, 27, 31, 32, 33, 76, C; trolleys 10, 11, 13, 34, 36; or either subway route.
Lunch: No facilities, but there are refreshment stands at the northwest and southeast corners.
E & D: To avoid steps, enter under archways to courtyard on south, east or west sides and go to corners of building to use elevators to all 7 floors.

This is where you'll learn how Philadelphia works.

Our City Hall is the largest City Hall in the country, and till 1987, the tallest building in Philadelphia. Its vast size and beauty always amaze visitors. Philadelphians, unfortunately, take it for granted. They're hardly aware of what goes on inside, unless they get in trouble. And, unfortunately, the building is now in need of much refurbishing. The goal is to have the job completely done in time to celebrate in the year 2001 the centennial of City Hall's completion.

City Hall took 30 years to finish, and it cost over $23 million. Just take one look and you'll understand why.

If you're on your own, the best place to start is at the northeast corner, the direction William Penn faces from his perch on top of City Hall. The statue and the tower underwent major restoration in the late 1980s.

The cantilevered stairwells at each of the building's four corners are six stories tall. They were designed by Thomas U. Walter, who designed the dome of the U.S. Capitol.

Take the stairs or an elevator to the second floor. The Mayor's Reception Room (202) is where dignitaries are greeted, proclamations are presented and official ceremonies are held. Walk in, look at the gold-leaf ceiling, the magnificent chandelier, the Honduras mahogany paneling, the portraits of many former Philadelphia mayors and the carpet with the City Seal woven into its center. The Mayor's Office is just around the corner.

Another example of our ornate City Hall is Room 400, the City Council Chamber. **City Council** usually meets on Thursday mornings at 10. Its 17 members are elected every four years to serve (beginning January 1992, 1996, and so forth) a simultaneous term with the Mayor. It's fascinating to see what goes on when they meet. Groups of 10 or more should make reservations by calling the Assistant to the President of City Council at 686-3432.

A bust of City Hall's architect, John McArthur, Jr., is also visible from the fourth floor. Go midway along the south corridor and look up the steps in the interior stairwell. Look on the wall for the marble statue of Mr. McArthur. If he had lived to see the building completed, surely he would have gotten a better place for this tribute.

Court Sessions are open to the public. There are over 40 courtrooms in City Hall for criminal and civil cases. This is an excellent learning experience for school children. For one thing, it shows them why they should stay out of trouble. For another, it might prompt your son or daughter to become an attorney, a court stenographer or court officer. Visiting arrangements must be made in advance for groups of no more than 20 (larger groups will be divided) by calling the Public Information Office of the Philadelphia Court of Common Pleas and Municipal Court at 686-7932. Discretion should be used in choosing the types of cases that youngsters observe.

Arrangements can also be made for small groups of high school students or adults to observe **Traffic Court** hearings on weekdays. Requests must be put in writing at least a month in advance to the President Judge of Traffic Court, **800 Spring Garden Street**, Phila., PA 19123. Use school or organization stationery to make your request and give two or three dates when your group could attend. This can be an invaluable experience for anyone who drives.

Back to City Hall. A trip here isn't complete until you see William Penn atop the **City Hall Tower***. Philadelphia's founder was cast in bronze by sculptor Alexander Milne Calder. The statue stands 37 feet tall and weighs 26 tons. Take an elevator on the north side to the seventh floor, and then follow the lines directing you to the tower elevator.

When you've returned to the ground, walk through City Hall's courtyard (assuming the restoration is completed). There are maps of Philadelphia, plaques commemorating historic events in Philadelphia and the history and development of Centre Square and City Hall.

If you have specific questions while you're at City Hall, visit the Mayor's Action Center in Room 143.

FIRE ADMINISTRATION BUILDING
3rd and Spring Garden Streets—19123
592-5952

Hours: By reservation only, weekdays, except holidays, 2 to 4 P.M. Allow 45 minutes.

Tours: Scheduled for groups of no more than 50, at least elementary school age. One adult must accompany every 10 children. All tour requests must be made at least a few weeks in advance by writing to the Deputy Commissioner of Operations at the above address.

Cost: Free.

SEPTA: Buses 5, 43; Market-Frankford Subway-Elevated.
E & D: Complete wheelchair access.

The Philadelphia Fire Department has a contemporary administration building where special care went into the design and construction. These details will be explained as you tour the facility. You'll see the rooftop helipad and learn about the special facilities that are always ready here in case of a disaster.

Every call for medical units and fire engines in Philadelphia is received and dispatched from the Fire Department Communications Center which is located in the basement of the building. The center always elicits amazement and respect from visitors.

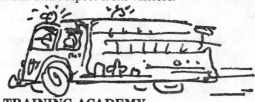

FIRE TRAINING ACADEMY
Delaware River and Pennypack Street—19136
335–8060

Hours: Weekdays, 10 to 4. Closed holidays. Allow at least one hour.
Tours: Scheduled for groups of no more than 50, at least elementary school age. One adult must accompany every 10 children. It's best to visit when there's a class in training.
Cost: Free.
SEPTA: Bus 20.
E & D: Wheelchair access.

This is where you learn how to be a firefighter.

In Philadelphia, if a child's father is a fireman and if his grandfather was or is a fireman, chances are he or she will be a firefighter. It runs in the family.

Try to arrange a tour of the Academy while there's a class in training. It's exciting to watch future firefighters practicing how to climb ropes, use ladders and squirt the hoses. You might also see a class of veteran firefighters getting advanced training in the latest firefighting methods.

FIRE MARINE UNIT #15
Delaware and Washington Avenues on Delaware River
(U.S. Coast Guard Station)
592–5952

Hours: By appointment only, daily, anytime. Allow 20
   minutes.
Tours: For group tour arrangements, see Fire Adminis-
   tration Building. All visitors must be school age.
Cost: Free.
E & D: Wheelchair access.

The fire marine unit at the new U.S. Coast Guard Station is where firemen are stationed aboard the "Delaware," one of Philadelphia's three fireboats. (The
"Bernard Samuel" and "Franklin" are stationed on the
Schuylkill.)

You'll see the 80-foot red boat and the special uniforms
worn by the firemen. A fireman will tell you about his job
on the waterfront. In addition to fighting blazes on the
Camden or Philadelphia side of the Delaware River, the
firemen fight oil spills, help distressed boats and aid in
rescue operations.

FIRE HOUSE—Local Installation
592–5952

Hours: Daily, anytime. Allow at least 20 minutes.
Tours: Visit on your own, or schedule in advance for a
   group visit. For group tour arrangements, see Fire Administration Building.
Cost: Free.
Other: Fire Prevention Week is always the full week that
   includes October 9. It commemorates the great Chicago fire of October 9, 1871. All firehouses hold Open
   House. There are also home fire drills and a series of
   educational programs to promote fire safety. Watch the
   newspapers for a schedule.
E & D: Wheelchair access.

Fire prevention is the best way to fight a fire. Nothing
impresses that on a child more than a visit to a firehouse.
There are 60 fire houses in Philadelphia. The equipment
varies with the size of the station. Your local fire house
might have a hook and ladder truck, medical unit, the
battalion chief's car and, of course, the red fire engines.

A fireman will talk to your group and tell you about his job. When you go on a class tour, ask the fireman about the Junior Fire Patrol Program.

The Fire Department's Fire Prevention Division (592–5967) also conducts, in conjunction with the city's Department of Recreation (686–3600), a Fire Safety Day Camp for three weeks in July. Youngsters from six to 12 are urged to sign up at their local recreation center. If chosen, they'll go by bus for the one day camp at the Fire Training Academy. In addition to touring the Academy, activities include indoor and outdoor education on home fire safety.

POLICE ACADEMY
State Road and Ashburner Street—19136
686–3380 (Police Community Relations)

Hours: Weekdays, 10 to 4. Closed holidays. Allow one hour.
Tours: Scheduled for groups of no more than 30, at least 3rd grade. Write at least 2 weeks in advance to the Philadelphia Police Commissioner, Police Administration Building, 7th and Race Streets, Phila., PA 19106.
Cost: Free.
SEPTA: Buses 70, 84.
E & D: Wheelchair access.

This tour gives visitors a bird's-eye view of the modern facility in which "Philadelphia's finest" receive their 13-week training. You'll see the gymnasium and training areas, and you'll learn about the rigorous curriculum.

The canine unit also trains here. If you're lucky, one of the dogs will give you a demonstration.

You might also see a display of firearms, recruits at physical training, lectures on crowd control or patrol procedure.

POLICE ADMINISTRATION BUILDING
7th and Race Streets—19106
686–3380 (Police Community Relations)

Hours: Weekdays, 10 to 4. Closed holidays. Allow one hour.
Tours: Same procedure for scheduling and reservations as the Police Academy.
Cost: Free.

SEPTA: Buses 47, 48, 61, Ben FrankLine route 76 or Market Street routes.

Other: National Police Week is usually celebrated the second Saturday in May with Open House from 10 to 3. Everyone is invited to see drill teams, the bugle corps and firearms displays. You can tour the building and perhaps ride in a police vehicle.

E & D: Wheelchair access.

Legend has it that the "Roundhouse" was designed with a pair of handcuffs in mind because of its shape.

Tours are geared according to the group's age level. You'll learn about chemical analysis and ballistics. You might see the communications center, a lie detector machine, fingerprinting or any number of other methods of crime prevention being put to work.

POLICE MARINE UNIT

Delaware and Washington Avenues on Delaware River (U.S. Coast Guard Station)
686-3380 (Police Community Relations)

Hours: By appointment only, daily, anytime. Allow 30 minutes.

Tours: Same procedure for scheduling and reservations as the Police Academy.

Cost: Free.

E & D: Wheelchair access.

Everybody gets a thrill out of seeing the Police Marine Unit and the city's fleet of police boats that are moored here. The river patrol's diving gear and headquarters are also here. The marine unit patrols both the Schuylkill and Delaware Rivers.

If the weather's right, and if you're lucky, one of the unit's scuba diver police officers will demonstrate diving techniques.

While you're here, plan to stop by Fire Marine Unit #15.

POLICE STABLES

8600 Krewstown Road—19115
685-0389

Hours: Weekdays, 8 to 4. Allow at least one hour.

Tours: Scheduled for groups of no more than 60 at a time, and an adult must accompany every 10 children. Call at least one week ahead. Your tour will be confirmed by a return call.

Cost: Free.
SEPTA: Bus 19.
E & D: Wheelchair access to observe outdoor activity only. If you want to enter the stables, one adult must be able to accompany each person in a wheelchair.

Since the city's mounted police force was reinstated in 1972, the handsome horses and their riders-in-blue have become a friendly and familiar sight.

A Mounted Training and Services Tour familiarizes you with patrol and stable headquarters in Northeast Philadelphia.

An officer will give you a tour of the stable. He'll show you how the horses are saddled, how the riders are trained, and how the horses are prepared for duty. If the blacksmith is in, he'll show you how he puts shoes on horses. This tour is a must for everyone who loves horses.

WATER POLLUTION CONTROL PLANT
1) Southwest: 8200 Enterprise Avenue—19153
2) Southeast: 25 E. Pattison Avenue—19148
592-6300

Hours: Weekdays, except holidays, 10 to 4. Allow one hour.
Tours: Scheduled for groups of no more than 25 adults, college or senior high school students. Call a few weeks in advance for reservations.
Cost: Free.
SEPTA: 1) Bus 68. 2) A block from bus G stop at Front and Pattison.
E & D: Much of these tours is outdoors and there's a lot of walking. You'll also go into several buildings. There's limited wheelchair access to everything but the laboratories.

If you're an environmentalist, engineer or technician, this tour will be given to you in technical terms. If not, you'll learn about ecology and water pollutants in simple, easy words. Either way it's a sophisticated look at the environment and what we can do to hurt it or improve it.

Philadelphia's Southwest Water Pollution Control Plant is a contemporary facility and ranks among the finest of its type in the country. It's also one of the largest—one-and-a-half miles long and a half-mile wide.

You can see the sedimentation basins, the digester tanks, a separate airblower building and the laboratories that are used for analysis and experimentation. And don't forget the sludge heaters and grit building that are also involved in wastewater treatment.

The Southeast Plant, at half the size but equally modern and efficient, opened in 1986. The tour is similar, but there are no digester tanks or sludge heating here.

WATER TREATMENT PLANTS
1) Belmont—Ford Road and Belmont Avenue—19131
2) Queen Lane—3545 Fox Street—19129
3) Samuel S. Baxter—9001 State Road—19136
592–6300

Hours: Weekdays, 10 to 4. Tours can sometimes be scheduled on weekends. Closed holidays. Allow one hour.
Tours: Groups of up to 35 are scheduled weekdays. Professional groups can sometimes be scheduled on weekends. All individuals and groups must call in advance.
Cost: Free.
SEPTA: 1) Buses 38, 44, 85. 2) Buses R, 32. 3) Buses 70, 84.
E & D: No wheelchair access. There's considerable walking.

If you're interested in ecology, you should visit a water treatment plant, because this is a splendid way to learn how Philadelphia deals with pollutants in the water.

Our drinking water is the most purified in the country. You can follow the process in any one of our plants' modern pushbutton facilities. The Baxter Plant is one of the largest in the country.

Water filtration starts directly at the river and the process continues until it's ready for you to drink. The pollution becomes apparent when the filter is washed clean of all non-purified elements. You'll learn how water comes from the river to how it gets to your home.

Tours of Federal Installations

Over 3,000 Federal government workers serve you from their offices at the 10-story **WILLIAM J. GREEN FEDERAL BUILDING** at 600 Arch Street.

You can contact your United States Senators and Congressman through their offices here.

Information is available from the regional offices of the Internal Revenue Service, Passport Agency, the Social Security Administration, the General Services Administration and a Federal Job Information Center. You can even tour the National Weather Service.

For general information about these and other government offices and services, call the Federal Information Center at 800–347–1997. (There are other Federal offices at different locations in the city. Refer to the Blue Pages at the back of the Bell of Pennsylvania White Pages phone directory.)

The Federal Building can be reached by **SEPTA** bus 48. It's just one block from any Market Street route.

The **elderly and disabled** can avoid steps by entering the building from 6th or 7th Streets. Once inside, there's complete wheelchair access.

A 22-story Federal Courthouse adjoins the Federal Office Building on the Market Street side.

Note: A **U.S. Government Bookstore** is at 100 North 17th Street at Arch in center city. You can browse here, or purchase practically every publication that is printed by the United States Government. The current list of hardbacks, paperbacks and pamphlets available from Washington numbers over 20,000. Fifteen-hundred of them are on display here. A "New Books Catalogue" is published four times a year and describes the currently most popular titles. It's available free from the bookstore. The subjects are as varied as the public library's.

The bookstore's hours are weekdays, except holidays, from 8:30 to 4. If you're interested in a specific title, call 597–0677 to see if it's in stock.

UNITED STATES COURTHOUSE
601 Market Street—19106
597-9368 (Clerk's Office)

Hours: Court is in session weekdays, except holidays, 9:30 to 4:30. Allow at least 30 minutes.
Tours: Individuals can report to the Clerk's Office, Room 2609, for trial information. You'll be directed to a court session. School groups, at least 5th grade, are scheduled in advance. All groups must call 2 weeks ahead for a date. You will then be directed to confirm your request in writing.
Cost: Free.
Lunch: There's a large cafeteria in the adjoining Federal Office Building.
SEPTA: Any Market Street route.
E & D: Complete wheelchair access.

Twenty-nine Federal judges, five U.S. magistrate judges and three bankruptcy judges preside here over criminal and civil cases for the U.S. District Court for Eastern Pennsylvania.

They hold trials in the 28 courtrooms at the handsome high-rise U.S. Courthouse. The building also houses the U.S. Court of Appeals for the Third Circuit.

The court facilities are modern, comfortable and secure. Each courtroom has its own jury room and individual chambers for the judge, the official court reporter and the clerk. Holding cells for defendants are on most floors, and they're directly accessible to courtrooms and elevators. So unless a defendant is free on bail, you'll never meet one in the corridors.

A courtroom visit is a worthwhile educational experience for anyone interested in the legal profession and criminal justice system.

AGRICULTURAL RESEARCH SERVICE
U.S. Department of Agriculture
600 E. Mermaid Lane
Wyndmoor, PA 19118
233-6595 (Information Desk)

Tour Day is once a year on a weekday in April. Tours are by reservation only for groups of no more than 40, at least junior high school level. Call after January 1 for the date and additional information.

Cost: Free.
SEPTA: Bus X. There's ample space for parking.
E & D: Complete wheelchair access.

The U.S.D.A. Research Center is a unique city "farm" where scientists work to help consumers. This isn't a traditional farm. The "farmers" here are researchers looking for ways to develop new and improved products, upgrade nutritional value, open new domestic and foreign markets, expand existing ones, reduce marketing costs, eliminate health-related problems, use waste products that are potential pollutants and provide improved quality and economy to the consumer—you and me.

The commodities include animal fats, dairy products, fruits, hides and leather, maple sap and syrups, honey, meats, potatoes and other vegetables.

Your tour will include stops at four of the 14 laboratory stations, if it's pertinent to your reason for being there. You could see a 15-minute film on the Agricultural Research Service, and there will be time for questions and answers.

DEFENSE PERSONNEL SUPPORT CENTER
2800 South 20th Street—19101
737-2311

Hours: Weekdays, 9 to 4. Closed holidays. Allow one hour.
Tours: Scheduled for groups of 20 to 30, at least 12 years old. Call at least 2 weeks in advance.
Cost: Free.
Lunch: Arrangements can be made when scheduling tour to bring-your-own or purchase lunch at the cafeteria.
SEPTA: Buses G, 2, 17.
E & D: No wheelchair access.

Uniforms for all branches of the United States Armed Forces are manufactured here. You'll see these garments being produced, and you'll visit the testing labs for government clothing textiles and medical supplies.

The local Defense Personnel Support Center can boast about something they do that no one else in the world does. They have a hand-embroidery flag shop where each seamstress works an average of three months to complete one flag. This is where all hand-embroidered flags for the

317

President, his Cabinet and officers of general rank are made.

This is also the facility that provided some billion dollars worth of food, clothing and medical supplies for U.S. forces in the Persian Gulf War.

FEDERAL RESERVE BANK
OF PHILADELPHIA
100 North 6th Street—19106
574-6114 (Public Information)

Hours: The ground floor Eastburn Court is open to the public, weekdays, 9 to 3. Closed holidays.
Tours: Groups of no more than 30 high school or college students, or adults interested in banking or related work, are scheduled by calling a month ahead.
Cost: Free.
SEPTA: Buses 47, 48, 61, Ben FrankLine route 76, or 2 blocks from Independence Hall.
Other: The ground floor 180-seat auditorium is the site for a concert series from October to April, the Philadelphia International Film Festival* late in July, as well as other occasional public events. Call for a schedule.
E & D: You can avoid steps by entering from 7th Street.

The Federal Reserve Bank isn't like any other bank. It's not a commercial bank. It's a bank for financial institutions, and it's governed by the Federal Reserve System.

The Federal Reserve Bank of Philadelphia serves a district that includes Eastern Pennsylvania, Southern New Jersey and all of Delaware. You can come here to purchase U.S. Savings Bonds and Treasury securities. You'll see the tellers' booths on the ground level of the Eastburn Court.

The Federal Reserve Bank is a monumental eight-story building which covers a whole city block. It's built around two sun-lit courts.

Alexander Calder's 100-foot "White Cascade" mobile is suspended from the Eastburn (East) Court facing Independence Mall. You can't miss it; it's the largest mobile in the world. (Calder's grandfather was the noted sculptor of City Hall* and the William Penn statue.)

Rare U.S. coins and currency are also on permanent display in this court. And, you can push a button and see a three-minute video show on the Federal Reserve Bank.

Combining this visit with a tour of the U.S. Mint*

across Independence Mall provides on-site education about money flow in the United States.

NATIONAL WEATHER SERVICE
William J. Green Federal Building
600 Arch Street—19106
627-5575

Hours: Weekdays, 1 to 3. Allow 30 minutes.
Tours: Scheduled for groups of no more than 20, at least 5th grade level. Call at least one week ahead. Hold the line patiently till the recorded weather forecast is finished.
Cost: Free.
E & D: Wheelchair access.

Sometimes we love them, sometimes we hate them. But we always rely on them. Who? The weather forecaster.

Here at the weather bureau, a staff of meteorologists issues general, marine and aviation forecasts every six hours, 24 hours a day, and you can see how they do it.

A tour of the office highlights forecast and communications procedures, weather maps and charts. (Since this is a forecast office only, you won't see any weather instruments.)

You'll also see the operation of radio station KIH 28 that's broadcast 24 hours a day from and by the National Weather Service. If your radio is equipped with a Public Service band, tune in to 162.475 megahertz. You'll hear weather reports, updated hourly, along with the marine forecast, travelers' advisories and storm warnings. And, you'll hear educational tapes about the weather and forecasting.

The weather people spend time providing members of the legal profession with certification of weather on specific dates. Building contractors try to use long range forecasts as an aid to estimating contract and construction deadlines.

And unless you were born before 1871, the weatherman can check the records for the temperature and precipitation on the date of your birth.

Remember: An **asterisk (*)** indicates that the same place or event appears elsewhere in the book with more details. Look in the Index for additional pages.

PHILADELPHIA NAVAL BASE
End of South Broad Street—19112
897–8775 (Public Affairs)

Hours: Friday at 10 A.M. by appointment only. Allow
one-and-a-half hours.
Tours: Call or write a few months in advance to the Public Affairs Office at the Base. A bus that seats a maximum of 45 is provided on arrival. All tour-goers must
be at least 8 years old.
Cost: Free.
SEPTA: Buses C, 17.
Other: United States citizens only.
E & D: Everyone remains on the Naval Base bus for the
tour. It cannot accommodate wheelchairs.

The Philadelphia Naval Base is a city within the city
on 713 acres where the Schuylkill River meets the Delaware. The nation's largest aircraft carrier, the U.S.S. Sara-
toga was completely overhauled here. The U.S.S.
Kittyhawk and the U.S.S. Constellation are currently being overhauled.

The Naval Base is a fascinating place to visit for anyone interested in ships, the waterfront, life at sea, or the
life on a military base.

A public affairs representative and a bus will meet your
group at the base entrance. Your guide will point out the
various ships, the shipbuilding center, the drydocks and
the land facilities. He'll identify the mothball fleet's assorted craft including battleships, an aircraft carrier, sub-
marines, cruisers, destroyers, tugs and cargo ships.

Note: If you would like to board a Navy or Coast Guard
vessel, or if you want to find out more about the Armed
Forces, turn to "May" in Chapter 19.

UNITED STATES MINT
5th and Arch Streets—19106
597–7350

Hours: Monday to Friday, 9 to 3:30. Closed holidays. Al-
low 45 minutes.
Tours: They're self-guided at your own pace.
Cost: Free. No samples.
SEPTA: Buses 48, 50, Ben FrankLine route 76, or Mar-
ket Street routes.

Other: There is a sales counter where you can buy commemorative medals and uncirculated coins.
E & D: Complete wheelchair access.

It's hard to imagine that most of the coins in the United States are made right here in Philadelphia. Of the country's four mints, ours is the largest.

The Mint has a self-guided audio visual tour that explains the stages involved in making nickels, dimes, quarters and pennies...all of which we take for granted. You'll see the processes of pressing, cleaning, inspecting, counting and bagging.

Five coin denominations are manufactured at the country's biggest money factory. This is the mint that made the Bicentennial coins now in circulation which are double-dated 1776–1976. It's also where the John Wayne commemorative medals were made, and more recently a U.S. Coast Guard Bicentennial Medal and a commemorative to mark the 50th anniversary of Mt. Rushmore.

A museum in the mint exhibits historical objects related to coin-making. And don't miss the seven Tiffany stained glass mosaics that depict the coinage processes of ancient Rome. The circular murals were preserved from the former Philadelphia mint when it closed in 1969.

While you're in the neighborhood, stroll around the corner to see the bust of Benjamin Franklin* on Arch Street, just below 4th. He was made out of 80,000 Philadelphia copper pennies.

UNITED STATES POSTAL SERVICE
2970 Market Street—19104
895–8817 (Public Information Office)

Hours: Weekdays, 10 to 3. Closed holidays and no tours scheduled in December. Allow one hour.
Tours: Scheduled for groups of 10 to 30, at least 13 years old. One adult must accompany every 10 children. Call or write at least a few weeks ahead. You'll set the tour date and then be told to send a letter to confirm.
Cost: Free.
SEPTA: Buses 9, 21, 30, 31, 42 or Market Street trolley and subway-elevated routes.
E & D: There are steps at entrance and considerable walking in hectic areas. Visitors in wheelchairs should enter at Chestnut Street. Arrangements can be made in advance for a few people to use elevator.

Do you know how eight million pieces of mail are handled in Philadelphia every day? And how they're sorted for delivery to your door? You'll find out when you visit the Main Branch of the Philadelphia Post Office.

A tour of the building lets you chart the various stages of mail processing from the time it's deposited in a mailbox until it's bundled for delivery to its destination.

The mailman who makes box collections drops his pickup bags at the post office. They go by conveyor belt to the collection center for sorting and separating. The letters are then automatically canceled at the rate of 20,000 per hour. Next they're sorted according to ZIP codes at the rate of 60 per minute. Then they're bundled and labeled and sent down the chutes to a platform for final pick-up and area delivery.

If all this sounds exhausting, we haven't even mentioned what happens to Special Delivery and the 35,000 pieces of first class mail scanned each hour by the Optical Character Reader. Or the multi-position letter sorting machine that sorts 36,000 pieces in an hour.

Stamp collectors will be interested in the **Philadelphia Philatelic Center** of the United States Postal Service. It's located at the 9th and Market Streets Post Office. Hours are 8 to 4:45 on weekdays and 9 to 3:45 on Saturdays.

The Center sells American commemoratives, mini-albums, opening day cachets and a variety of items of interest to philatelists. Call 895–8981 to see if they have what you're looking for.

Many of the same items are also available at the **B. Free Franklin Post Office** in Franklin Court* at 314 Market Street. This is also where all outgoing mail gets specially hand-canceled, and there's an interesting Postal Museum.

ACADEMY OF MUSIC
Broad and Locust Streets—19102
893-1935

Tours: By appointment only, during the orchestra season from October to May. Allow one hour. Reservations are necessary at least a week in advance. Groups can be accommodated, but no one under 12 is permitted.
Cost: Arranged when making tour reservation.
SEPTA: Buses C, 27, 32, 90; Broad Street Subway.
E & D: There is no wheelchair access for the tour, and there's a good bit of walking.

The Academy of Music is the home of the world-famous Philadelphia Orchestra*, and as part of the tour, you can stand on the stage where the orchestra performs. Then you can walk backstage, through the ballroom, the reception room, and the dressing rooms of the orchestra and their guest performers. If you would like, you can try out some of the Academy's 2,929 seats.

The Academy, which was designed by Napoleon LeBrun and Gustav Runge and opened in 1857, has a 20-foot-deep well in the basement. The well is also on the tour.

Hopefully, you'll come back again when the Academy is filled with beautiful music and beautiful people.

And don't forget to look for the Walk of Fame* outside on Broad Street.

BOY SCOUTS OF AMERICA
Philadelphia Council
22nd and Winter Streets—19103
988-9811

Hours: Weekdays, 8:30 to 4:30. Allow 30 minutes.
Tours: Groups of up to 50 can be scheduled. Call or write in advance to the Public Relations Office for a group tour. Individuals can stop by to browse.
Cost: Free.
SEPTA: Buses 7, 32, 48.
E & D: 8 steps at entrance prevent wheelchair access, but the building's exterior can be admired from the sidewalk. Ask about scout troops with special programs to accommodate boys with any type of disability.

The Philadelphia Boy Scout Council was founded in 1910 and completed construction of its own headquarters building in 1930. The Italian Renaissance-style structure houses administrative offices for the camping, activities, training, advancement and specialized programs that include more than 38,000 youth members in 895 Philadelphia cub, scout and explorer units. It's the oldest continuously used Boy Scouts office in America.

Scouts and friends of scouting from around the world take great pride in this building. Its entrance facade is inscribed, "Youth Prepared Safeguards the Nation... This house dedicated to the training of boys for useful leadership."

The building is covered inside and out with the many symbols of scouting. Look for the 12 points of the Scout Law, the universal Scout Badge, all of the merit and Veteran Scout badges along with several more noteworthy inscriptions.

You'll also see the seals of Philadelphia, Pennsylvania and the United States. The Golden Book of Scout Heroes is exhibited under glass, and a cabinet display includes assorted emblems, flags, medallions, statuettes and citations of local scouting. This is the only place for members of the Boy Scouts' "Order of the Arrow" to explore the complete history of that elite group.

A life-size bronze statue of "The Scout" looks out to the Benjamin Franklin Parkway as it greets you in front of the building. It was sculpted in 1937 by Dr. R. Tait McKenzie, whose works are also exhibited at the Lloyd P. Jones Gallery*.

COMMUNITY COLLEGE OF PHILADELPHIA
1700 Spring Garden Street—19130
751-8040

Hours: Weekdays, 10 to 5. Closed school holidays. Allow one hour.
Tours: Groups of up to 15 should call a week ahead.
Cost: Free.
SEPTA: Buses 2, 43.
E & D: Complete wheelchair access. Enter at ramp on 17th Street side of old U.S. Mint building.

High school students and prospective college students of any age will benefit from this tour. You'll hear about the diverse course offerings available in day and evening programs, and you'll see some of the up-to-date facilities used by those attending classes.

High tech areas like the TV studio and the computer-aided drafting labs used by architecture students are always interesting to see. If you're a would-be or accomplished artist, you'll want to see the art department and ceramics studios.

You'll be impressed by the preserved grandeur of the old United States Mint building and marvel how it has been adapted to classroom, library and academic use.

You can combine your tour with a visit to the Rotunda Gallery*. If you would like to know what concerts and plays are being presented at the Community College, call the Student Activities Office at 751–8210.

MASONIC TEMPLE
1 N. Broad Street—19107
988–1917

Tours: Weekdays, promptly at 10, 11, 1, 2, and 3. Saturdays (except July and August) at 10 and 11. Closed July 4, Thanksgiving, Christmas, New Year's. Allow one hour. Call ahead if you're coming with 20 or more.
Cost: Free.
SEPTA: Any route to City Hall.
E & D: There are 10 steps at the entrance. The tour includes a lot of walking and steps. An elevator is available, and 3 wheelchairs are available.

If you haven't been on a fancy movie set, you can pretend you're on one when you visit the Masonic Temple, because this place is unbelievable.

The Masons keep deep, dark secrets about their organization. Their secrecy is symbolized by two handsome Egyptian sphinx figures that flank the members' entrance on Broad Street. Each month, members from 92 lodges in the Philadelphia area hold their meetings here.

The building is the headquarters for the Pennsylvania Masonic Order. It was designed by a 27-year-old member, James A. Windrim, and it was dedicated in 1873. Windrim planned each of the seven huge Lodge Halls to represent a period in history. These halls are among this country's finest examples of Corinthian, Ionic, Italian Renaissance, Norman, Gothic, Oriental and Egyptian architecture.

Renaissance Hall, the most modern of the Temple's styles, will remind you of a three-story 15th century Italian cathedral with its marble columns and stained glass windows bearing the symbols of Masonry. The perfect hieroglyphics of Egyptian Hall were copied from eight Temples in Egypt.

The museum collections associate early Philadelphia and America to the Masonic Order. There are assorted emblems, gavels, symbolic jewels, decorative chinaware and an apron embroidered by Madame Lafayette. President Washington wore the apron when he laid the cornerstone of the new United States Capitol building in ceremonies that were in part Masonic ritual. Special exhibitions in the museum change every three months.

The Masonic Temple's cornerstone was opened a few years ago. Construction tools and objects of the day from 1873 are beautifully preserved and on display in the museum.

PENNSYLVANIA COLLEGE OF PODIATRIC MEDICINE
8th and Race Streets—19107
629–0300 Ext. 219 (Public Relations)

Hours: Weekdays, 9 to 4. Allow one hour.
Tours: Scheduled for groups, at least 4th grade level, with at least one adult for every 15 students. Call at least 2 weeks ahead.
Cost: Free.
SEPTA: Buses 47, 61.
E & D: The tour includes a lot of walking, but there's wheelchair access.

Podiatry applies to foot health and the proper medical and surgical care of human feet. There are only seven colleges of podiatric medicine in the United States, and you can visit one right here in Philadelphia. The college grants the degree of Doctor of Podiatric Medicine to students who successfully complete its four-year curriculum.

Your tour of the six-story education building covers several facets of contemporary teaching. You'll visit classrooms, laboratories and the Foot and Ankle Institute where 100 patients are treated every day by upperclassmen and professional staff. You'll see the instructional communications center that enables students to witness surgery by closed-circuit TV.

While you're here, stop by to see the Shoe Museum*. Happy walking!

PENNSYLVANIA S.P.C.A.
350 E. Erie Avenue—19134
426-6300 Ext. 27

Hours: Weekdays, 10 to 3.
Tours: Call several weeks ahead to schedule groups of 10 to 35, at least middle school age. Allow about 20 minutes for tour and 45 minutes for humane education program.
Cost: Free.
SEPTA: Buses 47, 50; trolley 56.
E & D: Wheelchair access for tour. Humane education program is in 2nd floor auditorium reached by stairs.

When you visit the Society for the Prevention of Cruelty to Animals you'll see the garage where rescue equipment and animal transport vehicles are kept and the receiving area where animals are checked in and given physicals. There are kennels for puppies, kittens, guinea pigs, hamsters and other creatures that turn up at the S.P.C.A. There's even a stable for horses.

Weather permitting, you'll visit the bird sanctuary and feed the resident chickens, ducks and geese.

If you attend a humane education program, you'll learn about proper pet care, the animal-human bond, the work of the S.P.C.A. and pet safety. Of course, some animals will attend too. (If your group can't get to the S.P.C.A. for this program, they'll bring it to you. Read about that later in this chapter.)

Everyone leaves with a souvenir and information on proper pet care.

PHILADELPHIA COLLEGE OF TEXTILES AND SCIENCE*
School House Lane and Henry Avenue—19144
951-2851 (Public Relations)

Hours: October to mid-May, weekdays, 9 to 4. Closed holidays. Allow one hour, and an additional hour if you include a visit to the Goldie Paley Design Center*.
Tours: Groups of high school students or adults should call at least 2 weeks ahead to schedule.

Cost: Free.
Lunch: Reservations can be made at the same time for the student cafeteria.
SEPTA: Bus 32.
E & D: No wheelchair access. The tour goes into a few buildings and there's considerable walking and steps.

Let a knowledgeable student be your guide at the country's oldest and largest college of textiles. This is where students major in textiles, science and business while they earn a four-year Bachelor of Science degree.

You won't visit any of the classrooms, but you'll get an insider's view of the laboratories and learn about other facets of the 90-acre campus.

The emphasis of the tour is on textiles, but it can be designed to coincide with the interests of your group. You'll see a fragment of thread on its way to becoming a fabric. That includes the process of spinning, dyeing, design-making, silk screening, card weaving, hand or commercial weaving on a variety of looms.

In the Apparel Research Center you'll be introduced to a variety of mannequins and machinery.

You'll leave this tour with a greater appreciation of your wardrobe.

THE PHILADELPHIA INQUIRER and PHILADELPHIA DAILY NEWS
400 N. Broad Street—19101
854–5501 (Public Affairs Office)

Hours: By appointment only. Allow one hour.
Tours: School groups of 10 to 30, 7th to 12th grades, will be scheduled by written request from the teacher to: Public Affairs Dept., The Philadelphia Inquirer and Daily News, Phila., PA 19101. Give your preferred date and an alternate.
Cost: Free.
SEPTA: Buses C, 43; Broad Street Subway.
E & D: No wheelchair access. There's considerable walking.

Journalism students will be interested in tours of The Philadelphia Inquirer and Daily News. Philadelphia's major morning newspaper has a daily circulation of 500,000; on Sundays it's 995,000. The Daily News has a daily circulation of 228,000.

When you visit the newspapers' headquarters you'll see the work that goes into putting out a major daily paper and a tabloid. You'll tour the newsrooms. You'll see reporters at work covering the metropolitan desk, national and foreign news. Practically everything in today's newsroom is processed on video display terminals.

You'll see the production facilities, and you'll find out what it means when they say: "Roll the presses."

If you can't get to tour The Philadelphia Inquirer and Daily News, read further in this chapter about bringing the newspaper to you. And we don't mean home delivery.

PHILADELPHIA STOCK EXCHANGE
1900 Market Street—19103
496–5200

Hours: Action on the trading floor is weekdays, 9:30 to 4.
Tours: You're on your own to observe. See below.
Cost: Free.
SEPTA: Any Market or Chestnut Street route to 19th.
E & D: No wheelchair access.

This is the nation's oldest stock exchange, and one of the busiest. Transactions are made on more than two thousand securities and options. Eight foreign currency options traded here have put the Philadelphia Stock Exchange in the international marketplace.

Even though you can't go directly on the trading floor, there's much to learn and observe. The Philadelphia Stock Exchange is the most modern exchange in the country. It moved to its new headquarters in 1981.

The building alone deserves a visit. It's built around a block-long, eight-story, enclosed skylit atrium. Stock and options trading can be viewed through window walls dividing the hectic marketplace from the lush, green, lower-level garden.

The atrium has 6,000 plants, 23 varieties of trees, nine pools, seven fountains and wonderful seating areas.

Watch the people on the trading floor and try to figure out the various roles they play. Look at the ticker tapes and try to read their codes.

The exchange's reception area is on the street level. Brochures are available here that explain how to better understand the stock exchange.

Business Tours

CUNNINGHAM PIANO CO.
5427 Germantown Avenue—19144
438–3200

Tours: By appointment only, Monday to Friday, 9 to 3.
Allow one hour. Call a week ahead to schedule groups
of up to 10.
Cost: Free.
SEPTA: Buses H, XH; trolley 23.
E & D: Wheelchair access to showroom only. Factory is
on the 2nd floor.

Cunningham Piano Co. started manufacturing pianos
in 1891 and continued until the 1940s.

Today, pianos are restored in their factory around the
corner on Coulter Street to the tune of a thousand a year.
(No pun intended.) This is the only factory of its kind in
Philadelphia.

Your tour starts in the showroom where you'll see several kinds of new and used pianos. Do you know the difference between a spinet, grand, console, upright and player
piano? If you don't, you'll find out quickly from the 60 or
so models on display.

Twelve pianos at a time are usually in various stages
of restoration or repair at the factory. Old-world craftsmen may be replacing a sounding board, rebuilding a key-
board or adjusting strings. Many of the employees have
been here 25 or 30 years and they're proud to show you
their work.

Next, you might want to visit some of the historic sites
along Germantown Avenue (see Chapter 3).

FOOD DISTRIBUTION CENTER
East of Broad Street, from Packer to Pattison Avenues
3301 Galloway Street—19148

Cost: Free.
SEPTA: Bus G.
E & D: No wheelchair access. There are steps and a good
bit of walking on either tour.

The city's Food Distribution Center moved from its

cramped and outmoded Dock Street headquarters in 1959 (now the site of the Society Hill Towers at 2nd and Locust Streets).

Today this $100 million, 380-acre complex is a good example of how a large city's food distribution should operate. The Center has food processing, warehousing, wholesaling and distribution. The occupants range from a banana importer and a dairy producer to a variety of meat, poultry and fish packers. Over 10,000 people work here day and night.

You can visit the wholesaling centers as follows:

Fruit and Produce
336-3003

Hours: By appointment only. Allow 45 minutes.
Tours: Scheduled for groups of 10 to 20, college students or people involved in the food industry. Call one month in advance.

The hustle and bustle of activity starts here at 4 A.M. Bushels and baskets of farm-fresh fruits and vegetables are brought in by the 40 wholesalers who occupy the row. Retail merchants, hucksters, restaurant buyers and thrifty housewives arrive before the sun rises to buy the day's or week's provisions. Tours are led by the terminal manager. He might focus on shipping, food handling, display or whatever the particular interest of the group.

Seafood
336-1051

Hours: Weekdays, by appointment only, 8:30 to 9:30 A.M. Allow 30 minutes.
Tours: Scheduled for groups of 20 to 25, at least 4th grade. Call at least 2 weeks in advance.
Other: Insurance is required for all tour-goers. The floors are slick and wet. Wear sneakers or rubber-sole shoes.

Seafood is the only thing that's sold in this market, and most of it is gone by 9:30 in the morning. The procedures of receiving and delivery will be explained. And all of the different varieties of seafood and fish will be pointed out.

PHILADELPHIA PRETZEL MUSEUM
1100 S. Delaware Avenue—19147
463-1880

Hours: Monday to Saturday, 10 to 4.
Tours: Call 2 weeks ahead for groups of pre-schoolers to seniors. Allow 45 minutes.
Cost: $1.
SEPTA: A short walk from buses 63 or 64. There's plenty of free parking.
Other: This is a pretzel bakery and gift shop as well.
E & D: Everything is on one level within a small area.

What beans are to Boston, grits are to Atlanta, pralines are to New Orleans, and soft pretzels are to Philadelphia. This is where you can watch them being made, try twisting one yourself and see them immortalized in a colorful museum.

Start your visit by viewing a short film on the origins and ingredients of pretzels. All would-be pretzel makers get a turn at twisting in order to qualify for an "official pretzel twister" hat.

Watch in the bakery itself as the dough goes from a huge vat through various stages and machinery to a tray of finished pretzels. They come in all shapes and styles here, from traditional to braids, sticks and hearts. You really can't capture the flavor of Philadelphia without having a soft pretzel!

SAMUEL YELLIN METALWORKERS
AND YELLIN MUSEUM
5520 Arch Street—19139
472-3122

Hours: By appointment only, April to November, weekdays, 9 to 3. Allow one hour. (There's no air-conditioning in summer.)
Tours: Up to 25 can be scheduled by calling or writing in advance. All visitors must be at least high school seniors and interested in the fine arts, ornamental metalworks or blacksmithing.
Cost: Free.
SEPTA: Bus 31 or Market Street elevated train to 56th and Market; bus G to 56th and Arch. There's plenty of street parking space.

Other: Dress comfortably and appropriately for visiting an ironworks studio.
E & D: No wheelchair access.

A visit to Samuel Yellin Metalworkers is a multi-faceted experience. The two-story Spanish-style building dates from 1920 when Samuel Yellin opened his shop. Mr. Yellin died in 1940, but his studio continues to create masterpieces in metal in the same tradition.

A first-floor museum houses hundreds of samples of Yellin craftsmanship and fine examples of metalwork from around the world. Locks, keys, altarpieces, gates, railings, andirons, lighting fixtures and purely decorative objects are embellished with sculpted asps, birds, animals, flowers, leaves and ornamental patterns.

Yellin ironwork can be seen across the country. In center city Philadelphia you can see the exquisite designs at the First Pennsylvania Bank entrance on the southeast corner of 15th and Chestnut Streets, the Curtis Institute of Music* at 1724 Locust Street, the iron-clad red doors of St. Mark's Church at 1625 Locust Street, and the Rosenbach Museum* at 2010 Delancey Street.

Samuel Yellin Metalworkers also has a library on wrought iron art and architecture and a medieval-style room with many of Mr. Yellin's favorite furnishings and artwork. The blacksmiths and metalworkers in the upstairs ironworks use many of the tools that Samuel Yellin used more than 60 years ago. While much of their current work is in iron, other metals such as bronze, stainless steel and aluminum are used. Depending on what's in production, you might be lucky enough to see iron being shaped by one of the many tools or methods that make the art possible.

TERMINI PASTRIES
1523 South 8th Street—19147
334–1816

Hours: Daily for business, 8 A.M. to 8 P.M.
Tours: By reservation only, weekdays, 9 to noon. Call a week ahead for groups of no more than 25, with 4 adults accompanying any group of children. Allow about 30 minutes. No tours are scheduled around holidays.
Cost: Free, but we think you'll be tempted to purchase a reminder of the visit.
SEPTA: Bus 47; trackless trolley 29.

Other: Wear appropriate clothes to be in a bakery and standing for entire tour.

E & D: Everything is on street level.

Tantalizing pastries have been rising from the ovens of this South Philadelphia family bakery since 1921. The second generation has joined in the all natural and hand-made preparation of popular items like chocolate whipped cream cake, strawberry shortcake, brown derby cake with a whipped cream center, donuts, strudel, napoleons, muffins, sticky buns and gingerbread men.

More exotic temptations are a fresh fruit ambrosia, clove-flavored "bones" (only in October) and zuccardi cookies from Sicilian recipes, sfogliadelli from Naples and a "stork's nest" from Northern Italy.

Their most famous product, though, is the cannoli. You can see cannoli-making on Wednesday, Thursday and Friday mornings. If you're well-behaved on the tour, you'll get a sample. A cannoli is sinfully delicious.

What you'll see at Termini's depends on the day and the season, but whatever you see will be tempting.

VINTAGE INSTRUMENTS
1529 Pine Street—19102
545–1100

Hours: Weekdays, 10 to 5; Saturday, by appointment. Allow 30 minutes.

Tours: Call ahead to arrange visit for groups at least high school age.

Cost: Free.

SEPTA: Buses 27, 32, 40.

E & D: No wheelchair access. There are 6 steps at the entrance and tour is on 4 floors of a grand old townhouse.

In a time when electronic music has become popular, it's special to find a workshop that maintains a part of Philadelphia and its classical musical tradition. Some of the wind and string instruments here are as old as the 17th century, and the house itself dates from 1860 when Philadelphia was already recognized for the fine instruments being made here.

The proprietor collects, appraises, restores, buys and sells with an international reputation. He also conducts. . .tours. What was once an elegant dining room now houses violins, violas, cellos, lap organs, antique harmoniums, lutes, lap organs and concertinas. There are tubas and a hall full of harpsichords. Another floor contains banjos, guitars and more unusual fretted instruments.

Try to schedule your visit when the violin maker is at work. You'll be intrigued by the detail and skill that goes into restoring an instrument or a bow. Indeed, this tour is music to the ears of any fine music lover.

Audience Television Show

If you would like to be part of a television audience, you can do it at WCAU-TV Channel 10, City Avenue and Monument Road in Bala Cynwyd.

Channel 10: The People airs on Sunday morning at 8 A.M., but it's taped the preceding Tuesday evening at 7:30. Pat Battle is host to local guests who talk about local issues, especially those involving minority communities. The audience participates with questions and comments. If you would like to participate, call ahead to 668–5697 and find out in advance what the topic will be on a date you'd like to attend. You'll have to allow about an hour-and-a-half at the studio. Reservations are necessary.

Tours to Go

Many Philadelphia businesses and organizations will bring their programs to you.

Their shows might be educational, they might be entertainment, or they might be both. There are several programs on tour from the city's performing arts groups, museums and sports teams. The selection is plentiful and often there's no charge.

Films, slide programs and lectures are available to please any audience. Reservations for most of them must be made at least a month in advance.

Reminder: An **asterisk (*)** indicates that the same place or event appears elsewhere in this book with more details. You'll find that place in the Index.

BELL OF PENNSYLVANIA offers without charge a 20-minute slide-lecture entitled, "A Vision of a Better

Tomorrow: Modern Technology of the 90s." A question and answer period follows. It's available for civic, social and religious groups of 30 and more. Call the Bell Speakers Bureau at 466–4111 for details or to schedule your event.

The **FREE LIBRARY OF PHILADELPHIA*** loans films and videos to anyone over 18 years old with a library membership card. They have over 2,000 16mm features, documentaries, short subjects and cartoons. The only condition to borrowing is that you can't charge admission or ask for donations when you show.

The films, which must be ordered through the Video and Film Department of the Central Library (686–5367), can be picked up and deposited there or at the Northeast, Northwest or West Philadelphia Regional Branches.

The Free Library also loans VHS videocassettes from a growing collection that now numbers over 3,000. They can be borrowed for seven days once you've signed the library's videocassette service agreement card and meet their requirements.

Same day service is available in the browsing collection at the Central Library from the Video and Film Department. Pick-ups can also be made at the three regional branches with reservations made a week in advance. It's best to reserve in advance from all branches.

Catalogues are available for reference at the Central Library and three regional branches.

Hours at the Central Library Video and Film Department are weekdays, 9 to 5.

INDEPENDENCE NATIONAL HISTORICAL PARK* offers two ways to preview the park experience and both are free.

School and civic groups can borrow a 12-minute, pre-visit slide program called **"The Independence Experience."** It has 60 slides in a carousel, a cassette tape and a copy of a script that can also be ordered in Spanish. The program is geared to 5th and 6th graders but it's appropriate for anyone planning to visit the National Park. The package is available on a first come, first served basis, so it's a good idea to request the kit at least a month before your group intends to see it. Write to: Pre-Visit Kit, Independence National Historical Park, 313 Walnut Street, Phila., PA 19106.

Independence National Historical Park also loans to

schools and civic groups the 16mm, 28-minute film **"Independence"** that's shown at the Visitor Center*. Again, requests are filled in the order they receive them, so plan your private show a few months ahead. Write to: Visitor Center "Independence" loan, Independence National Historical Park, 313 Walnut Street, Phila., PA 19106.

Both the film and the slide program must be returned within 10 days of receipt so be sure to plan your schedule accordingly.

The **PENNSYLVANIA S.P.C.A.*** brings animals along when it brings its Humane Education Program to groups of senior citizens on down to youngsters four years old. The topic is geared to the age or school grade of the audience. Call 426–6300 Ext. 27 as far ahead as possible to arrange this event for a weekday or early evening of your choice.

The **PHILADELPHIA FIRE DEPARTMENT** has a fire prevention program that's worthwhile for any school, community, civic or residential group. A Philadelphia firefighter will address your audience at your locale on the warning signs of a fire, prevention measures and safety tips. Call the Fire Prevention Division at 592–5982 to schedule this very important discussion.

THE PHILADELPHIA INQUIRER and **DAILY NEWS*** sends staff members and journalists to address interested groups. Write at least a month in advance to the Public Affairs Department, The Philadelphia Inquirer and Daily News, Phila., PA 19101. Tell them your group, the topic and the type of speaker you would like, business or editorial, and they'll give you an informative program.

The **PHILADELPHIA RANGER CORPS*** leaves Fairmount Park with its environmental education programs. Two of the rangers will come to address your classroom or group of 20 to 40 elementary to middle-school age youngsters in a 45- to 60-minute hands-on lesson. Topics include "The Impact Monster," "Portable Park" and "P is for Park, F is for Fun." These clever Park Rangers can also bring a bit of the outdoors in for adults who don't otherwise get out. Such programs might involve the concepts of ecology, artifacts from Fairmount Park, or a talk about the unique statuary and buildings in the park. Call the scheduling officer at RANGERS (726–4377) at least a few weeks in advance for more information and to plan their visit with you.

The **PHILLIES*** will include you on their road trip schedule. You have a choice from the Phillies Film Library of an annual 30-minute "Phillies Highlights" production, baseball instructionals for would-be professionals or films about All-Star games and World Series spectaculars. Call 463–6000 Ext. 292 for details. There's a small charge to cover mailing and your deposit is returned when the borrowed film is returned.

The Philadelphia Zoo* sends its **ZOO ON WHEELS** to schools, camps. libraries and churches within a 50-mile radius of the big zoo. Four topics are available to choose from for audiences of five-year-olds through adults. There's also a special program just for pre-schoolers. Of course, four or five live animals come along for the hour-long show. Call the Zoo (243–1100 Ext. 224) at least three months in advance for fee information and to request a registration form.

Many of Philadelphia's performing arts groups and museums have shows "to go." Here are some of them.

The **ACADEMY OF NATURAL SCIENCES*** takes its "Eco Show on the Road" to schools, homes or any institutions where the audience won't exceed 350. You have a choice of different auditorium (50 minutes) or animals-only (25 minutes) shows. They all include a speaker-naturalist, slide presentation and five or six live animals. There's a fee for "Eco Show on the Road." Call the Academy's Education Department at 299–1060 for details. The critters are happiest when they go on tour.

FREEDOM THEATER* travels to schools, churches, prisons, community groups and career conferences. You can choose from their repertoire a play that can be anywhere from 15 minutes to a full-length, full-scale production. The fee is charged accordingly. Call 765–2793 (ask for Public Relations) at least two months in advance to make arrangements.

Groups interested in history, and particularly in the Civil War, can invite volunteers from the **G.A.R. CIVIL WAR MUSEUM*** to address their meeting. One or two "soldiers" in full dress will gather up items from the museum or from their personal collections to include as part of the 90-minute program. Call the museum at 673-1688 for additional information.

GERMANTOWN THEATRE GUILD goes on the road with three one-person plays: "I, Amelia" on the life of Amelia Earhart, "Frederick Douglass" and "Sojourner Truth." Audiences of middle-schoolers through senior citizens enjoy these one-hour shows which can be followed by a question and answer period. You don't need a formal stage, but you do need to call at least a month in advance. Performances can be scheduled for day or evening. For additional information, call 842-0658 or 688-5842.

Another period of history can be brought before large audiences by a representative of the **HOLOCAUST AWARENESS MUSEUM***. Accompanied by a survivor of the Holocaust, and with artifacts from the museum, this is a vivid, personal and emotional hour-long program. Call 635-6480 for details if you know a large group that would benefit from this museum visit "to go."

PHILADELPHIA THEATER CARAVAN* takes its professional shows for children and young adults to audiences of at least 50 in schools, libraries, churches, recreation centers, camps, club or organization gatherings. There's a set fee for each production, and they all last about one hour. For available dates and rates, call 898-6068.

PHILADELPHIA MARIONETTE THEATER* will pack up its puppets and bring them to your gathering. Choose a show of fantasy or humor. This isn't just kids stuff—you'll be fascinated by the variety. For details on arranging a visit from the Marionette Theater, call 879-1213.

HEDGEROW THEATER* (565-4211) and the **PEOPLE'S LIGHT AND THEATRE COMPANY*** (647-1900) also have children's theater that goes on tour. Hedgerow's touring company has a repertoire of four or five plays that go to schools, community centers, festivals and the like. They require two or three months notice. People's Light and Theatre Company does an original production each year in April and May geared to school groups kindergarten through sixth grade or youngsters seven to 12. They start booking in September so call ahead as far as possible. There is a fee for both of these presentations.

The **PHILADELPHIA MUSEUM OF ART*** brings you a 45-minute mini-slide tour on one of 11 topics that you're free to choose from. If you can supply the screen, an art museum guide will supply everything else to give you a memorable tour. These slide programs are $35 to groups within a 45-minute drive of the museum. For topics and reservations, call at least a month ahead to the Museum's Park House Guides office, 787-5449.

PLEASE TOUCH MUSEUM* has **Traveling Trunks** for rent. Each trunk is chock-full of objects that provide hands-on learning experiences on any of 24 subjects. Some of them are The Circus, Dinosaurs, Native Americans, The Four Seasons, India, Space, Water, Puerto Rican Panorama, Step Into Art, Children's Health and Head to Toe (Clothing from Around the World). A teacher's guide is also included with explanations and activity suggestions.

The trunks are available for two-week rentals, and a one-hour introductory show can be scheduled for an additional fee. Call the museum (963-0666) for fee information and reservations for a traveling trunk.

THE QUIET RIOT COMEDY THEATER* can't keep this quiet. The two-person company will appear at your school, club or community gathering with a 45- or 90-minute comedy show. For details, call 885-8825, or write to them at 131 Woodland Road, Wyncote, PA 19095.

The **UNIVERSITY MUSEUM*** has "mobile guides" who take artifacts and treasures to third grade to sixth grade audiences in the Philadelphia Public Schools. A mini-museum on "Woodland Indians" or "Ancient Egypt" becomes a part of the host classroom. For details, call the Volunteer Services Office at the Board of Education at 299-7774. There is a fee for the program, and they'll explain it. If you would like to volunteer as a "mobile guide," call the museum at 898-4277.

YOUNG AUDIENCES OF EASTERN PENNSYL-VANIA introduces local students from kindergarten through high school to the performing arts. Professional musicians, singers and dancers from Philadelphia's finest companies present auditorium programs for up to 350 students to demonstrate string instruments, brass, per-

cussion or woodwinds and to perform opera, dance, jazz or orchestral numbers. Poetry workshops, mime, puppetry and theater are performed by a professional cast as well. Smaller hands-on workshops with 10 to 40 students allow greater audience participation and frequently come before or after the auditorium program. All of the programs are 45 minutes.

Young Audiences arranges for school programs anywhere in Southeastern Pennsylvania, the Lehigh Valley and South Jersey. More than 20 ensembles and 70 different artist-teachers are available to visit your locale. For further information, call 977-7707 or write to Young Audiences of Eastern Pennsylvania, 2400 Chestnut Street, Suite 1410, Phila., PA 19103. Reservations should be made early in the school term, or at least a month in advance.

At least three of Philadelphia's **dance groups** will perform at the place and time of your choice. Their programs are as flexible as their well-trained bodies. In each instance, there is a fee depending on the size of the company, distance traveled, accompanists and so forth.

GERMANTOWN COUNTRY DANCERS* go on tour evenings and weekends with a full-length program of English and American country dances and American colonial dances in traditional costume. The audience usually joins in after the show. Allow as much notice as possible. For more information, you can call 844-3259.

PHILADELPHIA CIVIC BALLET COMPANY*
goes on tour with "Dance, the Language of Movement."
Four or five professionals dance in the 45-minute show
at public and parochial schools in and around Philadelphia, for private groups and organizations. Over 800,000
youngsters and adults have seen the program since it
started in 1971. Call 564–1505 for details and make reservations as early as possible in the school term.

PHILADELPHIA DANCE COMPANY* goes on
tour to schools, community groups and senior citizen
centers with a 45- to 60-minute concert-lecture-
demonstration program. Arrangements must be made at
least six weeks in advance. Call Philadanco (387–8200)
for details.

Chapter 14.
Philadelphia at Play.

Spectator Sports

Philadelphia is fortunate to have a professional team and first-rate facility for every major sport.

And because Philadelphia's a college town, there's a full schedule of college games for every sport you can think of. And some you wouldn't think of. Like cricket.

Our sports complex is just 10 minutes from City Hall at the southern end of Broad Street.

The **Spectrum**, opened in 1967, has a seating capacity of over 17,000. **Veterans Stadium**, opened in 1971, can seat over 65,000 for baseball and 73,000 for football. John F. Kennedy Stadium, opened in 1926, used to seat as many as 102,000, but no longer seats anyone. (The **elderly and disabled** should refer to Chapter 16 for helpful information regarding these stadiums.)

The best **SEPTA** routes to the complex are bus C south on Broad Street or the Broad Street Subway south to Pattison Avenue. Check with SEPTA for special express trains and other routes to the stadiums.

Sports events are also held at the Civic Center's Convention Hall, 34th Street and Civic Center Boulevard, and at the Palestra, 33rd near Walnut Street.

Tickets for sporting events are available at the stadiums, at the respective team's office, at Ticketron outlets (call 885–2215 for the Ticketron location nearest to you, or 800–233–4050 to order tickets), at Ticketmaster (call 336–2000) and at commercial ticket agencies.

Don't forget to check the Calendar of Annual Events in Chapter 19 to keep up with sporting spectaculars like the Penn Relays, the Army-Navy Football Game, the BIG FIVE Tournament and the U.S. Pro Indoor Tennis Championships that take place every year.

BASEBALL—PHILLIES
Veterans Stadium (ticket office)
463–1000 (ticket, inclement weather and
daily game information)

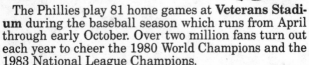

The Phillies play 81 home games at **Veterans Stadium** during the baseball season which runs from April through early October. Over two million fans turn out each year to cheer the 1980 World Champions and the 1983 National League Champions.

There are day games, night games, occasional twi-night doubleheaders and mid-week afternoon businessperson specials.

You can get tickets at one of 75 ticket agencies in and around Philadelphia, at the Phillies ticket office at the stadium or in the lobby of Mellon–P.S.F.S. Bank at Broad and Chestnut Streets. Call the Phillies to find out which is most convenient.

Since the Phillies ticket sales are completely computerized, you get the best available tickets from whichever location you buy them. You can even purchase by phone using any of three major credit cards. Your tickets will be mailed if time permits, or held at the "will call" window at the stadium.

Tickets range from $10 for field box seats to $1 general admission for children 14 or under when accompanied by an adult buying a general admission ticket for $4. You can take advantage of Family Day with special $1 reductions. There are always special reductions available for senior citizens. There are often group rates for 25 or more on specific dates. For group information (25 or more) and season tickets call 463–5000 or write Phillies Group Service, Box 7575, Phila., PA 19101.

Groups of 40 to 80 can also reserve the 400-level superboxes, "Philadelphia Suite" or "Legends," for a sit-down or buffet-style dinner during the game. Call Group Service as early in the season as possible to make these arrangements.

If you would really like to go first class, call the Stadium Restaurant (271–2300) for reservations to dine and watch the game from the glass-enclosed restaurant above the first base line. If you would like to see the Phillies at a time and place of your choice, see Chapter 13 on tours "to go."

The Phillies' two Phanavision scoreboards constantly dance with names, numbers, pictures, songs, cheers, games and cartoons. You can have a birthday party at the Vet, and YOUR NAME can be on the scoreboard. The entertainment continues at your seat. (Call 463–1000 for these plans, too.) The Phillie Phanatic is also a constant source of amusement.

The Phillies are as big on promotions as they are on winning. There are events like T-shirt Day, Hat Day, Beach Towel Day and Glove Day. There are many special occasions to celebrate during baseball season.

BASKETBALL—76ERS
The Spectrum
339–7676 (ticket office at Veterans Stadium)

The 76ers play 41 home games at the **Spectrum** from late October to April. When you see them, you'll be watching some of the best and the brightest basketball stars of the National Basketball Association. They're the 1983 World Champions and the 1989–1990 Atlantic Division Champs. Star forward Charles Barkley was Most Valuable Player of the 1991 All Star game.

If the game doesn't provide enough excitement for you, the promotions and special programs will. The half-time shows are colorful, and special nights are designated for children 14 and under. The purchase of any full-price ticket guarantees youngsters a 76ers ski cap, equipment bag, basketball or jacket on certain promotional days.

Tickets are $6 to $25, and group rates are available in advance for groups of 25 or more. Call or write the 76ers Group Sales Office at Veterans Stadium, P.O. Box 25050, Phila., PA 19148.

There are more opportunities to watch top-notch basketball in Philadelphia each winter. The **BIG FIVE** (LaSalle, University of Pennsylvania, St. Joseph's, Villanova and Temple) play at their respective campuses, except LaSalle which plays at the Civic Center. Call 898–4747 for a schedule and ticket information.

BOXING and WRESTLING

Boxing is a sometimes occurrence at the **Spectrum**. When important bouts aren't on the local schedule, the Spectrum provides closed circuit television viewing of them. World Wrestling Federation matches are at the Spectrum, too, usually on Friday or Saturday nights. For a recorded announcement of what's coming up in the ring at the Spectrum, call 389–5000. Ticket prices vary with the event. Group rates for 25 or more are available by calling 336–3600.

Wrestling is also on the agenda at Convention Hall at the Civic Center, 34th Street and Civic Center Boulevard (686–1776 or 823–7280). Call or watch the newspapers for announcements.

CRICKET

Did you ever wonder where Americans got the game of baseball? It's derived from cricket, a game played with a ball and stick that originated and still draws huge crowds in countries of the British Commonwealth.

In cricket, the batter scores as many runs as possible after a hit by going back and forth between two wickets, or bases, that are 22 yards apart. Eleven men play on each team and their uniforms are long white pants and white shirts. You can generally distinguish a team by the color of its players' hats or sweaters, and you can pick out the wicket keeper because he wears gloves. That's cricket.

The **Prior Cricket Club** (878–2552) plays its matches on Saturdays and Sundays from late April through September at Cedar Grove Cricket Field, Edgely Road east of Belmont Avenue in West Fairmount Park. Starting times vary from noon till 2 and games often last five or six hours.

Commonwealth Cricket Club (748–0707) has a similar season and they compete on the cricket field in front of Memorial Hall.

They meet teams from all along the East Coast, Canada, Jamaica, Australia and Great Britain. Call any weekend during the season for a specific schedule. These events are free to the public.

FOOTBALL—EAGLES
Veterans Stadium (ticket office)
463–5500 (ticket information)

The Eagles are Philadelphia's long-time popular delegation to the National Football League. Since Philadelphia is, was and will always be a football town, fans will brave the rain, cold and the snow to cheer the "Birds" on to victory. The Eagles wound up the 1980 season against Oakland in Super Bowl XV, they were division champions in 1981 and made it to the play-offs in 1988, 1989 and 1990.

Sixteen games are on the schedule from September to December. Eight are at home on Sunday afternoons with 1 or 4 P.M. kick-off at **Veterans Stadium**. Tickets are $30, and there are group discounts for 25 or more.

One or two pre-season games are played in August at the Vet. These seats are available at the same prices.

HORSE RACING

Philadelphia Park, on Street Road (Route 132) between I-95 and Roosevelt Boulevard, in Bensalem, PA (639–9000), features afternoon flat racing year-round. The first race is at 1 P.M. You can bet on the thoroughbreds five days a week, Friday to Tuesday, from February through May. The track is open daily, except Thursdays, the rest of the year. You can also make reservations to have lunch in the clubhouse. Admission is $3 and it includes parking. There's no admission charge if you arrive after the seventh race.

Garden State Park, just across the Benjamin Franklin Bridge on Route 70 in Cherry Hill, New Jersey (609–488–8400), has thoroughbred racing from February to early June. Post time is Wednesday to Friday at 7:30 P.M. and Saturday and Sunday at 1 P.M. Harness racing is at Garden State from September to December, with the first race at 7:30 P.M. Tuesday through Saturday.

Admission is $2 for the grandstand, and $3 for the clubhouse and the Phoenix Dining Room. Garden State is a state-of-the-art race track and entertainment center that opened in 1985. The physical beauty of the track and the exclusive restaurants are worth a trip in itself.

If you can't get to a racetrack, you can do your betting off-track at **Philadelphia Park O.T.B.** It's located in the lower level at 7 Penn Center at 17th and Market Streets in center city. Admission to the grandstand is $1; the clubhouse is $2. Tuesday is Ladies Day when women are admitted free. The doors open at 11:30 A.M. when there's a 1 P.M. post time and at 6 P.M. for a 7:30 post time (or 7 P.M. on Sundays). All of the races are simulcast from Philadelphia Park, as well as from The Meadows in Pittsburgh, Penn National in Harrisburg and Pocono Downs. Call 246–1556 for the schedule.

This is a rather high-class, high-tech gambling parlor. Bets are placed at windows or on machines. Video screens are everywhere. Lunch, dinner and Sunday brunch are served in the Clubhouse Turf Club Dining Room and reservations are suggested (246–1567). Refreshments are also available in the grandstand one level below. Proper attire is required: men must wear long trousers and a shirt with collar; women are not permitted to wear tank tops.

Philadelphia also hosts two of the country's most prestigious **HORSE SHOWS**. You can attend the **Devon Horse Show** each spring and the **American Gold Cup** in September. Both are described in Chapter 19.

ICE HOCKEY—FLYERS
The Spectrum (ticket office)
465-4500 or 755-9700 (ticket information)

The Flyers play 40 games at the **Spectrum** from October to early April. Tickets are from $12 to $28. Many of the Spectrum's 17,211 seats are sold out to season ticket holders, but a number of seats go on sale for each game.

Tickets are sold at all Ticketmaster locations and at the 14 Showcase Stores in malls throughout the area.

Some of the Flyers are fearless Canadians. Others are Czech, Swedish and American. The 20-minute periods move as quickly as the puck that speeds across the ice. Tempers flare, so be prepared to witness some fights. The Flyers have been Patrick Division Champions at the end of the 1983, 1985 and 1986 seasons.

If you're lucky enough to go to a game, be sure to dress warmly. The playing floor chills even the hardiest of fans.

LACROSSE—WINGS
The Spectrum (ticket office)
336-3600
336-2000 (Ticketmaster)
389-9543 (group and season tickets)

Indoor lacrosse took off in Philadelphia when the Major Indoor Soccer League began in 1987. The Wings were world champions in 1989 and 1990.

With only five home games scheduled at the **Spectrum** in January, February and March, tickets are in big demand. In fact, Philadelphia sports fans make this the best attended team in the league. Tickets are $10, $15 or $17.50, and there are money-saving season plans.

If you're familiar with outdoor lacrosse, this is a similar game but it's even quicker, tougher and more hard-hitting. Five forward players go at the opposing goalie in four 15-minute quarters. All-in-all, the game lasts two hours, and the play is fast and furious. You won't be disappointed by the action.

REGATTAS
The Schuylkill Navy
No. 4 Boat House Row, Kelly Drive
978–6919

Rowing races along the Schuylkill River are on 10 weekends from spring to late fall. Among the annual events are the May Dad Vail Regatta (the world's largest intercollegiate regatta), the Independence Day Regatta and the Frostbite Series in November.

The Schuylkill sculling course is close to center city in scenic Fairmount Park*. Its calm, sheltered flow makes it one of the world's most popular rivers for regattas. Artist Thomas Eakins has immortalized sculling on the Schuylkill; the United States Postal Service issued a commemorative stamp honoring it.

Most races begin north of the Strawberry Mansion Bridge and end 2,000 meters downstream towards center city. You can watch the races from the Schuylkill Grandstand on Kelly Drive (about a mile-and-a-half west of Boat House Row) or from anywhere you choose along the river's eastern shore. You might decide to follow the races while biking along the Kelly Drive bike path. Of course, there's no admission charge to watch any of these events.

There are few things more graceful than these sleek shells skimming rapidly across the water. If you walk by the 19th century boat houses on Boat House Row (just west of the Museum of Art and the Azalea Gardens), you'll be able to examine the shells. A single shell can cost rowers $10,000.

Ten boat clubs comprise Boat House Row, and they all have open memberships. If you've ever considered joining the Schuylkill Navy, call to find out which club might be appropriate for your schedule, skills, competitive or recreational rowing interests.

For a schedule of the season's regattas, look in the newspapers or call the Schuylkill Navy headquarters.

RUGBY

Rugby bears some resemblance to football, but no forward passing or blocking is allowed. This is another sport most Americans have never seen. You can watch first-class rugby any Saturday afternoon from March through May and early September through November at the

Memorial Hall field, Belmont and Parkside Avenues in West Fairmount Park. It's free and wholesome sports entertainment, and in Philadelphia rugby has gone coed.

The **Philadelphia-Whitemarsh Rugby Football Club** (642-9899) and any of the nearly 50 rugby clubs within 50 miles of Philadelphia compete in two 40-minute periods per game beginning at 12:30 P.M. Neither team of 15 is allowed more than two substitutes in the non-stop period. And then it's only for an injury. Competition continues till around 5 P.M. Call the club for a schedule, and come out and see the action.

SOCCER

The **PHILADELPHIA SOCCER 7** provides an opportunity to see outdoor college soccer each fall. Drexel (590-8945), LaSalle (951-1605), Philadelphia Textile (951-2852), St. Joseph's (660-1712), Temple (787-7445), University of Pennsylvania (898-6151) and Villanova (645-4121) are pitted against each other and visiting teams from along the East Coast. There's no admission charge to attend most of these games. Call the school closest to you to find out when you can see them play.

TENNIS

Professional tennis comes to Philadelphia each year. The **U.S. PRO INDOOR TENNIS CHAMPIONSHIPS** pit 48 of the world's top male players against each other in eight sessions of singles and doubles at the Spectrum for a week in the end of January or early February. Tickets are $15 to $40 for individual sessions. Call 947-2530 for details, or watch for newspaper announcements.

Top women players from around the world compete for five days in November at the Civic Center in the **KISS-100 TENNIS INVITATIONAL**. Call 800-331-KISS for ticket and schedule information.

If you've never seen tennis played on grass, watch for newspaper announcements each summer for **NATIONAL GRASS COURT TOURNAMENTS** at the Germantown, Merion and Philadelphia Cricket Clubs. Not only is this a terrific opportunity to see top players, but it's also fun to see any of the country's few and finest grass court clubs that are usually open to members only.

Participation Sports

CITY OF PHILADELPHIA
Department of Recreation, 685–0150 or 686–3612
Fairmount Park Commission—Division of Recreation,
685–0051 or 685–0052

The Department of Recreation, along with the Fairmount Park Commission, coordinates and supervises hundreds of activities for young people and their parents.

Philadelphia has nearly 200 recreation centers and playgrounds. There are over 80 swimming pools, an abundance of tennis courts, golf courses, ball fields and ice skating rinks, all of which are strategically located throughout the city. There are facilities for just about every sport you could want to try, and the activities are continuous throughout the year.

BASEBALL

Baseball is the most popular non-professional sport in Philadelphia. Each year, almost 50,000 people play in the city's programs in three major divisions on a thousand teams in almost 200 leagues competing in 8,000 games. So you see, when we say "baseball" in Philadelphia, we really mean baseball.

"A" and "B" divisions (uniformed and non-uniformed) are coached by Recreation Department staff and volunteers. The "Independent" division consists of teams that are privately sponsored by churches, clubs and businesses.

Age divisions are for players 12, 14, 16 and 21 and under. The teams compete at neighborhood ball fields throughout the summer in order to earn a place in the citywide playoffs for the annual championship.

With this kind of organization, there's no excuse for anyone interested in baseball not to be out there playing.

BASKETBALL

Some of the country's top basketball players are graduates of Philadelphia's Department of Recreation programs.

Players and teams should register at local playgrounds for indoor league competitions in the winter and outdoor leagues that compete in the summer. Boys and girls from under 10 to under 18 are divided into age groups with league games leading to citywide playoffs and a championship. N.C.A.A. rules are used, but the length of time periods is determined by age.

BICYCLING

The city's bicycling program has grown in accordance with the popularity of the sport. There are 23 miles of scenic bike paths in Fairmount Park, alone. You can ride the paved routes along the Kelly and West River Drives, in the Wissahickon Valley from Ridge Avenue to Rittenhouse Street, for five-and-a-half miles of gravel bridle path along Forbidden Drive adjacent to the Wissahickon*, the eight miles paved along Pennypack Creek and on trails in other parts of the park.

Special biking events are planned by the city from March to October. They include a Bike Safety Rodeo and rides with local celebrities and professional groups. Call the Fairmount Park Commission (685–0051) for information.

Bike tours of the Wissahickon or Pennypack Park can also be scheduled for groups with the Philadelphia Ranger Corps*. These tours are tailored to the interest and ability of the participants. Everyone must have their own bicycle. Call RANGERS at least a month ahead for specifics on these adventures.

If you don't own a bike, you can rent one by the hour or by the day at Plaisted Hall, No. 1 Boat House Row on the Kelly Drive just west of the Art Museum. The shop is open year-round, weather permitting, daily in warm months and weekends only in winter. Call 236–4359 for hours, specific rates and deposit requirements. The bike rental shop will give you a map of bike trails in Fairmount Park.

If you would like to join an enjoyable bike ride, the Bicycle Club of Philadelphia (440–9983) leads an easy recreational Sunny Sunday Afternoon Bicycle Ride every Sunday starting at noon from Plaisted Hall. Riders bring their own bicycles and learn the rules of the road while taking a leisurely three or four-hour excursion. B.C.P. offers other bike treks in and around Philadelphia, too, so call them for additional information.

Other, more vigorous bike trips are sponsored by American Youth Hostels (925–6004).

If you're an avid bike rider and would like to ride with fellow bicyclists or work on improving conditions for bike riders in Philadelphia, write to the Bicycle Coalition of the Delaware Valley, P.O. Box 8194, Phila., PA 19101, or call them at BICYCLE. Members in the Coalition receive newsletters, an annual biking wall calendar, commuter and touring service and discounts at area bike shops. Thanks to their efforts, bicyclists can now pedal across the Benjamin Franklin Bridge, and SEPTA initiated a bike-transit program to accommodate bicyclists. They have the city building and improving more and more bike routes, and they also publish a helpful Regional Commuters' Bike Map.

BLOCK PARTIES and PLAY STREETS

The City of Philadelphia wants you to have fun. They'll close off a street temporarily so you can have a **Block Party**. All you have to do is submit an application along with a petition representing more than 75 percent of the block's residents who want the party. The city must receive the request at least three weeks before the planned event. There's a $5 fee for the permit. For additional information and an application form, write to the Contract and Permit Office of the Highway Division, Philadelphia Streets Department, 820 Municipal Services Bldg., Phila., PA 19107. Or call 686–5501.

If you live on a residential block with a lot of children, you might want to have it closed to traffic on summer days. This is a good idea especially if you're getting a fire hydrant spray cap (described later in this chapter under "Swimming").

The city must receive all applications for **Play Streets** from April to early June and streets can be closed off from June through August. Call 978–2720 for additional information about Play Streets.

BOATING

Few American cities offer boating on a placid river in a beautiful park near the center of town. Philadelphia does, at the East Park Canoe House, Kelly Drive south of the Strawberry Mansion Bridge (225–3560). You can rent rowboats or canoes by the hour ($10) daily from mid-March till the end of September and weekends only in October and November. Refreshments and souvenirs are also available. The hours are 11 to 8, but it's a good idea to call ahead and be sure. (There are no boat rentals when regattas are taking place on the Schuylkill.) One member of your crew must be at least 16.

Philadelphia is also home to the country's oldest active canoeing club. If you'd like to know more about the club, its history, canoeing and kayaking, plan to attend the annual open house at Philadelphia Canoe Club on the first Saturday in July. The historic clubhouse is just east of the Schuylkill River at 4900 Ridge Avenue. Call 487–9674 if you'd like to know more.

It doesn't matter if you're going out for serious rowing or for relaxation. Boating along the Schuylkill River is fun on a beautiful day.

Happy sails to you!

BOXING

If you're anxious to test your strength and physical fitness, the Department of Recreation gives you a chance in their non-competitive amateur boxing program. Boxing rings are located at 10 centers throughout the city where at least one exhibition is held annually.

The bouts consist of three two-minute rounds. The pairings are determined by age (four groupings from ages 10 to 18), weight (12 classes from 90 to over 181 pounds) and experience.

CHESS

Chess players are attracted in droves to neighborhood tournaments at recreation centers, followed by district and citywide playoffs.

The city encourages chess playing, so there's an annual citywide tournament. Contestants are divided into seven age groups from Pee Wee (12 and under) to Senior (over 18). International rules govern the play.

FISHING

Bring your own equipment (it doesn't have to be fancy) and try your luck.

A license is required if you're over 16. It costs $12.50 for a calendar year if you live in Pennsylvania, or $2.50 if you're a senior citizen. (If you're over 65 you can purchase a lifetime license for $10.50.) Non-residents pay $20.50, or $15.50 for a seven-day tourist license. You can get your license at a local sporting goods store. (Check in the Yellow Pages for a location near you and call ahead to be sure.)

The Schuylkill River (from Manayunk through Fairmount Park, center city and southwest Philadelphia) and F.D. Roosevelt Lake (20th Street and Pattison Avenue) have carp, catfish, muskellunge, panfish, sunfish, striped bass and yellow perch.

Five miles of the Wissahickon (from Germantown Pike to the Walnut Lane Bridge) and Pennypack Creek (from State to Pine Roads) are stocked with trout in mid-April and several more times before Labor Day. Sometimes the catch is good at Concourse Lake (44th Street and Parkside Avenue). Check in advance with the Fairmount Park Commission; they might be able to tell you where the fish are biting.

They also sponsor the two-day annual Fall Festival Fishing Contest when thousands of dollars of fishing equipment is awarded as prizes. Call 685–0051 for the dates and details.

GOLF

Philadelphia has six public golf courses which are in operation year-round. They are John F. Byrne, 9500 Leon Street in the Far Northeast (632–8666); Cobbs Creek and Karakung (36 holes), 72nd Street and Lansdowne Avenue (877–8707); Juniata, M and Cayuga Streets also in the Northeast (743–4060); Walnut Lane, Walnut Lane at Magdalena Street (482–3370) and F.D. Roosevelt, 20th Street and Pattison Avenue (462–8997). All of them can be reached by SEPTA.

Golfing fees from March 1 to December 1 are $14 on a weekday and $16 on weekends and holidays, except at Cobbs Creek where it's $1 more. In December, January and February, it's $1 less. There are seven categories for season passes at special prices enabling play at any of the courses. There's a reduced twi-light rate for teeing off after 4:30 P.M. There's a reduced nine-hole rate at Byrne, Juniata and F.D.R. Single and double carts are available at all of the courses, and each course has a snack bar and pro shop.

HIKING

Here's a sport that requires no special equipment other than sturdy shoes and uncomplaining feet. Hiking is something you don't have to practice. You compete only with yourself.

The Department of Recreation's Wanderlust Hiking Club offers supervised four- to eight-mile hikes along scenic trails in and around Philadelphia every Saturday afternoon at 1 or 1:30. For a schedule of weekly routes, call 685-0150.

Other hikes are organized locally by American Youth Hostels (925-6004) and the Batona Hiking Club (659-3921). Call them for details.

HOCKEY

Philadelphia has hockey fever. Some of us remember when millions of fans turned out to celebrate each time the Flyers won the Stanley Cup. Thousands of those fans (and their sons) also participate in hockey programs which are sponsored by the city's Department of Recreation, including clinics led by members of the Flyers.

There are street, floor and ice hockey leagues for boys. They're divided into teams according to age. The street and floor games are played at neighborhood centers, while the ice hockey battles are fought at the Cobbs Creek, Rizzo, Scanlon, Simons and Tarken rinks (see "Ice Skating" in this chapter).

All of the leagues follow traditional rules. Parents don't have to worry about dental bills because the rules prohibit malicious play.

HORSEBACK RIDING

Over 80 miles of bridle paths wind through Fairmount Park, the Wissahickon and Pennypack Park. And every mile of them is great for horseback riding.

If you don't have your own horse, there are stables listed in the Yellow Pages under "Riding Academies." Call them for hours, rates, directions and additional information.

And by all means, "get a horse."

ICE SKATING

The Department of Recreation holds sessions at five outdoor ice skating rinks two or three times a day from mid-December to the beginning of March.

The rinks are Cobbs Creek at Cobbs Creek Parkway and Walnut Street (748-3480), Scanlon at J and Tioga Streets (685-9893), Simons at Woolston Avenue and Walnut Lane (685-2888), Tarken at Frontenac and Levick Streets (685-1226) and the Ralph Rizzo, Sr. Rink under I-95 at Front Street and Washington Avenue (685-1593).

There's a nominal charge to skate: adults, $2; children under 16, $.50; senior citizens, $1. (Spectators are charged $.25.) Ice hockey clinics and instructions are sometimes provided. An annual ice extravaganza at the Scanlon rink casts over a hundred skaters from the neighborhood on the last three nights of the season.

Also, frozen creeks and ponds are sometimes declared safe for skating by the Fairmount Park Commission. They include (only when the park police say it's okay) the Wissahickon at Valley Green, sites along Pennypack Creek, and Concourse Lake at 44th Street and Parkside Avenue.

You have a choice of places to skate indoors throughout the year. Call ahead for their rates and hours. You can rent skates at most of these rinks, which is a good idea for children with rapidly growing feet and for children who want to find out how much they like the sport before investing in a pair of skates.

You can skate at the University of Pennsylvania Class of '23 Rink at 3130 Walnut Street (898-1923), providing the Penn ice hockey team isn't playing there.

The Wissahickon Ice Skating Club at Willow Grove and Cherokee Avenues (247-1907) is open to the public on Friday, Saturday and Sunday evenings.

JOGGING and RUNNING

If you would rather jog than walk, you can go out on your own when it's convenient. Jogging is non-competitive and you go at your own pace. All jogging trails in Fairmount Park are posted with half-mile markers. One of the most popular is the eight-and-a-half mile loop starting at No. 1 Boat House Row on Kelly Drive.

Running, on the other hand, pits you against other runners in competition. Special events in Fairmount Park bring runners together in organized races throughout the spring and fall seasons. Most runs are five or 10 kilometers, and they originate in front of the Art Museum and continue onto West River Drive.

If you're a competitive runner, you might also want to inquire with the Department of Recreation about the annual 10-mile Broad Street Run on the first Sunday in May. There's a $12 entry fee.

For additional information, call the Department of Recreation or Fairmount Park Commission Division of Recreation, or jog by No. 1 Boat House Row (Plaisted Hall) west of the Art Museum.

PLAYGROUNDS

The Department of Recreation operates over a hundred playgrounds reaching into all parts of the city. In the summer some of them are supervised for group games, organized sports and arts and crafts projects. Call to find out which is most convenient for you.

Smith Memorial Playground was established in 1899 as a lasting memorial to Richard and Sarah Smith's son, Stanfield. Their trust fund enables youngsters to frolic indoors and outside among a potpourri of amusements. The house contains a mini-village where small fry under five learn to drive mini-cars through mini-streets with pint-sized traffic meters, street lights and buildings. Another playroom, a reading room and a nature den provide additional entertainment resources.

The playground itself is for children under 12, with a smaller playground within it that's reserved for pre-schoolers. It's landscaped with a variety of equipment from small swings and climb-ons to a sliding board for 10. There's an outdoor wading pool and a swimming pool for youngsters to enjoy from June 1 to mid-August. There are picnic groves and a refreshment stand that's open from mid-May to Labor Day from 10 to 2:30.

Smith Memorial Playground is in East Fairmount Park. It's about a two-block walk from the **SEPTA** bus 32 stop at 33rd and Oxford Streets. You can drive to it by turning onto Fountain Green Drive (at the Grant Statue) from Kelly Drive and make the next three right turns. Hours for the house are Monday to Saturday, 10 to 3:30, and the playground is open 9 to 4 in winter and till 4:45

in summer. It's closed Sundays, Good Friday, Thanksgiving, Christmas and New Year's. If you have any questions, call 765-4325.

ROLLER SKATING

Philadelphians have joined the trend to skate. It's another fun way to get your aerobic exercise.

Several indoor, year-round "Skating Rinks" are listed in the Yellow Pages. Call for hours, rental information and rates.

Get rolling!

SLEDDING and SKIING

There are advanced hills and beginner's slopes in Fairmount Park for folks who want to participate in either of the above activities. Bring your own vehicle, even if it's only a homemade slab of cardboard or a trash can lid.

Among the most popular hills are those in Burholme Park at Cottman and Central Avenues, Clifford Park at Wissahickon Avenue and Walnut Lane, Tacony Creek Park at Roosevelt Boulevard and F Street, Cobbs Creek Park at Haverford and Lansdowne Avenues and Bennett Hill at 7300 Emlen Street near Allens Lane.

And don't forget the Belmont Plateau near the Playhouse in the Park, behind the west entrance of the Art Museum, and the hills at the public golf courses.

Fairmount Park is also ideal for cross-country skiing. If you're a beginner on the slopes, try renting equipment from any of the shops listed in the Yellow Pages under "Skiing Equipment."

Novice down-hillers would be wise to ski the small hills of Fairmount Park before heading for the big slopes. There are several ski areas within a short distance of Philadelphia, and there are dozens of them in Pennsylvania. Write to the Pennsylvania Bureau of Travel Marketing, Room 453 Forum Building, Harrisburg, PA 17120, for maps and information on ski trails, ski schools and accommodations. Or, call the Pennsylvania Bureau of Tourism at 800-VISIT-PA (847-4872). Also, refer to the Philadelphia Yellow Pages for ski tours.

SOCCER

The country's fastest growing sport is enjoying increased popularity in Philadelphia. Young people of both sexes are playing soccer, so soccer clinics are sometimes part of the fall and winter recreation programs at neighborhood centers. Outdoor leagues are available for boys from nine and under to 16 and under, and for girls from 10 and under to 16 and under.

In addition, a major indoor soccer program for boys and girls 19 and under begins in January at city recreation facilities and school gymnasiums. There are frequent competitions in three age categories.

An annual Soccer Field Day draws youngsters from all over the city to Vogt Recreation Center on the day after Thanksgiving. Everyone gets a chance to test their soccer skills like dribbling, passing and shooting accuracy. Awards are presented to the highest scorers.

SOFTBALL

There's a citywide softball tournament for boys in all age divisions. Slo-Pitch and Fast-Pitch Tournaments are held at neighborhood recreation centers. The tournaments eventually go on to semi-finals and city finals.

Girl's softball leagues play throughout the summer in three age groups for Slo-Pitch and Fast-Pitch. They use shorter pitching distances. There are league playoffs for boys and girls at the end of the season.

SUMMER CAMPS

Summer camps are a specialty in Philadelphia. The Department of Recreation sponsors several day camps at various locations for thousands of children. Registration is required for all camp programs. A nominal fee is charged, lunch is usually provided, and transportation is often arranged.

There are one-week periods for seven- to 11-year-olds at Camp Overbrook on the grounds of St. Charles Seminary at City Line and Wynnewood Road. The camp program here includes organized nature study, hikes, arts and crafts, singing, stunts, storytelling, campfires and games.

The P.D.R. Swimming Day Camp is for youngsters who already know how to swim but want to improve their skills and train in aquatics. Youngsters six to 12 years old can attend. Call 685–0156 for additional information.

Golf Camp is for boys and girls 12 to 18 years old. There are four weeklong camp periods in July and August from which to choose. Golfers from any of the encampments can play in a three-day tournament that ends the season.

Additional summer camps include the Summer Arts Camp (see Chapter 9) and Carousel Camp for the disabled (see Chapter 16). William Penn overnight camp takes 350 boys and girls from nine to 11 years old on each of four two-week encampments in the Poconos.

Call the Department of Recreation (685–0150) or get the details on any of these camping opportunities at your neighborhood recreation center or playground.

As if this wasn't enough, the Fairmount Park Commission runs six outdoor day camps for boys and girls from eight to 12 years old. Each camp schedules three two-week sessions during the summer. Again, registration is necessary and there's a small enrollment fee to pay for refreshments, supplies and camp trips. The activities include swimming, crafts, drama, games, camp songs and some camp trips. Check with the Fairmount Park Commission (685–0051) for the camp location nearest you.

SWIMMING

The Department of Recreation operates 80 outdoor pools at neighborhood centers throughout the city. The Fairmount Park Commission has four. You can swim alone or together with friends or family in special events that are scheduled according to the pool and its location. The pools are open daily all summer. For specific hours, call 686–3615.

Most pools hold a variety of programs that include Swim-to-Live classes, family night, splash parties, meets, modified water polo, water carnivals and life-guarding for certification. Swim meets place swimmers of all ages in competition for individual championships.

If you aren't close to a swimming pool this summer, take advantage of the city's refreshing **street shower program**. Starting June 1 and depending on the city's water supply, 2,500 spray caps are distributed free of charge through neighborhood police stations. A cool spray of water shoots out when the cap is attached to an all-orange fire hydrant.

Applications for spray caps are available at your district police station. A cap and permit is given to any responsible adult who fills out the simple form.

The low flow spray caps protect children and property

while they save water and preserve water pressure. It's against the law to open a fire hydrant any other way.

TENNIS

If you want to play tennis, there's no excuse for not playing it in Philadelphia.

Over 100 all-weather courts are in Fairmount Park (685–0051), and free instruction is offered to children on weekdays throughout the summer. Call for a schedule and locations that are convenient to you.

Another 150 all-weather courts are at various Department of Recreation sites throughout the city (685–0150). Some of the courts are equipped for nighttime playing.

More than 4,000 youngsters participate in the Department of Recreation/National Junior Tennis League of Philadelphia each summer. There's a minimal fee to enroll. Boys and girls from ages eight to 18 play at beginner, intermediate and advanced levels. Rackets and balls are provided by the instructors. Of course, you can bring your own. Each participant also gets a team T-shirt.

Morning and afternoon clinics are held at 70 locations from late June through August. A round-robin tournament in August determines who the city champions will be. Some have gone on to Middle States junior rankings...which is pretty good, if you're up on tennis. If you would like to sign up, or know someone who would, call 686–3612 or 424–5300 (July and August only).

The Fairmount Park Commission sponsors an annual Fairmount Fall Festival Tennis Championship, the largest amateur tennis tournament held in the Philadelphia area, at the Chamounix courts in late September. There are junior singles events and adult events including singles and doubles for men and women. Call (685–0051) in August for information and to request an entry blank.

A once-a-year Saturday clinic attracts hundreds of young tennis enthusiasts. It's held in conjunction with the U.S. Pro Indoor Tennis Championships* at the Spectrum. Call 947–2530 for details. Some of the best players in the world conduct this clinic.

TRACK AND FIELD

Kids from all over the city are keeping fit by doing dashes, jumps, sprints and relays. At the latest count, over 15,000 boys and girls have participated in local, district and citywide contests. There's an indoor and outdoor season with many meets.

The Little Quaker Track Meet brings together boys and girls five to nine years old to do sprints, relays and field competitions. Other events include development meets, summer relays, the Jesse Owens Meet, Hershey Foods Meet and the U.S. Youth Games.

The Recreation Department's annual coordinated Track Carnival is indoors in January. It features a Handicapped Meet and an Age-Group Meet with a variety of events.

TUMBLING AND GYMNASTICS

Over 45 recreation centers sponsor fall and winter programs for boys. They're divided into four age groups: small fry (nine and under) to advanced (14 to 18). Dual, district and citywide meets are held.

Girls can compete in an equally lively tumbling program. Their meets also precede a city championship.

VOLLEYBALL

Almost 100 teams play volleyball throughout the year at city facilities. Intermediate players are up to age 15, juniors to 17, and 18 and over for seniors. There are local competitions at all levels.

If none of the preceding sports turns you on, maybe one of these will interest you:

AEROBICS classes are at several neighborhood recreation centers. Call the one nearest you to see if an exercise program is on the schedule.

DOG FRISBEE contests are sponsored each summer by the Department of Recreation. If your dog is good at catching frisbees, you can participate together as a team. Call ahead (685–0151) for the dates so you don't miss this June event. Start practicing now and sign up at your neighborhood center early in June.

RACQUETBALL and **SQUASH** are popular sports in Philadelphia, but they're limited to playing at private clubs where you can buy time by the hour. Racquetball and squash clubs are listed in the Yellow Pages.

If you're still not motivated, take another look at the chapters on "The Arts" and "History" and think about becoming an artist or a scholar.

Chapter 15.
Philadelphia for Children.

Many of the attractions described throughout this book are suitable for children. But this chapter is about the places and events that are designed *especially* for children. Grown-ups are welcome, of course, and they're requested to adequately supervise their little folk.

Reminder: An **asterisk(*)** indicates that the same place or event appears elsewhere in the book with more details. You'll find that place in the Index.

Just Watching

CONCERTS

Children can enjoy the **PHILADELPHIA ORCHESTRA*** just as their parents and grandparents did when they were young. Conductor William Smith makes music fun at the **Academy of Music***. Each concert features narration, illustration, ballet, choral groups or an unusual solo.

The Philadelphia Orchestra gives one-hour **Concerts for Children**, ages five to 11 years old, on five Saturday mornings at 11 during the concert season.

Tickets are $16 to $69 per seat for the series, and all seats are reserved. These concerts are sold in advance by subscription, but tickets are available for individual concerts at the Academy's box office prior to each concert.

Three **Come and Meet the Music Concerts** are during the school year for middle and high school students. A theme chosen each year corresponds with a school curriculum. Tickets for these concerts are available individually from $4 to $12.

Call the orchestra's education office at 893–1978 for additional information.

One or two children's concerts are also presented outdoors by the Philadelphia Orchestra in the summer at the **Mann Music Center***. These performances always feature talented young soloists and there's no charge to attend. Watch the newspapers for announcements of these concerts, or call 567–0707 early in the summer for details.

A combination of music and books is the main attraction at the **Free Library of Philadelphia's*** popular **Book Concerts for Children**, ages six to 13. Each concert has a theme and includes some facet of the performing arts. It could be a fairy tale, a dance or an adventure story told with music. Nine of these programs are presented at the **Logan Square Main Library** during the school year. They last from 60 to 90 minutes, with time to visit the library before and after the concert.

Reading lists and lending books, which are available after the concerts, encourage youngsters to follow up on the musical programs they've just heard. It's a creative as well as painless way to combine reading, music and the arts for children who aren't inclined towards these subjects. Call 686–5372 for a schedule and details.

ARTS AND SCIENCES

The **Philadelphia Museum of Art*** (763–8100) has workshops that enable pre-schoolers and school-age children to discover the museum and explore various art techniques. The museum also has free one-hour Family Programs, especially for children six to 12 and their parents, each Sunday at 11:30 A.M. and 1 P.M. There's no charge to attend these programs but tickets are necessary. They're distributed on a first-come, first-served basis each Sunday morning at the West Information Desk.

The **Institute of Contemporary Art*** (898–7108) has Saturday afternoon Children's Day events to coincide with their exhibitions. Gallery talks and art happenings are planned especially for youngsters 13 and under.

The galleries at **Moore College of Art*** (568–4515) and the **Pennsylvania Academy of the Fine Arts*** (972–7600) also have children's activities in conjunction with their current shows. Call them to find out what's scheduled.

The **Academy of Natural Sciences*** (299–1000) is the ultimate indoor stop for little people who love animals and want to know more about them. The exhibits, live animal shows and children's classes are described in Chapter 7. Outside In is described later in this chapter.

All of the **Franklin Institute*** (448–1200) is for children of all ages. But a special program just for children under seven years old is on Saturday and Sunday mornings at 11:15 in the **Fels Planetarium***. It's a nifty way to learn about the phases of the moon, the stars and what's happening in the skies. Several package plans are available including admission to the Planetarium. All children must be accompanied by adults.

FILMS

The **Free Library of Philadelphia*** (686–5322) has free films at the Main Library and many of the branch libraries. There are film programs for pre-schoolers on weekday mornings, and after school for their older brothers and sisters. Films relating to current holidays or special themes are shown in late afternoons and early evenings at some branch libraries. There are afternoon showings during the summer.

The **University Museum*** (898–4015 or 222–7777) shows all kinds and lengths of films for children on Saturday mornings at 10:30 from October through March. They're chosen especially for children from eight to 14 years old.

LIVE AND ON STAGE

American Theater Arts for Youth (563–3501) is a non-profit theatrical company of professional adult performers produced by localite Laurie Wagman, and Laurie really knows what young people like to watch.

Theater Arts for Youth presents musical shows that are especially related to school curriculums for children of all ages. Prepared study guides are included for teachers.

Most of the audiences are filled with groups, but the public is invited, too. Most of the school-year productions are weekdays (at 10 A.M. and 12:30 P.M.) and Saturdays (at 11 A.M.) at the theater in the Port of History Museum*. A seven week summer series has morning shows twice a week. Tickets are $5.75 and group rates are available. Reservations are necessary.

The repertoire changes each year, but "Babes in Toyland" is an annual fall classic. Be sure to call for the schedule, and give the young folks a real treat.

Annenberg Center* (898–6791) presents three productions a year in a top-notch **Theater for Children** series. Dynamic companies from around the world bring four performances of each show to the Zellerbach stage on Fridays and Saturdays. A fourth family entertainment production is scheduled over the winter holidays. Recent shows have included children's opera, giant puppets, mime and movement theater. Study guides are available for each production. This is a popular series. Get your schedule early in the fall so you won't miss anything.

Bristol Riverside Theater* (788–7827) has children's theater two or three Saturdays a month from September to late May. It's especially for youngsters four to 10 years old. A special winter holiday production is geared through seventh graders. Call for the schedule and reservations.

Hedgerow Theater* (565–4211) has plays for children three to 11 scheduled year-round. Tickets are $4 and group rates are available. Call for the dates and to order tickets.

Philadelphia Theater Caravan* (898–6068) takes its theater for children on the road. Go back to Chapter 13 and read about it in "tours to go."

The **Philadelphia International Theatre Festival for Children** is five full days at the end of May (including Memorial Day weekend). There are over a hundred performances of theater, mime, puppetry and dance along with acrobatics, juggling, face painting, balloon art and street performances. Professional children's theater companies from around the world are here to perform at the fete, and everything is geared to children.

Most of the events take place at Annenberg Center*. Some are at International House* and MTI Tabernacle Theater*. Individual tickets for all performances are $6. Discounts are available for groups and if you purchase tickets for more than one show. Call the Annenberg box office (898–6791) early in the spring for information. (Groups should call 898–6683.)

Plays and Players* (735–0630) has plays for children. Four original and/or classic plays are presented from September to June, each on two consecutive Saturdays at 11 A.M. and 1 P.M. and one Sunday at 12 and 2 P.M. They're planned for an audience of pre-schoolers to fifth graders. Tickets are $2.50 for children and $3.50 for the adults who accompany them. Find out what's coming up and give a child a treat.

Children's Musical Theater at Valley Forge Music Fair* (644–5000) is on Wednesdays in July and August at 11 A.M. and 2 P.M., and occasionally on Saturdays during the rest of the year and during school holidays.

A rollicking musical with charming costumes and scenery is presented in-the-round. Tickets are usually $5. Group rates and series rates are also available (call 296–9820).

Youngsters never seem to get enough of "Cinderella," "Pinnochio," "Alice in Wonderland" or "The Wizard of Oz." If your children will be home this summer, give them this joyful entertainment. If you can't wait till summer, check the newspapers or call to find out what's scheduled during the rest of the year.

The **Free Library of Philadelphia*** has free **Story Hours for Children** at the Main Library's Children's Department and at neighborhood branch libraries. These Story Hours spark the imaginations of Philadelphia children from pre-school through elementary school ages. The Library's animated reading program takes youngsters into a world of fantasy. It encourages children to become interested in books.

Pre-registration is required for pre-school Story Hours. They're usually one morning or afternoon during the week at specified branch libraries throughout the city. Story Hours for school children are scheduled for 4 P.M. Bedtime Story Hours are after dinner at some neighborhood libraries. Youngsters are invited to attend in pajamas, listen to stories and go home ready for bed. The schedule is available each month at the Free Library. Or call your local branch (listed in the Philadelphia White Pages) or the Office for Work with Children at 686–5372.

This project, alone, shows that Philadelphia is a great city for children. (The Free Library's extensive Children's Department is described in Chapter 11.)

ALMOST LIVE AND ON STAGE

Children love puppets, so Philadelphia has puppet shows. The **Philadelphia Marionette Theater*** performs in its fantasyland at Playhouse in the Park in West Fairmount Park. A one-hour performance includes puppets, live organ music and a marionette show from a happy repertoire of four new shows each year that's guaranteed to make you smile.

Tickets are $4.50, with group rates available. Reservations are necessary. Curtain is weekdays at 10:30 A.M. (except in September), and there are occasional Sunday shows. Call 879-1213 or watch the newspapers for a schedule. Don't miss this fabulous opportunity to have someone pull the strings for you.

If you're still looking for something to do "just watching," go back to Chapter 13 and consider a tour of a pretzel museum, a money factory or a bakery.

Joining the Fun

When the weather is nice, it's nice to be outdoors, exploring nature and visiting some animals.

The **Foundation for Architecture*** (569-3187 or 569-TOUR) arranges **Children's Walks** just for groups of youngsters ages seven to 12. A choice of four center city routes is available and each tour is supplemented with an activity workbook. These walks are guaranteed to stimulate children's interest in buildings, architecture and landscape. There are occasional regularly scheduled tours for children as well. Call to schedule your group or to find out when your youngster can join a tour.

Within the **Philadelphia Zoo*** is a two-acre **Children's Zoo** where youngsters can touch and feed the animals and be right there when the zookeeper takes care of the creatures. The inhabitants are also known to perform for their little visitors.

Daily events (except in winter from December to March) include sea lion demonstrations, cow milking, sheep dog demonstrations, pony rides and an animal show.

The Backyard Bugs Exhibit is a discovery center that invites children to learn while having fun as they touch and listen to the likes of ants, bugs, a beehive, walking sticks, giant hissing cockroaches and tarantulas. Sounds like *real* fun!

Admission to this special little zoo is included with admission to the big zoo.

Another zoo with a petting zoo for children is in Norristown. The **Elmwood Park Zoo*** is described under Montgomery County in Chapter 17.

And, if you can do it, plan a day at **Great Adventure***
in New Jersey (also described in Chapter 17) where thousands of wild animals roam the safari park.

Guided and/or informal **nature walks** are healthy and
fun for people of all ages. They can be enjoyed at Andorra Natural Area, Morris Arboretum, Pennypack Environmental Center, Schuylkill Center for Environmental
Education and Tinicum National Environmental Center,
all described in Chapter 7. Workshops and special events
for youngsters are planned at Andorra, Pennypack and
Schuylkill Center.

Another kind of nature extravaganza just for youngsters is the **Children's Garden at Longwood Gardens***
(388–6741). Little people from age two and older love to
navigate through a lush maze, climb the "ruins" of a
stone cottage, explore a vine-covered hideaway and exit
through a "tunnel" of foliage. Some of their favorite crea-
ture friends are there in topiary form along the way.

Within the **Academy of Natural Sciences***
(299–1060) is a Children's Nature Museum called **Outside In**. It's a mini-museum created for youngsters 12 and
under who, along with their adult chaperones, can explore nature by using all five of their senses. It's billed
as the "touchable world of woodlands, streams, beaches
and quarries. It's where you meet some of the creatures
who live in these outdoor spaces."

There are live animals to touch, environments to sample, sounds to make and natural objects to examine.
Everything is cleverly designed to involve visitors while
they enjoy learning about nature and their surroundings.

Hours at Outside In are weekdays, 1:30 to 4 P.M.,
weekends and holidays, 10 to 5. Children must be with
an adult. Groups are admitted with advance reservations
only. Admission to Outside In is included with admission
to the Academy.

PLEASE TOUCH MUSEUM at 210 North 21st
Street (963–0666) was the first museum in the country
designed especially for children seven and younger.
(Please Touch is directly across from the Franklin Institute's new Futures Center.)

Everything at Please Touch is meant to be explored,
touched, climbed on, tried on or played on. The Cultural
Corridor provides hands-on exhibits from a variety of cul-

tures. Calliope teaches about sound. The Nature Center houses small animals to watch and pet. The Tot Spot is for toddlers to crawl around and explore. You can be anything you want to be when you use your imagination and try on masks, hats, costumes and uniforms on hand.

Programs in the informal 120-seat Virginia Evans Theater might include music, mime, puppets, films or storytelling that's guaranteed to intrigue any small-fry crowd. Workshops are also scheduled regularly. Special exhibits are always fun and educational, too. There's a new topic every six months or so. A special room is also available at Please Touch for children, parents, educators and students. It's a place to find books, games, work kits and objects that help explain mysteries like magnetism, electricity, fossils and webs.

It's only natural that children are comfortable and curious at Please Touch and their learning is uninhibited. Their social skills benefit, too, as they meet and play with others their size. And parents will learn about their children too!

Hours at Please Touch are daily, 9 to 4:30, except Thanksgiving, Christmas and New Year's when it's closed. Children must be accompanied by an adult (one adult for every three children), and groups are requested to make reservations. No strollers are allowed on the gallery floor.

Physically and mentally **disabled** youngsters also benefit from Please Touch. It's recommended for handicapped children 12 and under. All exhibits have braille signage. There is complete wheelchair access.

Cost is $5, and group rates are available on weekdays

only. Again, group reservations are necessary. Admission is "pay as you wish" on Sundays from 9 till 1. Membership allows free admission, a quarterly newsletter, invitations to preview events, and shop discounts. Gift packages are available, too.

Please Touch also rents "Traveling Trunks" (see Chapter 13). A museum shop has high quality, low price books, games and toys reflecting the Please Touch environment.

Another museum especially for children 10 and under is in suburban Montgomery County. **CHILDVENTURE MUSEUM**, at 3364 Susquehanna Road in Dresher (643–9906), has several rooms of hands-on, try-on exhibits. In the storybook room children don costumes of their favorite characters and participate in a popular tale. A slide and sound room projects images related to accompanying music. An almost true-to-life hardware store and a grocery store encourage the appropriate participation. Workshops are scheduled frequently in conjunction with the exhibits, holidays or particular events. Any group wanting a special presentation must schedule in advance. All groups of 15 or more are requested to call before coming. **Hours** are Tuesday to Saturday, 10 to 4; Sunday, 12 to 4. **Cost** is $3.50, and group rates are available for 12 or more with reservations.

Summer camps and **recreation programs** offered by the City of Philadelphia are described in Chapter 14, along with professional sporting events you can watch from the sidelines.

The ultimate educational and recreational park for children three to 13 is **Sesame Place**. Since it's in Bucks County, you can read more about it in Chapter 17.

This is as close as anyone can come to guaranteeing your child will be busy and happy.

Chapter 16.
Philadelphia for the Elderly and Disabled.

This chapter is especially for people who have limited walking ability or are confined to wheelchairs. A disability shouldn't necessarily preclude visiting historic, educational and recreational attractions in Philadelphia. In many instances there are attractions just for people with disabilities.

A concerted effort has been made throughout this book to specify for the elderly and disabled the accessibility to each attraction. They are described as having "wheelchair access" or "no wheelchair access" based on a building's entrance, door widths and connections between floors.

"Complete wheelchair access" means that not only is the entrance level and manageable, but also there are special restroom facilities, elevators and other considerations. Details are given where it's pertinent. If further information is desired, call ahead before you visit.

You'll recognize the International Symbol for Accessibility at all public places where there are no architectural barriers and where all conveniences are at an accessible height.

You'll also appreciate the curb cuts and sidewalk ramps at all center city intersections in Independence National Historical Park, along the Benjamin Franklin Parkway, on the Chestnut Street Transitway (which also has depressed curbs midway on each block), on Walnut, Market, Juniper and Filbert Streets and John F. Kennedy Boulevard, and at most prominent city intersections where there are public buildings nearby.

Wherever special provisions are made for the visually and hearing impaired, they, too, are mentioned.

You can also write or call the **Mayor's Commission on People with Disabilities**, Room 143 City Hall, Phila., PA 19107 (686–2798). They can provide additional details on hotels, places of worship, branch libraries, banks, post offices, government office buildings and other places frequently visited.

Hearing impaired people with telephone-teletype equipment can call the City Hall TTY phone at 564–1782.

The office is anxious to help Philadelphians and visitors to the city. They'll also refer you to agencies serving people with specific disabilities.

The **Mayor's Commission on Services to the Aging** is at 1401 Arch Street, Phila., PA 19102 (686–3504).

Special Services

SEPTA

Call SEPTA at 580–7365 to get fare information for senior citizens and the disabled, or write to SEPTA Special Services, 130 South 9th Street, Phila., PA 19107.

Those with Telecommunication Device for the Deaf equipment can call SEPTA's TDD phone at 580–7812, weekdays from 8:30 to 4:30, for schedule, route and fare information.

Special ID cards from SEPTA enable disabled persons to ride SEPTA vehicles at half-fare during off-peak hours. Application forms are available from the 130 South 9th Street office.

Special fares for senior citizens are described under "SEPTA" in Chapter 1.

There are three steps to get on or off the SEPTA buses and trolleys. The first step is approximately 12 inches from the ground. The next two are less. Many of SEPTA's bus routes use wheelchair-accessible vehicles. Again, call SEPTA Special Services for information on these routes or to request a special vehicle on your route.

SEPTA Paratransit is a special van service for people unable to use regular SEPTA vehicles. It operates daily door-to-door and by reservation only. All riders must be registered with SEPTA. Write to the 9th Street office for Paratransit information, or call 580–7000.

A number of free brochures are available from SEPTA to benefit the elderly and disabled. These include a Transit Guide to Metropolitan Philadelphia for the Disabled (in print, cassette or braille), How to Ride SEPTA's Wheelchair Lift Buses, a guide to the Paratransit service and a guide to the wheelchair-accessible bus routes. Call 580–7000 or 580–7712 (TDD) if you know anyone who would benefit from these services.

ASSOCIATED SERVICES FOR THE BLIND
919 Walnut Street—19107
627-0600

The transcription of correspondence to braille, large-type copies or tape recordings of your material are provided for a nominal fee for supplies by Associated Services for the Blind.

A training program is available to newly blinded people. Call for details.

Sense-Sations, the A.S.B.'s unique shop for people who have difficulty reading print, has clever as well as practical tools for the blind and vision-impaired customer. The merchandise includes magnifiers, canes, braille wristwatches, talking calculators, speech synthesizers for computers, large-type playing cards, books, games and kitchen utensils. Braille playing cards are free for blind people from this agency. A mail/phone order catalogue is available for those who can't get in to the store.

Ask about other services, like job placement, instruction in mobility, computer training, daily living skills and cooking classes that are provided by Associated Services for the Blind.

CAROUSEL HOUSE
685–0160 (Department of Recreation)

The city's Department of Recreation, under auspices of Carousel House, sponsors year-round indoor and outdoor programs for disabled Philadelphians at its facility in West Fairmount Park.

A summer camp run by Carousel House in Fairmount Park is a rewarding experience for youngsters with developmental disabilities who participate in recreational, educational and therapeutic activities. There are two three-week encampments in July and August.

Reservations are necessary for all Carousel House events and activities. If you know someone who should be taking advantage of these activities, call the Department of Recreation for programs and the dates to enroll.

ELWYN–NEVIL CENTER
FOR DEAF AND HEARING IMPAIRED
4031 Ludlow Street—19104
895–5509 (TDD: 895–5695)

This agency provides several vital services to deaf, hearing impaired or communication-disordered people, as well as their families, friends, employers and co-workers. The staff is concerned with deaf people as well as people who can hear and are interested in the hearing impaired.

Among the services offered are vocational and personal

counseling, social work, information and referral. Also, there's referral within Elwyn Institutes for speech and language therapy, audiology, and vocational evaluation and training. They can help you contact government, public and private agencies providing special services. They can provide a list of religious services, social organizations and recreational clubs for the deaf. They occasionally sponsor workshops and seminars, and they can refer you to classes for sign language whether you hear or not.

The Center is open weekdays from 8:30 to 4:30.

A Deaf and Hearing-Impaired Senior Citizen Group (for those 55 and over) is also at the Center. There's a popular "drop-in" room, bi-weekly meetings, frequent social events, educational events and trips. The members are from throughout the Delaware Valley. Call 895-5567 (voice or TDD) for more information.

FREE LIBRARY OF PHILADELPHIA
Library for the Blind and Physically Handicapped
919 Walnut Street—19107
925-3213

Talking books, records, tapes, large print books and braille books are available along with traditional library materials from this special branch of the Free Library. Books and brochures on blindness are also at the Library for the Blind and Physically Handicapped.

The resources are available to anyone who can't read ordinary print or hold a book because of a temporary or permanent visual or physical disability. (If you're ordering records or tapes, be sure your home audio equipment is compatible with the library's.)

This facility was built especially for the physically disabled. It has level entrances, restrooms, and phones to accommodate the blind and physically limited visitor. Hours are weekdays, except holidays, 9 to 5. If you can't get to this branch of the library but would like to use its resources, ask about having materials mailed to you.

Materials and services for the hearing impaired are at the Central Library on Logan Square and at six branch libraries. A teletype machine at the Central Library's General Information Department enables deaf people to converse with the library staff. You can call the Library's TTY phone at 561-0942.

For access to the Free Library at Logan Square, refer to the next section of this chapter.

FREE LIBRARY OF PHILADELPHIA
Homebound Services
686-5411

Individuals who can't get to the library can request an application to qualify for the library to deliver its books to them at home. You must be a Philadelphia resident and have a disability that keeps you housebound. As many as six books, including those with large print, can be borrowed for as long as six weeks. If you know someone who could take advantage of this terrific opportunity, call, weekdays between 9 and 5, for more information.

HUTCHINSON GYM POOL
University of Pennsylvania
33rd and Locust Streets—19104
898-8383

The University of Pennsylvania offers a special opportunity to people who enjoy swimming, but have a physical disability. Hutchinson Gym's pool has depths of three-and-a-half to 10 feet and is equipped with two lifts to lower swimmers into the water. Anyone in a wheelchair or on crutches can take advantage of this if they can swim and are accompanied by an adult swimmer. There's no admission charge for this year-round activity.

The pool hours are weekdays, except holidays, noon to 6; weekends during the school year, noon to 5. Call a day in advance to confirm this and to be sure a lifeguard will be on duty. The east entrance of the Hutchinson Gym has a ramp, and the two parking spaces closest to this entrance are designated for the physically disabled.

RADIO INFORMATION CENTER
FOR THE BLIND (RICB)
919 Walnut Street—19107
627-0600 Ext. 207

More than 4,000 blind or print-handicapped people within a 50-mile radius of Philadelphia tune in daily to RICB's closed-circuit FM radio station. They hear readings from daily newspapers, magazines and books and live talk shows featuring useful information. Some call-in shows offer the audience a chance to air their questions and comments.

Broadcast hours are weekdays, 5 A.M. to 11 P.M.; Saturdays, 7 A.M. to 11 P.M.; and Sundays, 7 A.M. to 10 P.M.

RICB is a charitable non-profit radio station under the auspices of the Associated Services for the Blind (described a few pages ago). If you know a print-handicapped person who would benefit from this one-of-a-kind opportunity, call the station for an application. Radios, provided for an annual specified donation, enable listeners to help defray station expenses and to support its outstanding services.

If you have some spare time, call RICB and volunteer to read aloud for their listeners.

TRAVEL INFORMATION SERVICE
Moss Rehabilitation Hospital
1200 West Tabor Road—19141–3099
456–9600 (TTY: 456–9602)

The Travel Information Service at Moss is where you can get facts on hotels, ships, planes, trains and tourist attractions in the United States and abroad to make your travel easier. They can tell you where you'll have wheelchair access, and where you won't. For the cost of postage and handling, they'll send you information on several travel destinations or topics.

They're not a travel agency, but if you would like the Service to assist you with a trip, call them with the idea of your proposed itinerary. They won't book any of your accommodations, but they can offer invaluable suggestions and information, as well as contacts for other agencies and travel services for the disabled.

A **Resource and Information Center** at Moss offers a variety of materials on all aspects of physical disability and rehabilitation. The library has information on special programs for the disabled, job possibilities, services, facilities, benefits and the legal rights of the physically impaired. You can find information on making a home more accessible, clothing more comfortable and adaptability more complete. The resources are in pamphlets, books and magazines.

The Resource Center has complete wheelchair access, but if you can't get to the Center, call for additional information. The hours are weekdays from 9 to 5.

This facility offers invaluable information to people interested in the physically disabled.

Access to Theaters and Stadiums

Each of the following theaters, stadiums, special attractions and gathering places is mentioned more than once elsewhere in this book. They are popular sites for events in sports, visual and performing arts.

Museums and arts groups with specific programs and exhibits for the disabled are described with that attraction under "E & D."

ACADEMY OF MUSIC
893–1930 (box office)
893–1935 (manager's office)

Arrangements must be made in advance for people who plan to attend an event in a wheelchair. The best thing to do is buy designated seats in the parquet circle where the seat can be removed to accommodate a wheelchair. Ushers will assist with seating.

There are six steps at the main entrance on Broad Street. Call ahead to the box office so an usher will meet you at the ramped entrance on the Academy's south alley. Restrooms on the main floor have complete wheelchair access.

"Audio-Aid" headsets are available at no cost to individuals with a hearing impairment. Call ahead during business hours to the manager's office and arrange for a headset during the concert you plan to attend.

ANNENBERG CENTER AT THE UNIVERSITY OF PENNSYLVANIA
898–6791 (TTY: 898–7803)

All of Annenberg's theaters and restrooms are accessible to wheelchairs. Call ahead for special arrangements to enter at the most convenient door. There's limited space in each theater for individuals to remain in wheelchairs, and ushers will assist others into regular seats.

Viewers with up to 75 percent hearing loss can enjoy shows at Zellerbach Theater with a "magic eye" that gets sound signals through infrared light from the theater's master sound system. $2 rents the device for individual seats prior to each performance.

For information on all Annenberg Center services and programs for the disabled, call 898–6791.

FREE LIBRARY OF PHILADELPHIA
686-5322

The Central Library at Logan Square is accessible to wheelchairs. There are automatic doors at the front entrance and six low steps in three tiers. A ramped entrance at the 20th Street end of Wood Street on the library's north side is always open. Designated parking is on Wood Street.

Call the Free Library for information on the branch libraries (30 of them are wheelchair accessible), and read the beginning of this chapter for the library's special services for the disabled.

INDEPENDENCE NATIONAL HISTORICAL PARK
597-8974 (voice or TDD)

A large print brochure is available on "Accessibility" at the I.N.H.P. Call for the location most convenient to pick one up, or write to I.N.H.P., 313 Walnut Street, Phila., PA 19106. The Visitor Center and Liberty Bell Pavilion are the only buildings in the Park with complete wheelchair access. More information is in Chapter 2.

INTERNATIONAL HOUSE
387-5125

As you enter from Chestnut Street, there are eight steps in two tiers that take you to the main floor shops. You can avoid those steps by following the outdoor plaza to a ramped entrance on the building's east (37th Street) side.

There are four low steps at the entrance to Hopkinson Hall in the International House.

MANDELL THEATER AT DREXEL UNIVERSITY
895-2528

A ramp at the Chestnut Street entrance allows access to the building without climbing steps. There are several steps into the auditorium, or there is special level access to the audience left side where room is allocated for six wheelchairs. For assistance with wheelchairs, ask for the house manager on arrival. Complete wheelchair access to restrooms.

MANN MUSIC CENTER
567-0707

Complete wheelchair access with restrooms at ground level. An eight- by 130-foot ramp eliminates steep walking and steps. It goes from the top of the Center and parking areas directly into the balcony.

MTI TABERNACLE THEATER
382-0600

There are eight steps if you approach from Chestnut Street. Call ahead to enter at west side of theater where there is a ramp and no steps. Special seating arrangements can be made in advance for people in wheelchairs. Restrooms are wheelchair accessible.

PAINTED BRIDE ART CENTER
925-9914

Complete wheelchair access. Call ahead and space is reserved at the front of the theater for people who wish to remain in wheelchairs.

PALESTRA
898-6151

The main entrance (west side) is level. An area in the upper stands, Section 219, is set aside for eight wheelchairs. These spaces must be reserved in advance. Ushers will assist others into seats. Restrooms are accessible.

PHILADELPHIA CIVIC CENTER
823-5600

For **Convention Hall**, **Civic Center Plaza** and **Pennsylvania Hall**: there's a driveway entrance adjacent to each building of the Civic Center complex where the door is at street level. Once inside, the main floor is level and there is elevator service to other levels. Restrooms are wheelchair accessible.

SHUBERT THEATER
732-5446

Entrance and orchestra seats are level, but it's necessary for those who must remain in a wheelchair to get specific aisle seats. (No one can remain in a wheelchair for a performance.) Restrooms can be reached by elevator.

SPECTRUM
336–3600 (ask for box office)
TDD: 389–9500

When buying tickets for any event, specify if a spectator will be in a wheelchair. Call the box office at least a week prior to an event to request "primary" seating in a section designated for people in wheelchairs. (Two companions can accompany each wheelchair-bound spectator in these sections.)

To reach a level entrance of the Spectrum, approach the building's east or west side from 10th Street. Special parking is designated for the disabled. A ramp enables you to enter to the main floor without climbing steps. Doors 1 and 9 are built specifically to accommodate wheelchairs. Restrooms, telephones and water fountains nearby are designed for the wheelchair-bound.

If you are to remain in a wheelchair for the event and do not have "primary" seating, go directly to the Information Booth (behind Section U on the main level) on arrival. A folding chair is provided for the person accompanying the wheelchair-bound. You'll then go to the special seating area behind Row 21.

VALLEY FORGE MUSIC FAIR
644–5000

Check with a parking attendant to be directed to a level entrance. Visitors can remain in wheelchairs around the audience perimeter. There are restrooms for the physically disabled.

VETERANS STADIUM
Phillies, 463–1000; Eagles, 463–5500

There is one curb step from the adjacent parking lots to the entrance gates. Everything else is accessible by ramps and an elevator. The seats most convenient for fans in wheelchairs are in the 300s sections and reached from Gate D. Restrooms nearby have complete wheelchair access. When you buy tickets, specify that they're for disabled persons in wheelchairs. To arrange in advance for special parking, call 686–1776 Ext. 84–200.

WALNUT STREET THEATER
574–3550

The entrance to the orchestra section is level, but you should call ahead to arrange to remain in a wheelchair or to be transferred to your aisle seat. Restrooms are on the balcony reached by elevator or the lower level reached by stairs.

An "audio loop" throughout the theater enables better hearing for those wearing a hearing aid adaptable to the telecord.

YM & YWHA at 401 S. Broad Street
545–4400

There are several steps at the Broad Street entrance. Call ahead or have someone ask the front door attendant to open the Pine Street entrance where there's a ramp and lift. Once inside, there's complete wheelchair access.

Chapter 17.
Beyond Philadelphia.

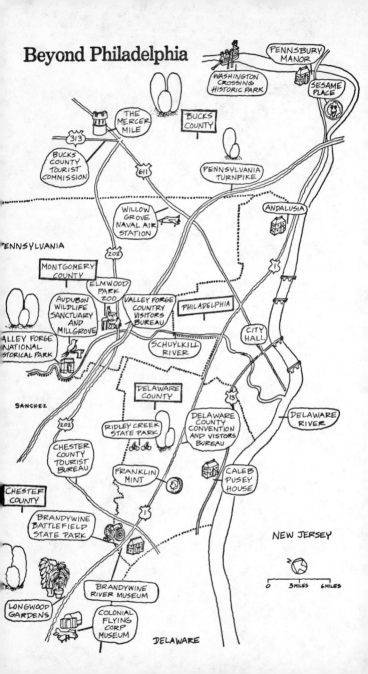

Beyond Philadelphia

PENNSBURY MANOR

WASHINGTON CROSSING HISTORIC PARK

SESAME PLACE

THE MERCER MILE

BUCKS COUNTY

313

BUCKS COUNTY TOURIST COMMISSION

611

PENNSYLVANIA TURNPIKE

ANDALUSIA

WILLOW GROVE NAVAL AIR STATION

PENNSYLVANIA

202

MONTGOMERY COUNTY

ELMWOOD PARK ZOO

VALLEY FORGE COUNTRY VISITORS BUREAU

PHILADELPHIA

AUDUBON WILDLIFE SANCTUARY AND MILLGROVE

1

VALLEY FORGE NATIONAL HISTORICAL PARK

SCHUYLKILL RIVER

CITY HALL

SANCHEZ

13

DELAWARE COUNTY

DELAWARE RIVER

202

RIDLEY CREEK STATE PARK

DELAWARE COUNTY CONVENTION AND VISTORS BUREAU

CHESTER COUNTY TOURIST BUREAU

FRANKLIN MINT

CALEB PUSEY HOUSE

CHESTER COUNTY

BRANDYWINE BATTLEFIELD STATE PARK

1

NEW JERSEY

LONGWOOD GARDENS

BRANDYWINE RIVER MUSEUM

COLONIAL FLYING CORP MUSEUM

DELAWARE

0   3 MILES   6 MILES

A book could be written on Philadelphia's neighboring counties: Bucks, Chester, Delaware and Montgomery.

This chapter attempts only to highlight the most outstanding and popular attractions that are within an hour's drive of center city Philadelphia. You'll see some of America's most beautiful farmland and countryside. In most cases, you'll have to provide your own transportation. Or you can check with the suburban train and bus routes. (The more accessible museums and tours are included with the appropriate chapters.)

Additional information is available from the Philadelphia Convention and Visitors Bureau* or the tourist bureau of each county.

Bucks County

ANDALUSIA
Just north of Philadelphia, on the Delaware River
Andalusia, PA 19020
848–1777 (Cliveden)

Hours: By reservation only, Tuesday to Saturday, 10:30, 12:30 and 2. Allow one hour.

Tours: One guide takes up to 8 visitors, and up to 40 can be scheduled for each time. Reservations are absolutely necessary. Call or write a month ahead to Cliveden*, 6401 Germantown Avenue, Phila., PA 19144.

Cost: $9 per person, and a minimum of $63.

E & D: There are 3 steps at the entrance and the tour is on the main floor.

Andalusia's main house was the first great example in this country of Greek Revival architecture. It sits on a 220-acre estate. The home was redesigned in 1834 by Thomas U. Walter for its owner, Nicholas Biddle. It's still owned by his descendant, James Biddle, who established the Andalusia Foundation and, in conjunction with the National Trust for Historic Preservation, opened the house to the public.

Go no further if you've never been to Athens to see the Theseum. Andalusia's riverside facade is an exact copy of the Greek structure. You'll get a lovely view of the Delaware from its portico.

Your tour of Andalusia includes the yellow parlor, ottoman room, library, music room, study, hallway and dining room with its enormous Duncan Phyfe mahogany table. Other furnishings are original Hepplewhite, Sheraton and Federal pieces. An exquisite fireplace is in every room. The magnificent chandeliers were never electrified. (Inside plumbing and electricity were installed in 1915.)

Art work at Andalusia includes oil paintings by Thomas Sully and Gilbert Stuart. There are rare engravings and busts of Napoleon and Alexander Hamilton.

Other original 19th century buildings on the estate include the cottage, pump house, billiard room and grotto. The grounds are especially beautiful in the summer when boxwood and rose gardens are in bloom.

THE MERCER MILE

Doylestown is the charming early 19th century town that serves as Bucks County's seat. Dr. Henry Chapman Mercer (1856–1930), an eccentric historian, architect, anthropologist, archaeologist and tile maker, lived and left his legacy there in the shape of three fantastic buildings and their contents within a mile of each other. The signs are strategically located to direct you, but you can't miss the towering structures.

Fonthill
East Court Street and Swamp Road (Route 313)
Doylestown, PA 18901
348-9461

Hours: Monday to Saturday, 10 to 5; Sunday, 12 to 5. Call for tour times. Closed Thanksgiving, Christmas, New Year's. Allow one hour.
Tours: Guided tours only. Groups of up to 12 depart throughout the day. Larger groups are divided. Reservations are suggested for all visitors, and groups of 10 to 50 must make reservations in advance.
Cost: Adults, $4; senior citizens, $3.50; students, $1.50; children under 6, free. Group rates by reservation.
E & D: Fonthill is multi-level and there are stairs everywhere. No wheelchair access.

Dr. Mercer designed and built his first building, his home, in the summers of 1908 to 1910. He acted as his own architect, employed eight to 10 unskilled day laborers and was among the first builders to use reinforced concrete.

Fonthill resembles a Tudor castle. It's decked with towers and turrets and filled with Moravian tiles from Dr.
Mercer's factory, and others collected from his travels
abroad. All of his designs were fascinating. Plans were developed from the doctor's recollections of buildings overseas and his desire for showplaces. He started building
from the inside, and the outside followed as a conse-
quence. Fonthill is built around an 18th century farmhouse. You really have to see it to believe it!

Moravian Pottery and Tile Works
East Court Street and Swamp Road (Route 313)
345–6722

Hours: Daily, 10 to 5 (last tour at 4) and doors close at
4:45. Closed major holidays. Allow 45 minutes for tour.

Tours: All visits begin on the hour or half-hour with a
15-minute slide slow and talk on the history and
production of the Tile Works. Call in advance to confirm
all visits and to schedule groups of no more than 30.

Cost: Adults, $2.50; senior citizens from outside Bucks
County, $2; students, $1; children under 6 and Bucks
County senior citizens, free.

Other: Approximately 300 varieties of tiles produced
here today are available for sale at the tile shop.

E & D: The entrance is level, enabling wheelchair access
to the first floor. The 2nd floor is reached by stairs.

This huge factory is another one of Dr. Mercer's fantastic designs. The building was completed in the summers
of 1910 to 1912.

Your guide, as well as the slide show, will tell you about
the different tiles that have been manufactured during
the company's history. You can walk through the plant
and see the original kilns and tools and some of the original tiles—including the ones that tell Bible stories. You'll
also see tiles as they're being made today by ceramists
working for Bucks County.

Tiles from Dr. Mercer's factory have been used for deco-
ration everywhere from the Capitol at Harrisburg, Pennsylvania, to the National Press Club in Washington, D.C.

Mercer Museum
Pine and Ashland Streets
345–0210 (Bucks County Historical Society)

Hours: Monday to Saturday, 10 to 5; Sunday, 1 to 5. Closed Thanksgiving, Christmas, New Year's. Allow at least one hour.
Tours: You're on your own. Pick up a self-guided tour brochure and see the orientation exhibit. Call in advance if you're coming with 20 or more.
Cost: Adults, $4; senior citizens, $3.50; students, $1.50; children under 6, free. Group rates by reservation.
E & D: An elevator that holds one wheelchair enables limited access to all but one level.

This is where you can find over 40,000 colonial artifacts representing at least 50 crafts. In a separate exhibition gallery, shows change twice a year with themes relating to Bucks County.

You'll see a conestoga wagon, stagecoach, horse-drawn fire engine, whale boat, log cabin and schoolroom, along with the tools and machinery needed for survival, education, recreation, clothing making and the trades.

The world's largest collection of its type is housed in an equally extravagant building. Dr. Mercer's Americana fills the museum he designed and built from 1914 to 1916. It, too, is made entirely of concrete and it, too, must be seen to be believed!

Dr. Mercer's museum was also his castle.

The **Spruance Library** of the Bucks County Historical Society (345–0210) adjoins the Mercer Museum. It houses the Bucks County archives dating from 1682 to the present, a huge collection of Bucks County history and genealogy, as well as vast collections on early American crafts, trades, industries and folk art.

The library's holdings include almost 20,000 books as well as an extensive collection of maps, manuscripts, photographs, newspapers, microfilm and other source materials. They preserve the history of Bucks County and interpret the collections of the Mercer Museum and Fonthill. All research must be done at the library. Hours are Wednesday to Saturday, 10 to 5. Admission is the same as for the Mercer Museum (and included with admission to the museum).

JAMES A. MICHENER ART MUSEUM
138 S. Pine Street
Doylestown, PA 18901
340-9800

Hours: Tuesday to Friday, 10 to 4:30; weekends, 10 to 5. Closed major holidays. Allow one hour.
Tours: Call at least 2 weeks ahead for groups of 10 to 60, children or adults.
Cost: Adults, $3; senior citizens, $2.50; students, $1.50; under 6, free. Group rates arranged in advance for 15 or more. Children 12 and under admitted free with an adult on Sundays till 1 P.M.
E & D: Complete wheelchair access. One wheelchair is available.

Spend some time browsing at the James A. Michener Art Museum and you'll have done time in the century-old Bucks County jail. When reincarnated in the fall of 1988 as a museum and arts center, Charles Kuralt was there to feature it on his CBS "Sunday Morning" show. Also present was Bucks County writer and Pulitzer prize winner, James Michener, who made his art collection available to the museum named in his honor.

Since its founding, visitors have come to the museum in droves to view exhibitions of masterpieces from the permanent collection and shows of works by regional artists, sculptors and craftspeople.

Special exhibitions change every few months. Call to find out what's being shown currently. The Michener Museum is across from "The Mercer Mile" and it's easy to combine your visits with a joint admission ticket.

PENNSBURY MANOR
Route 9
Morrisville, PA 19067
946-0400

Hours: Tuesday to Saturday, 9 to 5; Sunday 12 to 5. Closed all holidays except Memorial Day, July 4 and Labor Day. Allow at least one hour.
Tours: Start with the 15-minute slide-show orientation in the Visitor Center. Period-costumed guides lead tours at least once an hour through the manor house, outbuildings and gardens. In January and February, guided tours are limited to 11 A.M. and 2 P.M.

Tuesday to Saturday, and 2 P.M. Sunday. Groups of 18 or more should call ahead to schedule tour and group rate. Tours in any of 8 foreign languages can be scheduled 2 weeks in advance.

Cost: Adults, $2.50; senior citizens and groups with reservations, $1.75; children 6 to 17, $1; under 6, free.

E & D: Complete wheelchair access to all but the 2nd and 3rd floors of the manor house. Gardens are ramped; paths are packed gravel. Wide-tire wheelchairs are available. Signed tours can be scheduled in advance.

You'll feel welcome at William Penn's beautiful country plantation, 24 miles north of Philadelphia on the Delaware River. If you use I-95, it's roughly a 50-minute drive from Independence Hall.

Penn and his second wife, Hannah, entertained here. When you see the plantation, you'll see why. You'll see how Hannah set the table with damask, pewter, silver and glassware. And you'll see the kitchens where vast quantities of food were prepared.

While the family spent only two years here, Penn meticulously planned the house and gardens down to the last detail. The manor house was rebuilt on its original foundations in 1939, and it looks exactly as it did when Penn occupied it in 1700 and 1701. The mansion, with its setting on the river, is so realistic that you'll find it hard to believe it was rebuilt.

The furnishings are in the Jacobean style, and they include what is probably Pennsylvania's largest collection of 17th century antiques. Everything in the mansion reflects Penn's fine taste.

You'll also see the stable, the ice, smoke, bake and brew houses. The kitchen and formal gardens are a lovely part of the visit. The scenery changes according to the season. Special events take place on frequent Sunday afternoons. Living history demonstrations might include blacksmithing, open hearth cooking or woodworking.

SESAME PLACE
100 Sesame Road (just off Route 1); Box L579
Langhorne, PA 19047
757-1100 (recording) or 752-7070

Hours: Early May to early October, daily. Hours vary with week, weekend, holiday weekend and so forth, so it's best to call ahead. To avoid summer crowds, arrive early or later in the day. When the park is full, it's closed till the crowds diminish and others can be admitted.

Tours: Groups of 25 or more should write or call 752–4900 for reservations and to arrange special rates.

Cost: Adults, $15.95; children, $17.95; children under 2, free. Computer tokens are 3 for $1. Parking is $3 and adjacent to the entrance.

Lunch: The Food Factory and Captain Ernie's serve reasonably priced food that's good for you and tastes good. And, you can watch the preparation.

Other: Most of Sesame Place is outdoors so try to come in good weather. In warm weather, bathing suits are necessary for children because some of the play elements involve water. Lockers are available. Mr. Hooper's Store has Sesame Street toys, games, books, puzzles, dolls and clothing.

E & D: Complete wheelchair access. Call ahead to schedule your visit (752–4900).

The ultimate play-and-learn park designed especially for three- to 13-year-olds and their parents is just 20 miles northeast of center city Philadelphia.

Forty outdoor play elements have youngsters push, climb, pull, slide, crawl and "swim" through the likes of Rubber Duckie Rapids, Rainbow Pyramid, the Sesame Streak, Slippery Slope, the Count's Ballroom, the Monster Maze, Oscar's Obstacle Course, Big Bird's Court and Bert's Balancing Beams. (The author of this guidebook has been seen trying them, too.)

The indoor computer gallery challenges the most nimble of minds with 70 games, puzzles and scientific riddles.

Hands-on science exhibits in the Sesame Place Studios make it fun and easy to learn some of the concepts of television production. This is where visitors see themselves on closed circuit television in a replica of the Sesame Street studio. Jim Henson's Sesame Street Muppets also perform on stage, in person. Don't miss Big Bird, Bert & Ernie and the Honkers.

Sesame Island is a tropical entertainment paradise for kids. Ride an inner tube down Big Bird's Rambling River, board the Good Ship Sesame, tour Ernie's Waterworks, play on sandcastle beach and don't miss the exotic bird review and Oscar's trashcan bandstand on stage at

Paradise Playhouse.

We're fortunate that the Children's Television Workshop and Busch Entertainment Corporation chose our area for the country's first educational play park.

WASHINGTON CROSSING HISTORIC PARK
Routes 32 and 532, on the Delaware River
Washington Crossing, PA 18977
493–4076

Hours: The park is open daily, 9 A.M. to sunset. The buildings are open Monday to Saturday, 9 to 5; Sunday, noon to 5. The buildings are closed Martin Luther King Day, Easter, Columbus Day, Thanksgiving and New Year's.

Tours: A 30-minute film, "Washington Crossing the Delaware," is at 9, 10:30, 12, 1:30 and 3. A 45-minute tour follows at 9:30, 11, 12:30, 2 and 3:30. Groups of 10 or more should call at least 2 weeks in advance.

Cost: The film is free. For Thompson-Neely House, Mahlon K. Taylor House and Old Ferry Inn tour: adults, $2.50; senior citizens, $2; children 6 to 17, $1. Group rates by reservation only.

Lunch: Picnic pavilions can be rented by groups when making reservations.

E & D: The Visitor Center, some historic buildings and the Wildflower Preserve are accessible. Call for details.

This 500-acre state park (35 miles north of center city Philadelphia) is the site where George Washington crossed the Delaware River on December 25, 1776, to launch the Revolutionary attack on Trenton.

An exact copy of Emanual Leutze's famous painting, "Washington Crossing the Delaware," is on display at the Memorial Museum. It's also the place to listen to a short narrative of these momentous events and see the film noted above. (Why was George Washington standing in the boat?)

The Thompson-Neely House was the riverside headquarters for the Revolutionary forces. It's where Washington and his officers met to plan the fateful assault.

They say Washington dined at the Old Ferry Inn before he took his historic boatride. (Did he stand up all the way?) The Mahlon K. Taylor House belonged to a founder of the town of Taylorsville, also known as Washington Crossing. All of these historic buildings are restored and furnished from the colonial period.

The Boat Barn houses four replicas of the durham boats. These are one of the types of boats Washington and his troops used to make their famous crossing.

The Frye Spinning House is where occasionally you can see a demonstration of that colonial craft.

A 100-acre Wildflower Preserve is at the **Bowman's Hill** section of the park. You'll pass endless varieties of Pennsylvania trees, plants and flowers on its 22 miles of hiking trails. Call at least a month in advance to schedule a one-hour tour for groups of no more than 30. The teacher-naturalist can emphasize plants, animals or both. The talk and walk will be geared to the group's age level.

Bowman's Hill is where you'll get a magnificent view of the Bucks County countryside and a chance to pretend you're a soldier guarding your territory along the river. **Bowman's Hill Tower** is open April through October, daily, 10 A.M. to 4:30 P.M., and weekends only in November. Cost: adults, $2; senior citizens, $1.50; children, $.50; group rates by reservation, and reservations are absolutely necessary for groups of 10 or more.

Picnic tables and benches are situated throughout the park. Large groups can make reservations to rent any of the five pavilions. Ice skating is allowed when conditions make it safe.

What else should you see in Bucks County?

Bucks County is known for its 13 covered bridges and its quaint historic towns. **FALLSINGTON** is a colonial village that's built around a 17th century Friends Meeting House where William Penn worshipped. Many of the town's homes are from Penn's time, and the Stagecoach Tavern is also restored. Fallsington is at Tyburn Road, off Route 1. Guided tours of Fallsington can be scheduled. Call 295–6567 for details.

PEDDLER'S VILLAGE is a recently built community of antique shops, boutiques and restaurants in Lahaska, off Route 202. It's five miles south of the original artists' colony of **NEW HOPE**. This charming little town is only 35 miles north of Philadelphia. New Hope is lined with galleries, workshops, studios, shops and restaurants. (It's the town that Sausalito copied.)

You can ride a **mule-drawn barge** along the Delaware Canal, daily from early in April to mid-November. Call 862–2842 for hours and cost.

You can ride one of the country's few remaining steam-powered trains, the **New Hope & Ivyland Railroad**, from the restored New Hope Station to Lahaska. It's a nine-mile, 50-minute round-trip that no railroad buff will want to miss. Call 862-2332 for schedules and fare information.

Spend some time browsing among the shops for a delightful afternoon or evening. New Hope's historic landmarks are clearly identified.

Bucks County Tourist Commission
152 Swamp Road (Route 313)
Doylestown, PA 18901
345-4552

Chester County

COLONIAL FLYING CORP. MUSEUM
New Garden Airport
Newark Road
Toughkenamon, PA 19374
268-2048

Hours: By appointment only, weekends, 12 to 4. Allow 45 minutes.
Tours: Someone is available to answer questions at the museum.
Cost: Adults, $1; children under 12, $.50.
E & D: The museum is on 2 levels with ramp entrances and connections.

Did you ever visit a museum on the corner of an airfield? This one is. The Colonial Flying Corp. Museum has an unusual collection: an assortment of interesting bicycles, motorcycles, engines, cars and planes. There are seven automobiles that date from 1909 to as recently as 1950. The small airplanes are vintage World War II.

An annual Air Show is the second weekend in June (rain date the third weekend) when bystanders witness airobatics and parachute jumps and there's an open house at the museum. Call for the date and details.

To get your bearings, the museum and flying field are less than a mile south of Route 1, three miles west of Kennett Square, and six miles from Longwood Gardens.

LONGWOOD GARDENS
Route 1
Kennett Square, PA 19348
388–6741

Hours: Gardens: daily, 9 to 6 (till 5 in winter). Conservatories: daily, 10 to 5. Evening hours for special holiday displays and cultural events. Half-hour fountain displays are Tuesday, Thursday and Saturday nights at 9:15 from mid-June through August, when the conservatories also remain open till 10:30 P.M. Allow at least 2 hours.

Tours: All guided tours are scheduled in advance with the Group Visits Office and payment is due a week ahead. A 90-minute gardens tour or a 2-hour Peirce-duPont House and gardens tour is available for groups of 15 or more any day from 10 to 3. Tours are conducted indoors in inclement weather. At least one adult must accompany every group of 10 youngsters with or without a guided tour.

Cost: Adults, $8; children 6 to 14, $2; under 6, free. Group rates are available for 30 or more when making tour reservations.

Lunch: The Terrace Restaurant offers self-service informality or casual restaurant dining. Call 388–6771 for information or reservations.

Other: Wear comfortable shoes. No pets, bicycles or camera tripods are allowed. The Visitor Center provides a multi-image slide orientation. The Gift Shop sells film, books, stationery and plants.

E & D: Wheelchairs and special maps are available at the entrance, and there's access to the grounds and most buildings.

If you were visiting in Europe, you would go hundreds of miles out of your way to see the late Pierre S. duPont's estate. Longwood Gardens is less than an hour's drive from center city Philadelphia.

There are over 350 public acres (including four acres under glass) of magnificent gardens with all of the trees, plants and flowers carefully identified. There's a maze of hedges to navigate through, a conservatory and greenhouse, a bonsai room, experimental and "sample" gardens, fountain displays, a lily pond and water gardens. They're all in various stages of bloom throughout the year. There's a garden just for children that's described in Chapter 15.

You're bound to relax at Longwood Gardens, so while you're there inquire about their concerts, lectures and theater productions. Or, call ahead and plan your visit according to seasonal displays or another special event. Picnic facilities are also available, and bring your camera.

WAYNESBOROUGH
2049 Waynesborough Road
Paoli, PA 19301
647–1779

Hours: Mid-March to Christmas, Tuesday and Thursday, 10 to 4; Sunday, 1 to 4. Allow 45 minutes.
Tours: Groups of 10 or more should call at least a week ahead.
Cost: Adults, $3; senior citizens and students, $2; children under 6, free.
Lunch: Picnic facilities are on the grounds.
E & D: One step at the entrance and another into the kitchen. Slide show is on the 2nd floor.

This is where Revolutionary War hero Anthony Wayne was born (probably in a log cabin on the site) in 1745 and lived (except when away at battle) till he died in 1796. Seven generations of the family resided at Waynesborough till 1980, and now it's maintained by the Landmarks Society.

The original section of Waynesborough dates from around 1745. Additions were made in 1765, 1810 and 1902, but the furnishings are from the 18th century and some belonged to the Wayne family. A 20-minute slide show fills in details on the history of the house, the occupants and the era.

Don't leave without knowing why General Wayne is better known as "Mad Anthony."

WHARTON ESHERICK STUDIO
Box 595
Paoli, PA 19301
644–5822

Hours: By reservation only, March through December, Saturday, 9 to 5; Sunday, 1 to 5. Groups of 5 or more can be scheduled weekdays.
Tours: All visits are by one-hour guided tour scheduled

in advance. Directions to museum will be provided with tour confirmation.

Cost: Adults, $5; children under 12, $3. $25 minimum for weekday tour.

E & D: Limited wheelchair access.

In 1913, Wharton Esherick, a native Philadelphian, moved to an old stone farmhouse near Paoli in Chester County. He studied painting at the Pennsylvania Academy of the Fine Arts. Esherick spent the rest of his life here, painting scenes of the rural surroundings, sculpting and making furniture.

His studio and collection looks today as it did when he died in 1970. Over 200 paintings, woodcuts, prints, wood, stone and ceramic sculptures, furniture and furnishings are displayed. The five-level studio itself was 40 years in the building. When you see each detail, you'll know why.

Esherick's work has been exhibited around the world and is in permanent museum collections throughout the country. It's a special experience to visit his studio, and see his work and the way he lived.

Chester County is rich in flora and fauna.

The **STAR ROSE GARDENS** of Conard-Pyle Rose Company, on Route 1 south of Kennett Square (869–2426), is the place to see infinite varieties of star roses. The gardens are open to the public from late May to early fall, daily, from dawn till dusk.

The **SWISS PINE GARDENS**, in Malvern (933–6916), is lush with authentic Japanese and Polynesian gardens, herbs, heaths, heathers and a fern trail. A wild bird pond is popular in migratory seasons. This arboretum and wildlife haven is open weekdays, 10 to 4; Saturday mornings, 9 to 12. It's closed holidays and in inclement weather. This is a delightful hike for adventurous souls, but it's not recommended for people with walking disabilities. No strollers or children under 12 are permitted.

Chester County is also mushroom growing territory. In fact, it's the center for the nation's mushroom industry. You'll see indications of this from the roadside stands, signs and the unusual long, low buildings in Kennett Square, Toughkenamon and along Route 1.

You can tour a museum with a scale model mushroom

farm at **PHILLIPS MUSHROOM PLACE** on Route 1 in Kennett Square (a half-mile south of Longwood Gardens). Allow 30 minutes for the visit which includes a short film on mushroom growing, followed by seeing the real thing. Hours are 10 to 6 daily and groups should call ahead for reservations (388–6082). Cost: adults, $1.25; senior citizens, $.75; children 7 to 12, $.50; 6 and under, free; a busload, $10.

There are more historic sites that are fun to explore in Chester County.

The **CHESTER COUNTY HISTORICAL SOCIETY** at 225 N. High Street in West Chester (692–4800) is where archives are preserved and regional antique furnishings, clocks and decorative arts are exhibited. Hours for the museum and library are Tuesday, Thursday, Friday and Saturday, 10 to 4; and Wednesday, 1 to 8. Admission to the museum is $2.50 for adults and $1.50 for students. Group rates are available for 10 or more when making reservations. There's an additional $4 fee to use the library (which includes museum admission).

You can also stop at the historic **CHESTER COUNTY COURTHOUSE** in West Chester, and at the Chester County Tourist Promotion Bureau on West Gay Street. While you're there, ask about the **PAOLI MEMORIAL GROUNDS** in Malvern and the **FREEDOMS FOUNDATION** near Valley Forge.

If you would like to go on an all-day tour of historic homes, buildings and landmarks in Chester County, ask about the annual Chester County Day that's usually held the first Saturday in October.

Chester County Tourist Promotion Bureau
117 W. Gay Street
West Chester, PA 19380
344–6365

Brandywine Valley Tourist Information
Route 1
Kennett Square, PA 19348
800–228-9933

BRANDYWINE BATTLEFIELD STATE PARK
Route 1
Chadds Ford, PA 19317
459–3342

Hours: The grounds are open daily, 9 to 5. The Visitor
Center and houses are open Tuesday to Saturday, 9 to
5; Sunday, 12 to 5. Closed some holidays.
Tours: Guides are available to answer questions. Tours
can be arranged on arrival at the Visitor Center.
Cost: Adults, $3; senior citizens and groups with reser-
vations, $2; children 6 to 17, $1; under 6, free.
E & D: The houses are level with the ground; steps lead
to the 2nd floors. There are many hills and gravel paths.

This is where George Washington and the American
Revolutionary troops suffered defeat at the hands of the
British on September 11, 1777. Re-enactment Weekend
is celebrated at the park annually in September. Call for
a schedule of the events.
The Lafayette and Washington Headquarters are restored and furnished from the period. Picnic facilities are
also available throughout the 52-acre park.

BRANDYWINE RIVER MUSEUM
Route 1
Chadds Ford, PA 19317
459–1900

Hours: Daily, 9:30 to 4:30. Closed Christmas. Allow one
hour.
Tours: Call the tour coordinator at least 2 weeks ahead
to schedule a one hour tour for school or adult groups.
Cost: Adults, $4; senior citizens 65 and over, $2.50; students, $2; children under 6, free. Group rates available
by reservation.
Lunch: A self-serve 120-seat restaurant is open 11 to 3.
Group reservations are suggested.
Other: The Museum Shop sells art and environmental
books, gift items, stationery and reproductions.
E & D: Complete wheelchair access. There's a wheelchair
entrance and elevator that enables access to all floors.

This 19th century grist mill on the Brandywine Creek has been restored and converted under the auspices of the Tri-County Conservancy of Brandywine, into one of America's most popular art museums. It opened in June, 1971, as a three-story gallery connected by a glassed-in silo. 1984 saw the completion of a three-story brick, glass and wood addition. It's a masterpiece in design.

The works of Howard Pyle, three generations of Wyeths (N.C., Andrew and Jamie) and others of the Brandywine School have lured a steady stream of visitors from 80 nations.

The Conservancy and the museum are dedicated to the preservation of the Brandywine and the land that is the artists' inspiration. The permanent and the changing exhibits reflect ecology, land and water conservation.

The museum is an enchanting natural environment for concerts, lectures, antique shows and a fall harvest market in the courtyard.

After you visit the museum, leave through a cobblestone courtyard and follow the mile-long nature trail into the museum's surrounding acreage. You'll be self-guided through woods, meadows and swamps toward **John Chadd's historic home**. The interesting flowers and shrubs are labeled.

CALEB PUSEY HOUSE
Landingford Plantation at 15 Race Street
Upland, PA 19015
874–5665 or 876–9206

Hours: May through October, weekends, 1 to 4. Closed holidays. Arrangements can sometimes be made for groups to visit at other times. Allow 30 to 45 minutes.
Tours: Groups of 5 or more are scheduled if you call or write in advance.
Cost: Adults, $1; children under 12, $.75.
E & D: The grounds are level and there's one step at the entrance.

Caleb Pusey was Pennsylvania's first historian and the manager of the colony's first English industry, a mill at Landingford Plantation. Grain was ground here, and lumber was sawed for the colonists.

Pusey, who built this two-room stone home in 1683, was visited at home by his friend William Penn. See what the 17th century way of life was like in Pennsylvania. See what is said to be the oldest remaining home of any English settler in the colony.

Other attractions on the 12-acre tract include an 1849 school house (now a museum and gift shop) and the log house.

FRANKLIN MINT MUSEUM

Route 1 (4 miles south of Media by-pass)
Franklin Center, PA 19091
459–6168

Hours: Tuesday to Saturday, 9:30 to 4:30; Sunday, 1 to 4:30. Closed major holidays.
Tours: You're on your own with a self-guided tour. No reservations necessary, but groups are requested to call or write in advance.
Cost: Free.
Other: The Franklin Mint Gallery Store sells original Franklin Mint collectibles such as jewelry, sculpture, precision die-cast models and porcelain dolls that you can't buy elsewhere.
E & D: Museum is on one level, but there are several steps at the entrance. A ramp enables complete wheelchair access.

The Franklin Mint Museum, founded in 1973, is a coin-shaped gallery and showplace for the current and former products of the Franklin Mint itself, founded in 1968. You'll see not only the finished objects, but also exhibits that explain their artistic creation and manufacturing.

The Franklin Mint is the world's largest maker of high quality collectibles. What they make here today are our heirlooms of tomorrow. You'll see cases of dolls, jewelry, home accessories, porcelains, glassware, commemorative coins, books and arms reproductions. You'll see medals depicting the "Medallic History of Mankind," the presidents of the United States and the works of William Shakespeare.

In fact, we think this is the biggest collection of collectibles you'll ever see in one place. If you're a collector, or interested in collections, you'll want to make the 45-minute drive from center city Philadelphia to the Franklin Mint Museum.

RIDLEY CREEK STATE PARK
Sycamore Mills Road
Media, PA 19063
566–4800

Hours: The park is open daily, 8 A.M. till sunset. The office is open Memorial Day to Labor Day, daily, 8 to 4; weekends only the rest of the year.
Cost: Free, unless you partake in any of the concessions.

Less than an hour's drive from center city Philadelphia is a 2,600-acre state park with some unusual features. It has playgrounds, picnic and barbecue facilities, nature trails and markers for walking, horseback riding and bicycling. There are stables to rent horses, streams for trout fishing and a farm that takes you back 200 years.

Colonial Pennsylvania Plantation
Ridley Creek State Park
Media, PA 19063
566–1725

Hours: Weekends during Daylight Saving Time, 10 to 5; Eastern Standard Time, 10 to 4. Closed December through March. By reservation only, Tuesday to Friday, for group tours. Call ahead to be sure, and to ask about special events.
Tours: Call weekdays (9:30 to 1:30) or write a month in advance to schedule groups of 15 to 80.
Cost: Adults, $2.50; senior citizens and children under 12, $1.50. Family rate for parents and 2 or more children, $6.50. Group rates for 10 or more, $1.50.
Other: Wear sturdy shoes.
E & D: Call in advance to arrange wheelchair access. There's one steep gravel hill and everything else is level.

You can already tell that Ridley Creek State Park is far from the ordinary. In fact, the Bishop's Mill Historical Institute has recreated and manages within the park an 18th century plantation and working farm that operates today (just as it did in the 1700s).

The colonial-costumed volunteers and a farmer work on the 112-acre plantation using the tools and methods of 200 years ago. You'll witness the everyday life of a farm family as they tend their livestock and fields. Cows, horses, sheep, pigs and chickens live here. Watch as the

staff cuts curd for cheese, bakes bread, spins flax, prepares
the noon meal at the hearth and does whatever else is on
the day's agenda.

What else is there to see in Delaware County?

The **DELAWARE COUNTY INSTITUTE OF SCI-
ENCE** is at 11 Veterans Square (566–5126) in the center
of Media, Delaware County's seat of government. The Institute was founded in 1833. Its formidable red brick
home dates back to 1867.

This museum features a wide range of mineral collections, a herbarium of Delaware County plants, mounted
birds and animals, fossils, shells, corals and an unusual
collection of microscopes. The library has an extensive collection of natural science books and periodicals.

Admission is free. Hours are Monday, 10 A.M. to noon
and 7:30 to 9:30 P.M., and other times by appointment.
Group tours can be arranged. Call 566–3491 for additional information.

The **MUSEUM OF MOURNING ART** is in Drexel
Hill at the non-denominational Arlington Cemetery. This
unique collection is housed in the cemetery's main building, a replica of George Washington's Mount Vernon
estate.

What is mourning art? The collection includes a 19th
century horse-drawn hearse, artwork, jewelry, books and
clothing all related to mourning. This lively tour traces
how people have mourned since the 16th century, and how
customs and attitudes towards life and death have
changed through the centuries.

Tours are free and by appointment only. Call 259–5800
for additional information, directions and reservations.

And there's lots more to see in Delaware County, especially if you're a history buff.

The **1724 COURTHOUSE** at 5th Street and Avenue
of the States in Chester is the oldest public building in
continuous use in the United States.

OLD SWEDES CEMETERY is an 18th century
burial ground and the oldest Swedish cemetery in
America.

The **JOHN MORTON HOUSE**, built in 1654 and fully restored, is a reminder of the Swedish settlement in the county.

The **THOMAS MASSEY HOUSE**, built in 1696 and restored, is a reminder of Pennsylvania's English Quaker settlement.

GOVERNOR PRINTZ PARK is named for Johann Printz, the man who founded Pennsylvania's first permanent settlement of white men at this site in 1642.

Delaware County Convention & Visitors Bureau
200 E. State Street, Suite 100
Media, PA 19063
565-3679 or 565-3666 (24-hour "Funline")

Montgomery County

AUDUBON WILDLIFE SANCTUARY
and MILL GROVE
Audubon and Pawlings Roads near Route 363
Audubon, PA 19407
666-5593

Hours: The grounds are open daily, except Monday, from 7 A.M. to dusk. The house is open Tuesday to Saturday, 10 to 4; Sunday, 1 to 4. Closed Mondays, Thanksgiving, Christmas, New Year's.

Tours: You're on your own, but groups of 12 or more should call 2 weeks in advance to arrange for an introductory talk.

Cost: Free.

Other: No food allowed. Bicycles are permitted on the main road only.

E & D: Wheelchair access to Mill Grove's first floor only. The 2nd and 3rd floors are reached by steps.

John Audubon was an artist and naturalist who lived from 1785 to 1851. He was the first person to paint birds and wildlife with naturalism. The Audubon Society was founded in 1905 for the preservation of wildlife. A bird called Audubon's Warbler is also named after him.

John Audubon made his home in America on this 130-acre estate overlooking Perkiomen Creek, two miles north of Valley Forge National Historical Park.

You can walk along several miles of wooded hiking trails where Audubon walked. And you can visit his home,

Mill Grove, which is now a memorabilia museum. All of Audubon's published works are on display.

ELMWOOD PARK ZOO
Harding Boulevard
Norristown, PA 19401
277–3825

Hours: Daily, 10 to 4. Closed Thanksgiving, Christmas, New Year's.

Tours: You're on your own. No reservations necessary. Groups of up to 30, at least school age, can call a few weeks ahead to schedule 45- to 60-minute tour. One adult must accompany every 10 youngsters, and larger groups will be divided into smaller groups of 10.

Cost: Free. Donations accepted.

Lunch: Bring your own, or buy something at the refreshment stand that's open in warm weather. Picnic facilities are available.

E & D: Limited wheelchair access.

Norristown, the Montgomery County seat, is a borough of more than 30,000 people. It also boasts of a municipal zoo with a population in the hundreds.

There are deer, elks, goats, llamas, lambs, lions, monkeys, prairie dogs and a huge aviary with many bird species. A children's zoo within the zoo enables visitors to pet the farm animals. (The children's zoo closes in winter so the animals can go inside to stay warm.) A realistic exhibit recreates North American animal life at the time of the Revolution.

If you're within a 15 mile radius, Elmwood Park also has a "traveling zoo." Call the curator several weeks in advance to schedule this hour-long live animal presentation at your location. The fee depends on the program and the audience.

GLENCAIRN MUSEUM
1001 Cathedral Road
Bryn Athyn, PA 19009
947–9919

Hours: By appointment only, weekdays, 9 to 5.

Tours: Call in advance to schedule 2-hour tour at 10 A.M. or 2 P.M. for groups of up to 20. A self-guided tour is the 2nd Sunday of each month, except July and August, from 2 to 5 P.M. Children under 12 must be with an adult.

Cost: Adults, $3; children and students, free.

E & D: There are 2 steps at main entrance. Cloister entrance is level and can be used, except in inclement weather, by special arrangement. An elevator goes to all 9 floors and can accommodate one wheelchair.

In Chapter 5, you read about the Bryn Athyn Cathedral and the work that went into its unique building. Now you can visit the equally unusual home of the man who supervised the Cathedral's construction. (If you're combining visits to both locations, schedule the museum first.)

Glencairn, the Romanesque-style former home of Raymond and Mildred Pitcairn, was built from 1928 to 1939. The same principles and craft shops were used to create a unique family home as well as a depository for the family collection of medieval objects. The multi-level structure itself is embellished in stone, wood, glass and metal with artistic symbols of the teachings of the New Church.

The main floor looks as it did when it was occupied by the Pitcairns. It serves as a community and cultural center. Rooms on the upper floors are individual galleries housing art and artifacts of Egypt, the Near East, Far East, Greece and Rome, French sculpture and stained glass of the 12th century, American Indian objects, and the medieval collection. If you're in a contemplative mood, don't miss the Chapel and the Cloister.

VALLEY FORGE NATIONAL HISTORICAL PARK
Route 23 and North Gulph Road
Valley Forge, PA 19481
783-1076 (bookstore) and 783-1077 (information)

Hours: The park is open daily from 8:30 A.M. to dusk. The Visitor Center and Washington's headquarters are open from 8:30 to 5. Allow at least 3 hours.

Tours: Visit on your own, or from April through October call the park concessionaire (783-5788 or 265-6446) for details on a cassette tour to take in your car or a guided tour by bus.

Cost: It's free if you visit on your own, except $1 to enter Washington's headquarters. Charges vary for car cassette and bus tours.

Lunch: There are plenty of picnic areas.

E & D: There's one step into the Visitor Center and a ramp into the auditorium.

George Washington and his 11,000 weary troops survived the cold winter of 1777–1778 here.

Today Valley Forge Park is a 3,000-acre scenic national park filled with dogwood trees, botanical gardens and reminders of the American Revolution.

Start your tour at the Visitor Center. A 15-minute historic orientation film is presented on the hour and half-hour from 9 to 4:30. A museum is here, too.

Also visit Washington's headquarters, the Memorial Chapel, Bell Tower and National Memorial Arch. What once was the soldiers' winter encampment grounds are now hills dotted with cannons, trenches, forts, log cabins, reconstructed soldiers' huts, markers and monuments.

WILLOW GROVE NAVAL AIR STATION
Route 611
Horsham, PA 19090
443–1776

Hours: By reservation only, Thursday and Friday at 10. Allow 90 minutes.
Tours: Call or write to the station's Public Affairs Office at least 6 weeks in advance. Groups of 10 to 30 (including chaperons), at least 6 years old, can be scheduled. One adult must accompany every 4 children. Individuals or smaller groups should call a few days ahead to see if there's a tour group they can join.
Cost: Free.
Lunch: Ask about arrangements to eat at the fast food restaurant on the base.
E & D: Complete wheelchair access.

Anyone who loves airplanes will love this tour. You'll get to board a military aircraft if one's available. You'll stop by the air operations department to see the radar equipment room and (if your group isn't too large) the air traffic control tower. You'll also visit the base firehouse to see the special engines that are always on the ready at the airport.

No trip to the Willow Grove Naval Air Station is complete without a ground inspection of the World War II aircraft display. If you can't arrange to take the tour at

Willow Grove, you can see the old planes from the parking lot on Route 611.

What else should you do in Montgomery County?

See the **MAIN LINE**. It's where some of the nation's grandest estates are located. Why the name? It was, and still is, the "main line" for the Pennsylvania (now Con-Rail) Railroad's commuter route from center city Philadelphia to the western suburbs. We told you about the stops back in Chapter 1.

The train tracks are parallel to Lancaster Pike (Route 30), the original route to the **PENNSYLVANIA DUTCH (or AMISH) COUNTRY** of Lancaster County.

Valley Forge Country
Convention & Visitors Bureau
Box 311
Norristown, PA 19404
278-3558 or 800-441-3549
275-4636 (24-hour "Fun Line")

The Amish Country

It would be an oversight not to mention a few of the famous attractions that are just beyond Philadelphia, and within an hour or two of center city.

AMISH COUNTRY in Lancaster County, Pennsylvania, is about one-and-a-half hours west of Philadelphia on Route 30 beyond Chester County. If you saw the movie "Witness," you had a glimpse of the Amish Country. It's the locale of towns such as Bird-in-Hand, Blue Ball, Intercourse, Lititz, Paradise and Smoketown in some of America's most beautiful farm regions.

Amish Country is a mecca for antique and hand-made quilt shoppers, and for gourmands of German-style cooking followed by fresh fruit or shoofly pies.

You'll be enchanted by the Amish people, their dress, buggies, one-room schoolhouses and colorful hex signs that adorn their barns. Stop by the Mennonite Information Center (717-299-0954) just off Route 30, or the Pennsylvania Dutch Convention & Visitors Bureau at 501 Greenfield Road, Lancaster, PA 17601 (717-299-8901 or 800-735-2629) for some good and plenty information.

HOPEWELL FURNACE, a National Historic Site, is west of Philadelphia beyond Valley Forge and just a few miles south of Birdsboro on Route 345. It's about an hour-and-a-half from center city Philadelphia.

The village was founded in 1771 as an ironmaking community to supply cannon and shot for the Revolutionary forces. Today Hopewell Furnace looks as it did from 1820 to 1840, and is part of the National Park Service. It's open daily, from 9 to 5, year-round except Christmas and New Year's (with "living history" programs in July and August) so you can get a true picture of how you might have lived in such a community at the time. Guided tours are scheduled for school groups of 15 or more. Admission is $2 for visitors 17 to 61 (younger and older are free); a family rate is $5. For details write to the Superintendent at Hopewell Furnace National Historic Site, R.D. 1, Box 345, Elverson, PA 19520, or call 582-8773.

HERSHEY (Chocolate City), Pennsylvania, is a two-hour drive west from Philadelphia. It boasts three seasons and 23 acres of floral displays in the Hershey Hotel **Rose Gardens and Arboretum**; 36 rides (including a Kiss Tower), entertainment and 11 acres of native North American wildlife at ZooAmerica in **Hersheypark** (open mid-May to September); the **Hershey Museum of American Life**; and a magical ride through Hershey's **Chocolate World** where you'll follow a cacao bean on its way to becoming a Hershey Bar. And Hershey is no doubt the world's only city where streetlights resemble chocolate kisses. For details write to Hershey Information & Reservations Center, 300 Park Boulevard, P.O. Box 860, Hershey, PA 17033, or call 800–HERSHEY.

State of Delaware

The state of Delaware is less than an hour's drive south of Philadelphia.

Among its attractions are the **HAGLEY MUSEUM** at Routes 141 and 100, three miles north of Wilmington. It's on the 200-acre site of a 19th century industrial community where the DuPont Company began almost two centuries ago. Indoor and outdoor exhibits take you through the original black powder mills to learn the industry's evolution from colonial times to the present.

E.I. duPont built a country house here for his family in 1803. You can tour **"ELEUTHERIAN MILLS"** and admire generations of the duPont family's furnishings from the 19th century. Plan to spend at least three hours.

Call (302–658–2400 Ext. 259) or write to the Tour Office, Hagley Museum, Box 3630, Wilmington, Delaware 19807 for details. Reservations are required for groups of 15 or more.

WINTERTHUR MUSEUM is nearby on Route 52 in Winterthur, Delaware 19735. Henry Francis duPont's fabulous 200-room mansion-museum built in 1839 is also open to the public. It's filled with the largest and finest collection of early American (1640 to 1840) furnishings and accessories.

Call (302–888–4600 or 800–448–3883) or write for hours, admission charges and details about train rides and tours of various parts of the house-museum and beautiful gardens.

State of New Jersey

Head east from Philadelphia across the Delaware River and you're in New Jersey.

Directly across the river from Penn's Landing, is Camden's sparkling new attraction, the **NEW JERSEY STATE AQUARIUM**, scheduled to open in the spring of 1992. Some tanks are already full, fish are swimming and final touches are underway as the new centerpiece for Camden's waterfront prepares for its first visitors. We won't tell you anymore. You'll have to see this for yourself.

SIX FLAGS GREAT ADVENTURE, in Jackson, New Jersey, about 45 minutes from center city Philadelphia, has America's largest safari park. It's open from late March through October.

You can actually drive your car through a natural habitat that has been recreated for more than 2,000 wild animals from around the world. Be sure to bring a camera!

The entertainment theme park has thrill rides (including the Great American Scream Machine) for the entire family, roaring rapids, a log flume ride, a "dream street," restaurants and arenas for regularly scheduled superstar concerts, musical revues, a Bugs Bunny extravaganza and aquatic shows. The 15-acre Adventure Rivers offers 12 water-raft rides without the need to change into a swim suit. A one-price ticket for children or adults, for the theme park or combination theme park and safari, includes everything but refreshments and souvenirs and the superstar shows.

Missing Great Adventure is like being in Los Angeles and not seeing Disneyland. Call 908–928–1821 for information, concert schedules, special events and group sales.

WHEATON VILLAGE is just off of Route 47 in Millville, NJ 08332. It's 42 miles south of Philadelphia by way of the Walt Whitman Bridge, or 35 miles west of Atlantic City by way of the Black Horse Pike and Route 552.

Wheaton Village has roots that date to 1739 when Southern New Jersey's first successful glass factory was founded. Years later, Dr. T. C. Wheaton acquired the Shull-Goodwin Glass Company of Millville and gave it his name. His son and grandson have painstakingly re-created a typical late-19th century glassmaking community so that the skill and tradition of South Jersey glassmaking is preserved.

A visit to Wheaton Village is a magnificent look into the past. You'll tour a vast Museum of American Glass with Victorian period rooms and glass treasures dating from 300 B.C. to today. You'll visit an exact replica of Dr. Wheaton's 1888 Glass Factory, and you'll see artisans making glass by hand. You can browse in the General Store, have something to eat and visit the crafts shops.

Wheaton Village is open daily from 10 to 5, except holidays, and January through March when it's closed Monday and Tuesday. A one-day admission ticket enables entrance to exhibits, crafts shops and the museum. Call 609–825–6800 or write for additional information.

For more New Jersey tourism information, call 800–JERSEY–7.

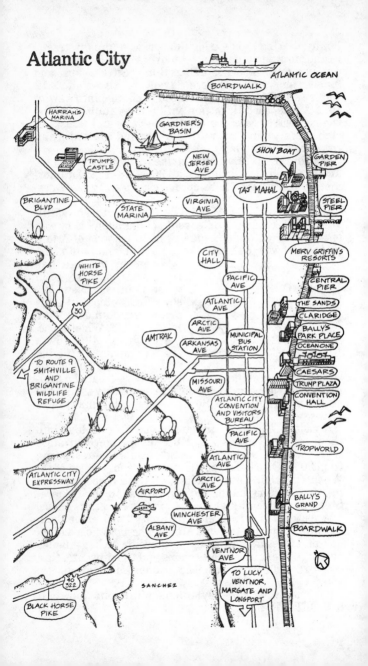

Atlantic City, New Jersey

Area code 609. ZIP code 08401.

The sun, sand and surf of the New Jersey coast are just about an hour from center city Philadelphia. Take a gambol to Atlantic City! For information, write or call the **Greater Atlantic City Convention and Visitors Bureau, 2314 Pacific Avenue** in Convention Hall, Atlantic City **(348–7100)**. The hours are 9 to 5 on weekdays.

You can drive to Atlantic City by way of the four bridges crossing the Delaware River from Philadelphia. Then head for the Atlantic City Expressway (a toll road), the Black Horse Pike (Route 322) or the White Horse Pike (Route 30).

NJ Transit (215–569–3752) and Greyhound (215–931–4000) buses to Atlantic City from center city Philadelphia depart frequently from the Greyhound-Trailways Bus Terminal at 10th and Filbert Streets (see Chapter 1). Fare for the 75- to 90-minute trip on NJ Transit is $10 one-way or $11.50 for the round trip. Greyhound fare is $8.50 one-way or $13.25 for the round trip. The buses come into Atlantic City at the **Municipal Bus Station, Arkansas and Arctic Avenues.**

Greyhound also runs buses directly to several of the casino hotels. Fares for most of these are $12 round trip. Call for schedules.

Or, if you would like to spend six hours in or around one of the major casino hotels, and if you're at least 21 years old, then take one of the frequent casino package trips from various locations in Philadelphia. The price for these is anywhere between $8 and $25 round trip, but you'll get most of the price back in quarters, meals and promotions when you get there. Look in the papers for ads about these trips. It's a good deal, but of course the hotels hope you'll spend your time gambling in their casinos.

Amtrak offers train service between Philadelphia and Atlantic City on the Atlantic City Express. Five round trips are made daily between 30th Street Station and the Amtrak station in Atlantic City at #1 Atlantic City Expressway (where the expressway meets Kirkman Boulevard). Call 800–USA–RAIL for the schedule and fare information and to make reservations.

Transportation in Atlantic City is best accomplished by taxicab, bus or jitney. Jitneys are mini-buses that take only as many passengers as they have vacant seats. They travel the length of Pacific Avenue from one end of Atlantic City to the other and to the marina casinos. The fare is $1. There's always a jitney in sight, and if you've never had the experience, it's a fun way to ride. NJ Transit buses travel the length of Atlantic Avenue, and the fare is $1.25.

Casino gambling, and the changes it has brought since gambling was approved by New Jersey voters in 1976, is something to see. The change is most evident in the luxurious new hotels. Casinos are a day and night activity. Hours are 10 A.M. to 4 A.M. on weekdays and 10 A.M. to 6 A.M. on weekends and holidays. The games are slot machines, blackjack at tables and on electronic machines, baccarat, craps, roulette and the wheel of fortune. Youngsters under 21 aren't allowed in the casinos.

The casino hotels give you a choice in size, theme and ambience. Entertainment abounds. Superstars appear at some of them, while others have glittering variety shows. All of the casinos have lounge acts. One has a giant indoor amusement park. There are 12 casino hotels in Atlantic City.

BALLY'S GRAND HOTEL & CASINO Boston and Pacific Avenues (347–7111 or 800–257–8677). All of the 518 rooms have an ocean view, as well as the glass-enclosed indoor pool that's part of the spa and health club. The casino covers 40,000 square feet. Three gourmet restaurants serve Chinese, Provincial Italian and steaks. There are two cafes, a buffet and a creamery. Top name stars appear at Bally's Grand Opera House (340–7200).

BALLY'S PARK PLACE CASINO HOTEL & TOWER Park Place and the Boardwalk (340–2000 or 800–225–5977). Bally's Park Place offers 1,300 guest rooms, complete wheelchair access, an outdoor swimming pool, a luxurious spa facility and a Park Cabaret Theater (340–2709 or 800–772–7777) presenting "An Evening at La Cage" nightly except Tuesdays since 1985. Dining choices include gourmet Italian, a steakhouse, 24-hour more-than-a-coffee shop and a spa cuisine cafe. The 60,000 square-foot casino is enhanced by waterfalls cascading parallel to lengthy escalators that go up from and back to the gambling floor.

CAESARS ATLANTIC CITY HOTEL CASINO Arkansas Avenue and the Boardwalk (348–4411 or 800–257–8555). Top-rate off-Broadway shows and big-name stars are headliners at Caesars' Circus Maximus Theater (348–4411 or 800–343–2550). Eleven restaurants, a smart shopping complex, rooftop tennis, a health spa, and a 60,000-square-foot casino are among the amenities at the 640-room hotel.

CLARIDGE HOTEL CASINO Indiana Avenue and the Boardwalk (340–3434 or 800–257–8585). One of Atlantic City's grand old structures was completely refurbished and given a new addition to create the "smallest, friendliest hotel casino." The Palace Theater presents Broadway shows and there's a Speakeeezy Cabaret (340–3700 or 800–752–7469). The Claridge has 504 guest rooms, six restaurants, a glass-enclosed year-round pool and health club, and a 30,000-square-foot, multi-level casino.

HARRAH'S MARINA HOTEL CASINO 1725 Brighton Boulevard (441–5600 or 800–242–7724). Harrah's sparkling building was the first casino hotel to rise on Atlantic City's bay. It has a beautiful, sweeping view of the marina, 750 guest rooms, nine restaurants and free indoor park-it-yourself space for your car. The entertainment is continuous nightly in the Bay Cabaret and Atrium Lounge. Harrah's Broadway by the Bay features big name stars (441–5165 or 800–242–7724). Car buffs will enjoy Harrah's world-famous automobile collection decorating the lobby and 44,000-square-foot casino.

MERV GRIFFIN'S RESORTS CASINO HOTEL North Carolina Avenue and the Boardwalk (340–6000 or 800–438–7424). Resorts was the first casino after gambling was approved in Atlantic City. The 680-room hotel with a 60,000-square-foot casino opened in May, 1978. Merv Griffin acquired it late in 1989. It features three gourmet restaurants, Le Palais, Capriccio and Camelot, as well as five other eateries. Mr. G's Lounge offers nightly entertainment. Superstar Theater (340–6830 or 800–438–7424) gets the superstars. Resorts is topped off with a roof-top year-round pool, health spa and squash club.

SANDS HOTEL CASINO AND COUNTRY CLUB
Indiana Avenue and Brighton Park (441–4000 or
800–257–8580). If you're overwhelmed by the size of the
larger casino hotels, The Sands might be more to your liking. It's set back from the boardwalk in a high-rise with
500 guest rooms, a 45,000-square-foot casino and its own
nearby 18-hole golf course. There's continuous music in
the Punch Bowl. Top stars like Cher, Liza Minelli and
Frank Sinatra appear at the Copa Room (441–4137 or
800–227–2637). There are four gourmet restaurants and
The Food Court offers a dozen moderately priced fast-
fooderies with international menus.

SHOWBOAT HOTEL AND CASINO Delaware
Avenue and the Boardwalk (343–4000 or 800–621–0200).
Outdoors the Showboat resembles a cruise ship; indoors
it's like you're in New Orleans. A Mardi Gras Showroom
and Lounge and the New Orleans Square Bandstand present jazz entertainment (343–4003 or 800–621–0200). A
60,000-square-foot casino, 516 rooms, 11 restaurants, a
youth care facility and a 60-lane bowling center are
featured.

**TROPWORLD CASINO AND ENTERTAINMENT
RESORT** Iowa Avenue and the Boardwalk (340–4000 or
800–257–6227). The 1,000-room TropWorld has two hotel
towers and a 90,000-square-foot casino. It also has 10
restaurants (several gourmet) and the Miss America Food
Court. The newest faces in stand-up comedy appear at
Comedy Stop at the Trop. Big-name stars are at Trop-
World's Showroom (340–4020 or 800–526–2935). Tivoli
Pier is a two-acre indoor amusement park, open weekends
only in winter, complete with ferris wheel, rollercoaster
and bumping cars (340–4396). There's a year-round
health club, tennis courts and an indoor and outdoor pool.

TRUMP CASTLE CASINO RESORT BY THE BAY
Huron Avenue and Brigantine Boulevard (441–2000 or
800–365–8786). Trump Castle on the marina treats
everyone like royalty. There's a three-acre recreation deck
with tennis courts, track, miniature golf and an outdoor
pool. There's free indoor parking for 3,000 cars, 700 guest
rooms, a 60,000-square-foot casino, complete health club,
six restaurants, continuous entertainment in the
lounges, nightly entertainment in King's Court Show-

room and Viva's Nightclub and monthly top star headliners in the Crystal Ballroom (800–284–8786).

TRUMP PLAZA CASINO HOTEL Mississippi Avenue and the Boardwalk (441–6000 or 800–677–7378) opened midway along the Boardwalk in 1984 with 550 rooms and 60,000 square feet of casino. There's nightly entertainment in the Casino Lounge, and Trump Showroom (800–759–8786) presents the likes of Paul Anka, Englebert Humperdinck and Tom Jones. Top sports events are held in the adjacent Convention Hall. Don't miss Ivana's Restaurant; it's one of the prettiest in town (and one of 11 places to dine at Trump Plaza). There's an indoor pool, outdoor tennis, a gym and spa, and a video arcade for the youngsters.

TRUMP TAJ MAHAL CASINO RESORT 1000 Boardwalk at Virginia Avenue (449–1000 or 800–825–8786). If you're in Atlantic City, it's hard to miss "the eighth wonder of the world," the biggest, most opulent and newest of all the Atlantic City casino hotels. Ten restaurants have exotic themes and international menus that span the globe; nine white elephants and 70 minarets adorn the Boardwalk resort; the casino covers 120,000 square feet; there are 1,250 rooms. Top stars in the entertainment and sports world appear at the 5,000-seat Etess Arena (449–5150 or Ticketmaster 800–736–1420). You've never seen *anything* like the Taj.

There are dozens of other hotels, motels and bed and breakfast inns in Atlantic City that are convenient to the beach, boardwalk and casinos. For additional information, call the **Greater Atlantic City Convention and Visitors Bureau (348–7130)** or a travel agent.

There's more to see in Atlantic City, and these are some of the more popular attractions that might appeal to the entire family.

ATLANTIC CITY HISTORICAL MUSEUM (347–5844) is at the Atlantic City Art Center on Garden

Pier, on the boardwalk at New Jersey Avenue. (It's closed through 1991 for total renovations of the pier.) The exhibits include furnishings from old and bygone hotels, along with related art and sculpture. The postcards and similar memorabilia will appeal to nostalgia buffs. While you're here, visit the Art Center's two galleries. The exhibits, which change monthly, feature paintings, sculpture and photography by regional artists. Hours are 9 to 4 daily. Admission is free.

Atlantic City's **BOARDWALK** has been immortalized by the game of Monopoly and a song or two. Despite the fact that it's five miles of wooden boards and used primarily for walking, the name comes from Alexander Boardman. In the 1860s, Boardman came up with a plan of wooden platforms so people could remove wet sand from their feet before entering shops and hotels from the beach. Can you imagine what would have happened if his name was Alexander Metalman?

Bicycling is permitted on the boardwalk daily from 6 to 10 A.M. Beach badges are not necessary in Atlantic City. Life guards are on duty during the summer from 9:30 to 5:30 daily.

Another fun and relaxing way to see the boardwalk is from a **rolling chair**. Catch one anywhere between the Showboat and Bally's Grand, anytime from late morning till late at night, any day of the year. Fares are posted on the chairs.

Going to Atlantic City and not seeing the boardwalk is like going to New York City and missing Fifth Avenue. And seeing the boardwalk without sampling a salt water taffy is like visiting Philadelphia and not having a soft pretzel or a cheesesteak.

Atlantic City's tradition of outdoor amusement rides has been revived at **CENTRAL PIER** on the Boardwalk at Tennessee Avenue. Thirteen of the rides await you, including a charming restored carousel. Come for the fun of it, any day from Easter through September.

EDWIN B. FORSYTHE NATIONAL WILDLIFE REFUGE—Brigantine Division (652-1665) is on the mainland north on Route 9, about a mile east of Oceanville. Its 20,000 acres of protected land attracts almost 300 species of wildlife. Ducks, geese and an occasional bald eagle are spotted migrating to and from the south. Most of the area is coastal salt marsh, but there is brush and woodlands with wildlife trails, observation towers and a visitor center. If you don't have the proper footwear, stay in your car for an eight-mile auto tour around the preserve. Bird lovers should bring binoculars. Admission is $3 per vehicle. Hours are daily from dawn to dusk.

HISTORIC GARDNER'S BASIN (348–2880) is at North New Hampshire Avenue and the Bay in Atlantic City. It's a charming reconstructed maritime village with shops, outdoor exhibits, an aquarium, seasonal events and a restaurant.

Every youngster who has ever come to Atlantic City remembers Lucy. **LUCY THE ELEPHANT** (823–6473 or 822–6519), at 9200 Atlantic Avenue in Margate, is now a National Historic Landmark. Lucy was built in 1881 as a real-estate promoter's dream to lure visitors to the Jersey shore. Lucy has been restored, and in warm-weather months you can climb up and around inside her six-story structure. Call for hours and cost.

Of course, if you're going to be in Atlantic City the first week of September, try to see some of the parades and competitions that make up the annual **MISS AMERICA PAGEANT**. And if you're lucky, get tickets for the finals and crowning of the new Miss America that takes place on Saturday night at the Convention Center (344–5278).

NOYES MUSEUM on Lily Lake Road in Oceanville (652–8848) is adjacent to the Edwin B. Forsythe National Wildlife Refuge. It's a perfect setting for their collection of handmade decoys. There are decoy carving demonstrations, a permanent contemporary American art collection and changing exhibitions. Hours are Wednesday to Sunday, 11 A.M. to 4 P.M. Admission is $2 for adults, $1 for senior citizens, and $.50 for students and children. It's free on Fridays.

A 900-foot "oceanliner" **OCEAN ONE** (347–8086) is permanently anchored at the Boardwalk and Arkansas Avenue. Its decks include a self-service food court, sit-down restaurants, exhibits, amusements and a mall with more than 150 shops.

STORYBOOK LAND (641–7847) is 10 miles west of Atlantic City on the Black Horse Pike (Routes 40 and 322) in Cardiff. Fifty buildings, displays and animals bring fairy tales and nursery rhymes to life. There are also rides, a playground, a petting zoo, picnic areas and a snack bar. Call for a schedule of admission, hours and seasonal events.

The **TOWNE OF HISTORIC SMITHVILLE** is also on the mainland on Route 9, about 20 minutes and 12 miles north of Atlantic City. Founded in 1787, Smithville today is a charming conglomeration of some 30 specialty and craft shops, a recreation of the historic Old Village working community that was built around the county's first Quaker Meeting House, and the popular dining attraction of Smithville Inn (652–7777). Just across Lake Meone, another 18th century village of 35 shops and restaurants has been recreated at **THE VILLAGE GREENE** (652–3111). A bridge connects the two villages.

There are several noteworthy and popular restaurants in Atlantic City, in addition to those in the casino hotels. Here are a very few representing a choice of cuisines and ambience. Some are closed in the winter. So call them for specific hours, dress code, reservations and credit card information.

Abe's Oyster House 2301 Atlantic Avenue (344–7701) is a local landmark serving fresh seafood and prime beef for more than a half-century.

Angeloni's II 2400 Arctic Avenue at Georgia (344–7875)

is a few blocks off the beaten path, but reservations are a good idea. Italian specialties, seafood and grilled beef are the specialties with a big wine list.

Baltimore Grille 2800 Atlantic Avenue (345-5766) is a casual place for pizza and reasonably priced Italian food. It's noisy and fun and you might have a jukebox at your table. Bring the family.

Dock's Oyster House 2405 Atlantic Avenue (345-0092) serves outstanding fresh seafood and steaks. The owner is the chef, his wife is the hostess and they're the fourth generation here at Atlantic City's oldest restaurant. People drive from New York and Philadelphia to enjoy dinner here, so it's a good idea to make reservations.

Frisanco's 3426 Atlantic Avenue (345-0606) is another popular place for gourmet Italian specialties and seafood.

Irish Pub 164 St. James Place at the Boardwalk (345-9613) is a 19th century-style friendly, moderately-priced saloon that serves sandwiches, steaks, chops, Irish specialties and Irish entertainment day and night.

Knife & Fork Inn Atlantic and Pacific Avenues (344-1133) has been serving gourmet fresh seafood and steak dinners to the Jersey shore's elite since 1927.

Le Grand Fromage 25 S. Pennsylvania Avenue (347-2743) is casual for reasonably priced Italian and American dinners.

Los Amigos 1926 Atlantic Avenue (344-2293) features authentic Mexican cuisine and decor for lunch (except Sunday), dinner and late night snacking.

Orsatti's 22 S. North Carolina Avenue (347-7667) is another Atlantic City landmark for fresh fish, steaks and Italian specialties.

Pal's 3810 Ventnor Avenue (344-0366) also serves seafood, veal and Italian specialties. Come casual or dressed up. Reservations are a good idea.

Peking Duck House 2801 Atlantic Avenue at Iowa

(344–9090) is known for Peking duck carved tableside and fried ice cream for dessert. Elegant decor for Szechuan, Mandarin and Cantonese gourmet cuisine.

The White House 2301 Arctic Avenue (345–1564). You shouldn't visit Atlantic City without trying a steak sandwich or submarine from The White House. If you don't know what that is, it's all the more reason to try one. Be prepared to wait. There are some booths, but most of the service is take-out.

As we said, this is just a small sampling of places to eat in Atlantic City. One thing for sure, you won't go hungry!

Chapter 18.
Restaurants. Nightlife.

There are so many good restaurants in Philadelphia, an entire book could be written about them. In fact, some have been.

This chapter describes two hundred places to dine in Philadelphia. They represent a broad spectrum of appeal.

No attempt has been made to rate the restaurants. Food and atmosphere are subjective, and service can vary in the best of them. Reviews are only as good as the occasion for which they are written. Instead, an idea of the menu is given, along with the ambience and unique features of each establishment. An indication is given if they're moderately priced or expensive, casual or formal, avant-garde or traditional, romantic or for the family, for fun or for business.

Several categories for dining are described at the end of the chapter. You can refer to these as a quick reference.

Restaurant descriptions include a code for the credit cards they accept: American Express (AE), Carte Blanche (CB), Diners Club (DC), Discover (DS), MasterCard (MC) and Visa (V).

"BYO" means bring your own wine or liquor if you want a drink with your meal, because the restaurant doesn't have a liquor license.

Every effort has been made to include the major restaurants in Philadelphia, as well as some that are lesser known.

Our apologies to any that were missed.

Bon appetit!

A Multitude of Restaurants

Alla Letizia 1915 E. Passyunk Avenue, 755–7552. A charming, intimate storefront restaurant on a bustling South Philadelphia retail block, seats 74 in two rooms on two levels. White lace, pink linens and fresh flowers set the mood. Italian food is all cooked to order by the owner, Maria. Dinner served daily, except Monday, followed by homemade gelati, capuccino and espresso. (MC,V)

Alouette 334 Bainbridge Street, 629–1126. Elegant French and New Asian cuisine (prepared by the owner-chef), a fine wine list, candlelight and fresh flowers make for refined dining for lunch weekdays, dinner daily and Sunday brunch. An outdoor courtyard with just six tables in warm weather. Closed Tuesdays. Reservations. (AE,DC,MC,V)

American Diner 4201 Chestnut Street, 387–1451; 435 Spring Garden Street, 592–8838. Return to the '50s in authentic silver diners at both locales. Juke box music, vintage dress on the staff, booths and counters for reasonably priced pancakes, burgers, sandwiches, meatloaf and mashed potatoes, milkshakes, homemade pastries and the like. Casual and funky, fun for breakfast, lunch and dinner daily till late. (No cards)

Astral Plane 1708 Lombard Street, 546–6230. Another off-beat, fun place to dine with Victorian ambience and an international menu that changes regularly. Reservations. Lunch weekdays; dinner daily; Sunday brunch. (All major cards)

Azalea 4th and Chestnut Street in Omni Hotel, 931–4260. Regional American fare is featured in this newest of dining rooms in the historic area. Daily for breakfast, lunch and dinner overlooking the National Park. Reservations suggested for weekends. (All major cards)

Barrymore Room Broad and Walnut Streets, 19th floor in Hotel Atop the Bellevue, 893–1776. One of Philadelphia's most beautifully restored rooms is popular for afternoon tea, cocktails and after theater. (All major cards)

Between Friends 17th and Vine Streets in Wyndham Franklin Plaza Hotel, 448–2768. The Continental menu changes monthly at this elegant and refined dining room in the city's largest hotel. An international buffet or à la carte selections are available for lunch weekdays, dinner is Tuesday to Saturday, and there's Sunday brunch from 10 to 2. Reservations suggested. (All major cards) More casual dining at the Wyndham Franklin Plaza is at **The Terrace** incorporating part of the big atrium lobby.

Boat House Row Bar in the Rittenhouse Hotel, 546–9000. Resembles a Schuylkill boat house and filled with local rowing memorabilia. Huge beer and ale selection, barrels of peanuts, hand-carved sandwiches, soups and salads in a fun-filled atmosphere. Large screen TV for special events and scheduled evening entertainment. Lunch and dinner and a popular "happy hour." (All major cards)

Bogart's 17th and Walnut Streets in Latham Hotel, 563-9444. Seafood, fowl and beef dinner specialties, with several tableside preparations, all in an elegant Casablanca atmosphere. Breakfast, lunch and dinner daily and Sunday brunch. (All major cards)

Bookbinder's, Old Original 125 Walnut Street, 925-7027. Philadelphia's long-standing famous restaurant outside of Philadelphia, frequented by visiting movie stars, athletes, politicians and local celebrities as well as tourists. Seafood is the specialty, but the menu includes beef and chicken. There are model fire engines, unusual wall decor and photographs of people you know. The lobster tank and dessert are also special. Lunch and dinner daily. Pricey. Reservations. Group arrangements for up to 250. (All major cards)

Bookbinder's Seafood House 215 S. 15th Street, 545-1137. The fourth generation of the Bookbinder family presents outstanding seafood along with prime steaks and other special dishes. Another Philadelphia landmark popular with business people, celebrities and tourists. Close to the Academy of Music and City Hall. Arrangements for large and small groups. (All major cards)

The Bourse at Independence Mall East. A variety of restaurants fill the 3rd level of this beautifully restored 1890s structure. **Saladalley** features a wine bar, homemade soups and deluxe salad bar. **Bain's** features hefty sandwiches. **Grand Old Cheesesteak** has cheesesteaks and hoagies. **Lots a Licks** dips homemade ice cream. **Cafe Berretta** has Italian pastries and espresso. **Athens Gyro** has Greek fare. **City's Best** serves burgers, ribs and fries. **Mandarin Express** has Chinese food. **International Sausage Shop** has what the name says. **Parinda** is French for salads, sandwiches and soup. And for dessert, **Hot Chips Cookie Company** is just how it sounds. You can eat while overlooking tiers of shops and activity below. **La Coupole** (described later in the chapter) is on the lower level reached from the 4th Street side. There's something for everyone to enjoy a casual lunch or dinner at The Bourse.

Brigid's 726 N. 24th Street, 232-3232. A cozy new little spot for dinner, except Sunday, behind a neighborhood bar near the Art Museum. A fireplace in winter; seats just 26. Specialties include duck Chambord and salmon Rushdie from a mostly European-style menu. (All major cards)

The Broadway at the Bellevue Broad and Walnut Streets in the Bellevue, 732-3737. Late breakfast, lunch and dinner daily à la New York-style deli. Tables and booths, friendly waiters, theater posters, lots of bustle, hearty selections of overstuffed sandwiches, smoked fishes, grilled garlic steaks, platters and home-made desserts, pickle bowls and you've got the picture. Come hungry! (All major cards)

Cafe Cosmo 12th and Locust Streets, 627-7004. Chic and contemporary with lots of marble and huge windows facing the street. Mostly wholesome Italian fare. Veal, chicken, pasta and pizza specialties for lunch, except Sunday, and dinner daily. Casual, with a separate bar and cafe. (AE,DC,MC,V)

Cafe Nola (as in New Orleans, LA) 326-330 South Street, 627-2590. Head to South Street (where everyday is Mardi Gras) for Cajun and Creole cuisine, the likes of fresh seafood, jambalaya, gumbo, "popcorn," Po' Boy sandwiches, an oyster bar and fresh baked desserts. Have lunch Tuesday to Saturday, dinner daily, and Sunday brunch with fresh baked biscuits and Bananas Foster. (All major cards)

Caffé Bene 602 S. 2nd Street, 925-8373. Spacious, chic "post modern" interior with black and white tile floor, turquoise walls, and a large open kitchen; outdoor cafe tables to sit and watch the South Street scene. Italian menu with antipasti, insalate e zuppe, polenta e risotto, pasta, pesce e carne. Dinner every night from 5 P.M. Adjoins the **Roxxi** for entertainment and dancing till late. (All major cards)

Callowhill 1836 Callowhill Street, 557-6922. A former union hall in Franklintown near the Art Museum, tastefully converted to a contemporary, well-designed bi-level restaurant with French and American cuisine at reasonable prices. All wines by the glass or bottle. Lunch Tuesday to Friday; dinner except Sunday; Sunday brunch. Live jazz on weekend evenings. (AE,DC,DS,V,MC)

Capriccio 17th and Locust Streets in The Warwick, 735–9797. A patisserie, sandwich, coffee, capuccino, espresso, frozen yogurt of the day and Ben & Jerry's ice cream shop that's also a popular meeting place and newsstand. Open daily from 7 A.M. till at least 10 P.M. (All major cards for over $10)

Carolina's 261 S. 20th Street, 545–1000. A huge storefront bar in one room is popular with the neighborhood crowd; the dining room is equally bustling and fun. Trendy, noisy and friendly for good, basic American and international food at popular prices. Reservations. Lunch weekdays; weekend brunch; dinner daily. (All major cards)

Catalina 2001 Hamilton Street in Korman Suites Hotel, 569–7500. Contemporary, bright decor with casual, resort-like atmosphere. Popular, fresh American cuisine with unique pizzas, grilled fish, and create-your-own stir-fry. Big screen TV in a big bar area. Breakfast, lunch and dinner daily. Reservations. (All major cards)

Cent' Anni 770 S. 7th Street, 925–5558. Old World Italian cooking in the heart of South Philadelphia's Italian neighborhood. Specializing in a variety of veal dishes, pasta, seafood, large portions and complimentary desserts. Dinner daily. (All major cards)

Chameleon 1519 Walnut Street, 636–4435. An upscale cafeteria, food shop and bakery for breakfast or lunch, except Sunday, from 7 A.M. to 6 P.M. The menu changes daily for a creative, wholesome variety at reasonable prices. An airy bi-level dining room with oak panelling and casual atmosphere. (All major cards)

Charlie's Water Wheel 1526 Sansom Street, 563–4155. Help yourself to the tasty meatballs and pickles while standing on line to order plump sandwiches and hoagies. (Fresh roasted turkey on marble rye is my favorite.) Then fill your tray with the huge variety of complimentary condiments and a choice of fresh fruit. Mostly for take-out but a few tables. No frills for a hearty lunch, except Sunday. Be sure to say "hi" to Charlie. (No liquor, no coffee, no cards)

Chart House 555 S. Delaware Avenue at South Street, 625-8383. Welcome aboard this dazzling Penn's Landing edition of an eatery that's known throughout the country for fresh seafood, prime rib, steaks, a huge salad bar and even bigger desserts. A big cocktail deck and bi-level dining areas with nautical motif and fabulous waterfront views. Dinner daily; Sunday brunch. Set your own mood, romantic or for a family celebration. Reservations. (All major cards)

Chautauqua 8229 Germantown Avenue, 242-9221. Tucked neatly in the second floor rear of the Chestnut Hill Hotel, Chautauqua offers a bright and cheery nightly dinner experience. The dining room menu is mostly French with entrees including seafood, venison, veal, chicken and beef. The bar is casual with lighter Thai cuisine served. Reservations suggested. (All major cards)

Chef Theodore 1100 S. Delaware Avenue, 271-6800. Large and informal storefront room in a shopping plaza facing the waterfront. Big portions, reasonably priced, seafood and Greek specialties. Reservations suggested for dinner Tuesday to Saturday, 4 to 11, and Sunday, 1 to 10. Come on your birthday; the staff will sing to you. (All major cards)

Chiyo 8136 Germantown Avenue, 247-8188. Choose chopsticks or flatware to dine on an authentic Japanese dinner served in the traditional style by waitresses in kimonos. You'll sit at a low table, but you can keep your shoes on. Closed Monday and Tuesday. Reservations. BYO. (No cards)

Ciboulette 1312 Spruce Street, 790-1210. Sophisticated, contemporary decor in a center city townhouse around the corner from the Academy of Music. Elegant Provencal French cuisine from a fixed price (choice of three, four or six courses) or à la carte menu. Dinner, except Sunday. Seats about 40; reservations suggested; not recommended for youngsters. (AE,DC)

City Tavern 2nd and Walnut Streets, 923–6059. The National Park Service has carefully recreated the 18th century tavern that was frequented by Ben Franklin, Thomas Jefferson and our famous forefathers. Read more about it in Chapter 2. You can relive the colonial atmosphere and enjoy a delightful "early American" (or 20th century, if you must) lunch or dinner daily. Group arrangements for up to 200. A treat for the whole family. (AE,MC,V)

The Commissary 1710 Sansom Street, 569–2240. Bright and cheerful gourmet cafeteria with carrot-covered walls and a wonderful array of salads, soups, pastas, entrees, pastries and wines that change daily for breakfast, lunch, dinner and anytime snacks. Seating is at tables or a comfortable counter. Almost everything can be packaged to go from The Commissary or its adjacent Market. (All major cards)

Copabanana 4th and South Streets, 923–6180. Welcome to Mexico. . . South Street style. It's neon, glitter, funky and very casual for Tex Mex and Islands fun food. Open daily for lunch and dinner till very late. A great place to dine, drink and South Street people watch. (All major cards)

Corned Beef Academy 400 Market Street, 922–2111; 18th and Kennedy Boulevard, 568–9696. Informal and friendly for hearty weekday lunches of corned beef, brisket, turkey, ham, salami and tuna salad. (No cards; no liquor)

Cutters Grand Cafe and Bar 20th and Market Streets in Commerce Square, 851–6262. Stylish, handsome, airy and friendly with Rousseau-esque paintings, a huge bar selection, West Coast-style menu and daily specials. Salads, soups, pasta, poultry, beef, seafood and mesquite grill preparations. Sinful desserts and a choice of beverages and coffees. Lunch and dinner daily. (AE,DC,MC,V)

D'Angelo's Ristorante Italiano 256 S. 20th Street, 546–3935. A sophisticated restaurant on a sophisticated retail and dining block. Family-operated and popular with folks in this upscale neighborhood. Authentic

Italian cuisine and especially good pasta. Lunch weekdays; dinner except Sunday. (AE,DC,MC,V)

Daniels at the Riverfront Delaware River at Poplar Street, 925–7000. Watch the ships go by as you dine on large portions of beef, veal, chicken and seafood and make your own salad from a 20-foot boat buffet. Bring the family. Reservations suggested. There's parking for boats if you radio ahead, and a **dinner theater** that's listed later in this chapter. Lunch Tuesday to Friday; dinner except Monday; Sunday brunch. (All major cards)

Dante and Luigi's 762 S. 10th Street, 922–9501. One of South Philadelphia's longstanding, reasonably-priced traditional Italian-style restaurants. Authentic atmosphere. Lunch and dinner daily 11:30 A.M. to 8:45 P.M. (except Sundays in July and August) share the same menu. (No cards)

Déja Vu 1609 Pine Street, 546–1190. Dining in this center city townhouse is formal, intimate, classic French and fixed price. Seating for 30, so reservations a must. Dinner, except Monday, and lunch Tuesday to Friday (call at least a day in advance). (All major cards)

Deux Cheminées 1221 Locust Street, 790–0200. A beautifully restored 1890 mansion and former Princeton Club is the elegant setting for French cuisine, prepared by the owner-chef, from a menu that changes with the season. Fixed price or à la carte dinner daily. Reservations. (D,M,V)

Dickens Inn 421 S. 2nd Street, 928–9307. Dining at Dickens Inn is the closest you'll get in Philadelphia to an English pub. In fact, it's modelled on and managed by its namesake by the Tower of London's Thameside. Roast beef, Yorkshire pudding, and steak and kidney pie are among the "veddy British" specialties. There's also Continental fare and a fresh fish cart from which to choose. Vegetables come family-style. Lunch and dinner daily. (All major cards)

DiLullo 7955 Oxford Avenue in Fox Chase, 725–6000. The decor is contemporary Italian at its best; the cuisine is Northern Italian as it would be if you were there. Everything is fresh and basic and you can see the pasta being made. Gelati is prepared daily on the premises. It's worth the trip from center city! Dinner daily. Reservations a good idea. (All major cards)

DiLullo Centro 1407 Locust Street, 546–2000. Another stunning decor and menu featuring Northern Italian and Continental fare. Diners "in the know" often choose risotto. A private wine cellar can accommodate private parties. Pricey and elegant for a special occasion. Lunch weekdays and dinner except Sunday. (All major cards)

Dimitri's 3rd and Catherine Streets, 625–0556. A neat, clean and casual corner restaurant in Queen Village that seats just 28 for dinner every night from 5:30. The floors are black and white tile, tables are marble and the walls a mellow yellow. A small marble counter encloses the compact open kitchen and grill. Everything is fresh and cooked to order Mediterranean-style. (Dimitri uses olive oil instead of butter.) At least five varieties of fresh fish, chicken and lamb are always available from the grill. The prices are reasonable. BYO. No reservations, but you can wait at the counter or on benches outside. (No cards)

DiNardo's 312 Race Street, 925–5115. Famous for Baltimore-style hard-shell crabs and other seafood specialties. Informal and fun. Lunch and dinner from 11 A.M. till 10 P.M., Friday and Saturday till 11, and Sunday dinner only from 4 to 8:30. (All major cards)

Diner on the Square 19th and Spruce Streets, 735–5787. Open 24 hours every day for typical diner food and ambience at an atypical diner locale just off Rittenhouse Square. (No cards; no liquor)

The Dining Room and **The Grill** 17th and Chestnut Streets in Ritz-Carlton Hotel, 563–1600. Gracious dining and superb food are certain at either Ritz-Carlton restaurant. The Dining Room is more formal and elegant for Continental cuisine; The Grill more clublike for hearty beef and seafood. Breakfast, lunch and dinner and a sumptuous Sunday brunch. Reservations a must for both restaurants. (All major cards)

Dock Street Brewing Co. 18th and Arch Streets in Two

Logan Square, 496–0413. Booths, cherry wood, brass, a lengthy bar and brewery on site make this a handsome, popular restaurant with Parkway businessmen. Hearty fare for lunch and dinner includes charcoal-grilled steaks, seafood and sandwiches. (All major cards)

Downey's Front and South Streets, 629–0525. A lively and spirited drinking house and Irish dining saloon. The bar is from a former Dublin bank, the walls are covered with memorable newspapers, and there's an old-time radio collection of proprietor and former broadcaster Jack Downey. Lunch and dinner daily; Sunday brunch. There's an oyster bar, outdoor tables, and TV at the bar. Popular with ballplayers and visiting celebrities. Also famous for their Irish whiskey cake. (All major cards)

Eden 3701 Chestnut Street in International House*, 387–2471. An upscale cafeteria-style restaurant with an imaginative, healthy menu that changes daily for lunch and dinner. There are soups, salads, quiche, gourmet burgers, stir-fry and grilled fish and chicken. Convenient to Annenberg Theaters and University City cultural sites. A casual bar and outdoor dining on the plaza. (All major cards)

El Mariachi 135 S. 24th Street, 567–6060. Mexican fun food and spirited music compliments of the six owner-brothers. Small and informal. Seats just 34 downstairs in south-of-the-border ambience, so call ahead for lunch Tuesday to Friday and dinner, except Sunday. Try the mole poblano or carni tampiquana, finished off with flan or bananas flambe. (All major cards)

Empress Dining Cruises Unfortunately, the steamboat sank at Penn's Landing during the winter, after Chapter 1 (page 21) was written but before this chapter was completed! We hope she'll be cruising again soon for your dining pleasure.

European Dairy Restaurant 20th and Sansom Streets, 568–1298. If you're kosher, or don't want meat, this no frills restaurant is just right. You can get borscht, kugel, kreplach, latkes, blintzas, gefilte fish, kasha, salads, omelets, smoked fish or fresh fish in season. Hours are Sunday to Thursday, 11 to 9; Friday till 3. BYO. (AE,DC)

Falls Catfish Cafe 4007 Ridge Avenue, 229–9999. A century old wining and dining place just above the Schuylkill River in the East Falls neighborhood. There's a great old-fashioned bar and a dining room that seats around 40. The menu includes fanciful salads, pasta, stir-fries and steak, but the real specialties are fish, as in catfish, pan-fried or blackened. Fun and friendly for lunch weekdays and dinner, except Sunday. (MC,V)

Famous Delicatessen 700 S. 4th Street, 922–3274. A Philadelphia institution for generations for a fun and informal bagel and lox brunch, hefty sandwiches, scrambled egg concoctions, knishes and kugels. It's the "in" place on Sunday to see local celebrities, politicos and friends. David, your host, is equally famous for his Famous 4th Street chocolate chip cookies sold on the premises (naturally), at Reading Terminal Market and elsewhere. Daily 7 A.M. to 6 P.M.; Sunday till 3. (No cards)

Flying Fish 8142 Germantown Avenue, 247–0707. Don't let this fish get away. It's served fresh and every which-way for lunch Tuesday to Friday and dinner, except Sunday. If you must have other than seafood, there are grilled burgers for lunch and chicken and steak for dinner. Comfortable, casual Chestnut Hill locale. (No cards)

Founders Broad and Walnut Streets in Hotel Atop the Bellevue, 790–2814. Breakfast, lunch and formal dinner in a magnificent domed room on the hotel's 19th floor that offers skyline views. French and continental cuisine served with style. Ask about pre-theater dinners and a weekly dinner-dance. Nice for a special occasion. (All major cards)

Fountain Restaurant One Logan Square in Four Seasons Hotel, 963–1500. A truly elegant and leisurely dining experience from an international menu, fixed price or a la carte. The menu changes daily. An equally beautiful view to the outside overlooking Logan Circle and the Swann Fountain. Popular for business breakfasts weekdays; lunch except Sunday when there's a magnificent Sunday brunch; dinner daily. Reservations recommended. (All major cards)

Fratelli 1701 Spruce Street, 546–0513. An ever-popular establishment of the Rago family (known by three generations of those in the know around Rittenhouse Square). Hearty home-style Italian cooking of good quality and value. Veal, pasta, chicken and seafood specialties followed by rich desserts and real gelati. Separate dining areas are casual to more casual for lunch except Sunday and dinner daily. Reservations are suggested. (All major cards)

Friday, Saturday, Sunday 261 S. 21st Street, 546–4232. The blackboard menu changes daily, but always has the consistently good regular items like the famous cream of mushroom soup and rack of lamb. The ceiling is canopied in fabric, the tables are close, the food is creative and the Rittenhouse Square crowd is equally colorful. No reservations taken, but cocktails at the intimate upstairs "Tank Bar" are worth the wait. You can dine upstairs, too. Lunch weekdays; dinner daily. (All major cards)

Gaetano's 705 Walnut Street, 627–7575. Tom and Inez welcome you to their lovely restaurant as if it were their home. In fact, it's on the ground floor of a centuries-old townhouse, seats just 48, and is filled with period furnishings and antiques. The fixed price five-course dinner, Tuesday to Saturday, is Italian and very fine. Reservations are necessary; not recommended for children. (All major cards)

The Gallery at Market East* There are no fewer than 20 ethnic and popular fast food eateries with common seating in **The Market Fair** of The Gallery's lower level near 10th Street. Hours are 10 to 7 daily, till 8 on Wednesday and Friday, and noon to 5 on Sunday. Other restaurants in The Gallery include 2 Street Cafe, Guzzlers, McDonald's and Roy Rogers, as well as the restaurant and Food Court in Strawbridge and Clothier.

The Garden 1617 Spruce Street, 546–4455. Dine outdoors in warm weather in the lovely garden. Inside is a beautiful townhouse-restaurant with a charming, casual oyster bar, small intimate dining rooms and an elegant main dining room. The food is country French and Continental; the overall decor is Old English. Popular with sophisticated people who enjoy quality. Lunch weekdays, dinner except Sunday, and closed weekends in summer. Reservations recommended. (All major cards)

Girasole 1305 Locust Street, 985–4659. Bright and sunny as an Italian "sunflower," with fresh and light, reasonably-priced Italian cuisine. Delicious homemade pastas, carpaccio, innovative individual pizzas made in a visible wood-burning oven, focaccio and Italian bread served with olive oil are a few of the specials that make Girasole so good. Lunch weekdays and dinner except Sunday; convenient to theater and the Academy of Music. Friendly and upbeat. Reservations. (All major cards)

Harry's Bar & Grill 22 S. 18th Street, 561–5757. Comfortable and clublike with rich mahogany walls and bar adorned with hunt prints; manly elegance for mature tastes. Two floors of dining feature aged prime beef, fresh seafood and homemade pasta. Reservations suggested for lunch and dinner, weekdays only. (All major cards)

Hikaru 607 S. 2nd Street, 627–7110; 108 S. 18th Street, 496–9950. Sushi, sashimi and sukiyaki are the most popular choices in these authentic Japanese-style restaurants. Fun for the family (or with a date) to remove your shoes and sit tableside on the floor. Small and informal, but reservations a good idea. (All major cards)

Houlihan's Old Place 225 S. 18th Street, 546–5940. Fun, food and spirits are offered in colorful surroundings of arts, antiques, stained glass, bright fabrics, wood panelling and plants. The menu has something for everyone: finger foods for starters, heaping salads, gourmet burgers, exotic sandwiches, pastas, fajitas, chicken, seafood and beef. There are all-time favorite desserts, popular beverages and specialty drinks. The bar is usually jumping. Open for lunch and dinner daily till late; also a Sunday brunch. (All major cards)

Il Gallo Nero 254 S. 15th Street at Latimer, 546–8065. The three dining rooms are each small, pleasant and cosmopolitan. There's a cozy piano bar, and the food is Northern Italian from a menu that changes with the season. Homemade pasta and breads. Popular with sophisticates and musicians, and convenient to the Academy of Music. Lunch Tuesday to Friday; dinner Tuesday to Saturday.

Reservations. Not recommended for youngsters. (All major cards)

Irish Pub 1123 Walnut Street, 925–3311; 2007 Walnut Street, 568–5603. They live up to their name with an Irish-American menu that features what else but Irish stew. There are sandwiches and burgers at lunchtime, a varied menu for dinner and light snacks for late in the evening. Hardwood floors, a huge bar, high ceilings, oak beams and music make for a casual, fun time. Lunch and dinner daily. (AE,MC,V)

Italian Bistro 3401 Walnut Street, 387–7900; 2500 Welsh Road, 934–7700; at Franklin Mills*, 637–2400; Broad and Walnut Streets. A chain restaurant that does lunch and dinner daily, with cheerful, attentive service, bright ambience and attractive, tasty, reasonably priced food. The extensive menu offers everything Italian from antipasto to zabaglione. Fun for the family, business or a date. (AE,MC,V)

Jack's Firehouse 2130 Fairmount Avenue, 232–9000. A stately brick firehouse from the early 1900s enjoys new life as a popular restaurant and bar in the Art Museum area. American regional cuisine is featured in the main dining room with lighter fare served at the bar. Known, too, for their 18-bottle cruvinet. Reservations suggested for dinner in the dining room, served daily; lunch weekdays and brunch on Sunday. (All major cards)

Jake's 4365 Main Street, 483–0444. Contemporary and casual but elegant in the heart of Manayunk. You'll recognize it by the vegetables on the facade. A seasonal menu with American regional specialties. Everything is fresh and artfully presented. Lunch weekdays; dinner daily. Reservations suggested; seats just 65. (AE,MC,V)

Jamey's 4417 Main Street, 483–5354. Jamey's was among the first on the scene when Manayunk* went up-scale. A delightful, warm and friendly restaurant in shades of mauve that's helped the neighborhood grow. Fresh food; refreshing prices and presentation. A small bar and a good wine list. Lunch Tuesday to Saturday; dinner except Monday; Sunday brunch. Reservations a good idea. (AE,MC,V)

Jeannine's Bistro 10 S. Front Street, 925–1126. An informal French bistro that seats just 40 and serves affordable country French cuisine from a blackboard menu that changes daily. Upstairs from La Truffe. Dinner, except Sunday, and live music on Fridays. Reservations. (AE,MC,V)

Jimmy's Milan 39 S. 19th Street, 563–2499. One of Philadelphia's longstanding bars also serves some of Philadelphia's most consistently hearty and good food. Specialties are the house salad, veal, chicken and steak "Milan." There's never a dull moment at Jimmy's. Lunch weekdays; dinner except Sunday. Reservations. Not suggested for youngsters. (AE,DC)

Jim's Steaks 4th and South Streets, 928–1911. An art-deco steak shop in the heart of South Street. Take-out, stand-up or sit-down to enjoy super steak sandwiches and hoagies. Monday to Thursday from 10 A.M. to 1 A.M.; till 3 A.M. on Friday and Saturday; noon to 10 P.M. on Sunday. Closed Thanksgiving and Christmas. (No cards)

La Buca 711 Locust Street, 928–0556. The cuisine is Northern Italian with Tuscan specialties. Veal, chicken, fresh fish and pasta are plentiful. Popular for business lunches weekdays and family dinner, except Sunday. A downstairs location just west of Washington Square. (AE,DC,MC,V)

La Coupole 4th Street between Market and Chestnut in The Bourse, 440–0700. A country French bistro, reasonably priced with daily specials including cassoulet, and a wine list that changes weekly. Lunch weekdays; dinner, except Sunday. (AE,DC,MC,V)

La Famiglia 8 S. Front Street, 922–2803. The Sena family came from Italy to Philadelphia to bring us their fine Northern and Southern Italian cooking. The handsome bi-level room is comfortable and sophisticated. Reservations suggested for lunch Tuesday to Friday and dinner, from 5:30 to 10:30, except Mondays and when the family returns to Italy in August in search of new recipes. (All major cards)

La Grolla 782 S. 2nd Street, 627–7701. Tucked into Queen Village, this sophisticated little bar and trattoria seats only 60 in two pleasant rooms. The menu is mostly Northern Italian with interesting venison dishes, osso buco, risotto and homemade pasta among the favorites. Dinner is Monday to Saturday from 5 till 10, and midnight on the weekend. The name means "cup of friendship" and you'll find out why when you finish your meal. Ask about the seasonal festival dinners for seafood and game. (AE,DC,MC,V)

La Truffe 10 S. Front Street, 925–5062. An intimate fine French restaurant facing Penn's Landing. Classic cuisine or cuisine minceur in an elegant but country-flavored atmosphere. Pricey price-fixed or à la carte menu. Popular with Main Liners and Philadelphia sophisticates, but not recommended for children. Lunch Tuesday to Friday; dinner, except Sunday. Reservations. **Jeannine's Bistro** is upstairs. (All major cards)

La Veranda Pier 3 at Delaware Avenue near Market Street, 351–1898. Upscale dining in an airy contemporary interior or outdoors on the veranda. The views are great either way. Lunch and dinner daily for an appealing Italian menu where the pasta is made on the premises and everything is cooked to order. Reservations suggested. (All major cards)

Le Beau Lieu East Rittenhouse Square in Barclay Hotel, 545–0300. A comfortable hotel dining room, "the beautiful place" serves breakfast, lunch and dinner daily. The clientele is an interesting mix of the building's residents and guests, business people, occasionally some celebrities and Philadelphians looking for a well-prepared, well-priced meal. (All major cards)

Le Bec Fin 1523 Walnut Street, 567–1000. Everything here is exquisite, from the rich wall coverings, crystal chandeliers, tapestry chairs, colorful fresh flowers and French china, silver and glassware to the formal service and, of course, the magnificent classic French haute cuisine. The owner-chef, Georges Perrier, is internationally acclaimed. His restaurant is one of very few in the country to get very top awards from Mobil and AAA. Two seatings for lunch (fixed price or à la carte) at 11:30 and 1:30 weekdays; dinner (fixed price and five courses), except Sunday, at 6 and 9. Reservations a must. Cocktails and à la carte lighter fare are available with no reservations at Le Bar Lyonnais. (All major cards)

Le Bus 3402 Sansom Street, 387–3800. A bustling, crowded, informal, contemporary cafeteria on the University of Pennsylvania campus for innovative salads, homemade soups, quiche, pasta, sandwiches, specials of the day and wonderful fresh-baked breads and pastries. Ample portions, reasonably priced. Breakfast, lunch and dinner daily. (No cards)

Levis 507 S. 6th Street, 627–2354. Levis has been continually serving delicious hot dogs, fishcakes and cherry cokes at their earthy 6th Street location since the turn of the century. Casual and fun, daily from 11 A.M. to 6 P.M., and midnight on Friday and Saturday. Bring the kids. (No cards)

Liberties 705 N. 2nd Street, 238–0660. A casual restaurant and bar in Northern Liberties opened in the mid-1980s by the proprietor of a restored furnishings and interiors showroom down the block. A tin ceiling and walls, oak and tile floors, mahogany bar and wood booths for two or four make for a unique and fun environment. Popular salads, sandwiches, burgers and regional fare for lunch and dinner, except Sunday. Live jazz on Friday and Saturday from 8:30 P.M. Reservations suggested. (AE,DC,MC,V)

Liberty Place* Chestnut Street between 16th and 17th. More than a dozen eateries are at The Buffet food court on the second level of The Shops at Liberty Place. They surround a clean, contemporary and comfortable seating area to accommodate 500 for lunch or early dinner. Look for the likes of deli sandwiches, steak sandwiches, Chinese food, dairy dishes, pizza, Greek fare, salads, fish and chips, desserts and gourmet coffee. Hours are Monday to Saturday, 9:30 A.M. to 7 P.M. and Wednesday till 9 P.M.; Sunday, noon to 6 P.M.

Lickety Split 401 South Street, 922–1173. A forerunner of the South Street renaissance, Lickety has been serving creative, good food in a creative, fun atmosphere for two decades. A lively staff, upbeat music, good drinks and lots of funk. Dinner daily and Sunday brunch. Not recommended for youngsters. (All major cards)

Little Pete's 17th and Chancellor Streets, 545–5508. Nothing fancy here, but wholesome, moderately priced breakfast food, lunch and dinner sandwiches, platters and daily specials. Booths and a counter for business people, shoppers and neighbors on the go. Open 24 hours, everyday but Christmas. (No cards) A "dressed up" restaurant annex with similar menu and upstairs lounge is at 1904 Chestnut Street, 563–2303. It's open daily for breakfast, lunch and dinner till 11 P.M. and draws an eclectic crowd from neighboring apartments, businesses and the nearby movies. (AE,MC,V)

London 2301 Fairmount Avenue, 978–4545. A friendly restaurant and neighborhood pub that was a forerunner of trendy eateries in the Art Museum area. Continental and California-style cuisine and a good wine list for lunch and dinner daily and Sunday brunch. (All major cards)

Mace's Crossing 1714 Cherry Street, 854–9592. A tastefully restored carriage house that survived highrise encroachment on the Parkway. Popular at lunch weekdays for burgers and sandwiches; brunch weekends from 11 to 3; steak, veal or chicken for dinner daily till 10; bar food till after midnight. Also popular with young executives for drinks on the patio after work. (AE,DC,MC,V)

Magnolia Cafe 1602 Locust Street, 546–4180. Dine casual New Orleans-style in a beautiful old townhouse for lunch weekdays, dinner daily, and weekend brunch. Try Cajun and creole specialties like crawfish and shrimp popcorn, jambalaya gumbo, blackened chicken, fried catfish, hushpuppies and cornmeal muffins. Choose your meal to the size and tanginess of your liking. (AE,MC,V)

Main Street Cafe 4245 Main Street, 487–7025. A friendly, casual neighborhood bar-cafe in Manayunk. Reasonably-priced, creative menu for American fare.

Funky bright colors on the walls covered with the owner's contemporary artwork. Lunch and dinner, except Monday; Sunday brunch. (AE,MC,V)

Mara Brothers 1533 S. 11th Street, 334–7722. At least one of the brothers Mara, Carmelo and Alessandro, from Turin, Italy will greet you and prepare your dinner nightly at their trattoria-style South Philadelphia rowhouse restaurant. Dining is on two floors in two homey rooms that seat about 60. Pastas are homemade or imported from Italy. For those who can't decide, there's a sampler. Choosing an entree and dessert is a tougher choice. Reservations necessary. BYO. (AE)

Marabella's 1420 Locust Street, 545–1845. Contemporary, colorful and casual decor for fresh, festive, reasonably-priced Italian-style fare and fresh grilled fish. Two levels of dining and a big-screen TV over the bar. Popular and fun after work, before or after a concert or show, with the same menu at all hours for lunch and dinner daily. (AE,DC,MC,V)

Marrakesh 517 S. Leithgow Street, 925–5929. Dinner (daily from 5:30 to 11) at Marrakesh is a Moroccan ceremony that begins with a kettle of warm water and terry towels to wash your hands. Why must your hands be clean? Because there are no utensils here. Extra towels are provided for your lap. Dress casually, and be prepared to relax on cushions around a low, hammered brass table. Come with friends for this traditional seven-course meal that starts with salad, followed by bastilla (stuffed pastry), a whole chicken, lamb, couscous, fresh fruit, baklava and mint tea or Turkish coffee. Reasonably fixed priced. Reservations. (No cards)

Marra's 1734 E. Passyunk Avenue, 463–9249. The third generation of the Marra family carries on the tradition of making their own pasta and specialties like mussels, veal marsala, fisherman's delight, fettucini pesto genovese and an array of pizzas. The ambience is casual and friendly, and the bar is stocked with a huge variety of wine and beer at what's reputed to be South Philadelphia's oldest Italian restaurant. Lunch Tuesday to Saturday; dinner except Monday. (No cards)

Meiji-En Pier 19 North, Callowhill Street at Delaware Avenue, 592–7100. Picture a huge pier jutting out over the Delaware with fabulous views of the waterfront from the dining room, a teppanyaki room for tabletop cooking, a sushi bar, a tempura bar, and spacious piano lounge. Meiji-En has all of the above for dinner daily and a man-size Sunday brunch. A smorgasbord of Japanese food with popular American fare as well. Fun for a family gathering, business or a romantic evening. (AE,DC,MC,V)

Melrose Diner 1501 Snyder Avenue, 467–6644. A South Philadelphia landmark that's open 24 hours, seven days a week with menus that are appropriate to the time of day or night. Good food, good people, counter seating and large booths to share. (No cards; no liquor)

Metropolis 1515 Locust Street, 546–1515. Lively and contemporary with American fare including "small" plates, salads, pasta, pizza, "large" plates and specially prepared low-fat items. A large bar and three tiers of dining for lunch weekdays, dinner daily, and Sunday brunch. (All major cards)

Mezzanotte 1701 Green Street, 765–2777. Upscale, urban chic for reasonably-priced Italian food. Good antipasto, homemade minestrone, creative individual pizzas, pasta, and a choice of entrees. Open daily for lunch and dinner from 11:30 A.M. to 11:30 P.M. Sidewalk cafe dining in summer. Casual and fun; attracts folks from the Art Museum neighborhood and from the suburbs. (All major cards)

Michael Jack's 8th and Market Streets in Market Place East, 829–2424. Sports fans won't want to miss this eating, drinking and entertainment establishment that honors the 18-year career of Phillies baseball star Michael Jack Schmidt. The restaurant opens daily at noon for lunch and dinner with a menu of popular foods like salad, sandwiches, seafood, chicken and steak. **Philadelphia's Original Sports Bar** is an enormous two-level entertainment complex with a dance floor, an assortment of bars, live music and a huge sports arcade. Have fun! (All major cards)

Middle East 126 Chestnut Street, 922–1003. Philadelphia's original for Middle Eastern cuisine (with American favorites tossed in) and exotic belly dancers and musicians who entertain every night. Lunch by reservation only; dinner daily till very late, and there's never a dull moment. **The Comedy Works** is upstairs. (All major cards)

Monte Carlo Living Room 2nd and South Streets, 925–2220. Finely prepared Italian cuisine goes just right in the elaborate mirrored, candlelit dining room, lavished with plush furnishings and crystal chandeliers. Men are requested to wear a jacket and tie. Dinner daily; reservations suggested. Fixed price or à la carte. Not recommended for youngsters. Cocktails and dancing in the upstairs lounge, Tuesday to Saturday. (AE,DC,MC,V)

Morton's One Logan Square (19th Street, south of Parkway), 557–0724. Philadelphia has the steakhouse made famous in Chicago. Man-sized portions of aged prime beef, veal, chicken and seafood shown to you tableside before being prepared to your liking. Oversized, beautiful fresh vegetables, too. Everything is à la carte. Reservations suggested for lunch weekdays and dinner daily. Bustling, businesslike and sophisticated. (All major cards)

New Deck Tavern 3408 Sansom Street, 386–4600. Two old rowhouses neatly restored on the University of Pennsylvania campus to resemble an Irish-style pub. Wood panelling and old brick decor with a lengthy bar and several dining rooms. Popular Irish and American specialties for a lively crowd. Open daily from 11 A.M. till 2 A.M., except some Sundays in summer. (AE,MC,V)

94th Aero Squadron 2750 Red Lion Road, 671–9400. A jeep and an airplane are stationed on the lawn and that's for openers to create the ambience for the 94th Aero Squadron. It's on the edge of Northeast Philadelphia Airport, and part of the fun while dining is watching the runway activity and tuning in to the control tower. Lunch and dinner daily and a Sunday brunch buffet. All-American favorite meals and a special menu for youngsters. Also a cocktail lounge and dancing. (All major cards)

Noodles 8341 Germantown Avenue, 247–7715. You guessed it! They specialize in pasta here, hot and cold varieties. They also have great ice cream. Informal and friendly with a blackboard menu that changes every few weeks and an open kitchen separating the two dining areas. Open for breakfast, lunch and dinner daily, except Monday. In the heart of Chestnut Hill. BYO. (All major cards)

North Star Bar 27th and Poplar Streets, 235-STAR. Near the Art Museum and attracting an eclectic crowd for ample portions of reasonably-priced, well-prepared fresh food and a nightly entertainment schedule. Call to find out who's performing this week. Informal and fun at the bar and two dining rooms from 5 P.M. every night. (AE,MC,V)

Norm's 3301 S. Galloway Street, 336–4848. If you're looking for something really different, here's an institution in the midst of the Food Distribution Center*. Everything is fresh for breakfast and lunch weekdays from 1 A.M. to 2 P.M. or Sunday "brunch" from 9 to 5. A huge counter and several tables for very casual, good eating from an extensive menu. Have fun! (No cards; no liquor)

Odeon 114 S. 12th Street, 922–5875. A mahogany panelled 19th century florist shop enjoys new life as this chic marble-topped bar and multi-level bistro restaurant featuring fine French food. The cruvinet offers more than a dozen wines. Convenient for Forrest Theater-goers and center city business types. Lunch weekdays, dinner except Sunday. Reservations. (AE,MC,V)

Osteria Romana 935 Ellsworth Street, 271–9191. The main dining room is bright, white and simple with an old tin ceiling and tile floor. A balcony with additional seating overlooks it. The menu is authentic Roman-Italian with several choices of meats, fishes, and pastas cooked al dente. Dinner, except Monday, in the heart of the Italian Market. Known for their special holiday meals at Passover. Also, if you give them 72 hours notice for a party of six or more, they'll prepare an ancient Roman specialty, roast suckling pig. Make reservations; leave the kids at home. (AE,MC,V)

Palladium 3601 Locust Walk, 387-3463. At street level of a wonderful Tudor-style building that personifies Ivy League on the Penn campus. A crackling fire at the bar in winter; an outdoor cafe in summer. The menu is international. Everything is made fresh, from the bread and pasta to the ice cream. Lunch weekdays; dinner except Monday, except in summer when they're closed weekends. Reservations recommended. (All major cards) The sibling **Gold Standard** gourmet cafeteria is downstairs for inexpensive breakfast, lunch and dinner weekdays during the academic year. Wholesome fresh foods and home-baked goodies are featured.

Palm 200 S. Broad Street in The Bellevue, 546-PALM. Surround yourself with caricatures of famous Philadelphians as well as local politicos and celebrities in real life. The place for power lunches and hearty dinners of prime beef, lobster, veal, lamb and their famous home-fried potatoes. You get steak with the sizzle if you're lucky enough to get a table. Reservations a must. Closed Sunday. (AE,DC,MC,V)

Palumbo's Nostalgia 807 S. 9th Street, 574-9091. The celebrities who have appeared at the adjoining **Palumbo's** adorn the walls of this traditional Italian restaurant in the Italian Market area. The portions are large, the prices are reasonable, and you might see some famous people. Lunch and dinner daily. (All major cards)

Panorama 14 N. Front Street in Penn's View Inn, 922-7800. A polished marble floor, white tablecloths and a huge scenic wall mural bring Italy to mind even before discovering the creative and budget-minded menu. The recipes are mostly Milanese. The wine bar offers 120 choices by the glass or bottle. Lunch weekdays and dinner daily. Reservations suggested. (AE,DC,MC,V)

Pat's King of Steaks 1237 E. Passyunk Avenue, 339-9872. Many have tried, but none have duplicated the aura of Pat's. It's almost as famous as the Liberty Bell. Drive by anytime, day or night, for a steak sandwich to go. Or, stand outside to eat with the other aficionados. Dress formal or casual. (No cards; no liquor)

Pizzeria Uno 509 S. 2nd Street, 592–0440; Locust Street between 17th and 18th, 790–9669. Pizza aficionados have discovered Chicago's legendary deep dish pizza in Philadelphia. It comes in a variety of styles and two sizes. You can eat it here or take it home partially baked, fully baked or frozen. There are also appetizers, soups, salads, fun foods, burgers, sandwiches, fancy beverages, beer, wine and booze. The decor is fun and informal with tile floors, booths for "famous" people and tables for small or large parties of young or old diners. (All major cards)

Pomodoro 17th and Parkway in The Windsor, 981–5555. Angles and curves are juxtaposed with warm colors, displays of beautiful fresh vegetables and bright light from huge windows overlooking the Parkway to give Pomodoro a sophisticated and friendly ambience. The antipasto is tempting, the hearty Italian-style food is imaginative and tasty, the bar is stylish and well-stocked. A popular new spot for lunch weekdays, dinner daily and a leisurely Sunday brunch. (All major cards)

Primavera 146 South Street, 925–7832. A sibling of its neighbor, Monte Carlo Living Room, Primavera seats 40 and serves basic Italian cuisine and daily seafood specials for dinner except Monday. You might have to wait, but it's worth it. No reservations are taken. (No cards)

Priori's 10th and Wolf Streets, 339–9358. The third generation of South Philadelphia's Priori family chefs presides over the kitchen making home-style, reasonably priced Italian dishes including calamari, mussels, meatballs and veal specialties. Small and earthy, seating only 20, for lunch, Tuesday to Friday, and dinner except Monday. Buon Appetito! (No cards)

Ralph's 760 S. 9th Street, 627–6011. A family-managed and family-oriented restaurant that's been a landmark since 1900. Chicken Sorrento, veal rollatini, linguini pescatore and mussels are some of the popular items. Homemade Italian cooking from the same menu for lunch and dinner daily. (No cards)

Reading Terminal Market 12th and Arch Streets, 922–2317. The market is known for its bakeries, butchers, fish stalls, fruit and produce stands. (Read more about it in Chapter 21.) But there's also a variety of informal restaurants in the terminal. You can choose international specialties for a moderately priced breakfast or lunch from among: Aunt Sadie's Deli, Basic Four Vegetarian Snack Bar, Bassetts Ice Cream, Bassett's Original Turkey, Coastal Cove, Delilah's, Down Home Diner, Famous 4th Street Cookie Co., Fireworks, Franks-A-Lot, Glick's Salads, Le Bus, Middle Eastern Cuisine, Old City Coffee, Olivieri Prince of Steaks, Olympic Gyro, Pasta Natale, Pearl's Oyster Bar, Salads Unlimited, Salumeria, Sandwich Stan, Sang Kee Peking Duck, Spataro's Sandwiches and Buttermilk, Stella's Deli, Stoltfus Snack Bar, Sushi Bar, 12th Street Cantina, Wok Shop and Your Bagel Place. The Reading Terminal is a fun place to visit and it's unique. The eateries are open every day, except Sunday. Most have their own seating, and there are central seating areas with live music entertainment at lunchtime. Go grazing; try one course at each.

Restaurant School 4207 Walnut Street, 561–3649. Founded in a center city brownstone in 1974, the Restaurant School recently moved to its wonderful and much larger new home in West Philadelphia. It combines a mid-19th century restored mansion with an addition housing classrooms, school facilities and, of course, **The Restaurant**. Your waiter or waitress is a student who is learning the fine art of serving. (The Restaurant itself is a classroom for the school.) His or her classmates have planned the fixed price menu, bought and prepared the food. Come for dinner Tuesday to Saturday, from 5:30 P.M., with two seatings on the weekend when reservations are a must. (All major cards)

Rindelaub's 128 S. 18th Street, 563–3993. A regular following shows up for breakfast from 6 A.M., lunch, tea or coffee breaks. The cakes and pastries are known around town. There are also eggs, sandwiches and platters. You'll want to take some goodies home or to the office, too. (No cards)

River Cafe 4100 Main Street, 483–4100. Huge restaurant and dance club (Wednesday to Sunday) in a restored 19th century stone mill overlooking the Schuylkill in

Manayunk. Grilled steaks, chops, burgers, pasta and seafood specialties. Lunch and dinner daily, with a game room in case you have to wait. Casual and fun for the family. (AE,MC,V)

Roller's 8705 Germantown Avenue, 242–1771. Come to the top of the hill in Chestnut Hill for a delightful lunch, Tuesday to Saturday; Sunday brunch, except in summer; and dinner except Monday. The menu and presentation are fresh and creative, the ambience is bright and friendly, the kitchen is in view as are the outdoors through mostly glass walls. Reservations suggested for dinner. (No cards)

Ruth's Chris Steakhouse 260 S. Broad Street, 790–1515. The "home of serious steaks" started in New Orleans in 1965. Today, aficionados of prime beef in cities around the country are enjoying Ruth's quality and success. In Philadelphia, it's in a restaurant built into the former lobby of an office building. Aged and hand-cut steaks arrive at your table sizzling to perfection. For those who prefer, seafood selections are available along with side dishes of grand proportion. Everything is à la carte for lunch weekdays and dinner daily. Reservations suggested. (All major cards)

Saladalley 1720 Sansom Street, 564–0767; The Bourse, 627–2406; 4040 Locust Street, 349–7644; on Temple University campus and suburban locations. If you're looking for healthy food and a casual atmosphere, here's a place with a bottomless salad bar, fresh-baked breads, gourmet soups and a few hot, vegetarian, pasta, beef, chicken and seafood entrees. Hours vary at different locations for lunch, dinner and Sunday brunch that includes omelets. Wine by the glass. (AE,MC,V at some locations)

The Saloon 750 S. 7th Street, 627–1811. Splendid Victorian decor with magnificent woodwork in the heart of South Philadelphia. Outstanding Italian dishes and prime steaks. Interesting bars upstairs and downstairs. Lunch Tuesday to Friday, dinner except Sunday. Popular with an arty, business and political crowd; not recommended for youngsters. Reservations. (AE)

Samuel Adams Brew House 1516 Sansom Street, 2nd floor, 563–2326. Perched on the second floor above Sansom Street Oyster House, this cozy pub is an on-site brewery where vat you see is vat you drink. The food is traditional pub-fare. The in-house potables comes in amber, porter and gold, along with a large selection of other unique beers. Fun for lunch, dinner and happy hour, except Sunday, from 11 A.M. till 11 P.M. and later on weekends. (AE,MC,V)

San Carlo 214 South Street, 592–9777. The owner is Sandro and his mother is the cook. Everything is cooked to order from a European-Italian menu that always includes pasta, veal, chicken and a fish of the day. To the sound of Italian music, the decor is tones of pink and green with fresh flowers on all 13 tables and crystal chandeliers overhead. Reservations suggested for dinner daily. Buon Appetito! (AE)

Sansom Street Oyster House 1516 Sansom Street, 567–7683. Simple, panelled decor, earthy and good quality seafood since 1947 at reasonable prices. All of the fish is bought fresh daily. The colorful collection of oyster plates and ceramics is worth seeing, too. Come casual for lunch or dinner, except Sunday. (All major cards)

Seafood Unlimited 270 S. 20th Street, 732–3663. A bare basics dining room behind a fresh fish market for prepared-to-order fresh seafood. Very casual and moderately priced; attracts folks from the neighborhood for good wholesome food. Lunch and dinner daily. (AE,MC,V)

Serrano 20 S. 2nd Street, 928–0770. International home cooking at a moderate price in a casual, wood-floored, brick-walled long narrow dining room with a neighborhood bar. The ethnic menu features popular foods from Indonesia, Malaysia and Mexico, and blackboard specials change daily for dinner, except Sunday, and weekdays for lunch. Mondays feature multi-course, fixed price ethnic dinners that are always filling and fun. Reservations suggested. (All major cards)

1701 Cafe 17th and Locust Streets in The Warwick, 545–4655. A see-and-be-seen lobby restaurant, stylish dining room and cozy bar for daily breakfast, lunch, dinner and Sunday piano brunch. Live jazz on Friday and Saturday from 8:30 P.M. Contemporary American cuisine cooked to order at reasonable prices, weekend specials and outrageous bread pudding for dessert. (All major cards)

Sfuzzi 1650 Market Street at Liberty Place, 851–8888. Don't pronounce the "s" when you talk about this chic, bustling, tasteful Italian bistro that features focaccia with olive oil, the frozen Sfuzzi drink in four sizes, bowls of imaginative pastas, delicious thin pizzas, a three-cheese lasagna like none you've ever tasted, terrific antipasto and desserts like you've never seen. One wall of the multilevel dining area resembles Roman ruins, another is floor to ceiling glass. There's outdoor dining on the Liberty Place* terrace in summer. Reservations suggested for lunch weekdays; dinner daily; a bountiful weekend brunch. (DC,MC,V)

16th Street Bar & Grill 264 S. 16th Street, 735–3316. A neighborhood bar and restaurant for informal dining and drinking. Popular American and Mediterranean foods for lunch and dinner daily; Sunday brunch. Popular with center city sophisticates. (All major cards)

Smart Alex 36th and Chestnut Streets in Sheraton University City, 396–5556. Advertised as "an eating and drinking emporium for wild lunches, outrageous dinners and decadent drinks." Open daily near the Penn and Drexel campuses for breakfast, lunch and dinner from 7 A.M. to midnight. A big bar and a big screen TV. (AE,MC,V)

Society Hill Hotel 3rd and Chestnut Streets, 925–1919. A small, fun, airy, cheerful restaurant, piano bar and sidewalk cafe that's open daily from 11 A.M. to 2 A.M. (the kitchen closes an hour earlier). Creative burgers, cheesesteaks, sandwiches, salads and daily specials. Sunday brunch from 10:30 to 2 includes omelets. (Upstairs is Philadelphia's first bed and breakfast hotel.) (AE,DC,MC,V)

Spirit of Philadelphia Delaware River near Market Street at Penn's Landing, 923–1419. Come aboard (except in winter) for a delightful cruise along the Delaware River that offers, not only sightseeing, but also a plentiful buffet-style meal and entertainment. Lunch cruises are Monday to Saturday, noon to 2; Sunday brunch is 1 to 3; dinner is daily from 7 to 10. Reservations necessary. (AE,MC,V)

Strolli's 1528 Dickinson Street, 336–3390. Another South Philadelphia hideaway that's relatively small, serves good food at reasonable prices and is fun when the crowd around the bar starts to sing. Italian home-style cooking for lunch weekdays; dinner daily. (No cards)

Susanna Foo 1512 Walnut Street, 545–2666. Chinese cuisine that's as beautiful to look at as it is delicious to eat. Comfortable and sophisticated. You'll see why Esquire Magazine recently called Susanna Foo best Chinese restaurant in the country. Lunch weekdays; dinner except Sunday. Reservations suggested. (AE,MC,V)

Tacconelli's Pizzeria 2604 Somerset Street, 425–4983. Head to the Port Richmond section of lower Northeast Philadelphia for white pizza like you've never had before. The ingredients are all fresh, but the real secret is the 20- by 20-foot brick oven built in 1928 by proprietor Vince Tacconelli's grandfather. Very casual and open Wednesday to Sunday from 4:30 P.M. till the day's dough is used up. Bring the family. (No cards)

Tea Garden of Independence National Historical Park Chestnut Street between 3rd and 4th Streets, 597–7919. Each summer (from 11 A.M. through late afternoon) the Friends of I.N.H.P. operate an outdoor cafe for light refreshments such as 18th century "squash punch," iced tea and ice cream. The garden is adjacent to the Second Bank of the United States.

T.G.I.Friday's 18th and Parkway in Raddison Hotel, 665–8443; 2nd and Lombard Streets, 625–8389; 4000 City Line Avenue, 878–7070. A big and fun place for the whole family for any day of the week from 11 A.M. till 1 A.M., and for cocktails at the huge bar till 2. The bistro-style menu includes ethnic fun foods, finger foods, salads, burgers, sandwiches, and entrees guaranteed to please any appetite and make you smile. Reservations for large parties only. (All major cards)

Three Threes 333 S. Smedley Street, 735–4010. A charming little restaurant on a charming little street. Lunch weekdays, dinner daily and Sunday brunch are pleasant and relaxed in this converted townhouse that recalls college days. Continental menu, featuring veal, chicken, seafood and pasta dishes. Reservations recommended. (AE,DC,MC,V)

Top of Centre Square 1500 Market Street, 563–9494. A modern restaurant and cocktail lounge that's eye-level with neighbor Billy Penn. Marvelous views of the city and City Hall. Lunch weekdays and dinner daily for traditional American food. A Stouffer's operation (as in Top of the 666s at Rockefeller Plaza, New York). Reservations suggested. (All major cards)

Treetops 210 W. Rittenhouse Square in The Rittenhouse, 546–9000. Wholesome American cuisine for breakfast, lunch and dinner in a casual, bright setting overlooking Rittenhouse Square. Fixed price dinner specials. Popular with the folks on the Square. (All major cards)

Triangle Tavern 10th and Reed Streets, 467–8683. Yet another of South Philadelphia's famous neighborhood bar-restaurants. No frills decor. Specialties are mussels, veal scalloppine, homemade pasta and pizza. Reasonably-priced dinner, except Sunday, from 4 P.M. to midnight; local entertainment on Friday and Saturday after 8:30 P.M. (No cards)

210 210 W. Rittenhouse Square in The Rittenhouse, 790–2534. An elegant setting overlooking Rittenhouse Square. Classic French and contemporary cuisine served to perfection. Worthy of a celebration on a special occasion. Reservations. (All major cards)

Under the Blue Moon 8042 Germantown Avenue, 247–1100. A refreshing and imaginative eatery in Chestnut Hill since 1977. Colorful batiks, tile and light wood decor. The international home-cooking menu changes often for dinner from 6 P.M. Tuesday to Saturday. Reservations suggested. (No cards)

Upstares at Varalli 1345 Locust Street, 546–4200. Upstairs at the corner of Broad and Locust Streets with a view directly to the Academy of Music and Shubert Theater. Wholesome homemade pasta and Northern Italian specialties in plentiful portions. Lunch except Sunday; dinner daily. (AE,DC,MC,V)

Valley Green Inn Valley Green Road and Wissahickon Creek, 247–1730. A quaint, picturesque 19th century inn, in one of the most beautiful settings in Philadelphia. (See Chapter 8.) Have lunch, before or after a walk in the woods, or come for dinner. Open daily and for Sunday brunch. Dine on the porch when weather permits. American country cuisine always features fresh fish, chicken and beef dishes. Everything is made from scratch, including the mayonnaise! A lovely place for family gatherings, leisurely romantics and private parties. (MC,V)

Victor Cafe 1303 Dickinson Street, 468–3040. If you like opera, you'll love this cafe in the heart of South Philadelphia, because opera is served with every course. The record library has 25,000 selections, give or take a few. The third generation of family owners serve delicious Italian dinners every evening. Reservations suggested. (All major cards)

Villa di Roma 936 S. 9th Street, 592–1295. This informal, earthy, family-style Italian restaurant-bar is smack-dab in the midst of the Italian Market. The menu covers the entire back wall and there are abundant chicken, veal and pasta choices. Portions are large; prices are small. Lunch except Sunday; dinner daily. Be prepared to wait, especially on Sunday. (No cards)

Waldorf Cafe 20th and Lombard Streets, 985–1836. A center city neighborhood eatery with a small bar and casual dining room that seats no more than 40. Everything is prepared fresh and presented attractively. Sinfully rich homemade desserts. Lunch weekdays; dinner daily. Reservations suggested. (All major cards)

Walt's King of Crabs 804 S. 2nd Street, 339–9124. Philadelphia's seafood lovers have made an institution of this casual, moderately priced restaurant and bar. Hard-shell crabs, clams, mussels, shrimp and lobsters are served to order. Daily 11 A.M. to midnight; Sunday 2 to 10 P.M. (No cards)

Warsaw Cafe 306 S. 16th Street, 546–0204. This casual, chic and small restaurant resembles a European cafe. The menu features Eastern European cuisine from Hungary, Poland, Russia and Germany, and it and changes regularly. Lunch weekdays; dinner except Sunday. Reservations suggested; not recommended for kids. (AE,DC,MC,V)

White Dog Cafe 3420 Sansom Street, 386–9224. Popular with the University of Pennsylvania crowd, Annenberg theater-goers, and folks from all over who enjoy the funky, casual decor and interesting seasonal menu with American cuisine. Fills the downstairs of two old rowhouses, plus a contemporary, airy addition and more seating on the lower level. A large, lively bar, too. Unusual dining and community-minded events are also appealing. Ask what's coming up soon. And stop by **The Black Cat** next door. Breakfast weekdays; dinner daily; a popular weekend brunch. Reservations. (AE,DC,MC,V)

White Nights 8558 Bustleton Avenue, 745–1890. Head to Northeast Philadelphia where most of Philadelphia's Russian immigrants have settled and join about 300 others for an evening of fun, feasting and merriment. The name recalls the bright evenings in Leningrad. Russian-Jewish-style dinner (fixed price feast or à la carte) is served Friday, Saturday and Sunday nights to large and small parties seated at banquet-style tables. The music is live, and the dancing is lively. Reservations a must on Saturdays, especially. L'chaim! (No cards)

Zocalo 3600 Lancaster Avenue, 895–0139. A University City crowd and those-in-the-know head to Zocalo (a "plaza") for its bright decor, Mexican accents and artwork, friendly staff, and traditional and contemporary Mexican cuisine. Several rowhouse rooms, a bar and patio allow for comfortable dining. Some popular items include grilled corn on the cob, sopes, tacos, tortillas and Mexican salad. Lunch weekdays; dinner daily. Reservations suggested. Salute! (AE,MC,V)

Asian-American Cuisine

Chinatown* is the home of dozens of Chinese restaurants that feature traditional Chinese cooking, Cantonese, Mandarin and Sechuan-style food. To name a few: **Don Wong Coffee Tea & Restaurant** at 1022 Race Street (574–9503) features duck, noodles, pastries and, of course, coffee and tea. **Harmony Chinese Vegetarian** is at 135 N. 9th Street (627–4520). Guess what they serve at **Joe's Peking Duck House** at 925 Race Street (922–3277). **Joy Tsin Lau** at 1026 Race Street (592–7228) is known for everything from traditional to unique Chinese cuisine as well as dim sum. **New Imperial Inn** at 142 N. 10th Street (627–2299) also serves authentic dim sum daily for lunch. **Ray's Coffee Shop** at 141 N. 9th Street (922–5122) cooks everything fresh to order with artistic presentation, bright surroundings, upscale music and, of course, exotic, freshly brewed coffees (at non-Chinatown prices). **Tang Yean** at 220 N. 10th Street (925–3993) serves Oriental health cooking. There's no beef, duck, lamb or pork. There's chicken, seafood and a Chinese-style soyburger along with very fresh vegetables.

Delicate Thai preparation influences the cooking at several Oriental restaurants. **Queen's Orchid** at 1029 Race Street (922–2715), **Siam Cuisine** at 925 Arch Street (922–7135) and **Thai Garden** at 101 N. 11th Street (629–9939) are among the more popular spots.

We've already mentioned **Susanna Foo** earlier in the chapter. Among other Chinese restaurants with loyal followings to other-than-Chinatown locations are **Long's Gourmet Chinese Cooking** at 2018 Hamilton Street near the Art Museum (496-9928), **Tang's**, a long-standing tradition at 429 South Street (928–0188), and the huge **Hai Tien** at 16th and Washington Avenue (732–8970), owned by three families from China, Thailand and Vietnam. For a real Asian-American adventure, don't miss the adjoining Asian Shopping Mall.

For traditional Japanese restaurants, go back and read about **Chiyo, Hikaru** and **Meiji-En** earlier in the chapter. Or try **Shogun** at 1009 Arch Street (592–8288).

With the influx of Southeast Asians to Philadelphia, Vietnamese restaurants have joined the scene and become equally appealing for their basic decor, friendly service, low prices and carefully prepared foods. Several popular restaurants are clustered in the area around the Italian Markets near 8th and 9th Streets and Washington Avenue. To name a few: **Saigon Restaurant** at 935 Washington Avenue (925-9656). **Tu Do** at 1030 S. 8th Street (829-9122). **Vinh Hoa Vietnamese Restaurant** at 746 Christian Street (925-0307). **Van's Garden** was a forerunner at 121 N. 11th Street (923-2438).

Strictly Kosher

These restaurants are certified Glatt Kosher. Call them for hours and additional information.

Jonathan's 130 S. 11th Street, 829-8101. Middle Eastern food at a New York style-deli. No dairy food, but you won't believe the cheese cake!

Maccabeam 128 S. 12th Street, 922-5922. Another center city storefront restaurant for Glatt Kosher lunch and dinner. Traditional Middle Eastern and Israeli specialties enjoyed by an international clientele.

New York Delicatessen 2028 Chestnut Street, 496-1555. Cold cuts and kosher cooking blessed by a Rabbi for informal dining.

European Dairy Restaurant is described earlier in the chapter.

Dining with Heart

The following restaurants offer menu items that are lower in overall fat, cholesterol and salt. The heart-healthy choices have been planned in conjunction with the cardiology staff and dieticians at Thomas Jefferson University Hospital in center city.

Carolina's. Catalina. The Commissary. Day by Day, 2101 Sansom Street, 564-5540. DiLullo Centro. Fountain Restaurant at the Four Seasons. Jake's. La Buca. La  Truffe. Magnolia Cafe. Meiji-En. Sansom Street Oyster House. 1701 Cafe. Susanna Foo. Philadelphia Fish & Co., 207 Chestnut Street, 625-8605.

Coffee Break Time. Tea Time.

The English custom has caught on in Philadelphia. Here's where you can take a break in the afternoon for a leisurely cup of tea with traditional tea sandwiches, biscuits and scones. It's a good idea to call ahead for reservations (see Chapter 20 for Center City and Historic Philadelphia hotels).

The Swann Lounge at the Four Seasons Hotel. The lobby lounge at the Ritz-Carlton Hotel. The Barrymore Room at the Hotel Atop the Bellevue. Cassatt Tea Room and Lounge at The Rittenhouse Hotel. The lobby lounge at the Omni Hotel at Independence National Historical Park (Wednesday through Saturday).

For those with a sweet tooth, have tea or coffee with pastries as good to eat as they look, at any of the following center city locales. A few of them are described earlier in this chapter.

Cafe Brickworks 119 S. 19th Street, 977–9396.

Capriccio 1701 Locust Street in the Warwick, 735–9797.

The Commissary 1710 Sansom Street, 569–2240.

Espresso Bar at Borders, 1727 Walnut Street, 568–7400.

Jamison's Bakery and Cafe 1220 Pine Street, 735–2240.

More Than Just Ice Cream 1141 Pine Street, 574–0586.

Pink Rose Pastry Shop 4th and Bainbridge Streets, 592–0565.

Rindelaub's 128 S. 18th Street, 563–3993.

I Scream. You Scream.
We All Scream for Ice Cream.
Or Frozen Yogurt.

Here are a few places to stop for a frozen treat.

Bassetts (a Philadelphia original since 1861) at Reading Terminal. **Capriccio** at the Warwick for Ben & Jerry's, Vermont's finest all natural. **Gelateria** at 265 S. 17th Street for a daily selection of homemade gelato. **Haagen Daz** at 242 South Street, 30th Street Station and Franklin Mills for renowned ice cream, sorbets, cream floats and sundaes. **Hillary's** at Front and Chestnut Streets, 437

South Street, 1929 Chestnut Street and 34th and Walnut Streets in the Shops at Penn for dozens of exotic and traditional flavors, with a myriad of toppings, to eat in or take out. **Scoop de Ville** at Maron Candies, 107 S. 18th Street, where you can create your own ice cream or frozen yogurt flavor. **TCBY** at 4040 Locust Street in The Warehouse on the Penn campus, offering six flavors daily of "the country's best yogurt." **Thinny DeLites** at 1511 Spruce Street for four flavors daily of a no fat, no cholesterol cone, sandwich or dish treat to eat in or take out.

Dinner Theaters

These dinner theaters are in town or within an hour's drive of center city Philadelphia. They offer a hearty meal and popular shows. Call for a schedule of performances, reservations and directions.

Cavanaugh's Restaurant Help solve a murder-mystery while enjoying a four-course chicken, fish or steak dinner. 39th and Sansom Streets (662–5000).

Huntingdon Valley Dinner Theater Broadway musicals and comedies. 2633 Philmont Avenue, Huntingdon Valley, PA (947–6000).

Lily Langtry's Las Vegas-style musical revues. Sheraton Valley Forge Hotel, King of Prussia, PA (337–LILY).

Murder at Moriarty's Match wits with Sherlock Holmes over a four-course Saturday dinner. 1116 Walnut Street (935–3950).

Mystery Cafe Dinner Theater Gourmet dinner while you solve a mystery-comedy. 120 Lombard Street at Bistro Romano in Society Hill (238–1313).

Riverfront Dinner Theater Live Broadway musicals with a full-course dinner. Delaware River at Poplar Street (925–7000).

Upstairs at Torano's Musical hits with an Italian buffet. 11th and Christian Streets (923–4440).

Cabaret Theater. Comedy Clubs. A Night Club.

Bank Street Comedy Club 31 Bank Street in Old City, BANK–ST–1. Headliners from around-the country and local clowns, too. Part nightclub, part theater, good entertainment at low prices.

Chestnut Cabaret 3801 Chestnut Street, 382–1201. Seating for at least 400 for live entertainment a few nights a week. Some big names come here.

Comedy Works 126 Chestnut Street atop the Middle East Restaurant, WACKY–97. Philadelphia's oldest, largest and longest running comedy club. Stop in for laughs Wednesday (open stage), Thursday (local showcase), Friday and Saturday (America's top comedy talents).

Funny Bone 221 South Street, 440–9670. Monday is "open night" for 10-minute routines from local comics; comedians with a national reputation are on stage every other night.

Palumbo's 824 Catharine Street, 627–7272. The South Philadelphia night club where many well-known entertainers got their start. Frankie Avalon, Joey Bishop and David Brenner will confirm this.

All That Jazz. Blues. Folk. Or Rock. A Few of the Hot Spots.

The following restaurants and night spots have live musical entertainment. Some are ongoing gigs; others change nightly or weekly. Call them to learn who's scheduled. Some are described earlier in the chapter. Reservations are always a good idea.

Borgia Cafe 406 S. 2nd Street, 574–0414. Genuine 1920s French cabaret posters add to the downstairs bistro atmosphere with nightly live jazz and vocalists.

Brass Rail 3942 Chestnut Street, 222–4250. Local and New York jazz talent on Saturday nights; jam sessions on Monday nights.

Callowhill Street 1836 Callowhill Street, 557–6922. Live jazz on Thursday, Friday and Saturday nights.

Khyber Pass Pub 56 S. 2nd Street, 440–9683.

Liberties 705 N. 2nd Street, 238–0660. Live jazz Friday and Saturday nights.

North Star Bar 27th and Poplar Streets, 235–7827.

Ortlieb's Jazz Haus 847 N. 3rd Street, 922–1035. An unpretentious neighborhood bar in Northern Liberties that was the 1850s house of the Ortlieb's brewing family. Regular jam sessions as well as top talents appearing nightly. Cajun-Continental fare.

Roxxi 602 S. 2nd Street, 925–7999. Nightly entertainment followed by dance music.

1701 Cafe 1701 Locust Street in The Warwick, 545–4655.

Zanzibar Blue 301–305 S. 11th Street, 829–0300. Live jazz nightly, after-work jazz fests and a Sunday jazz brunch at this popular restaurant and jazz cafe.

Gotta Dance

Put on your dancing shoes. Get out your dance card. Head for the Barrymore Room at the Hotel Atop the Bellevue (sophisticated swing, big band sound). Monte Carlo Living Room. Polo Bay Club at the Warwick Hotel. Bobby Sox and Tooters at Market Place East, 8th and Market Streets. The Aztec Club (and entertainment complex) at 939 N. Delaware Avenue. Katmandu (a huge dance club, entertainment complex, bar and restaurant) on Pier 25 at Delaware Avenue and Willow Street. White Nights in Northeast Philadelphia.

Open 24 Hours

The following establishments serve all day and all night. Diner on the Square. Little Pete's at 17th and Chancellor Streets. Melrose Diner. Pat's King of Steaks. Good night! Good morning!

New Restaurants.
And Restaurants I've Missed.

Make your own listing in this space.

Chapter 19.
Calendar of Annual Events.

There are hundreds, maybe even thousands, of great events that take place in Philadelphia every year. After all, we've had over 300 years of experience at making things happen.

It's impossible to list all of them, so a few are highlighted in this chapter.

If your favorite event isn't here, write to me and we'll try to include it in the next edition of "A Guide's Guide to Philadelphia."

When you see an asterisk (*), that place or event is described elsewhere in the book. Look in the Index for the exact pages so you can get additional information.

Keep this guide handy, and refer to it as often as possible so you won't miss something special and have to wait a year for it to come around again.

January

New Year's Day is January 1.

There's at least one parade a month in Philadelphia, but Philadelphia is best known for its all-day, world-famous **New Year's Day Mummers Parade***. The magnificently costumed string bands, comics and fancy division perform the famous Mummers strut for two-and-a-half miles along South Broad Street from Snyder Avenue to City Hall. They start at 7:45 A.M. and continue till after dark. Wear warm clothing. (The rain date is the following Saturday.)

City and state tributes are held around January 15 to honor the late **Dr. Martin Luther King, Jr.** The third Monday of the month is a holiday.

Benjamin Franklin's Birthday is celebrated the weekend closest to January 17 with "Ben's Birthday Bash" festivities at the Franklin Institute Science Museum (448–1200). Call for information.

Edgar Allan Poe's 1809 birthdate is celebrated at the National Historic Site* on the weekend closest to January 19 and each Saturday this month. Call 597–8780 for the schedule.

The annual **Philadelphia International Auto Show** exhibits hundreds of new imported and American cars at the Philadelphia Civic Center (823–5600 or 823–7400) along with family entertainment and guest celebrities.

It's suddenly summer when you're at the annual indoor **Philadelphia Boat Show** at the Civic Center. This is a one-week exhibit of the latest in sailboats, yachts, power boats and boating accessories. More than 500 boats are displayed, making this one of the country's biggest boat shows.

The annual **Philadelphia Sportsmen's and Recreational Vehicle Show** is also at the Civic Center. It's your chance to see the latest in sports and equipment, camping, vacation and travel gear.

February

Look for announcements of activities to commemorate **Black History Month**. Or call the Afro-American Historical and Cultural Museum (574–0380) for a schedule of lectures, tours, visual and performing arts.

Don't forget your sweetheart on **St. Valentine's Day,** February 14.

Presidents' Day is celebrated the third Monday of the month, honoring the birthdays of **Abraham Lincoln** (February 12) and **George Washington** (February 22).

Presidential Jazz Weekend brings national and local performers to stages all over Philadelphia for a four-day-and-night immersion of music. Call the Presidential Jazz Hotline (636–4464) or the Philadelphia Visitors Center (636–1666) for a schedule of events.

The men's **U.S. Pro Indoor Tennis Championships*** are at the Spectrum for a week in February. Top players from around the world are here to compete in singles and doubles. A children's clinic is on Saturday morning. Call 947–2530 for dates and details.

If you're looking for a new decor or ideas for remodeling, stop by the Civic Center for the week-long **Philadelphia Home Show**. See the latest in tools and plans to make your home your castle.

The **Ice Capades** dazzles viewers of all ages at the Spectrum in a week of afternoon and evening shows. Call 336–3600 for time and price details.

The **Chinese New Year** brings crowds to Chinatown* for parades and special events that herald the start of the new year this month or next. You can also celebrate with a 10-course fixed-price Chinese New Year's Banquet prepared by chefs visiting from China and served at the Chinese Cultural Center. Call 923–6767 for details.

Ash Wednesday is February 24, 1993; February 16, 1994.

March

The Civic Center becomes a miraculous indoor garden wonderland for one week in March. Don't miss the thousands of flowers, plants and shrubs that are part of the **Philadelphia Flower Show**. Tickets can be purchased in advance at the Pennsylvania Horticultural Society* (625–8253) or at the door of the Civic Center (823–7400).

One of Philadelphia's favorite parades honor **St. Patrick's Day**, on the Sunday afternoon closest to St. Patrick's Day (March 17). The parade starts on the Benjamin Franklin Parkway at 20th Street, heads east to 17th, south onto 17th to Chestnut Street, and then east on Chestnut to Independence Hall. Wear green!

Women's History Month is a national event honoring women at home and at work. Citywide celebrations occur, highlighted by a day-long annual Women's Festival at the Bourse, 5th and Market Streets. Call the Mayor's Commission for Women (686–1570) for details.

Poetry Week is observed at various locations with literary events under the auspices of the American Poetry Center (546–1510). Call 800-ALL-MUSE, the 24-hour literary hotline, for information.

Ash Wednesday is March 4, 1992.

April

Daylight Saving Time arrives the first Sunday in April. Spring forward, fall back; lose an hour's sleep.

Good Friday is April 17, 1992; April 9, 1993; April 1, 1994. **Easter Sunday** is April 19, 1992; April 11, 1993; April 3, 1994. Philadelphia's annual **Easter Promenade** starts at noon at Rittenhouse Square, 18th and Walnut Streets.

Palm Sunday is the week preceding Easter Sunday. The Easter bunny makes an annual visit to Lore's Chocolates, 34 S. 7th Street (a block west of Independence Hall), where fresh candy is made and sold daily. On this one day a year, you can take a short tour of the factory and see Easter eggs get chocolate coated.

The Pysanky Expo at the Ukrainian Heritage Studies Center* features eggs of another kind. Hand-decorated Ukrainian eggs and fanciful eggs from around the world are shown, along with demonstrations, gifts for sale and ethnic foods. Call 885–2360 for additional information.

World-renowned chefs, sommeliers and cookbook writers visit Philadelphia for four days this month to meet, lecture, demonstrate and prepare meals for lucky local folks. It's called **The Book and the Cook**. If you would like to watch, have your favorite cookbook signed by its author, or partake in a gastronomic experience for breakfast, brunch, lunch, dinner, afternoon tea or wine-tasting, call the Philadelphia Visitors Center (636–1666) for details. Or plan to attend the two-day Book and the Cook Fair at Memorial Hall in Fairmount Park.

The annual **Philadelphia Antiques Show and Sale** has a five-day run this month. A benefit for the Hospital of the University of Pennsylvania, it's reputed to be the best show of its kind in the country. Guided tours, lectures and other special events are scheduled in conjunction with the show at the 103rd Engineers Armory, 33rd and Market Streets. For details, call 526-0850, or 387–3500 during the show.

If you missed the Mummers Parade in January, you

have a chance to see and hear the string bands this month at the **Mummers String Bands "Show of Shows."** More than a dozen bands don their New Year's finery for evening and matinee performances at the Civic Center. Tickets are sold by the local string bands or at the Civic Center box office (823–7400) prior to each performance.

The **Phillies*** begin their season at Veterans Stadium this month, and play continues till October.

The **Penn Relays*** are traditionally the last weekend of the month. The world's oldest and largest scholastic, collegiate and amateur track meet is at Franklin Field, 33rd and Spruce Streets. For information, call 898–6151.

Philadelphia's oldest (since the early 1920s) equestrian parade is the last Sunday of the month in the Valley Green section of Fairmount Park. The **Wissahickon Day Parade** starts at noon at Northwestern Avenue and continues on Forbidden Drive along the Wissahickon Creek past the Valley Green Inn. Hundreds of horses and carriages participate with English and Western riders. A carriage and horse competition precedes the parade starting at 10:30 A.M. at Harpers Meadow. For additional information, call 482–8130 or 828–7909, or Fairmount Park's recreation division at 685–0052.

The first weekend of **Friends Hospital Garden Days** (831–4772) is the last weekend of April. Feast your eyes on brilliant azaleas in more than 40 varieties. If you miss nature's show in April, you can catch it the first two weekends in May.

The **St. Walpurgis Night Festival** ushers in spring on a Saturday night of April at the American-Swedish Historical Museum*. There's a bonfire, folk dancing, refreshments and lots of fun.

Three days of singing, dancing, arts, crafts, exhibits and foods from around the world are at the biennial (in "even" years) **Philadelphia Folk Fair**. No less than 50 nationalities and all of Philadelphia's ethnic groups are represented under one roof at the Civic Center. For information, call the Fair's founder, Nationalities Service Center*, at 893–8400.

May

Law Day is May 1. The local Bar Association has special programs. Naturalization ceremonies take place at the United States Courthouse*.

Israel's Independence Day is celebrated with a Sunday parade down Chestnut Street. The route leads to Independence Mall where there's a day-long bazaar, entertainment and festivities. For details, call 922–7222.

Art exhibitions, concerts, parades, theater, films, dance and folklore events are all scheduled at venues throughout the city during the 12-day **Africamericas Festival** at the beginning of May. There are activities for adults and children; many are free. Call 790–9707 for dates, details and ticket information.

An **Azalea Day Festival** ushers in spring the first Sunday of May at the four-acre Azalea Garden* in Fairmount Park just west of the Art Museum. Thousands of multicolored azalea plants, rhododendrons, dogwoods, and spring bulbs bloom. **Friends Hospital* Garden Days** continue the first two weekends of May. Scores of varieties of azaleas cover more than 20 acres of the hospital's 99-acre grounds in Northeast Philadelphia. Call 831–4772 for the hours and group tour reservations.

Mother's Day is the second Sunday in May.

Later this month, on a Wednesday and Thursday, thousands of Philadelphians will flock to the **Rittenhouse Square Flower Market** to buy plants, flowers, lemon sticks, pizza, pita sandwiches and other goodies.

Philadelphia Open House is 17 days of tours by bus, by boat or walking to neighborhoods, private houses, gardens, historic and contemporary sites sponsored by the Friends of Independence National Historical Park. Call 928–1188 for details and don't miss this once-a-year opportunity to visit attractions that aren't usually open to the public.

Armed Forces Weekend is the third Saturday and Sunday in May at Penn's Landing. All branches of the military are represented with exhibits, demonstrations, aircraft and ships. Call 923–4992 for details.

The annual **Police Department Open House** is a Saturday of festivities, exhibits and tours at the Police Administration Building*. For details, call 686–3380.

Manayunk* Canal Day includes a parade and all-day festival the third Saturday of May. Watch for newspaper announcements, or call 483–7530.

May is for music. **Mozart on the Square** is a two-week festival that pays tribute to Wolfgang Amadeus Mozart with concerts at various locations around Rittenhouse Square. Several of them are free. Call 988–9830 and see Chapter 10 for details.

The **Devon Horse Show** opens at the end of the month at the Devon Fair Grounds on Lancaster Pike in Devon, PA. Some 2,000 horses and riders appear in one of the country's largest and finest outdoor shows. The nine-day event also includes an enormous country fair. Call 964–0550 for dates and details, and 688–2554 for tickets.

Memorial Day is the last Monday in May.
An observance is held aboard the U.S.S. Olympia*. Call 922-1898 for information.
Jambalaya Jam is the holiday weekend jazz celebration at Penn's Landing when the music and food of New Orleans come to the waterfront. It's Mardi Gras in May in Philadelphia! Call the Visitors Center (636–1666) for schedule and ticket information.
Old City* restaurants celebrate on Sunday and Monday of the holiday weekend with outdoor food vendors and street entertainers along the 100 block of Chestnut Street.

The **Philadelphia International Theatre Festival for Children*** presents indoor and outdoor performances for five days around Memorial Day at Annenberg Center. See Chapter 15 for additional information and be sure to take advantage of this great opportunity for youngsters.

Look for announcements about local fairs and festivals.

Elfreth's Alley Day* is celebrated the first weekend in June when dwellers on the nation's oldest continuously occupied residential street hold Open House. Call 574–0560 for hours and admission charges.

The **Head House* Crafts Fair** opens in mid-June at 2nd and Pine Streets and continues on Saturdays from noon to midnight and Sundays from noon to 6 P.M. through Labor Day weekend. Forty craftsmen demonstrate their skills in pottery, jewelry, batik, glassware, photography, prints, metal sculpture, leatherware, candles and woven goods. For more information, call 790–0782.

The annual Mid-summer Fair is a Saturday in June at the **American-Swedish Historical Museum***. A festival complete with maypole, folk dancing and authentic Swedish sandwiches celebrates Sweden's mid-summer day when the sun shines for 24 hours.

The **Rittenhouse Square Fine Arts Annual** at 18th and Walnut Streets is where over a hundred local artists display thousands of works on Wednesday to Sunday, 10 A.M. to 6 P.M., the first week of June. Call 634–5060 for additional information.

Stop by the **Visitors Center** at 16th and Kennedy Boulevard and pick up a schedule of free entertainment planned for popular locations during the summer. **Phillyfest** is hour-long noontime live entertainment weekdays mid-June through August adjacent to the Visitors Center at John F. Kennedy Plaza, and Wednesdays and Fridays at Commerce Square, 21st and Market Streets. Be there to enjoy jazz, big band and popular music, dance, sports celebrities and competitions and more. Call 636–1666 for a schedule.

Flag Day (June 14) is celebrated with a parade, special observances and ceremonies at the Betsy Ross House*.

Old Newsboys' Day brings celebrities and bands together on center city corners to raise funds for handicapped children.

Father's Day is the third Sunday in June.
More than 100 professional bicyclists from around the world compete in the annual **CoreStates U.S. Pro Cycling Championship**. Start-off for the 156-mile race is at 9 A.M. in front of the Philadelphia Museum of Art. The race takes a 14-mile route along Kelly Drive to "The Wall" in Manayunk. When you're not watching the cyclists whiz by, catch the Cycling Expo of biking equipment and clothing along the Benjamin Franklin Parkway. The activity lasts till mid-afternoon and it's exciting from wherever you eye the riders. Call 247–9136 for more details, and look for announcements in the local newspapers.

Mann Music Center* invites you outdoors for the summer season with the Philadelphia Orchestra. **Concerts by Candlelight*** open their season at **Laurel Hill** in East Fairmount Park. You're also invited to popular Dockside Concerts and Big Bands Live at **Penn's Landing***, and string band concerts at the **Mummers Museum***.

The **Mellon Jazz Festival*** brings jazz performers of world renown to Philadelphia for concerts at popular center city locales. Some of the events are free; others require tickets. Watch the local newspapers for dates and details, or call 561–5060.

The **Department of Recreation*** gears up for another full summer. Day camps are open, swimming pools are filled, play streets are closed to traffic and tennis lessons are underway.

The circus comes to town! Don't miss the **Ringling Bros. and Barnum & Bailey Circus** when they appear at the Spectrum (336–3600) in the greatest show on earth.

Visit the majestic ships and partake in the lively and free annual **Harbor Festival at Penn's Landing** (923–4992) the last Thursday to Sunday of the month. Don't miss the summertime fun down by the riverside.

July

Philadelphia's Freedom Festival celebrates America's independence in the city where it all began. Daytime and evening events in the days surrounding July 4 include a Great American Hot-Air Balloon Race, a Summer Mummers Parade, food festivals, concerts, an Independence Day Parade and, of course, fireworks. The traditional **Fourth of July** ceremony and pageantry gets underway at 10 A.M. at Independence Hall. The newspapers and the Visitors Center (636–1666) will keep you abreast of the schedules.

Philadelphia's French restaurants have their celebrations on **Bastille Day,** July 14.

Free and almost-free entertainment is in full swing for the entire summer. **Pop concerts** are at neighborhood parks and squares. **Big Band Live** concerts are at Penn's Landing. **Robin Hood Dell East*** joins the outdoor concert season. **International Folk Dancing*** is on Tuesday evenings at the Art Museum Terrace. The **Phillyfest*** of free entertainment continues weekdays at noon at John F. Kennedy Plaza, 16th Street and Kennedy Boulevard, and Wednesdays and Fridays at Commerce Square, 20th and Market Streets.

The annual **RiverBlues Festival** is the last weekend of the month at Penn's Landing. Performers come from around the country to share their music from the soul while restauranteurs serve up soul food. Call 636–1666 for ticket and schedule information.

Watch the **Schuylkill Regattas*** from the river's edge as college teams and crews compete in the summer.

You haven't been to Veterans Stadium to see the **Phillies** yet? Shame on you. Fireworks light up the sky following the game closest to July 4th. It's one of the season's most popular games.

August

Have you been to the **Robin Hood Dell East** or **Mann Music Center**? Did you rent a boat? Have you been to the **Head House Crafts Fair**? Have you taken a carriage ride through historic Philadelphia? Have you been to a concert or festival at Penn's Landing? Who says there isn't much to do in the summer in Philadelphia?

The annual **Philadelphia Folk Festival** is held rain or shine the weekend before Labor Day weekend at Old Pool Farm near Schwenksville, PA in Montgomery County. Call the Philadelphia Folksong Society* (242–0150 or 800–422–FOLK) for dates and details.

Events take place on the ground and in the air at the annual **Willow Grove Air Show**. Call the Willow Grove Naval Air Station* (443–1776) for the weekend dates. If you like airplanes, you'll love this event.

The Fairmount Park Commission sponsors an annual **"Pictures in the Park"** photography contest. Amateur shutterbugs of all ages can submit their favorite snapshots. (The judges are partial to those that relate to Fairmount Park.) Winners are exhibited next month during the Fairmount Fall Festival and several prizes are awarded. Call the Fairmount Park Commission (685–0052) for details, or pick up an entry form at the Visitors Center, 16th and Kennedy Boulevard.

September

Labor Day is the first Monday of the month.

The Old City Restaurant Association sponsors another **Old City Happening** on Labor Day and the Sunday before. Come down to the 100 block of Chestnut Street for international foods, entertainment and flea markets.

The **Hero Show** is the first weekend after Labor Day at the Civic Center. Top stars perform, there are motorcycle and firefighting feats and musical entertainment. Tickets are available at Room 486 City Hall and at police stations and firehouses. Proceeds are for scholarships for children of police and firemen who were permanently injured or who lost their lives in the line of duty. For information, call 686–3400.

The annual **Fairmount Fall Festival** features a few weeks of recreational and cultural activities in Fairmount Park and along the Benjamin Franklin Parkway. Call the Fairmount Park Commission (685–0052) for a schedule, or watch for newspaper announcements.

The festival welcomes fall with the Pennsylvania Horticultural Society's annual weekend **Harvest Show** at the Horticultural Center*.

Memorial Hall, 42nd Street and Parkside Avenue, is the showplace for the winning entries in the "Pictures in the Park" photography contest, which was held in August.

The **In-Water Boat Show** sails in for four days to the 10-acre boat basin at Penn's Landing with all types of pleasure craft and the latest in marine equipment. Call 449–9910 or 923–4992 for details.

The **Jewish New Year** is observed September 28, 1992; September 16, 1993; September 6, 1994. The **Day of Atonement** is observed September 25, 1993; September 15, 1994.

The **Germantown Hospital Equestrian Festival** featuring the American Gold Cup* and Grand Prix Horse Jumping Competition is a three-day weekend this month at the Devon Horse Show Grounds. There's a Fall Flower Festival as well. Tickets are available at the gate, or call 438–8383 for details.

The **Von Steuben Day Parade** in center city on the last Saturday of the month honors the German General who trained American patriots at Valley Forge. The **Puerto Rican Day Parade** the following day honors Philadelphia's Puerto Rican residents.

Football season gets underway with the **Eagles*** at Veterans Stadium and local college games.

October

The Jewish **Day of Atonement** is observed October 7, 1992.

Columbus Day is celebrated the second Monday of the month. There's always a parade on the closest Sunday and a Columbus Day Festival at Penn's Landing that follows. The Sunday **Pulaski Day Parade** on the Parkway and Chestnut Street in center city pays tribute to a Polish patriot's contributions to America. Call the Visitors Center (636-1666) or watch for newspaper announcements.

An annual **Ukrainian October Fest** is the first Sunday of the month at the Ukrainian Heritage Studies Center*. Exhibits, crafts demonstrations by native artisans, and ethnic foods are on the agenda. Call 885-2360 for additional information.

The **Fairmount Fall Festival** continues (see September). **Fall foliage** is magnificent this month at Morris Arboretum's* Fall Festival, in Fairmount Park, Valley Forge, Bucks County and anywhere you travel in the region.

Super Sunday is the second Sunday of the month. It's the original of the super block parties, started in 1970 and sponsored by the cultural institutions along the Benjamin Franklin Parkway. Exhibits, games, rides, crafts, entertainment, food and a flea market line the Parkway from Logan Circle to Eakins Oval in front of the Art Museum from 11 A.M. to 5 P.M. Call 665-1050 for additional information. See you there.

Chester County Day features tours that cover some 45 historic homes and landmarks (see Chapter 17).

The 1777 **Battle of Germantown** is re-enacted, along with a country fair, crafts and flea market, on the grounds of historic Cliveden*.

The ice hockey season opens with the **Flyers*** at the

Spectrum. The basketball season opens with the **76ers*** at the Spectrum. (The basketball floor is placed on top of the ice.) The Schuylkill and its shores are crammed on the Saturday of the annual **Thomas Eakins Regatta**. More than a thousand students participate from colleges across the country.

William Penn's Birthday is October 24. Philadelphia's founder is honored with special events and programs. There's a party at Pennsbury Manor*. Call the Visitors Center (636–1666) or watch the newspapers for details.

City firehouses hold Open House during **Fire Prevention Week** (the week including October 9). It's also the time to plan a fire drill at home and at the office.

Witches and goblins appear later this month (October 31) to celebrate **Halloween**. This is a fun time to visit the Italian Markets* and pick out a giant pumpkin to carve. There are hundreds of them at 9th Street and Washington Avenue. Haunted houses are open to daring visitors. Put on a costume and take a Halloween tour of Laurel Hill Cemetery*. See (the 1925 silent film) and hear (on the Curtis organ) "Phantom of the Opera" at Irvine Auditorium*. Watch for newspaper announcements. Don't get spooked!

The last Sunday night in October is when we return to **Eastern Standard Time**. Pick up that hour's sleep you lost in April.

Election Day is the first Tuesday after the first Monday of the month. Be sure to vote.

Veterans Day is November 11.

Old Fort Mifflin* is under siege again as 400 "soldiers" in Revolutionary War dress re-enact the battle and spend a weekend demonstrating colonial military games and camp life.

The annual **Philadelphia Craft Show** draws thousands to the Philadelphia Civic Center over four days to see the ceramics, jewelry, quilts, woodwork, clothing and weaving of 100 juried craftspeople from around the country. Call the Visitors Center (636–1666) or the Craft Show office (787–5448) for details.

The **Bach Festival** of Philadelphia* is underway. Call 247–BACH if you want to be part of this annual musical celebration.

Thanksgiving Day is the fourth Thursday of the month. Thousands of marchers parade down Market Street to 15th and then west on the Benjamin Franklin Parkway for the annual Thanksgiving Day Parade. There are bands, colorful floats and famous personalities. It's always fun to see Santa Claus arrive in Philadelphia (at the Art Museum around noon) for the holiday season. And it's more fun to be at the parade than to watch it on television.

And if it's Thanksgiving, it's **Tinkertoy Time** at the Franklin Institute Science Museum. Join the extravaganza for three days after Thanksgiving when the Benjamin Franklin National Memorial is the site of some major tinkering.

December

The midshipmen and cadets are in Philadelphia on the first Saturday of December for the **Army-Navy Football Classic** held each year at Veterans Stadium. Call 636–3477 for additional information.

For basketball* fans, the **Big Five** (LaSalle, St. Joseph's, Temple, University of Pennsylvania, Villanova) season starts with games at their respective stadiums.

Disney's World on Ice makes its appearance at the Spectrum the last week of the year. This spectacle is fun for the whole family. Call 336–3600 for dates and details.

This is also a special month for dog lovers. The Kennel Club of Philadelphia holds its annual **Dog Show** at the Civic Center. It's one of the few benched dog shows in the country where the participants can be admired close-up, and almost 3,000 animals will be there. Call 674–4532 or 823–7400 for the date and ticket information.

The Pennsylvania Ballet* returns to the Academy of Music every year during the winter vacation with the ever-popular **"Nutcracker."**

A 25-foot Menorah glows with a new light for each of the eight nights of **Hanukah**. It's at Independence Mall on Market Street across from the Liberty Bell Pavilion. The first night (December 20, 1992; December 9, 1993) is celebrated with music and latkes at sundown.

Christmas is big in Philadelphia. The holiday season starts early in the month with tree-lighting ceremonies and choral singing at City Hall, Rittenhouse Square and several other well-publicized locations.

The annual **Lucia Fest** takes place at both Old Swedes' Church* and the American-Swedish Historical Museum*. A candlelight procession on the first or second weekend of the month calls for participants dressed as a queen, page boys, elves, fairies and star boys. Booths display and sell Swedish crafts and foods following the traditional holiday season welcome.

The Fairmount Park Houses are splendid with their holiday finery. Special **Park House Christmas Tours** by trolley-bus are scheduled the first weekend of the month. Call the Art Museum's Park House guides (787-5449) for details.

Ebenezer Maxwell Mansion* hosts a Dickens Christmas Party in the Victorian spirit. All of Germantown is aglow when you take the **Holiday House Tours of Historic Germantown.** Call Cliveden* for details.

Longwood Gardens* is resplendent with lighted and decorated outdoor trees and thousands of poinsettias and Christmas flowers. A Holiday Greens Sale and Yule Fest are celebrated at **John Bartram's House and Garden*.**

A **live nativity scene** is in the yard at Old First Reformed Church*. The **Philadelphia Zoo*** (243-1100) celebrates both Hanukah and Christmas, too.

Philadelphia's major **department stores** go all out with entertainment. Strawbridge and Clothier recreates 26 scenes from Dickens' "A Christmas Carol." A Christmas Show with dancing fountains, animated characters and a tree with 100,000 lights draws hundreds of wide-eyed spectators to the grand court of John Wanamaker every day from mid-November through December. Mr. and Mrs. Claus are available for consultation.

The **Enchanted Colonial Village** comes to life in nine almost life-size animated scenes. Thanks to the Atwater Kent Museum*, you can revisit the refurbished magical village as it appeared in the old Lit Brothers Department Store three decades ago. Walk through the Enchanted Colonial Village any day this month (except Christmas) at Market Place East, on Market Street between 7th and 8th. Call 629-0222 for additional information.

General George Washington and his troops crossed the Delaware river on December 25, 1776 to defeat the British at Trenton. The historic trip is re-enacted on Christmas Day at **Washington Crossing Historic Park*.**

Kwanzaa is a week-long festival starting the day after Christmas and celebrated by many African-Americans. There's a parade and a variety of cultural happenings. Call the Afro-American Historical and Cultural Museum* (574-0380) for a schedule.

Merry Christmas! Happy New Year!

Chapter 20.
Hotels and Camping Out.

There are hotels and hostelries offering all kinds of accommodations for overnight visitors in Philadelphia. They range from the most luxurious to those appealing to the most budget-minded. The number of luxury hotels in center city has proliferated in just the past few years, along with the addition of some charming inns that dot the historic area. Bed and breakfasts are another popular alternative.

The following list includes features that are unique to each of these hotels. They are categorized according to their location. The AAA and Mobil ratings are current with publication of this book. We've noted the hotels with top ratings. In fact, some of the hotels are too new to be rated.

If you're planning a convention or a class trip, most of Philadelphia's hotels will provide group rates. Many have Vacation Packages and Weekend Plans. If you're traveling with youngsters, most hotels have special family plans for you, too.

For more information, visit or write to the Philadelphia Convention and Visitors Bureau*, 1525 John F. Kennedy Boulevard, Phila., PA 19102. Or see your travel agent.

Center City

These hotels are in the heart of Philadelphia. They're close to the cultural attractions on the Avenue of the Arts (Broad Street) and the Benjamin Franklin Parkway. They're a few minutes from the historic area. They're approximately three miles north of the sports complex and six miles from Philadelphia International Airport.

THE BARCLAY 237 S. 18th Street at Rittenhouse Square East, Philadelphia, PA 19103 (545–0300 or 800–421–6662). 244 rooms and suites (most with a refrigerator and some with 4-poster and canopied beds) in early American style. Posh but low key; facing Rittenhouse Square, near galleries and fine shops. Le Beau Lieu Restaurant and a cozy piano cocktail lounge. Valet parking.

HOTEL ATOP THE BELLEVUE 1415 Chancellor Court (Broad and Walnut Streets), Phila., PA 19102 (893–1776 or 800–222–0939). A grand European-style hotel from 1904 that's elegantly restored with 170 guest rooms and all modern amenities. The hotel occupies the top 7 floors around a skylit atrium and above 11 floors of offices and 3 floors of some of the most exclusive shops in Philadelphia. Member Preferred Hotels and Historic Hotels of America; AAA 4-Diamond. The Sporting Club is state-of-the-art. The exquisite Barrymore Room for afternoon tea and light fare, cocktails in the handsome Philadelphia Library Lounge, and classic French and Continental cuisine in the formal Founders. Also site of the Palm Restaurant and The Broadway deli (see Chapter 18).

FOUR SEASONS HOTEL One Logan Square, 18th Street and Benjamin Franklin Parkway, Phila., PA 19103 (963–1500 or 800–332–442). 375 luxury rooms and suites; 8-story world-class hotel with fine dining at the Fountain Restaurant and Swan Cafe overlooking Logan Circle. Careful attention to personal service, a concierge, spa and indoor pool. The only AAA 5-Diamond hotel in Pennsylvania and awarded 4 stars by Mobil Travel Guide.

HERSHEY PHILADELPHIA HOTEL Broad and Locust Streets, Phila., PA 19107 (893–1600 or 800–HERSHEY). 425 rooms; 25-story transient and convention hotel with ballrooms, meeting rooms, a 5-story atrium lobby, indoor pool, racquetball and health spa. Top 3 floors are exclusive rooms and suites with concierge service and access to executive business center. Cafe Academie for dining, and a cozy bar.
Note: Renamed **PHILADELPHIA HILTON & TOWERS** after September 1, 1991.

HOLIDAY INN CENTER CITY 18th and Market Streets, Phila., PA 19103 (561–7500 or 800–HOLIDAY). 450 contemporary rooms, indoor parking, outdoor pool, Coffey's Restaurant, Reflections Lounge. Two executive floors with concierge service. A good location if you plan to be visiting the Philadelphia Stock Exchange, Commerce Square, or the Benjamin Franklin Parkway sites.

HOLIDAY INN MIDTOWN 1311 Walnut Street, Phila., PA 19107 (735–9300 or 800–HOLIDAY). 160 rooms, indoor parking, outdoor pool, Walnut Street Bar & Grill, and a cocktail lounge. In the heart of the business, shopping and theater district; 2 blocks from City Hall.

KORMAN SUITES HOTEL AND CONFERENCE CENTER, 20th and Hamilton Streets, just north of Benjamin Franklin Parkway, Phila., PA 19130 (569–7200 or 800–626–2651). 250 rooms and suites in a luxury hotel, apartment, conference center complex for short- or long-term stays. Kitchenette and washer-dryer in every accommodation. A health club, paddle tennis and outdoor pool. Dining at Catalina. Complimentary van service to center city and historic area.

LATHAM 135 S. 17th Street at Walnut, Phila., PA 19103 (563–7474 or 800–LATHAM–1). 140 rooms, tailored for executives and with a concierge. Bogart's and Crickett for dining and drinking, and a "private" bar in most rooms. A quiet, fashionable, friendly hotel surrounded by fine shops. A block from Rittenhouse Square and Liberty Place.

QUALITY INN CENTER CITY 501 N. 22nd Street, Phila., PA 19130 (568–8300 or 800–221–2222). 275 moderately-priced rooms, free outdoor parking on premises, outdoor pool, Poor Richard's Restaurant and Logan's Tavern. A short walk to the Parkway museums.

QUALITY INN HISTORIC DOWNTOWN SUITES 1010 Race Street, Phila., PA 19107 (922–1730 or 800–221–2222). 96 suites, all with a kitchen, and furnished with Tai-Ming decor. Unique hotel interiors and locale. In the heart of Chinatown*, convenient to City Hall, Market East* and the Federal buildings. Business and conference facilities and a cocktail lounge. Complimentary continental breakfast.

RADISSON SUITE HOTEL 18th Street and Benjamin Franklin Parkway, Phila., PA 19103 (963–2222 or 800–333–3333). 285 luxury suites, each with a parlor, wet bar and terrace. Indoor parking and T.G.I. Friday's Restaurant, all in a circular white tower facing Logan Circle and convenient to Parkway museums and Penn Center. Affiliation with health club at Wyndham Franklin Plaza.

490

THE RITTENHOUSE 210 W. Rittenhouse Square, Phila., PA 19103 (546–9000 or 800–635–1042). 98 spacious and handsome rooms in an intimate, luxury hotel facing Rittenhouse Square. Topped off with an exclusive apartment tower, all in contemporary saw-tooth design. Emphasis on personal attention and service. Elegant dining in 210 facing the Square; casual fare in the airy Treetops, also overlooking the Square; soup, salad and sandwiches in the ambiance of an old rowing club at Boat House Row Bar; light fare at lunch and afternoon tea in the lobby Cassatt Tea Room and Lounge. Member Preferred Hotels; Mobil 4-Star and AAA 4-Diamond. Toppers health and fitness center with indoor, skylit pool. Designer shopping at Nan Duskin.

THE RITZ-CARLTON 17th between Market and Chestnut Streets at Three Liberty Place, Phila., PA 19103 (563–1600 or 800–241–3333). Opened November 1990 with 290 luxurious guest rooms, each with a marble bath, refrigerator and honor bar. A formal French Dining Room, The Grill for American regional fare, and the Lobby Bar that also serves afternoon tea. A fitness center and concierge add to the amenities. In the heart of center city and adjacent to the Shops at Liberty Place.

THE WARWICK 17th and Locust Streets, Phila., PA 19103 (735–6000 or 800–523–4210). 190 rooms in a luxury apartment building a block from Rittenhouse Square and two blocks from Liberty Place. Concierge and indoor parking. Dining at 1701 Cafe; dancing at Polo Bay; sinful ice cream, desserts and coffee at Capriccio.

WYNDHAM FRANKLIN PLAZA Two Franklin Plaza, 16th and Race Streets, Phila., PA 19103 (448–2000 or 800–822–4200). 750 rooms; 26-story modern and airy convention hotel, Philadelphia's largest. An underground garage; racquet ball, squash, tennis, basketball, health club with nautilus, outdoor running track and glass-enclosed pool. Between Friends and Terrace Restaurants and two lounges. Convenient to Parkway museums and Penn Center.

491

Historic Philadelphia

These hotels are also in Center City, but they're closer to Independence National Historical Park, other historic sites and Penn's Landing.

COMFORT INN AT PENN'S LANDING 100 N. Delaware Avenue, Phila., PA 19106 (627–7900 or 800–228–5150). 185 rooms and 9 suites moderately-priced at a location convenient to the historic sites and on the waterfront. No restaurant, but complimentary continental breakfast and free outdoor parking.

HOLIDAY INN INDEPENDENCE MALL 4th and Arch Streets, Phila., PA 19106 (923–8660 or 800–HOLIDAY). 364 rooms in historic Old City Philadelphia. Indoor parking, outdoor pool, Benjamin's Restaurant, Plain and Fancy Cafe and the Reunion Bar. Daytime concierge service.

INDEPENDENCE PARK INN 235 Chestnut Street, Phila., PA 19106 (922–4443 or 800–624–2988). A unique 36-room hotel (no 2 are alike) in a Victorian building that's on the National Register of Historic Places. Complimentary continental breakfast in the glass-enclosed courtyard; afternoon tea in the parlor. Contemporary amenities with 19th century character. Facilities for business travelers.

OMNI HOTEL AT INDEPENDENCE PARK 4th and Chestnut Streets, Phila., PA 19106 (925–0000 or 800–THE OMNI). All 155 rooms overlook Independence National Historical Park from this luxury hotel that opened November 1990. There's an indoor pool and health club, concierge service and the Azalea Restaurant for regional cuisine. Adjacent to the 5-screen Ritz Theaters, the Bourse and, of course, the National Park.

PENN'S VIEW INN 14 N. Front Street, Phila., PA 19106 (922–7600 or 800–331–7634). An intimate "new" 28-room (some with fireplace and jacuzzi) hotel that overlooks the Delaware River from Front Street just north of Market. Formerly a 4-story warehouse built in 1826 and now on the National Register of Historic Places. Complimentary continental breakfast; Ristorante Panorama for contemporary Italian cuisine and a wine bar.

SHERATON SOCIETY HILL One Dock Street (2nd and Walnut Streets), Phila., PA 19106 (238–6000 or 800–235–3535). Four-story red brick architecture designed to blend with the neighborhood. 365 rooms, underground parking, meeting rooms, indoor pool and health club, 24-hour room service and daytime concierge. AAA 4-Diamond. Hadley's Restaurant, Wooden Nickle Pub and a courtyard bar. Convenient to Penn's Landing, Independence National Historical Park, South Street and historic attractions.

SOCIETY HILL HOTEL 3rd and Chestnut Streets, Phila., PA 19106 (925–1394 or 925–1919). Philadelphia's smallest hotel has 6 single rooms and 6 suites, all with brass beds, dark wood furnishings and private bath with shower. It was built in 1832 to house longshoremen from around the world who were in port in Philadelphia. Totally renovated, it reopened in 1979 as an historic "bed and breakfast" and the first of historic Philadelphia's "boutique" hotels. The restaurant is described in Chapter 18. In the heart of Independence National Historical Park.

THOMAS BOND HOUSE 129 S. 2nd Street, Phila., PA 19106 (923–8523 or 800–845–BOND). Originally built by Dr. Thomas Bond (see Pennsylvania Hospital*) in 1769, with additions in 1824 and 1840, completely renovated and opened as a "bed and breakfast" in 1988. Now on the National Register of Historic Places, with 12 different colonial-style rooms and 20th century comforts. Breakfast included. Adjacent to Welcome Park* and in the heart of Independence National Historical Park.

University City

These hotels are convenient to the Civic Center, University City Science Center, major Philadelphia hospitals and the attractions of University City*. They're west of the Schuylkill River and 10 minutes from center city.

PENN TOWER HOTEL 34th Street and Civic Center Boulevard, Phila., PA 19104 (387–8333 or 800–356–PENN). 220 modern rooms, adjacent to the University Museum*, Philadelphia Civic Center*, Children's Hospital, the Hospital of the University of Pennsylvania and the university campus. Indoor self-parking, The Terrace Restaurant, Ideas Lounge and ample meeting facilities.

SHERATON UNIVERSITY CITY 36th and Chestnut Streets, Phila., PA 19104 (387–8000 or 800–325–3535). 377 rooms, outdoor pool, indoor self-parking, Smart Alex restaurant. Convenient to the Philadelphia Civic Center, University of Pennsylvania, Drexel University and the University City Science Center.

Philadelphia International Airport
South Philadelphia

These hotels are close to the Spectrum and Veterans Stadium, and Philadelphia International Airport. They're about 15 minutes from center city.

AIRPORT HILTON INN 10th Street and Packer Avenue, Phila., PA 19148 (755–9500 or 800–HILTONS). 238 rooms, outdoor pool, free parking on premises and free van service to and from the airport. Cinnamon's Restaurant and bar. Popular with ball players and sports fans because it's adjacent to the stadiums.

AIRPORT RAMADA INN 76 Industrial Highway, Route 291, Essington, PA 19029 (521–9600 or 800–228–2828). 290 rooms, free parking on premises, outdoor pool, restaurant, lounge, 24-hour coffee shop and 24-hour van service to the airport. Four miles south of the airport.

AIRPORT TOWER HOTEL 2015 Penrose Avenue, Phila., PA 19145 (755–6500 or 800–247–7676). 225 rooms in a round high-rise. A restaurant and lounge, heated outdoor pool, free parking on premises.

COMFORT INN 53 Industrial Highway, Essington, PA 19029 (521–9800 or 800–4–CHOICE). 150 rooms on 5 floors; an exercise room and complimentary continental breakfast. Three-and-a-half-miles south of the airport with 24-hour free van service.

COURTYARD BY MARRIOTT (800–321–2211). 150 rooms under construction and scheduled for completion late in 1991. A half-mile from the airport.

DAYS INN AT THE AIRPORT Two Gateway Center, 4105 Island Avenue, Phila., PA 19153 (492–0400 or 800–325–2525). 175 rooms, 4-story contemporary decor with a Seasons Cafe. Free parking; free van service to and from the airport.

EMBASSY SUITES HOTEL 9000 Bartram Avenue., Phila., PA 19153 (365–4500 or 800–362–2779). A half-mile from the airport with complimentary van service. All 265 "rooms" are a two-room suite. Indoor pool and health club. Ellington's Restaurant. Complimentary breakfast and manager's daily cocktail reception.

GUEST QUARTERS SUITE HOTEL One Gateway Center, 4101 Island Avenue, Phila., PA 19153 (365–6600 or 800–424–2900). 250 suites on 8 floors designed around an atrium. Indoor pool and health club, restaurant and lounge, complimentary breakfast and a cocktail reception. Free parking; free van service to and from the airport.

HOLIDAY INN AIRPORT SOUTH 45 Industrial Highway, Essington, PA 19029 (521–2400 or 800–HOLIDAY). 307 rooms, restaurant and a lounge, outdoor pool and free parking on premises. Three miles south of the airport.

HOWARD JOHNSON EXECUTIVE HOTEL 1300 Providence Avenue (I-95 and Route 320), Chester, PA 19013 (876–7211 or 800–654–2000). 115 rooms and adjacent restaurant, indoor pool and health club, complimentary breakfast. Six miles south of the airport.

PHILADELPHIA AIRPORT MARRIOTT 4509 Island Avenue, Phila., PA 19153 (365–4150 or 800–228–9290). 330 rooms, free parking on premises, indoor pool (in the lobby), 2 restaurants and a cocktail lounge. Van service to and from the airport.

RADISSON HOTEL AT THE AIRPORT 500 Stevens Drive, Phila., PA 19113 (521-5900 or 800-333-3333). Opened March 1991 with 350 rooms on 12 floors. Complimentary van service to and from the airport one-and-a-half miles away. Indoor pool and exercise facilities. Hampton Grill, a Sports Bar and Atrium Lounge with a piano bar.

City Line Suburbs

These hotels are 15 minutes from center city Philadelphia. They're convenient to the shopping on City Line Avenue. They border on Montgomery County* and they're a step closer to Valley Forge and the nation's largest shopping mall complex at King of Prussia.

ADAM'S MARK HOTEL City Line and Monument Road, Phila., PA 19131 (581-5000 or 800-444-ADAM). 515 rooms, free parking, indoor pool, outdoor pool, saunas, health club. Family dining in Appleby's, gourmet at The Marker, Quincey's for dancing to live music, Pierre's jazz lounge and the Sports Bar. Complete banquet, meeting and convention facilities.

HOLIDAY INN CITY LINE 4100 Presidential Boulevard, Phila., PA 19131 (477-0200 or 800-HOLIDAY). 345 rooms; 8-story contemporary design that was prefabricated in modules and assembled at the site. Free parking on premises, indoor pool and exercise room, meeting facilities, restaurant and cocktail lounge.

Northeast Philadelphia
Bucks County

The following hotels are within a half-hour drive of center city Philadelphia on either the Roosevelt Boulevard (Route 1) or the Delaware Expressway (I-95). They're convenient to Northeast Philadelphia Airport, the Greater Northeast shopping centers, Philadelphia Park Race Track and the Bucks County* attractions. They all offer free outdoor parking.

COMFORT INN BENSALEM 3660 Street Road at Route 1, Bensalem, PA 19020 (245-0100 or 800-458-6886). 140 rooms in a modern 3-story building. Complimentary breakfast, Easy Street Lounge with light menu, fitness room, game room, meeting rooms.

COMPRI HOTEL BUCKS COUNTY 3327 Street Road, Bensalem, PA 19020 (639-9100 or 800-4-COMPRI). 165 contemporary rooms, complimentary breakfast and late afternoon cocktails, outdoor pool and small gym. Sandwich menu for lunch and dinner.

HOLIDAY INN BUCKS COUNTY 4700 Street Road, Trevose, PA 19053 (364-2000 or 800-HOLIDAY). 215 rooms on 6 floors (top floor with concierge), Bensalem Beef Co. Restaurant, Legends Lounge, indoor pool, exercise and game rooms.

HOLIDAY INN NORTHEAST 3499 Street Road, Bensalem, PA 19020 (638-1500 or 800-HOLIDAY). 115 rooms on 2 floors (you can drive to your room), Bibsy's Restaurant, Stars Lounge and an outdoor pool.

HOWARD JOHNSON LODGE 11580 Roosevelt Boulevard, Phila., PA 19116 (464-9500 or 800-654-2000). 105 rooms (some with jacuzzi), adjacent restaurant, outdoor pool.

ROYCE HOTEL 400 Oxford Valley Road, Langhorne, PA 19047 (547-4100). 165 rooms in a contemporary highrise, indoor pool and health club, Remington's Restaurant and Fizz Night Club.

SHERATON INN NORTHEAST 9461 Roosevelt Boulevard, Phila., PA 19114 (671-9600 or 800-325-3535). 190 rooms, year-round indoor-outdoor pool, saunas, Plum Tree Restaurant and lounge.

TREVOSE HILTON 2400 Old Lincoln Highway and Route 1, Trevose, PA 19053 (638-8300 or 800-HILTONS). 285 rooms and suites on 6 floors, Seasons Restaurant, Atrium Cafe and Bumpers Lounge, indoor pool and health club.

Other Accommodations

BED & BREAKFAST OF VALLEY FORGE; ALL ABOUT TOWN—B & B IN PHILADELPHIA; ALL ABOUT THE BRANDYWINE VALLEY B & B P.O. Box 562, Valley Forge, PA 19481 (783–7838). Bed & Breakfast is a longtime European custom that provides comfortable, moderately priced, personalized lodgings in a private home. Now you can enjoy the same tradition in Philadelphia and its suburbs. This reservation service arranges at-home personalized accommodations for business people and tourists in unique, charming, historic and contemporary residences and inns. It gives you the opportunity to be part of a local family when you visit Philadelphia.

CHAMOUNIX MANSION INTERNATIONAL YOUTH HOSTEL West Fairmount Park, Phila., PA 19131 (878–3676). Built in 1802 as an elegant country home, Chamounix is just 15 minutes by car from center city, or walking distance from SEPTA bus 38 stop. Cooking facilities, bunks, mattresses and blankets are available, but bring your own linens. Sign in from 4:30 to 8 P.M. and out by 9:30 A.M. Room for 60 in summer and 40 the rest of the year (closed December 15 to January 15); groups and families accepted; reservations advised. Chamounix is chartered by American Youth Hostels, 38 S. 3rd Street, Phila., PA 19106 (925–6004). Membership is required of international visitors, but non-members can purchase a special guest card from A.Y.H. or at Chamounix and stay for two nights. They'll also provide information on biking, hiking, canoeing, sailing and skiing in the area.

CHESTNUT HILL HOTEL 8229 Germantown Avenue, Phila., PA 19118 (242–5905 or 800–628–9744). A four-story colonial-style country inn at the top of Chestnut Hill*. 28 rooms, including three two-rooms suites, all with 18th century reproduction furnishings and continental breakfast included. A meeting room and two restaurants, Chautauqua and J.B. Winberie.

INTERNATIONAL HOUSE* 3701 Chestnut Street, Phila., PA 19104 (387–5125). This super-structure residence is for the area's foreign and American graduate students, and a number of dormitory-style accommodations for transients are also available.

OLD FIRST REFORMED CHURCH* 4th and Race Streets, Phila., PA 19106 (922–4566). This restored church in historic Philadelphia provides mattresses and a light breakfast for nightly visitors (ages 18 to 26) in July and August. There's a three-night limit. Sign in from 5 to 10 P.M.; closes at midnight.

STATE CAMPGROUNDS INFORMATION Write or call the Department of Environmental Resources, Bureau of State Parks, P.O. Box 8551, Harrisburg, PA 17105–8551 (800–63–PARKS). Pennsylvania has 55 state park campgrounds and more than 7,000 campsites.

Elsewhere

Many other hotels and motels are within an hour's drive of center city Philadelphia. Many of them feature resort facilities, weekend get-aways, fine restaurants, night clubs and good quality accommodations. Some are less extravagant. A few of them are listed here.

Just to get your bearings, refer to Chapter 17 on Philadelphia's neighboring counties.

In **Bucks County** (in addition to those already listed with Northeast Philadelphia):

Bristol Econolodge Route 13 and PA Turnpike Exit 26, Bristol, PA 19057 (946–1100).

George Washington Motor Lodge PA Turnpike Exit 28, Trevose, PA 19047 (357–9100).

Holiday Inn New Hope Route 202, New Hope, PA 18938 (862–5221).

In **Chester County** (convenient to Valley Forge):

Courtyard by Marriott 762 Lancaster Avenue, Wayne, PA 19087 (687–6633 or 800–321–2211).

Great Valley Hilton Hotel & Conference Center One Liberty Boulevard, Malvern, PA 19355 (296–9800 or 800–HILTONS).

Guest Quarters Suite Hotel Valley Forge 888 Chesterbrook Boulevard, Wayne, PA 19087 (647–6700 or 800–424–2900).

Sheraton Inn Great Valley Routes 202 and 30, 707 Lancaster Pike, Frazer, PA 19355 (524–5500).

In **Delaware County** (in addition to those already listed near Philadelphia International Airport):

Brandywine River Hotel Route 1 and 100, Chadds Ford, PA 19317 (388–1200).

Chadds Ford Ramada Inn 1110 Baltimore Pike (Routes 202 and 1), Glen Mills, PA 19342 (358–1700).

Hotel Regency 1124 W. Baltimore Pike, Media, PA 19063 (566–9600).

Media Inn Providence Road and Baltimore Pike, Media, PA 19063 (566–8460).

St. David's Inn Route 30 (Lancaster Pike) and Radnor-Chester Pike, St. Davids, PA 19087 (688–5800).

In **Montgomery County** (also convenient to Valley Forge):

Budget Lodge 815 West DeKalb Pike, King of Prussia, PA 19406 (265–7200).

Courtyard by Marriott 1100 Drummers Lane, Valley Forge, PA 19087 (687–6700 or 800–321–2211).

Courtyard by Marriott 2350 Easton Road, Route 611, Willow Grove, PA 19090 (687–6633 or 800–321–2211).

Days Hotel 530 Pennsylvania Avenue, Fort Washington, PA 19034 (643–1111).

George Washington Motor Lodge PA Turnpike Exit 24, King of Prussia, PA 19406 (265–6100); PA Turnpike Exit 25, Plymouth Meeting, PA 19462 (825–1980); and PA Turnpike Exit 27, Willow Grove, PA 19090 (659–7200).

Guest Quarters Suite Hotel 640 West Germantown Pike, Plymouth Meeting, PA 19462 (834–8300 or 800–424–2900).

Holiday Inn Fort Washington 432 Pennsylvania Avenue, Fort Washington, PA 19034 (643–3000).

Holiday Inn King of Prussia 260 Goddard Boulevard, King of Prussia, PA 19406 (265–7500).

Plaza Valley Forge 1250 First Avenue, King of Prussia, PA 19406 (265–1500).

Howard Johnson Lodge Route 202 North and Gulph Road, King of Prussia, PA 19406 (265–4500).

Ramada Inn Commerce Drive, Fort Washington, PA 19034 (542–7930).

Sheraton Valley Forge Route 363 (North Gulph Road) and First Avenue, King of Prussia, PA 19406 (337–2000).

Stouffer Valley Forge Hotel Route 363 (480 North Gulph Road), King of Prussia, PA 19406 (337–1800).

Valley Forge Hilton 251 West DeKalb Pike, King of Prussia, PA 19406 (337–1200).

Crossing the Delaware River into **New Jersey** (area code 609), there's a **Cherry Hill Hyatt** (662–1234), a **Cherry Hill Inn Radisson Hotel and Conference Center** (662–7200) and a **Cherry Hill Sheraton Poste Inn** (428–2300). There's a **Courtyard by Marriott** in Mt. Laurel (273–4400). The closest **Holiday Inns** are in Cherry Hill, Gloucester, Maple Shade, Moorestown and Mt. Laurel. All of these hotels are within a half-hour drive of center city Philadelphia.

Chapter 21.
Useful Information.

Philadelphia Glossary. Shopping Tips. Architectural Notes.

In addition to all of the distinctive Philadelphia neighborhoods, customs and traditions you've already come to know, there are other terms and expressions you'll probably come upon. Here they are:

Antique Row includes some two dozen or more antique shops between 9th and 12th Streets on Pine Street. It's mecca for collectors, dealers and plain folks interested in things that are old and collectible.

Avenue of the Arts refers to the six blocks south of Broad Street from City Hall. It packs in several cultural institutions you've read about including the Historical Society of Pennsylvania, Library Company of Philadelphia, Opera Company of Philadelphia, Pennsylvania Ballet, University of the Arts, Shubert Theater, the Academy of Music and the Philadelphia Orchestra.

The **Bourse** was built as a merchants exchange in 1893 to 1895. Its grand scale and elaborate design were copied from the commercial exchanges of Europe where goods, commodities and services were bought and sold.

Some 1,500 members were allowed on the trading floor, a two-level balcony provided for spectators, a skylight provided bright daylight over the central core, and six floors of offices looked down on it all. The Bourse continued as a trading center till the Depression.

After two years of total restoration to its turn-of-the-century splendor, the Bourse reopened in 1981 as a one-of-a-kind office, shopping and dining complex. Overlooking Independence Mall, The Great Hall of The Bourse houses retail shops. The restaurants at The Bourse are described in Chapter 18.

Center City is Philadelphia's term for downtown. You can easily determine north, east, south and west from the compass in the center of the City Hall Courtyard. Remember, William Penn on top of City Hall faces northeast.

The **Chestnut Street Transitway** is the mile on Chestnut Street between 6th and 18th Streets. It's off-limits during the day to all traffic except buses. Motorists can use the transitway from 7 P.M. to 6 A.M. for one lane of traffic in each direction. This is a major shopping district of Philadelphia with department stores, boutiques, specialty shops, restaurants and fast food services. The tree-lined pedestrian walkway has extra-wide brick seating areas and protected bus stops.

Fabric Row is the 600 to 700 blocks of South 4th Street in Queen Village*. This is where you'll find shop after shop of fabrics with selections as good as the values.

Franklin Mills is the Philadelphia area's largest shopping mall. Nearly 250 stores and 30 food vendors fill more than 40 acres, reached from the Woodhaven exit of I-95 in Northeast Philadelphia. All of the shops offer discount, off-price or outlet shopping. Food courts at each end of the mall are designed to resemble a 1950s-style diner filled with rock and roll memorabilia and a sports establishment touting the local teams. Entertainment is ongoing at various stages within the mall. Look for a schedule when you arrive. Everything at Franklin Mills is planned to make your shopping fun.

Jeweler's Row is the 700 block of Sansom Street and its adjoining streets. This is a place to go for super selections and prices on diamonds, gold, silver and other beautiful things.

One Liberty Place, at 17th and Market Streets, is 61 stories tall. It's also the first building in Philadelphia's history that tops William Penn's statue on City Hall*. It was completed late in 1987. Two Liberty Place was completed late in 1990. It's 58 stories. The Ritz-Carlton Hotel opened at Three Liberty Place on 17th Street late in 1990. They're all connected to the **Shops at Liberty Place**, on Chestnut Street between 16th and 17th Streets. Some fifty fine shops, a pushcart pavilion, restaurants and a food court occupy two floors surrounding a glass-topped rotunda. A huge multi-level underground garage occupies the entire block under Liberty Place. Access is from 16th Street between Chestnut and Market or adjacent to the Ritz-Carlton Hotel. Helmut Jann was the architect of Liberty Place.

Since Philadelphia's skyline has changed so dramatically in the past few years, it would be remiss not to mention a few more of the notable skyscrapers that have been built. **Bell Atlantic Tower** reaches 53 floors high at 18th and Arch Streets. **Commerce Square** is two 41-story towers between 20th and 21st on Market Street. **Mellon Bank Center** is 54 floors at 18th and Market Streets. **1919 Market Street** (Blue Cross Tower) rises some 50 floors. **Two Logan Square** is 34 stories at 18th and Cherry Streets. Just imagine what William Penn must be thinking from his perch atop City Hall!

Market East stretches east along Market Street from City Hall towards Independence Mall. With major department stores, office buildings, a commuter tunnel, an abundance of "street art" (described in Chapter 9) and good design, it is likely the largest office and shopping center within a city in the country. A major street and sidewalk renovation was completed in 1988, giving Market East a dramatically new boulevard look.

Market Place East opened in 1988 on the north side of Market Street, between 7th and 8th Streets (Market East), as an office, retail, dining and entertainment complex surrounding a huge atrium. Its magnificent cast iron facade dates from the late 19th century. Secretary of State Thomas Jefferson's office occupied part of the site in 1793. J.B. Lippincott Publishers was on part of the block from 1863 to 1899. Lit Brothers Department Store bought the block between 1893 and 1907 and built their original store here. Lits closed in the early 1980s and the site was reborn later in the decade after completion of a monumental restoration. There are some 25 shops and restaurants at Market Place East, along with several memorabilia exhibits, the Enchanted Colonial Village* and a place to pick up visitor information.

The **Gallery at Market East** brought an enormous new shopping mall to center city at 9th and Market Streets. It's a four-story, glass-roofed, suburban-style mall of 100 shops anchored on either side by the major department stores of **Stern's** and **Strawbridge and Clothier**. You can shop under and over 10th Street while traffic flows across it. **Gallery 2**, including a **J.C. Penney**, 125 more shops and eating places, bright courtyards and fountains, extends the mall a block further west to 11th Street.

SEPTA's Market-Frankford Subway-Elevated trains stop at The Gallery, as well as the PATCO High Speed

Line and bus routes running on Market Street. Parking garages also connect directly with the shopping complex from Filbert Street.

The Gallery's lower level towards 10th Street houses dozens of fast food restaurants serving specialties from around the world. They circle a common seating area. (Additional restaurants occupy other sites in The Gallery.) The Gallery Market houses specialty food shops in the lower level near the 8th and Market Streets subway stop.

Shopping hours at most of The Gallery are Monday to Saturday, 10 A.M. to 6 P.M.; Wednesday till 8; and Sunday, 12 to 5.

John Wanamaker, at 13th and Market Streets, is center city's other major department store. Its bronze eagle in the splendid Grand Court has been a meeting place for generations of shoppers. Don't miss the Philadelphia tradition. Its pipe organ is described in Chapter 10. The Wanamaker Building has recently undergone a major restoration condensing the landmark store onto the first five floors and renovating the top seven floors into offices. John Wanamaker is open Monday to Saturday, 10 to 6; Wednesday night till 8; and Sunday, 12 to 5.

Wednesday night is the night some stores remain open late in Philadelphia. Most department stores are open late daily for advertised big sale events and holiday shopping from Thanksgiving till Christmas.

Other **major shops** and **specialty stores** line Chestnut and Walnut Streets, especially in the streets near Rittenhouse Square. We're partial to Sophy Curson, Toby Lerner and the Knit Wit. Fine European and specialty stores are on Walnut Street from the Square heading east. Among the choices are Borders Book Shop and Espresso Bar, Fila, Jaeger, Rodier, Talbots, Ann Taylor, Banana Republic, Gap, Burberrys, Laura Ashley, Descamps, Wayne Edwards, Allure, and Louis Vuitton. At Broad Street you'll find the exclusive, international Shops at the Bellevue, including Dunhill, Gucci, Pierre Deux, Polo/Ralph Lauren, and Tiffany & Co. And don't forget Nan Duskin for women at The Rittenhouse, and Boyd's for men at 1818 Chestnut Street.

The **Marketplace Design Center** at 2400 Market Street (561–5000) houses showrooms catering to designers and decorators. It's the place to go for ideas on the latest in home and office decor, but you'll have to be with a qualified professional buyer, or have a referral from one, in order to gain access. There's also a pleasant cafe for light dining.

The **National Register of Historic Places** is published by the U.S. Department of the Interior. It currently lists almost 56,000 sites and structures in the United States that are of architectural, cultural or historical importance.

A more selective list issued by the Department of the Interior specifies **National Historic Landmarks**. They come from the National Register, but are deemed more important because of their national significance.

There are almost 335 Philadelphia sites in the National Register and at least 62 local attractions are National Landmarks. Many of them are described in this book: the Academy of Music, John Bartram's House, Carpenters' Hall, City Hall, Cliveden, Elfreth's Alley, Founder's Hall at Girard College, NewMarket, Old Fort Mifflin, Pennsylvania Hospital, the U.S.S. Olympia and the Walnut Street Theater, to name a few.

Penn Center is west on Market Street from City Hall to 19th Street. What is now a complex of skyscraper buildings was once the Pennsylvania Railroad's Chinese Wall.

Penn Center Concourse is the underground complex of shops, banks, restaurants and the O.T.B. Parlor (see Chapter 14) with access from Richardson Dilworth Plaza of City Hall, office buildings, stairways from street corner locations, SEPTA train routes, and connecting by SEPTA commuter trains to the Market East station.

A new **Pennsylvania Convention Center** is under construction in the area north of Market Street and surrounding the old Reading Railroad Terminal whose shed will be resplendently restored to serve as a grand entrance to the new complex. The Convention Center is scheduled to open in 1994. It will occupy the area from Arch to Race Streets, between 11th and 13th, with an adjacent 1,000-room hotel at 12th and Market Streets.

The **Philadelphia Civic Center**, just 10 minutes from center city in West Philadelphia, is a multi-building, multi-function complex for sports events, conferences, conventions, exhibitions and trade shows. It's been the site of Presidential nominating conventions, high school and college commencements and shows for boats, dogs, flowers and just about everything imaginable. The Civic Center includes Convention Hall, the exhibition halls, underground parking garages and Pennsylvania Hall.

Philadelphia Scrapple. Get it fresh and spicy at Reading Terminal Market*.

The **Philadelphia soft pretzel.** Have one (with mustard) before you leave town. We guarantee you'll want more.

Reading Terminal Market (922–2317) has served Philadelphians with a unique shopping experience since 1893. It's located at 12th and Arch Streets, soon to be surrounded by the new Convention Center. No less than 80 merchants stock their stalls with fresh poultry, meat, seafood, baked goods, fruit, produce, pasta, spices, flowers, coffees, ice cream and dairy products. Amish farmers bring their Pennsylvania Dutch specialties from Lancaster County on Wednesday to Saturday, adding to the local color. Hours at the market are Monday through Saturday, 8 A.M. to 6 P.M., but get there at least an hour before closing time. It's easily accessible from any Market Street SEPTA route. Reading Terminal Market also provides a unique informal dining experience for breakfast, lunch or snacking. For more about that, see Chapter 18.

Richardson Dilworth Plaza is the wide-open, two-level vista with fountains, benches, trees and shrubs on City Hall's west side. It's another link to the Penn Center Concourse. The Plaza honors the late Mayor Richardson Dilworth, who led Philadelphia from 1956 to 1962.

Handy Phone Numbers.
Handy Addresses.

Philadelphia telephone area code: 215
Philadelphia ZIP code: 191 plus 2 digits

CITY HALL
Broad and Market Streets, Phila., PA 19107
686–1776
Mayor's Action Center
143 City Hall
686–2250 (Complaints)
686–3000 (Information)

EDUCATION
School District of Philadelphia
Public Schools, Board of Education, 299–7000
Archdiocese of Philadelphia
Office of Catholic Education, 587–3700
There are hundreds of private schools in the Philadelphia
area. See the Bell of Pennsylvania Yellow Pages under
"Schools."

EMERGENCIES
Police, Fire and Medical, 911
Poison, 386–2100
Suicide, 686–4420
See the Blue Pages "Guide to Human Services" in the
back of the Bell of Pennsylvania Philadelphia phonebook.

FEDERAL INFORMATION CENTER
800–347–1997

FREE LIBRARY OF PHILADELPHIA
Central Library—Logan Square, Phila., PA 19103
686–5322

GREATER PHILADELPHIA
CHAMBER OF COMMERCE
1234 Market Street, Suite 1800
Phila., PA 19107
545–1234

HEALTH
Mayor's Office for the Handicapped
686–2798

For crisis intervention services, hotlines, ambulances, and the like, see the Blue Pages "Guide to Human Services" in the back of the Bell of Pennsylvania Philadelphia phonebook.

INDEPENDENCE NATIONAL HISTORICAL PARK
Independence Hall
6th and Chestnut Streets, 627–1776
Independence Visitor Center
3rd and Chestnut Streets, 597–8974 or 597–8975

PHILADELPHIA CONVENTION AND VISITORS BUREAU
Philadelphia Visitors Center
1525 John F. Kennedy Boulevard, Phila., PA 19102
636–1666
24-hour "Events Hotline," 337–7777 (Ext. 2540)
Philadelphia Convention & Visitors Bureau
1515 Market Street, Phila., PA 19102
636–3300
800–321–WKND

PUBLIC TRANSPORTATION
AMTRAK-intercity rail service, 824–1600
Greyhound-Trailways bus service, 931–4000
SEPTA, 574–7800

SPORTS RESULTS
Philadelphia Inquirer Dial-A-Score, 854–2500

TICKETS FOR SPORTS AND THEATER
Ticketmaster charge-by-phone, 336–2000
Ticketron information, 885–2515

TRAVEL ASSISTANCE
Keystone Automobile Club
2040 Market Street, Phila., PA 19103
864–5000
Pennsylvania Bureau of Travel Marketing
800–VISIT–PA
Traveler's Aid Society
311 S. Juniper Street, Phila., PA 19107 (and branches)
546–0571

TIME   WEATHER
TIme 6–1212   WEather 6–1212

Notes.

INDEX

514

515

518

William Penn Tower (see City Hall)
Willow Grove Naval Air Station, 411–412, 479
Wilma Theater, 236, 274
Wings, 349
Winterthur, 414
Wissahickon, 138, 142, 172, 173, 183, 473
Wistar Institute Museum, 163
Wister, John, 59, 61
Women's History Week, 471
Woodford, 180
Woodlands, 76
Woodmere Art Museum, 215–216, 262
Workshop on the Water, 102, 135–136
World Affairs Council, 298
World Sculpture Garden, 136
Wrestling, 346
Wyck, 56, 62

Wyeths, N.C., Andrew, James, 203, 206, 404

Y Arts Council, 221, 235, 259
YM & YWHA, 128, 235, 386
Yearly Meeting Library, 286
Yellin, Samuel, Metalworks and Yellin Museum, 332–333
Yellow fever epidemic, 48, 55–56, 58–59, 60
Young Audiences of Eastern PA, 341

Zero Moving Dance Company, 236, 242
Zoological Gardens (see Philadelphia Zoo; see also Elmwood Park Zoo)

Notes.

Notes.

Notes.